THE OTHER NORFOLK ADMIRALS

The Other Norfolk Admirals

Myngs, Narbrough and Shovell

Simon Harris

Helion & Company Limited

Helion & Company Limited
26 Willow Road
Solihull
West Midlands
B91 1UE
England
Tel. 0121 705 3393
Fax 0121 711 4075
Email: info@helion.co.uk
Website: www.helion.co.uk
Twitter: @helionbooks
Visit our blog http://blog.helion.co.uk/

Published by Helion & Company 2017
Designed and typeset by Mach 3 Solutions Ltd (www.mach3solutions.co.uk)
Cover designed by Paul Hewitt, Battlefield Design (www.battlefield-design.co.uk)
Printed by Short Run Press Ltd, Exeter, Devon

ISBN 978-1-912174-22-5

British Library Cataloguing-in-Publication Data.
A catalogue record for this book is available from the British Library.

For details of other military history titles published by Helion & Company Limited contact the above
address, or visit our website: http://www.helion.co.uk.

We always welcome receiving book proposals from prospective authors.

Contents

List of Illustrations

Illustrations in colour

Ilustrations in black and white

List of Maps

Acknowledgements

A large number of individuals and institutions have helped me in the production of *The Other Norfolk Admirals: Myngs, Narbrough and Shovell.*

First and foremost among the individuals has been Professor Hughie Young who has worked tirelessly on the syntax of the book as well as checking many of the facts. In addition, as an eminent physicist and mathematician, he has produced a plausible hypothesis for the relative importance of longitude versus latitude as the cause of the catastrophe on 22 October 1707. I owe Hughie a great deal for his unfailing support and the book is dedicated to him.

Over the last 40 years, my wife Clare and our children Lucy and Charles have been greatly supportive in following in the wake of Myngs, Narbrough and Shovell from Tripoli to the Isles of Scilly. This included nearly drowning the family on a causeway between Tatihou Island and Saint-Vaast-la-Hougue whilst trying to trace the boat burning sequence of May 1692. My brothers, Timothy and Ralph accompanied me to Bantry Bay to study the battle of 1 May 1689. Clare, too, came up with the apt title of the book, *The Other Norfolk Admirals: Myngs, Narbrough and Shovell* with the greatest respect to Horatio Nelson.

Once again I am indebted to Derek Stone who has produced the excellent maps as he has done with all my books. Glenn Adams and Jez Batch have been unstinting with their time and expertise in scanning and photography. John Osborne whose wonderful cartoons have featured in many of my talks has kindly agreed to my using one in this book.

Many people have generously allowed me to photograph portraits of their illustrious ancestors. They include: the 8th Earl of Romney and his son David, descendants of Cloudesley Shovell's eldest daughter, Elizabeth; William Cartwright-Hignett and his mother Elizabeth, descendants of Shovell's youngest daughter, Anne; John Narbrough Hughes-D'Aeth [also his wife Catherine who went to great lengths to obtain a photograph of the James Narbrough portrait] and Richard Dixon, both descendants of John Narbrough's eldest daughter, Elizabeth.

Excellent illustrations for the book have been provided by: Her Majesty the Queen through the Royal Collection Trust; the British Library, London; the Guildhall Museum, Rochester; the Houses of Parliament Collection; the Isles of Scilly Museum; the London Metropolitan Archives, City of London; Mullock's Auctions Ltd, Shropshire; the Musée de la Marine, Paris; the National Archives, Kew; the National Maritime Museum, Greenwich; the National Portrait Gallery, London; the Norfolk Record Office, Norwich; the Rijksmuseum, Amsterdam; Sotheby's of New Bond Street, London; St James's Auctions Ltd, London. Two individuals from these institutions were particularly helpful. Tom Harper,

Curator of Antiquarian Mapping at the British Library and Steve Nye from the Guildhall Museum, Rochester went beyond the call of duty to help me. Valuable written material has been gleaned from: the British Library; the Huntington Library, San Marino; Kent County Archives; the National Archives; the National Maritime Museum; the Norfolk Record Office; Yale University Library. I am grateful to the staff of all these establishments who have helped me over the last 40 years.

The Reverend Ian Whittle, the incumbent of Cockthorpe and allied parishes has kindly allowed me to use a photograph of the baptismal entries of John Narbrough and Cloudesley Shovell. The Reverend Phil Blamire, from the neighbouring parish at Salthouse, has also kindly permitted me to use photographs of the marriage entry for Christopher Myngs' parents and also his two baptismal entries.

Duncan Rogers and his staff at Helion have been unfailing in their support during the production of *The Other Norfolk Admirals: Myngs, Narbrough and Shovell*. I am grateful to them all. Particularly so to Kim McSweeney and Charles Singleton who have been of the very greatest assistance to me.

I hope that I have not unintentionally infringed anyone's copyright, but if I have they have my apologies and naturally the matter would be corrected in any future editions of the book.

Introduction

For over half a century the three North Norfolk admirals Christopher Myngs, John Narbrough and Cloudesley Shovell served their monarch and country on the high seas. By tradition it is said that the Myngs and Narbrough families were related although there is no proof. In the second half of the seventeenth and in the first decade of the eighteenth century one or more of this naval triumvirate took part in the Anglo-Dutch Wars, the Nine Years' War and the War of the Spanish Succession. Myngs promulgated the career of Narbrough, taking him from ship to ship and effecting his promotion from post to post. Although it is likely that Shovell first went to sea with Myngs, on the latter's death, Narbrough stepped into the breach to promote Shovell's progress in the navy. Numerous relatives and friends of the three North Norfolk admirals served in their ships at a time when patronage was very much the order of the day.

Christopher Myngs came to the notice of Richard Badiley in the First Anglo-Dutch War and then made a name for himself with William Goodson in Jamaica and on the Spanish Main. 'Kit' Myngs, the Buccaneer, became a skilled leader of irregular forces both on land as well as on the sea. He was short, slightly built with a magnetic personality. Myngs' successful amphibious assault on Santiago de Cuba in 1662, was a classic of its type. Later in Campeche, he suffered serious wounds to his face and both thighs. Whilst serving in the Caribbean, Myngs learned a hard lesson after misappropriating funds more properly destined for the coffers of the state. Having been shipped back to England to face charges, his popularity in the navy saved him. Myngs had an unusual humanitarian attitude to discipline and was ridiculed for refusing to hang deserters.

In 1665, at the Battle of Lowestoft, Myngs as the vice-admiral in Prince Rupert's squadron, fired the first shots of the battle and weathered the Dutch. In the subsequent chase and rout of the unfortunate Obdam's fleet, Myngs was again prominent and was rewarded with a knighthood. The following year, 1666, at the Four Days' Battle, Myngs accompanied his patron Prince Rupert into the English Channel before returning to join Monck's main fleet on the third day of the battle. The following day, in brutal combat with Jan de Liefde's *Ridderschap*, Myngs was shot through both cheeks by a musket ball. Holding his shattered face together with his hands, Myngs refused to go below and continued the fight. Soon afterwards further shot penetrated his neck and settled in a shoulder. Myngs was forced to hand over command of his ship, the *Victory,* to his lieutenant, John Narbrough, and retired to a lower deck. Six days later, the 40-year-old Myngs succumbed to his wounds at his London home and the subsequent funeral was attended by his admirer Samuel Pepys. There can be little doubt that if Myngs had survived he would have risen to an even higher station in the Navy.

John Narbrough first started to make a name for himself as Myngs' lieutenant in the *Triumph*, at the Battle of Lowestoft and, as noted above, assumed command of the *Victory* after Myngs' fatal wounding at the Four Days' Battle. In 1667, he was part of John Harman's squadron to the West Indies. Narbrough took a prominent part in the successful action against the French at Martinique and was present at the later successful attacks on Cayenne and Surinam. Whilst fighting ashore in Surinam, he received a serious leg wound, with damage to a major nerve, which would trouble him for the rest of his life. In the years 1669–71, Narbrough took the *Sweepstakes* on a voyage of exploration, on behalf of Charles II, into the Pacific Ocean and up to Valdivia in modern day Chile. During the voyage, he showed formidable powers of leadership in persuading his reluctant crew to sail through the infamous Strait of Magellan as a lone ship. On the return journey Narbrough became the first Englishman to sail from west to east through the Strait.

In 1672, Narbrough became the second captain of the Duke of York's flagship, the *Prince*, at the Battle of Sole Bay. After the Duke was forced to transfer to another ship during the battle, Narbrough's fine seamanship extricated the badly damaged *Prince* from possible capture or destruction. The next year, at the Battle of Texel, his excellent performance as captain of the *St Michael* led to a knighthood. In the years 1673–79, Narbrough commanded a squadron in the Mediterranean to protect English merchant shipping from the vagaries of the Barbary corsairs. For part of the time he carried the rank of admiral and perhaps his greatest triumph of this period was the successful destruction of the Dey's shipping in Tripoli harbour, in 1676. Although Cloudesley Shovell has rightly received the lion's share of the praise for this successful operation, it should not be forgotten that Narbrough was in overall command.

On his return from the Mediterranean, Narbrough became a Commissioner of the Navy and did much to improve its administration. He was greatly respected by the astute Samuel Pepys and was an instigator of the introduction of selection of lieutenants by examination. Finally, the lure of sunken Spanish treasure off Hispaniola, which Narbrough had apparently been dreaming of for many years, proved to be irresistible and led to his demise from a febrile illness in his 48th year. As was the case with his patron Christopher Myngs, if Narbrough had not died prematurely, it is very likely that he would have held high command in the coming Nine Years' War. One of the main reasons that Narbrough is not better remembered is that no known portrait of him has survived.

Like John Narbrough, Cloudesley Shovell owed his first opportunity in the Navy to Christopher Myngs. It is probable that his first voyage was to the West Indies during his 12th year, in the *Centurion*, with Myngs as captain and Narbrough lieutenant. For a time the three men from North Norfolk served together and we know with certainty that Shovell was in the Caribbean with Myngs in 1663, and again with Narbrough in 1667. By tradition Shovell impressed his admiral by swimming through an enemy's line of ships with despatches in his mouth. Probably, he served in the *Triumph* at the Battle of Lowestoft in 1665 and in the *Victory* during the Four Days' Battle of 1666 when Myngs was mortally wounded. On the death of his first great patron, Narbrough then guided Shovell's nascent career, taking him from ship to ship. There is convincing evidence that Shovell was with Narbrough for the 1669–71 voyage into the Pacific Ocean. Certainly, Shovell was in the *Prince* with the Duke of York and Narbrough at the Battle of Sole Bay in 1672, and again with Lord Ossory and Narbrough, in the *St Michael*, at the final battle of the Third Anglo-Dutch War, the Texel.

No doubt whilst serving in the royal flagship at Sole Bay, Shovell came to the attention of the Duke of York who supported his early naval career until the two men fell out over James' Catholicism. In the years 1673–86, Shovell served in the Mediterranean, firstly under Narbrough, secondly under Arthur Herbert and finally with an independent command around the Straits. Narbrough persuaded the authorities at home, including the influential Samuel Pepys, to make Shovell the second-lieutenant of the *Henrietta* in 1673. Three years later, in 1676, Shovell led the famous boat-burning action against the four ships belonging to the Dey of Tripoli. This brought him to national attention with a special supplement added to *The London Gazette* describing the action. However, this caused a spectacular falling out with Pepys over the £100 medal Shovell persuaded the gullible Charles II to give him to mark the occasion. When his second patron, John Narbrough, went home Shovell seamlessly moved under the influence of the debauched Arthur Herbert. Surprisingly the two men got on well with Herbert helping to progress Shovell's career and saving him after he was forced, against standing instructions, to salute a Spanish admiral's flag in 1683.

In 1688, Shovell was part of Lord Dartmouth's fleet which failed to find and engage William of Orange's ships, under Shovell's erstwhile chief, Arthur Herbert. By now Shovell was in favour of the Protestant cause and very anti the deposed James II. In 1689, Shovell fought his first major action as captain of his own ship, the *Edgar*, under Herbert at the Battle of Bantry Bay and was very prominent in the fighting. Later, William III knighted Shovell in person at Portsmouth. 1690 saw the capture of Duncannon Castle in Southern Ireland and Shovell further enraged the deposed James II by shooting up his footguards, in the royal presence, in Dublin Bay. At the twin Battles of Barfleur and La Hogue, under the overall command of the irascible Edward Russell, Shovell played a starring role in the first action by breaking the French line. Only injury precluded him from even greater glory at the subsequent boat-burning off Saint-Vaast-la-Hougue and Tatihou Island. Shovell's contemporary and great rival, George Rooke, was only too happy to take his place. Like Arthur Herbert, Edward Russell was another man to appreciate Shovell's capabilities and did much to promote his career.

The Smyrna Convoy disaster of 1693 almost led to the abrupt termination of Shovell's sea career, as it did to those of his fellow admirals Henry Killigrew and Ralph Delaval. Matters did not improve the following year with the failure of the landings at Camaret Bay and the subsequent death of General Tollemache. In the mid-1690s, Shovell took part in the unpleasant warfare of the bombing of the French coastal ports which did little damage to the French economy whilst rendering many of the population homeless. Also at this time, he became an extra Commissioner of the Navy and a Member of Parliament. In 1702, Shovell was narrowly beaten to Vigo when George Rooke captured the Spanish plate fleet. Later, he was ordered by Rooke to bring the treasure home: this he achieved in appalling weather without losing any of the predominantly silver coinage. The following year, 1703, Shovell went out as Commander-in-Chief to the Mediterranean and on his return was lucky to avoid death in the Great Storm.

In 1704, Shovell played his part in the successful siege of Gibraltar and at the subsequent Battle of Malaga was largely responsible for the fact that Rooke's fleet was not defeated. After Rooke's retirement, in practical terms, Shovell commanded the fleet during Lord Peterborough's brilliant capture of Barcelona. Two years later, Shovell did his best to spur on the Duke of Savoy and Prince Eugene to take the vital French port of Toulon. It was through no fault of his that the siege failed and whilst returning home on 22 October 1707, Shovell's flagship, the *Association* was wrecked on the rocks to the south-west of the Isles of Scilly. This led to Shovell's demise in his 57th year.

Note

Dates in *The Other Norfolk Admirals* are given in 'Old Style,' in accordance with the Julian calendar, except that the beginning of each year is written as 1 January and not 25 March which was actually the case at the time. In continental Europe, the 'New Style' Gregorian calendar was in use and was 10 days ahead of the date used in England. Thus, to the English the Battle of Lowestoft was fought on 3 June 1665 and to the Dutch it was 13 June.

1

The Early Lives of the Three Admirals and the First Anglo-Dutch War 1625–1655

During the first quarter of the 17th century, there were a number of ports on the North Norfolk coast. Amongst them was Salthouse, the home of the seafaring Parr family, whose daughter, Katherine, married on 28 September 1623, a John Myngs of the parish of St Katherine's in the City of London. According to Laughton,[1] John Myngs was a near kinsman, if not son of Nicholas Mynnes, the scion of a long-established Norfolk family.[2] In the first year of Charles I's reign, 1625, a son was born to the union of John Myngs and his wife of two years, Katherine; the baby was baptised in St Nicholas Church, Salthouse on 21 November.[3] Over the next 40 years, the baby, Christopher, would become famous, as a swashbuckling buccaneer and then a knighted Stuart admiral, before his premature death at the Four Days' Battle of 1666. Christopher Myngs loved to boast that his mother was a hoyman's daughter and his father a shoemaker.[4] The reality was a little different: the Parrs were property owners as well as seafarers based on Salthouse and John Myngs, in reality, was a wealthy manufacturer of footwear.[5]

Today, the village of Salthouse is very different from the one Christopher Myngs knew as, in the middle of the 17th century, an embankment was placed across the 'Mayne Channel', leading to the demise of Salthouse plus the neighbouring Blakeney and Cley-next-the-Sea as working ports. Throughout his life Myngs owned property in Salthouse which in the fullness of time he passed on to his son, another Christopher. In 1698, a daughter, Mary, was buried in the nave of St Nicholas Church with the inscription: 'Here lieth interrd the Body of MARY MYNGS Daughter of the late Renown'd Sr Christopher Myngs She Departed this

---

1 Sir John Knox Laughton [1830–1915]: Professor of Modern History at King's College, London and co-founder of the Navy Records Society. He wrote nearly 1,000 biographies of naval personalities for the *Dictionary of National Biography*, including those of Myngs, Narbrough and Shovell.
2 The family name has been spelt in numerous ways: Myngs, Mings, Mins, Minn, Mine, Mynne, Mynnes, Mynge etc.
3 Norfolk Record Office (NRO): PD 23/1, Salthouse Parish Register. The *Dictionary of National Biography (DNB)*, Myngs [Knighton] states the 22nd.
4 A hoy was a small coastal sailing vessel, characteristically with a single mast.
5 *DNB*, Myngs [Laughton].

life 27 day of January Anno Dom: 169⅞.'[6] Today, in Salthouse, there are two houses which are claimed to be the former home of Christopher Myngs.

As the crow flies, just over six miles to the west of Salthouse is the hamlet of Cockthorpe where, at the font of All Saints Church, a baby boy was baptised on 11 October 1640, a little under 15 years after Christopher Myngs' own baptism.[7] The infant, named John, was the fifth child of Gregorie Narborough, who was probably the tenant of a Cockthorpe farm owned by the Calthorpes, the local landowners. Cockthorpe sits on an elevated plateau and was originally part of the church lands of the See of Thetford. In the 14th century, its rector and 'lord' was Roger Bacon, an ancestor of the polymath Francis Bacon, from whose family the land passed to the Calthorpes. It has been suggested that Gregorie was a lowly farm labourer,[8] although the Narborough family was an ancient one dating back to the 13th century. Unlike his father, John would drop the first 'o' in the spelling of his surname as he invariably demonstrated, in adult life, with his well-formed handwriting of letters and documents. In the introduction to this book, we have already seen that by tradition the Myngs and Narbrough families were related.[9]

A decade after the birth of John Narbrough, another child was baptised at the same font in All Saints Church, Cockthorpe. Thus, on 25 November 1650, the infant Cloudesley Shovell was christened: his parents were John Shovell and his wife Anne. It is likely that John Shovell was a small-time farmer, a tenant of the Calthorpes, who also owned land at nearby Morston. In 1801, there were only four houses, supporting six families with a total population of 32 persons in the hamlet of Cockthorpe.[10] A century and a half earlier, Cockthorpe was unlikely to have been appreciably bigger, yet it would spawn two famous Stuart admirals in John Narbrough and Cloudesley Shovell. Sometimes Christopher Myngs' name is added to those of Narbrough and Shovell making them the 'Cockthorpe Admirals', although there does not appear to be any firm evidence for this assertion. The Myngs family were very much associated with nearby Salthouse. Whilst the details of the origins of Christopher Myngs and John Narbrough are sparse, much more is known about those of Cloudesley Shovell.

The name Shovell is unusual and a multitude of exotic theories have been put forward to explain its origins. It has been suggested that it was derived from: Shuvaloff, a Russian noble family; Chauvel, a common name in Normandy; de Schoville, a family who followed William I from France.[11] However, the most likely explanation is that Shovell was an anglicised form of a Dutch or Flemish name such as Schouvel. Indeed, in the 16th century, many of the indigenous population of the Low Countries settled in Norfolk and the name Shovell first appeared in Norwich as early as 1554. In that year one John Shovell was admitted as a citizen of Norwich. 'Johes Shovell alien: indigena dyer apprentice: Willmi Morley jurat:

6   A. Linnell, *A Guide to St Nicholas Church Salthouse Norfolk*.

7   NRO: PD 493/1, Cockthorpe Baptismal Register.

8   J. David Davies, *Pepys's Navy* (Barnsley: Seaforth Publishing 2008), p. 99.

9   Florence Dyer, *The Life of Admiral Sir John Narbrough* (London: Philip Allan 1931), p. 2; Francis Blomefield, *County History of Norfolk*, Vol. 2 (London: W. Miller 1805 1808), p. 218.

10   *Blakeney Area Historical Society booklet*.

11   National Maritime Museum (NMM): Robert Marsham-Townshend (RMT) MS, MAT 6: correspondence relating to the Brereton and Shorting families.

et admifis est civis die veneris in festo Sci Mathei appli primo et Sedo Phi et Marie.' 'Alien indigena' meant that he was either born overseas or perhaps in England, but to foreign parents. This John Shovell, a dyer, was Cloudesley Shovell's great-great-grandfather.

Amongst the children of John Shovell, the dyer, was another John [Cloudesley Shovell's great-grandfather] who held several important positions in his home city of Norwich which culminated in his appointment as Sheriff in 1606.[12] In 1601, Nathaniel Shovell, a son of John Shovell, was baptised at St Saviours, Norwich and is likely to have been a son of John Shovell, the Sheriff. Nathaniel [grandfather of Cloudesley Shovell] appeared to have farmed in North Norfolk and on his death, in 1636, he bequeathed his lands at Morston to his son, another Nathaniel, and failing him to a younger son, John. Nathaniel the younger vanished from the scene so that the land at Morston passed to his brother, John, the father of Cloudesley Shovell. In essence, the Shovell family were 16th century refugees from the Low Countries who became dyers, held administrative posts in Norwich, before moving to farm in North Norfolk. In adult life, the excellent relationship Cloudesley Shovell enjoyed with Dutch seamen in particular might have been explained by his evident good nature and also by his family's continental origins.[13]

The maternal side of Cloudesley Shovell's family also came from the coastal region of North Norfolk. His mother was Anne Jenkenson, daughter of Henry Jenkenson of Cley-next-the-Sea by his wife Lucy, daughter of Thomas Cloudesley of the same village. At the time of Cloudesley Shovell's birth, Anne was 22-years-old and she also had a brother two years younger than herself, confusingly also called Cloudesley, who would later serve in the navy at the same time as his distinguished nephew. It is clear that the surname of his great-grandfather [Thomas] and thus the maiden name of his maternal grandmother [Lucy] was used as an unusual Christian name for the future admiral. In later life, Cloudesley Shovell would spell his name in a variety of ways; Cloudesley, Cloudsley, Cloudsly, Clowdisley, Clowdisly, Cloud, Clow, Clowd amongst others. In that era phonetic spelling was the order of the day.[14]

The date and place of the marriage of Cloudesley Shovell's parents, John Shovell and Anne Jenkenson is unknown, although it is likely to have occurred around 1645 during the general chaos of the English civil war. The union produced at least three children, sons Nathaniel, John and Cloudesley. Although Gilbert Crockatt, Cloudesley Shovell's eventual parish priest at Crayford,[15] recorded that he was the second son, in his deathbed will John Shovell listed Cloudesley after the other two boys. There are no baptismal records for either Nathaniel or John and Cloudesley Shovell's entry for 25 November 1650, in the Cockthorpe records, is decidedly odd. It is an interpolation written in the style of the 17th century and has been explained in two ways.[16] Firstly, according to Crockatt, the family were supporters

---

12   Timothy Hawse, *Norwich City Officers 1453–1835* (Norwich: Norfolk Record Society 1986).

13   Robert Marsham-Townshend, 'Parentage of Cloudesley Shovell', *Notes and Queries* (London: John Francis 19 January 1895), p. 41; Walter Rye, *Norfolk Families* (Norwich: Goose and Son 1913), p. 798; International Genealogical Index, Norfolk.

14   Marsham-Townshend, 'Parentage of Cloudesley Shovell', p. 41.

15   Cloudesley Shovell bought the May Place estate, Crayford, Kent in 1694.

16   Marsham-Townshend, 'Parentage of Cloudesley Shovell', p. 42; Gilbert Crockatt, *Consolatory Letter to Lady Shovell* (London: George Strahan 1708), preface.

of Charles I,[17] so that the baby may have been baptised in private by a Royalist clergyman. Secondly, the entry was added at the time of the Restoration, in 1660, or still later when Cloudesley was making a name for himself in the navy.

Despite the irregular baptismal entry there can be little doubt that Cloudesley Shovell was born in Cockthorpe. Crockatt, who knew the family well, merely stated that he was born in Norfolk. The anonymous author of Shovell's supposed *Secret Memoirs* is a little more specific in recording that he was born in a small town near Cley, which is compatible with Cockthorpe.[18] Certainly, in 1654, Cloudesley's father was living in Cockthorpe as this was recorded in his deathbed will as his place of abode.[19] Exactly where Anne and John Shovell lived in Cockthorpe is uncertain, although by tradition of the Brereton family, who were descendants, it was the Manor House. Indeed, in the 19th century, members of that family would visit the hamlet and point out the sites relating to their illustrious ancestor.[20] Cockthorpe Hall has also been associated with the family.[21]

Other places in England have claimed to be the birthplace of the future admiral. Amongst them are Yorkshire, Nottinghamshire, Linkinhorne in Cornwall and finally Hastings on the south coast of Sussex. In 1653, there were Shovells in Linkinhorne and it is possible one of the family had moved there from Norfolk prior to Cloudesley's birth. Hastings has also claimed to be the birthplace of Cloudesley Shovell and there is certainly a house or rather part of two medieval houses which traditionally have been associated with his mother or nanny. In 1736, a Captain William Russell used to point out this house in All Saints Street and asserted that he had played with the future admiral as a boy. This does not seem to have been likely.[22]

When Cloudesley Shovell was a little over three-years-old, his father John died, having made a deathbed will on 22 March 1654. 'John Shovell of Cockthorpe in the County of Norfolk Gent being sick of the sickness whereof he died but perfect in mind and memory.' His estate was left to his wife, Anne, with £100 to each of his three sons on their reaching 21-years-of-age. The next few years must have been difficult ones for Anne who had been widowed at 25 years and with at least three young children to bring up alone. No doubt the Jenkenson and Cloudesley families rallied around. Her father-in-law, Nathaniel Shovell, had been dead for nearly 18 years.

The next time we hear of Anne Shovell is on 8 February 1659 when she married a John Flaxman of Walcott, at nearby Gimingham. By this time Cloudesley was in his ninth year and his brothers, Nathaniel and John, were a little older. As the crow flies, Gimingham

---

17   Crockatt, *Consolatory Letter*, preface.

18   Anonymous, *Secret Memoirs of the Life of the honourable Sir Cloudesley Shovell* (London: 1708), p. 3.

19   Marsham-Townshend, 'Parentage of Cloudesley Shovell', p. 42; NMM: RMT MS, MAT 24, copies of the wills of the Shovell family.

20   Rachel Jones [Mrs H], 'Historic Memorials of the Norfolk Coast', *Fraser's Magazine* (September 1881), p. 333.

21   Cockthorpe Hall: *Eastern Daily Press*, 17 October 1986. There are no buildings dating from the middle of the 17th century still standing in Cockthorpe.

22   Marsham-Townshend, 'Parentage of Cloudesley Shovell', pp. 41–3; NMM: RMT MS, MATs, 5, 24, 29c: correspondence concerning the Shovell family in Cornwall, Shovell family wills, extracts from the *St Leonards and Hastings Gazette* for 1895 and 1914; Jones, 'Historic Memorials', p. 333; William Harvey, *History of the Parish of Linkinhorne* (Bodmin: written in 1727 and published in 1876); T. Brett, *St Leonards and Hastings Gazette*, 6 and 13 May 1893; *The Hastings and St Leonards Pictorial Advertiser and Visitors List* (Hastings: 1 January 1914).

and Walcott are respectively 18 and 25 miles east of Cockthorpe, but still in the County of Norfolk. It would seem likely that after her remarriage, Anne took her children to live with her new husband at Walcott. Sadly, the Walcott register showed that her sons, Nathaniel and John died within eight days of each other in February 1664. The fact that the two adolescent young men died in such a short space of time points to some sort of infection, 280 years before the era of antibiotics. The 13-year-old Cloudesley was most likely saved from the same fate by being away at sea with Christopher Myngs and John Narbrough.[23]

The new Anne Flaxman was to have several children by her husband, John, whose occupation is unknown. One of the children, another Anne, was baptised, at Holt, in late January 1672 and she would marry a Thomas Shorting, at Morston, the next village to the east of Cockthorpe, in 1691. Shorting, a well-known Norfolk name, was the Inspector of Customs at nearby Cley and there would be no less than 11 children of the union. Anne and John Flaxman must have moved back to North Norfolk, perhaps to Morston, where Anne had inherited land from her first husband, at some point before her daughter Anne's 1672 Holt baptism.[24] In later life, Cloudesley Shovell was a dutiful son towards his mother, Anne, and also greatly supportive of his half-sister, Anne, and her husband Thomas Shorting. In his will Cloudesley Shovell left the land he owned at Morston, at least in part inherited from his father, John, to his mother and his half-sister, Anne. His mother had the great misfortune to outlive her by now famous son by over 18 months and she was buried, at Morston, in June 1709, aged nearly 81 years.[25]

Nothing is known of the pre-naval education of Christopher Myngs and John Narbrough, although evidently both were intelligent men; the latter's handwriting is beautifully clear and he was also an accomplished artist. A little more is known in the case of Cloudesley Shovell as Gilbert Crockatt recorded: 'his parents having trained him up to such learning as their country schools afforded.'[26] Knowledge of education in Norfolk, prior to the restoration of the monarchy in 1660, is sketchy at best, although from 1581 it was a legal requirement for teachers to subscribe, this leading to a record of their domiciles. Unfortunately, the law does not appear to have been enforced and as women, who did not have to subscribe, did much of the educational work, the records are scanty. The most likely period of Shovell's life when he attended school was during his time at Walcott. In the late 17th century, there were schools at Happisburgh, Bacton, Knapton and Walcott itself. In addition, a school was declared at North Walsham in 1662. It is intriguing to think that Cloudesley Shovell might have attended a school in the same village, North Walsham, as an even more famous Norfolk admiral, Horatio Nelson. In all probability, the young Cloudesley could read and write before going away to sea. But it has to be recorded that his handwriting is difficult to read, unlike that of his mentor John Narbrough.[27]

After his school days, the suggestion that Cloudesley Shovell was apprenticed to a shoemaker is certainly a myth which was probably started by Doctor John Campbell in his naval history: 'apprentice to a mean trade I think that of a shoemaker, to which he applied himself

23   Marsham-Townshend, 'Parentage of Cloudesley Shovell', p. 42; IGI Gimingham.
24   Marsham-Townshend, 'Parentage of Cloudesley Shovell', p. 42.
25   NMM: RMT MS, MAT 24, will of Cloudesley Shovell.
26   Crockatt, *Consolatory Letter*, preface.
27   Edward Carter, *The Norwich Subscription Books 1637–1680* (London: Nelson 1937).

for some years.' Perhaps, Campbell confused the matter with Samuel Pepys' erroneous view that Christopher Myngs' father was a shoemaker. So a legend was created from shoemaker to admiral! In William Winks' 19th century book *Illustrious Shoemakers* [1883], Cloudesley Shovell was given pride of place with a fine portrait on the opening page and then the book continued: 'his parents were glad to send him to the village shoemaker to learn the art and mystery of making and mending boots and shoes.' There is absolutely no evidence for Cloudesley Shovell training as a cobbler.[28]

It is time to return to the early lives of Christopher Myngs and John Narbrough. Details of Myngs' initial career at sea are sparse, although it is likely that from about the age of 10 years he was involved with the coastal trade off East Anglia. As a young man, Myngs served for several years prior to 1648 with the Puritan clergyman, Thomas Brooks and as the latter was a chaplain in the Parliamentary fleet, Myngs must have seen naval service around the time of the civil war. In 1648, he signed a petition calling upon parliament to confront part of the fleet that had revolted and gone across to the Royalist cause. Amongst the other signatories were William Goodson and Richard Badiley with whom he would later serve.[29]

As with Myngs', records of John Narbrough's early career are sketchy. Tradition has it that he first went to sea with Myngs and that in the 1650s he made two voyages to St Helena, one to Guinea and spent two years around the Mediterranean in merchant ships. Probably, he was engaged on convoy duty in the trips to St Helena, as the East India ships were often accompanied home from that island in order to protect them from danger. Narbrough's time in the Mediterranean may well have involved trade with places such as Scanderoon and Smyrna in the Levant.[30]

In late 1651, Captain Richard Badiley was made responsible for the convoy which took merchant ships out to the Eastern Mediterranean. Myngs travelled with Badiley as a super-numerary officer in the 42-gun *Paragon*, formerly named the *Henrietta Maria* in honour of Charles I's queen. Their route took them to Cadiz, through the Straits, to Genoa and Leghorn [Livorno] before proceeding to the Levant.[31] By the onset of the First Anglo-Dutch War in 1652, Myngs was acting as the lieutenant or master of the *Elizabeth* under Captain Jonas Reeve who was still serving with Badiley. The origins of this war were complex: Cromwell bringing in the navigation acts;[32] George Ayscue's capture of 27 Dutch ships sailing for Barbados; Robert Blake's altercation with Maarten Tromp on 19 May 1652, off Dover, in

---

28   John Campbell, *Lives of the British Admirals*, Vol. IV (London: C.J. Barrington 1817), p. 238; John Charnock, *Biographia Navalis*, Vol. II (London: R. Faulder 1794–8), p. 16; William Winks, *Lives of Illustrious Shoemakers* (New York: Funk Wagnalls 1883), p. 5.

29   *DNB*, Myngs [Laughton, Knighton]; Dyer, *Narbrough*, p. 8; Bernard Capp, *Cromwell's Navy : The Fleet and the English Revolution 1648–60* (Oxford: Clarendon Press 1989), p. 31.

30   *DNB*, Narbrough [Laughton, Davies]; Dyer, *Narbrough*, p. 9.

31   The Strait of Gibraltar was known in the eras of Myngs, Narbrough and Shovell as the Straits or Streights. Traditionally, the English called Livorno Leghorn.

32   The navigation acts of 1651 restricted the use of foreign ships for trade between England and her colonies. Exports could be transported solely in English ships and imports carried only in English ships or those belonging to the country of origin of the merchandise.

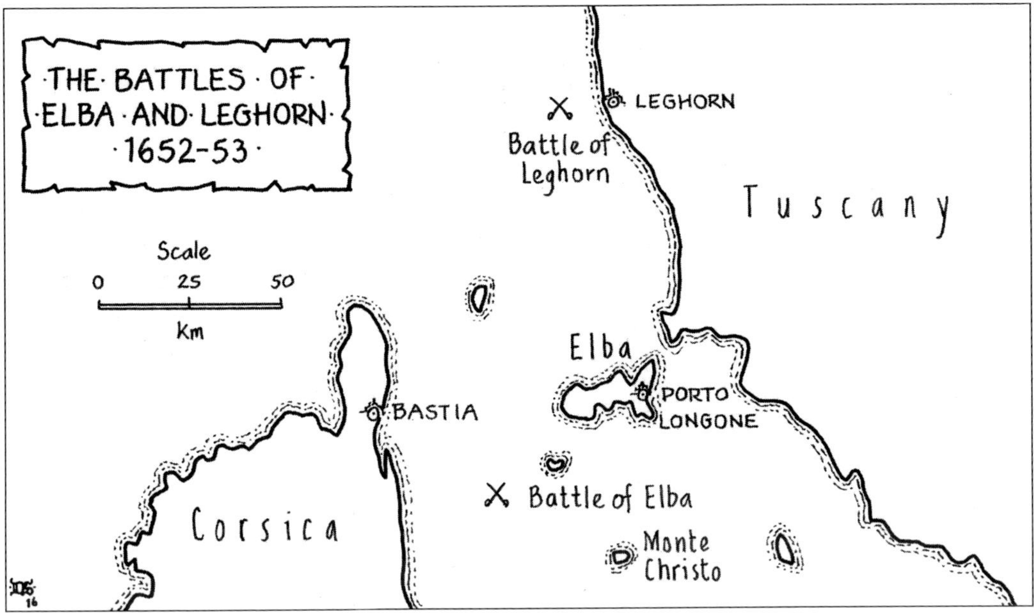

Map 1　The Battles of Elba and Leghorn 1652-1653.

the Battle of Goodwin Sands. George Monck, 1st Duke of Albemarle put it succinctly: 'the Dutch have too much trade and the English are resolved to take it from them.'[33]

On his way back from the Levant, during the late summer of 1652, Badiley hurried with his escort ships to come to the aid of Captain Henry Appleton who had been trapped by the Dutch with a small squadron and some merchant ships at Leghorn. On 28 August, Badiley ran into a superior Dutch fleet, under Johan van Galen, between Elba and Corsica and then the Battle of Elba or Monte Christo took place. At this juncture, Myngs appeared to be still in the *Elizabeth* with Jonas Reeve. Badiley ordered his three armed ships to close in on the stern of his flagship, the *Paragon*. It has been suggested that he was attempting to form a primitive line of battle, but in reality he was probably concentrating his small force for their own protection. The four merchant vessels under Badiley's convoy held back out of harm's way and sailed for Porto Longone, now Porto Azzuria, in Elba. The *Paragon*, the largest of the four English ships, received the bulk of Dutch fire and ended the day with 26 men killed as well as 57 wounded. The *Elizabeth* with Myngs aboard was thought to have fought well, although the *Phoenix* was successfully taken by the Dutch whilst most of her own crew were absent endeavouring to board another enemy ship. Meanwhile, claiming to be on his sick

---

33　*DNB*, Myngs [Laughton, Knighton]; Thomas Spalding, *The Life and Times of Richard Badiley* (Westminster: Archibald Constable and Co 1899), pp. 68, 98–9; Paul Kennedy, *The Rise and Fall of British Naval Mastery* (USA: Random House 1976), p. 48.

bed, Appleton declined to assist Badiley either with ships or his person. Understandably, Badiley was furious with this cowardly lack of support.[34]

Following the merchantmen, Badiley's warships retired to Porto Longone where they were blockaded by van Galen and his Dutch squadron. In fact the Dutch wanted to attack the English ships in harbour, but were forbidden to do so by the local governor despite a suitable financial reward being discretely offered. Badiley's wounded sailors were cared for and his ships repaired, whilst he expectantly awaited the arrival of Appleton and his few ships. The Dutch were able to increase the number of their ships and they plied between Leghorn and Porto Longone to stop any junction of the two English squadrons. After the Dutch withdrawal from Porto Longone, Badiley was able to make contact with Appleton at Leghorn and, at about this time, an order from London instructed Badiley to take overall command of all English vessels in the Mediterranean, no doubt to Appleton's chagrin.[35]

On St Andrews Day, 20 November 1652, the now Commodore Badiley arranged for the *Phoenix*, captured by the Dutch earlier in the summer, to be cut out from her anchorage in the outer roads of Leghorn and sailed out to sea. The Dutch captain of the *Phoenix*, the young Cornelis Tromp who will feature again in later chapters, was caught unawares dining with his officers. This most belligerent of men, in a most uncharacteristic manner, leapt overboard receiving a slash with a cutlass 'where a brave man is never proud of a scar.'[36] Ferdinando II de Medici, the Grand Duke of Tuscany, was offended by the removal of the *Phoenix* from his supposedly neutral port. Ten days later, off Dungeness, Maarten Tromp, father of Cornelis, defeated Robert Blake's fleet and so giving the Dutch temporary control of the English Channel. This indirectly made the position of the English ships at Leghorn even more problematical as the Grand Duke, already offended by the *Phoenix* affair, now favoured the Dutch in light of their recent Dungeness success.[37]

Appleton and his ships were given an ultimatum by the Grand Duke to leave his port and van Galen's considerably superior force was waiting for them just outside Leghorn. Badiley had come up with a scheme whereby he would sail towards Leghorn and then Appleton was to break through the Dutch ships to join him. If a successful junction were made, the two squadrons combined would have a better chance of seeing off the Dutch than as separate entities. Unfortunately, on 4 March 1653, van Galen's vessels, having spotted Badiley, made a feint towards the English, leading to a premature departure of Appleton's ships from Leghorn. Disaster immediately struck Appleton when one of his ships, the *Bonaventure*, blew up after a shot ignited her magazine. Only one English vessel was able to fight its way through to Badiley who had done his best to come to Appleton's assistance despite a contrary wind. The action was named the Battle of Leghorn and was a victory for the Dutch, although poor van Galen would later die from his shattered leg. Appleton had the indignity

---

34   Spalding, *Richard Badiley*, pp. 101–13; William Laird Clowes, *The Royal Navy a History from the Earliest Times to the Present*, Vol. II (London: Sampson Low and Marston 1898), pp. 161–3.

35   Spalding, *Richard Badiley*, pp. 119–26; Laird Clowes, *Royal Navy*, Vol. II, pp. 162–4.

36   Presumably a laceration of his buttocks or back.

37   Spalding, *Richard Badiley*, pp. 141–2, 162; Laird Clowes, *Royal Navy*, Vol. II, pp. 164–5.

of being taken prisoner by the Dutch.[38] Myngs is thought to have continued as lieutenant or master of the *Elizabeth*, still part of Badiley's squadron, during the action.[39]

It would not be long before the Grand Duke of Tuscany understood that he had been premature in throwing in his lot with the Dutch; in late-February 1653, he received news of Robert Blake's victory over Maarten Tromp at the Battle of Portland. Meanwhile, Badiley realised that his small, undermanned squadron, greatly damaged in the Battle of Leghorn, was in a hopeless situation in the Mediterranean and elected to return home. At Cadiz, he contemplated sending the *Elizabeth* and another small vessel back into the Mediterranean to act as commerce raiders against the Dutch. But on hearing their new orders, the crew of the *Elizabeth* promptly mutinied and 'no encouraging language, with a proffer of six months' pay,[40] nor laying before them the advantage like to come to the nation thereby, nor the danger of refusal according to the tenor of the 11th article of war, would work upon them.[41] Badiley was forced to drop his plan and set sail for England. Soon after leaving Cadiz, his squadron captured a Dutch merchantman, the *Augustine*, near Cape St Vincent. In order to sail her home, Badiley requested two English sailors from each ship to man her, these then to be replaced by Dutch prisoners. Two of the merchant ship captains refused to obey the order and Badiley was forced to overlook this gross insubordination. The sorely tried squadron eventually reached the Downs in May 1653.[42]

During the voyage home, Jonas Reed, captain of the *Elizabeth*, was killed in an action with a Dutch ship, leaving a destitute wife with seven children, and Christopher Myngs was appointed to his first command in Reed's place. Reed's death was reported to have been as the result of an action with the Dutch in the Straits and, if this is the case, Myngs would have faced the mutiny at Cadiz as the newly appointed captain of the *Elizabeth*.[43] Alternatively, Reed may have been killed in the engagement with the *Augustine*. On return to England the men of the *Elizabeth* insisted in being paid off, but the ship was soon refitted and re-manned.[44]

Myngs missed the English victory at the Battle of the Gabbard, fought off the coast of Suffolk on 2–3 June 1653. George Monck, Richard Deane and later Robert Blake with around 100 ships overwhelmed Maarten Tromp and Witte de With plus their Dutch fleet of a similar size. The Dutch were forced to flee to their own ports having lost around 20 ships. The only downside for the English was the death of Richard Deane. He is reputed to have taken it as a sign of imminent death when he found, on the eve of battle, that rats had eaten

38 Henry Appleton did his best to lay the blame for the defeat firmly at Richard Badiley's door. Also, he claimed that Badiley had ordered him to come out of Leghorn with his ships. Badiley was forced to appear before the Committee for Scottish and Irish affairs of which Oliver Cromwell was a member. In December 1653, Badiley was acquitted and eventually made a rear-admiral. The deeply unpleasant, but personally brave, Appleton was never employed at sea again.

39 Spalding, *Richard Badiley*, pp. 173–4, 186–211; Laird Clowes, *Royal Navy*, Vol. II, pp. 175–7.

40 Seamen were paid 10d a day during the interregnum and the rate remained the same for 150 years.

41 Spalding, *Richard Badiley*, p. 233.

42 Spalding, *Richard Badiley*, pp. 231–4.

43 Reed was reported killed, on 4 May 1653, in an engagement with the Dutch in the Straits [*CSP Dom, Int*, Vol. 140–1, petition 16 June 1653], yet Badiley's squadron was back in the Downs on 8 May 1653 [Spalding, *Richard Badiley*, p. 234]. There must be confusion with place or dates.

44 Laird Clowes, *Royal Navy*, Vol. II, p. 177; *DNB*, Myngs [Laughton, Knighton].

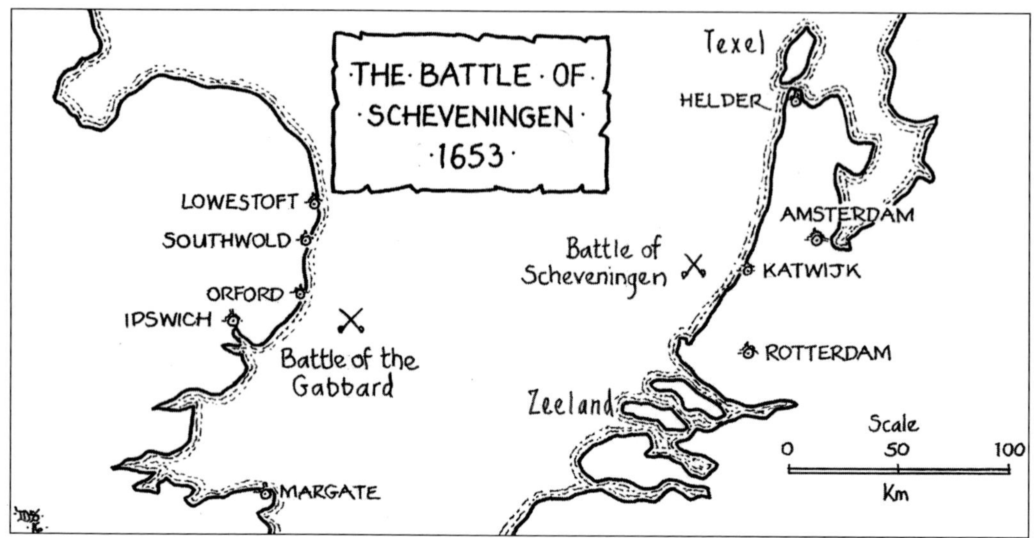

Map 2 The Battle of Scheveningen 1653.

away part of his doublet.[45] Peace negotiations were opened, but the English fleet having re-victualled set sail to successfully blockade the Dutch coast.[46]

In late July, the final bloody action of the Dutch war took place off Scheveningen and Christopher Myngs would play his part in the refitted *Elizabeth*. The English blockade rapidly produced hardship amongst the inhabitants of the Dutch coastal region. As the first step to breaking the blockade, on the 24th, Maarten Tromp left the River Maas with around 80 ships proposing to link up with Witte de With; he was in the Frisian Islands, commanding another 30 vessels, some 80 miles to the north. The English ships watching Texel noticed that de With had moved his ships to a position outside the port of Helder with a view to joining Tromp. George Monck, commanding the English fleet, after consultation with his flag officers, suspected that an attempt was to be made by the Dutch to amalgamate their vessels into a single fleet and acted accordingly. He sailed to the south and in the morning of 29 July, Tromp's ships were sighted.[47]

Tromps' first action was to turn away to the south-east to give de With the opportunity to escape into the open sea. At 5:00 p.m. on the 29th, Monck's leading ships caught up with the hindmost of Tromp's, just to the north of Scheveningen off Katwijk. Around 30 of Monck's ships attacked the Dutch who lost two ships and the fighting continued until darkness came down. The next day, the wind was so strong that little progress could be made by Monck and Tromp, although during the afternoon de With managed to join the latter. The Battle of Scheveningen opened at 7:00 a.m. on 31 July 1653, with the English fighting in three squadrons and the Dutch in five. Myngs was reputed to be at the battle,

---

45 Capp, *Cromwell's Navy*, p. 326.
46 Laird Clowes, *Royal Navy*, Vol. II, pp. 191–2.
47 Laird Clowes, *Royal Navy*, Vol. II, pp. 192–3; Spalding, *Richard Badiley*, pp. 280–3; David Plant, *The Battle of Scheveningen 1653* (self-published 2010).

but it is uncertain which squadron he was in.[48] There followed the most vicious and bloody battle of the whole war with the incomparable Maarten Tromp, the hero of the Dutch navy, succumbing to a musket ball in the heart, quite early in the action. Supposedly, he died with a prayer for his country on his lips. The English lost two flag officers; Thomas Graves was killed in the action and James Peacock would subsequently die from burns suffered at the hands of a fireship. The Dutch lost 14–30 ships and the English only two. Overall the action was considered to be an English victory and the war would come to an end at the Treaty of Westminster in 1654.[49]

In early October 1653, Myngs, still in the *Elizabeth*, transported the Vice-Chancellor of Poland, Jerome de Radziciowice Radzeieiowsky, with his party across the Channel to Dieppe. He had presented to Parliament a letter, from Queen Christina of Sweden, asking for the support of the English ambassador at Constantinople in his negotiations there. Radzeieiowsky's journey would take him through France to Genoa and then on to the Eastern Mediterranean. During the return journey from Dieppe, Myngs came across a fleet of Dutch merchant ships under convoy of two men-of-war and a sharp action ensued. The Dutch vessels were successfully taken by Myngs who escorted them into the Downs and, on 4 October, he reported the affair to the authorities. Two days later, parliament ordered that the Council of State take notice of the captain of the *Elizabeth* [Myngs] and consider the widow and children of the master who had been killed in the action.[50]

In November 1653 Myngs, in the *Elizabeth*, was part of a squadron that took Bulstrode Whitelocke to Gothenburg to become an extraordinary ambassador to Sweden.[51] He had been instructed by Oliver Cromwell to form an alliance with Queen Christina which allowed trade to pass through the Sound [Strait between Zealand and the Swedish province of Scania] and other commercial matters. Free access to the Sound was essential for English trade in the Baltic. It must have been a rough, late autumnal crossing as Whitelocke was seasick. However, he found time to talk to the mariners and watched them play: 'affording them now and then a douse in the neck, or a kick in jest ---- which demeanours please those kind of people.'[52] The *Elizabeth* was forced to remain at Gothenburg for some time by unfavourable winds and the crew suffered a great deal of illness. Myngs wrote that 90 men were sick and five more had died. On the way home, Myngs exchanged shot with a Dutch convoy, but was unable to take the matter further in view of the distressed state of his crew.[53]

Still in the *Elizabeth*, Myngs spent most of 1654 in the English Channel off the French coast. At the end of May, he was at Gluckstadt, Denmark, where two of his sailors quoted a

---

48   Two years later, Thomas Brooks, whilst promoting Myngs' career with the commissioners of the admiralty, indicated that he had served with William Goodson who was rear-admiral of the blue in the battle. This may indicate that Myngs was in Goodson's blue squadron at the time.

49   Laird Clowes, *Royal Navy*, Vol. II, pp. 193–9; John Barratt, *Cromwell's Wars at Sea* (Barnsley: Pen and Sword Books 2006), p. 154.

50   *DNB*, Myngs [Laughton, Knighton]; *CSP, relating to English Affairs at Venice*, Vol. 29, 1653–4, pp. 105–20.

51   His mother was Elizabeth Bulstrode. At his baptism, a godfather instructed that the child be named Bulstrode. When the priest demurred, the godfather insisted that he be christened Bulstrode or Elizabeth! Hence the unusual Christian name.

52   Capp, *Cromwell's Navy*, p. 246.

53   *DNB*, Myngs, [Laughton, Knighton]; Francis Davenport (ed), *European Treaties Bearing on the History of the United States and its Dependencies* (Washington: Carnegie Institute 1917), p. 22.

Rich Thursby, 'that 5,000 of the King of Scots' old soldiers had entered the army, and nearly as many more the navy, to cut the throats of those that stood for the protector and opposed them.'[54] Myngs was very much a supporter of Cromwell.

Myngs, aboard the *Elizabeth*, was again in the Channel during the early months of 1655. His former shipmate and friend, Thomas Brooks, endeavoured to persuade the commissioners of the admiralty to promote Myngs: 'he is a man fearing the Lord; a man of sound principles, and of blameless life and conversation; he is one of much valour, and has shown it again and again in several engagements and by the prizes he has taken. Vice-admiral Goodson and Vice-admiral Badiley,[55] if they were here, would underwrite this writing from their knowledge of him: more than I have written I have heard them say.' He also said that Myngs 'had brains on both sides of his head.'[56] Brooks was an influential Independent minister then based at St Margaret's, New Fish Street Hill, in the City of London and he was known to Oliver Cromwell.[57] In March 1655, Myngs brought back Bulstrode Whitelocke from Sweden and landed him at Gravesend. At this juncture Myngs was troubled by his drunken boatswain who disobeyed orders.[58]

Later in 1655, Myngs would renew his acquaintance with Admiral William Goodson in a warmer climate.

54   *CSP Dom, Int*, Vol. 73, 11 July 1654.
55   William Goodson [around 1609–10 to in or after 1680]. He was born in Great Yarmouth, Norfolk.
56   *CSP Dom, Int*, Vol. 128, 30 January 1655.
57   *DNB*, Brooks [Liu]. St Margaret's was destroyed in the Fire of London and never rebuilt. Today, the Monument stands on the site.
58   *CSP Dom, Int*, Vol. 34, 23 March 1655.

2

Kit Myngs the Buccaneer 1655–1663

The First Anglo-Dutch War came to an end in the spring of 1654, and this allowed Oliver Cromwell to turn his mind to challenging the omnipotent Spanish in the West Indies. He had his mind very much on Spain's land and trade. In December, a squadron of 17 warships and transport vessels left Portsmouth for the Caribbean under the command of Admiral William Penn. The transports carried 2,500 soldiers led by General Robert Venables who brought his domineering wife with him.[1] Early in the New Year, after a 35-day voyage, Penn's force arrived at Barbados and following a two month delay 3,500 volunteers were raised locally. Eventually, in April, the expeditionary force arrived off Santo Domingo in Hispaniola,[2] intent upon an amphibious landing on the jewel of the Spanish Antilles.[3]

Part of the force under Admiral William Goodson sought a landing point for the troops to the west. Finally, the men were landed all of 30 miles from Santo Domingo and with great difficulty attempted to find a way through the jungle to the town. Once the Spanish understood what was happening, they attacked Venables' unfortunate men and repulsed them. Total casualties from disease and enemy action were about 1,000 men. Faced with this catastrophe Penn and Venables decided to cut their losses and withdrew. In order to save face at home, after their failure in Hispaniola, they made an unopposed landing on nearby Jamaica and soon rid themselves of the few Spanish settlers living on the island. In July 1655, Penn sailed for England leaving Goodson with a few ships behind. Goodson sailed to Santa Marta, in what is today Colombia, and burnt the town with little gain of booty. Next stop was to follow the coast to the south-west as far as Cartagena, which he realised was too strong for him to attack and so he slipped back to Jamaica.[4]

Early in 1656, on 15 January, William Goodson was joined in Jamaica by his fellow Norfolk mariner, Christopher Myngs, who had sailed from England, in November 1655, in the year-old, 54-gun, *Marston Moor*. Myngs had had considerable difficulty in putting together a crew for his new ship. Firstly, there was a delay as Myngs could not be found and his absence was excused to the naval authorities by his friend, the Puritan preacher, Thomas Brooks. Brooks

---

1   Lucie Street, *An Uncommon Sailor a Portrait of Admiral Sir William Penn* (Bourne End: Kensal Press 1986), p. 77.

2   Modern-day Haiti and the Dominican Republic.

3   Florence Dyer, 'Captain Myngs in the West Indies', *Mariner's Mirror*, Vol. 18 (United Kingdom: Society for Nautical Research 1932), pp. 168–71.

4   Dyer, 'Myngs in the West Indies', p. 172.

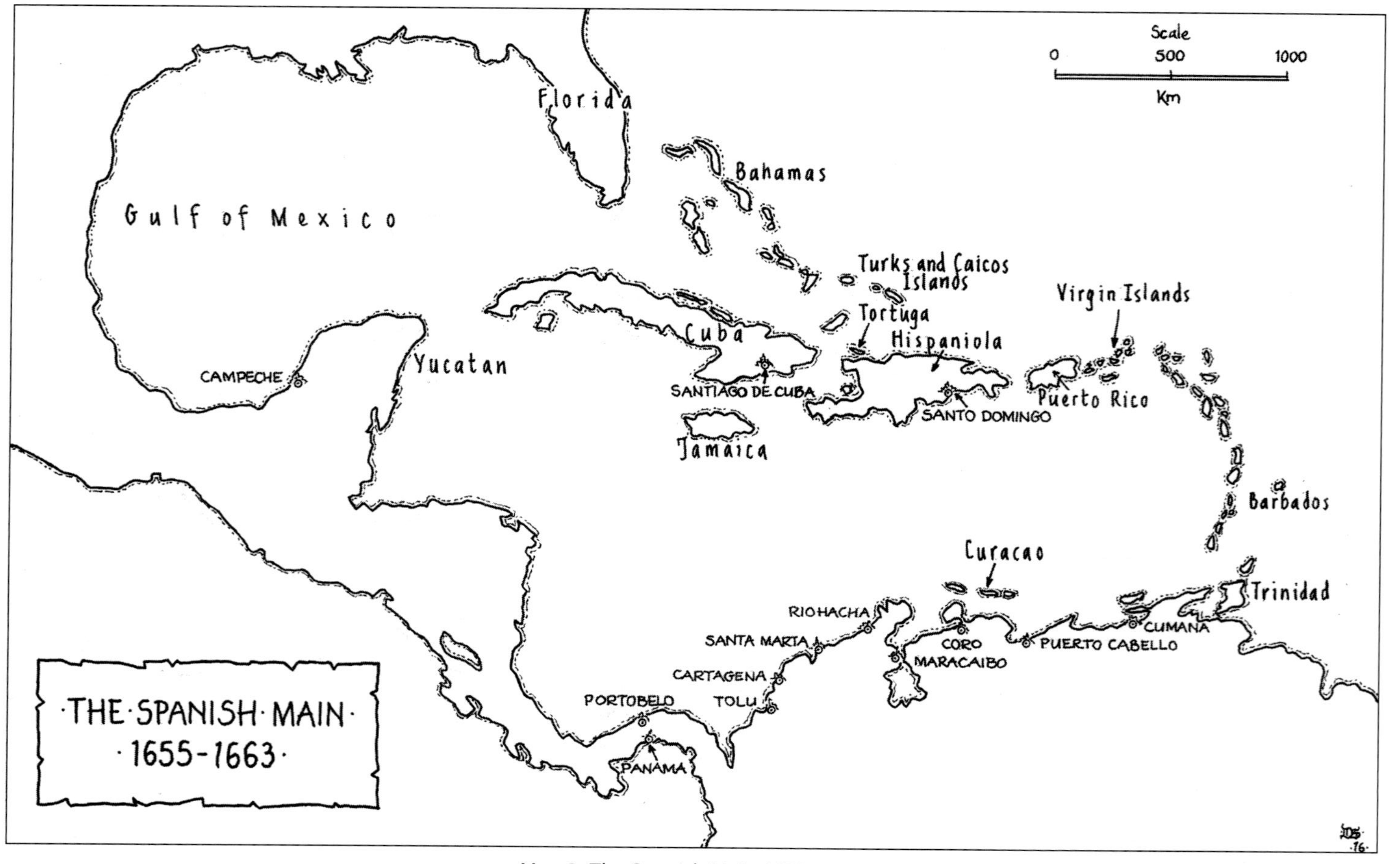

Map 3 The Spanish Main 1655-1663.

wrote: 'hopes his absence will be no prejudice to him, nor raise any frowns or clouds in their [the commissioners'] countenance. He can fancy he hears his horse dash, but a word to the wise is enough; hopes may apologise for him.' Secondly, the crew of the *Marston Moor* who had only recently returned from the Caribbean, had not been paid and mutinied. On taking up his command, Myngs realised that he had no chance of getting the old crew to serve again and sacked them. It was clear that 'if they [the old crew] were compelled to sail in the ship they might infect others with their baseness and fears.' Such was the high mortality rate in the West Indies, men were not keen to serve there, and some vowed to be hanged rather than go back. Myngs with his customary energy, then looked for a new crew from ships then at Portsmouth, found 30 men of the ship's complement of around 300, and sailed to Spithead where he said that he had enlisted a further 130 volunteers. Here he insisted that the navy agent pay his men immediately despite this being highly irregular. Myngs also denied having bribed the few men such as he had to serve. By foul means and fair, somehow he put together sufficient crew to sail the *Marston Moor* across the Atlantic. Some men were reputed to have been suspended from another ship for having struck an officer. Myngs was beginning to demonstrate his considerable man-management skills. Eventually, he sailed on 10 November 1655.[5]

During the spring, Goodson and Myngs made another attempt on the Spanish Main.[6] This time Riohacha was burnt with little plunder gained, and then they sailed down the coast to water at Santa Marta and finally on to Cartagena before returning to Jamaica. Little had been achieved and Goodson made further unsuccessful attempts on the Spanish Plate Fleet which was on route to Cadiz. Myngs ferried 1,400 planters with their wives, children and servants from the island of Nevis to inhabit Jamaica. In January 1657, Goodson sailed for England, to be followed a month later by Myngs. Myngs' three-ship force stopped off in the Bahamas to purchase 8,560 pounds of turtle meat at £107 for the crews to live on during their transatlantic crossing.[7]

Myngs, in the *Marston Moor*, arrived at Dover in July, paid off the crew, and then he took leave in order to marry. There is some doubt whether this was to his first wife Mary or to his second wife Rebecca Stone. Once more his faithful friend, Thomas Brooks, had to cover for him as he was still looking after his personal affairs when summoned by the admiralty. Brooks argued that the commissioners should permit Myngs as much leave as possible as '[Myngs] had given sufficient proof of his ability.' In any event Myngs' father, John, had already written to recall him from the country. Married life was to be short-lived, as by Christmas [1657] he was back on board his ship again, sailing for the West Indies. Oliver Cromwell had entrusted Myngs with £2,572-17s-11½d, which was to be used on the fortification of Jamaica. During the voyage, Myngs took six Dutch merchant ships and three victuallers which had infringed the navigation acts whilst trading with Barbados. To his fury, the admiralty court in Jamaica did not recognise the captured ships as prizes and the matter was referred back to England for adjudication. Myngs commented 'the worm will eat, ships will decay, decks will leak and goods be damnified, especially what requires present disposal.' It was not until 1659 that only one of the ships was officially deemed a prize and Myngs then had his paltry prize money.[8]

5   Dyer, 'Myngs in the West Indies', pp. 174–5.
6   Modern-day Florida, Central America and the north coast of South America.
7   Dyer, 'Myngs in the West Indies', pp. 176–8.
8   Dyer, 'Myngs in the West Indies', pp. 178–80.

On 2 March 1658, Christopher Myngs reached Jamaica and started to relish the fact that he was now the senior naval officer on the station and would be able to demonstrate his aptitude for leading the irregular buccaneer forces. In May 1658, four Spanish troopships came to anchor off the north coast of Jamaica and discharged 550 Mexican soldiers ashore. A month later, Myngs ferried the Governor, Edward D'Oyley, and the irregular forces, who soon put the unwanted invaders to the sword. The Spanish artillery pieces were carried back to the capital, Cagway,[9] and incorporated into its defences. Soon Myngs was on the move again, in this his first independent action against the Spanish Main. Poor Santa Marta was assaulted once more, followed by Tolu to the south-west. The icing on the cake for Myngs, was the interception of three Spanish merchantmen on route from Cartagena to Portobelo. Perhaps it was the captain of one these ships, a Spanish grandee with a long string of titles, who was so distressed to find that he had been taken by plain Kit Myngs! Later, the three ships were sold at a considerable profit to men who would soon become famous corsairs.[10]

After his excellent work with its rich reward, Myngs took his own ship the *Marston Moor*, together with the *Hector*, the *Cagway*, plus a large number of 'freebooters' on his next raid to the Spanish Main.[11] Early in 1659, Myngs tacked against the prevailing winds, further to the east than either he or William Goodson had sailed before. His small fleet appeared before the unsuspecting Spanish in Cumana now in Venezuela. Rapidly, Myngs' men sacked the port, before returning to their ships and sailing with a good westerly wind to Puerto Cabello. This speedy action precluded the possibility of any alarm reaching the unfortunate Spanish inhabitants overland. Puerto Cabello too was rapidly sacked before Myngs raced still further to the west and continued the destruction at Coro.

In the roads of Coro, Myngs found two richly laden Dutch merchant ships sailing under Spanish colours. Each ship contained at least 400 pounds of silver ingots belonging to the King of Spain with a value of £200,000–£300,000 plus, according to Myngs, minted money worth £50,000.[12] By the time the expedition had returned to Jamaica with the richest prize ever to reach the island, the 22 treasure chests had been broken open and much of their contents had been looted. It was rumoured that the crew had fought over the spoils.[13] Myngs argued that it was normal practice for irregular forces to help themselves to some of the treasure after a vigorous action such as this one. The Governor of Jamaica, D'Oyley, and the Jamaican court were far from happy with the situation. Myngs was suspended and sent home in his own ship, the *Marston Moor*, to be tried for his defrauding the state. D'Oyley stated: 'had suspended for disobeying his orders and plundering the hold of one of the prizes of 12,000 pieces of eight.' He continued that Myngs' behaviour was 'so unhandsome and contradictory' and 'he was so distasteful to the other officers of the fleet' that he did not think he would get a fair trial in Jamaica. 'There hath been a constant market with these goods on board the *Marston Moor* without any controule----.' Possibly the other sea officers were just plain jealous of Myngs' good fortune. The prevailing view was that Myngs had

---

9   Kingston, Jamaica.
10   Robert Searle, John Morris, and the Dutchman Laurens Prins.
11   Freebooters: lawless adventurers.
12   Total value in 2017 around £6,810,000.
13   It was not unheard of, during the Dutch wars, for the crews to be so keen to strip a damaged prize that they ignored orders to leave and drowned when it sank beneath their persons.

'lost his head' as the Jamaican authorities had refused to recognise the six Dutch prizes that he had captured on route to the West Indies.[14]

Myngs did not take his suspension lying down and counter-attacked by claiming that the charges had been trumped up by the Steward-General, one Cornelius Burough. Burough, a personal enemy of Myngs, 'agreed with those who thought that his sanity had been affected.' Also he was livid with Myngs for making an all too public comment on the deck of his ship that he, Burough, was a 'rogue and rascal.' Burough was not the only person to complain about Myngs, as the influential planter, Captain William Dalyson, wrote that if the truth were known Myngs 'would be found no better than he is, a proud vain speaking fool, and a knave in cheating the state and robbing merchants.' Strong words indeed from representatives of an island where corruption was endemic.

In the spring of 1659, the suspended Myngs arrived back in England and the following 1 June, after some investigation, he appeared before a Council of War consisting of 'the Lord General and 9 others.' After considering the allegations made by Burough, Myngs was asked for an explanation. 'He denied that he spoke any such words; what he spake was in passion and related to private differences between them, also denied the petition as to his being unfaithful to the State.' Myngs was cleared of all charges by a sympathetic hearing of the war council. It was highly unlikely that the authorities would wish to make an example of such a popular and brave naval commander whose growing reputation had preceded him. Of course this was the time of political unrest in the lead up to the Restoration of Charles II and the country had more important things on its mind. Myngs was sufficiently back in favour, by November 1659, to join four other captains in signing a letter to George Monck, which justified the army's dissolution of the Rump Parliament.[15]

Although it has been written that Myngs was back in Jamaica by the end of 1659,[16] this seems highly unlikely, given that he had signed the letter to Monck on 4 November. Indeed his movements during the period 1660–1 are obscure. Perhaps he was in Jamaica for part of the time and England for the rest of it. His movements in 1662 are much clearer. Myngs arrived at Port Royal in Jamaica, in August 1662, in his new command, the 34-gun *Centurion*. It is likely that Cloudesley Shovell was part of the crew of the *Centurion*, perhaps as a captain's servant, as we know that he was in the West Indies with Myngs in 1663.[17] Also on board his ship was the new Royalist Governor of Jamaica, Thomas, Lord Windsor, who had replaced Myngs' enemy Edward D'Oyley. Windsor brought with him instructions from the new king, Charles II, that if the Spanish refused to trade with them, force might be used. This was despite the fact that a peace treaty had been signed between the two countries three years earlier. Cleverly, Windsor tricked the Spanish into refusing to trade with the English and there were plenty of buccaneers around Jamaica who were all too ready to make the most of the situation.[18] They were a violent group of men intent on plunder and none too fussy how they got it. They were capable of the most abominable torture of their captives: men spitted on stakes over a fire; strung up by their genitalia; one would lick his cutlass

14 Dyer, 'Myngs in the West Indies', pp. 181–2.
15 Dyer, 'Myngs in the West Indies', pp. 181–4.
16 Dyer, 'Myngs in the West Indies', p. 184.
17 Historical Manuscripts Commission (HMC): Finch MS, Vol. IV, p. 388.
18 Buccanneer: originally meaning a piratical figure preying on ships in the Caribbean.

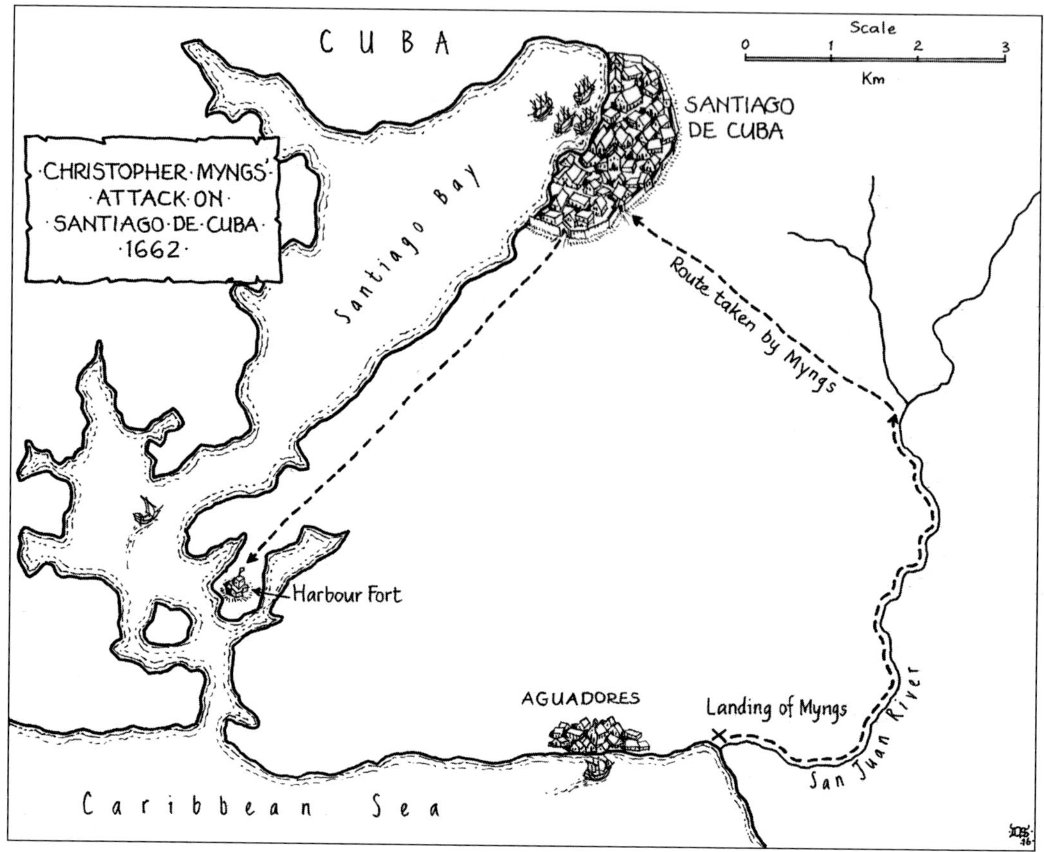

Map 4 Christopher Myngs' attack on Santiago de Cuba 1662.

blade clean of blood after killing Spaniards who did not speak fast enough on the rack; dishonouring female prisoners was the order of the day.[19] Soon Windsor, freely, started to hand out privateering commissions to all and sundry.

In this heady climate, volunteers were called for to strike against the Spanish in a raid upon Santiago de Cuba to the north of Jamaica.[20] This Cuban town was an advanced Spanish base for threatening the island of Jamaica and was a considerable irritant to its inhabitants. The leader of this action was to be the charismatic Myngs and such was his burgeoning reputation that within a few days no less than 1,300 men, with the smell of booty rich in their nostrils, came forward. As well as the two English naval vessels, the *Centurion* and the

---

19 It could be argued that the Spanish were getting their just deserts. In 1604, the Venetian ambassador in London wrote: 'news that the Spanish in the West Indies captured two English vessels, cut off the hands, feet, noses and ears of the crews and smeared them with honey and tied them to trees to be tortured by flies and other insects.' It was indeed a cruel era.

20 South-eastern Cuba. St Iago was the capital of half the island [Cuba] with a resident governor and bishop. Most of its commerce in the form of sugar, tobacco and hides was with the Canary Islands.

Griffin, there were 10 privateer vessels, one of which was commanded by the young Henry Morgan.[21] Myngs' little fleet left Port Royal on 1 October 1662, rounding western Jamaica in light winds, before a few days later sighting the Cuban coast. Here he found the dissolute Sir Thomas Whetstone, a nephew of Oliver Cromwell, whose debts had forced him to seek a new life abroad. Myngs joined Whetstone in order to gain knowledge of the dispositions of the Spanish, and then decided to make a surprise frontal attack on the port. On reaching the fortress guarding the entrance to Santiago de Cuba, Myngs was precluded from making an immediate assault by a weak, erratic wind. Instead, late in the afternoon of 16 October, he took his force to the village of Aguadores, at the mouth of the San Juan River. Here he was able to land around 1,000 men. He has left a record of what happened next:[22]

According to your Excellency's commands of the 21st of 5 bre (7 ber) we set sail from Point Cagaway (Jamaica) on the 22nd, but it was the 5th of October before we got sight of the castle of St Iago upon Cuba. We decided to land under a platform two miles to windward of the harbour, the only place possible to land and march upon the town on that rocky coast. We found no resistance, the enemy expecting us at the fort, and the people flying before us. Before we were all landed it was night. We were forced to advance into a wood, and the way was so narrow and difficult and the night so dark that our guides had to go with branches in their hands to beat a path. By daybreak we reached a plantation by a river's side, some six miles from our landing and three miles from the town, where being refreshed with water, daylight and a better way, we very cheerfully advanced for the town surprizing the enemy, who hearing of our late landing, did not expect us so soon. At the entrance of the town the Govenor, Don Pedro de Moralis, with two hundred men two pieces of ordnance, stood to receive us, Don Christopher, the old Govenor of Jamaica (and a good friend to the English), with five hundred more, being his reserve. We soon beat them from their station, and with the help of Don Christopher, who fairly ran away, we routed the rest. Having mastered the town we took possession of the vessels in the harbour, and the next day I dispatched parties in pursuit of the enemy and sent orders to the fleet to attack the harbour, which was successfully done, the enemy deserting the great castle after firing but two muskets. From 9th to the 14th we spent our time in pursuing the enemy, which proved not very advantageous, their riches being drawn off so far we could not reach it. The ill offices that town had done to Jamaica had so exasperated the soldiers that I had much ado to keep them from firing the churches. From the 15th to the 19th we employed ourselves in demolishing the forts. We found great stores of powder, 700 barrels of which we spent in blowing up the castle and the rest in country houses and platforms. The castle mostly lies level with the ground. It was built upon a rocky precipice, the walls on a mountainside some sixty feet high, there was in it a chapel and houses

---

21   The Welsh-born Henry Morgan was to become a notorious pirate on the Spanish Main in the 17th century.

22   David Marley, *Pirates Adventurers of the High Seas* (London: Arms and Armour Press 1995), pp. 28–32.

sufficient for a thousand men. We are now in safety in the harbour on our return to Cagaway.[23]

Myngs returned to Port Royal after his highly successful action against the Spanish, only to discover the Governor, Lord Windsor, was on the point of sailing for England, supposedly on health grounds. In his absence, Myngs found that he had been appointed to the newly formed Jamaican Council, which had decided to continue the aggressive policy towards the Spanish. A decision was taken by the Council for a further punitive expedition towards them, which would consist of freebooters from many nations plus a squadron led by Myngs. Early in the New Year of 1663, on 21 January, Myngs sailed in the *Centurion* with the *Griffin* and a selection of privateers for the coast of what is now Central America. They swept around Yucatan, past the dangerous shoals in the Gulf of Mexico, towards their goal of the port of Campeche.[24] Unfortunately, the *Centurion* became separated from the *Griffin* and some of the other privateers. Despite this, on the night of 8–9 February 1663, Myngs managed to land around 1,000 men at Jamula beach, some four miles west of Campeche. Undoubtedly, the 12-year-old Cloudesley Shovell was either with them, or left in the *Centurion* as by his own words he was with Myngs in 1663.[25]

In the early morning, the Spanish inhabitants were surprised to find a cluster of ships around and standing off the shore. Their surprise turned to consternation as Myngs, his sailors and a large force of violent freebooters poured out of the woods and down on to the city of Campeche. The 150 strong militiamen put up a stout resistance to the invaders, firing muskets with great effect from the top of the flat-roofed, stone houses. During this bloody action, whilst advancing up the main street, Myngs received serious wounds to his face and both thighs. He was carried back to his ship, the *Centurion,* whilst the fighting continued on land. Eventually, after two hours, the Spanish were overcome, with a loss of 50 men compared with 30 of the attackers killed. Many of the city's thatched houses were then torched. The next day a truce was agreed, in which Myngs, despite his wounds, was able to participate. In exchange for being allowed to fill his water casks, Myngs returned all but the six most important prisoners. On 23 February, Myngs sailed away with a considerable amount of plunder and no less than 14 Spanish vessels that he had taken in the harbour of Campeche. His small fleet struggled with its heavily-laden ships to get around Yucatan with the wind and current against them. It was not until 23 April 1663, that the *Centurion* finally reached their destination, Port Royal, described at the time as 'wickedest city on earth.'[26] Myngs was still suffering from his injuries, which were slow to heal, and that July the *Centurion* set sail for England. Christopher Myngs would eventually recover from his wounds to fight once more but he would never see the West Indies again. His time in the amphibious raiding of the Caribbean had been fruitful, bringing him wealth and a degree of notoriety.[27]

23   Historical Manuscripts Commision (HMC): Heathcote MS, pp. 34–5, Myngs letter to Lord Windsor Oct 19th 1662; Dyer, 'Myngs in the West Indies', pp. 185–7; Charles Firth, 'The Capture of Santiago, in Cuba, by Captain Myngs, 1662', *The English Historical Review* (Oxford: Oxford University Press, 1 July 1899), pp. 536–540.
24   Campeche wood was essential for the production of the best dyestuffs.
25   HMC: Finch MS, Vol. IV, p. 388.
26   Alexandre Exquemelin, *Buccaneers of America* (London: Folio Society 1972), p. 11.
27   Marley, *Pirates*, pp. 32–3.

3

The Second Anglo-Dutch War and the Death of Sir Christopher Myngs 1664–1666

Following his return to England, Christopher Myngs, in 1664, was given command of the 54-gun *Gloucester* and on 27 May he requested a John Myngs to be appointed surgeon to his ship. Clearly, this was a relative and most likely to have been his brother.[1] A few months later, Christopher Myngs moved briefly to the smaller 50-gun *Portland*, before transferring to the magnificent 76-gun *Royal Oak,* in which he would remain until early 1665. On the latter ship, Myngs raised his flag for the very first time as vice-admiral of the white, under Prince Rupert, in the Channel squadron. It is known that John Narbrough was with Myngs, as his lieutenant, in the *Portland* and the *Royal Oak.* Although there is no conclusive proof of Cloudesley Shovell's movements at this time, it seems more than likely that he was with Myngs in the *Portland* and the *Royal Oak* and possibly also the *Gloucester.*[2]

Tension between the English and the Dutch had not been dissipated by the peace of 1654, and matters deteriorated further after the Restoration. Interference with foreign trade was at the very heart of the matter. George Monck's apt comment still applied: 'the Dutch have too much trade, and the English are resolved to take it from them!'[3] The final rupture of relations came from the desertion of John Lawson by Michiel de Ruyter, when the two men had been co-operating against the Algerian corsairs; then Thomas Allin's unprovoked attack upon the Dutch Smyrna fleet off Cadiz was the last straw. The Second Anglo-Dutch War officially began in March 1665 and would continue until July 1667.

Late in April 1665 both protagonists were ready for war. Charles II bolstered with a hefty £2,500,000 grant from a tight-fisted Parliament was intent on a speedy success, followed by the destruction of Dutch maritime trade. The English fleet had 100 ships, 4,800 guns and 24,000 men.[4] In command was the king's brother, James, Duke of York, the Lord High

---

1   *CSP Dom, Charles II*, Vol. 4, 27 May 1664.
2   *DNB,* Myngs [Laughton, Knighton], Narbrough [Laughton, Davies].
3   Kennedy, *British Naval Mastery*, p. 58.
4   Strictly speaking, as Scotland and Ireland had been incorporated into the Commonwealth in 1652, it was the British rather than English navy.

Map 5 The Second Dutch War 1665-1667.

Admiral of England,[5] in the 80-gun *Royal Charles* with William Penn as his chief advisor and John Harman as captain. Prince Rupert of the Rhine, York's royal cousin,[6] led the van with the white squadron, and Edward Montagu, Earl of Sandwich, commanded the blue squadron in the rear. Other experienced officers from the time of the Commonwealth, such as John Lawson and George Ayscue were in the fleet. Charles II thought that George Monck, Duke of Albemarle, was too important a person for the safety of the state to be put at risk

---

5   The Lord High Admiral of England from 1660–1673. He had never before commanded a fleet or seen a sea battle. William Penn made decisions in York's name.

6   Interestingly, neither Charles II nor the Duke of York liked their cousin, Prince Rupert.

in battle and he was kept on shore. Christopher Myngs was vice-admiral of the white, in the ancient 44-gun *Triumph*,[7] manned by 380 men and leading Prince Rupert's squadron. John Narbrough was his lieutenant and almost certainly Cloudesley Shovell was with them as either a captain's servant or gentleman volunteer.

The Dutch had 107 ships,[8] 4,864 guns and 21,556 men under the command of the aristocratic Jacob van Wassenaer, Lord of Obdam. He, poor man, was suffering from gout and was forced to sit in a chair on the poop of his ship during the battle! The Dutch command structure can only be described as shambolic with the competing interests of the five different admiralties,[9] and the involvement of the Grand Pensionary of Holland, the strong-willed Johan de Witt, making executive decisions over the fitting out of the fleet. In the end petty provincial jealousies led to the necessity of the formation of no less than seven squadrons, each with its own three flag officers.

Both the English and the Dutch were dependent on incorporating armed merchantmen to bolster their fleets. Just how well these vessels would fight was problematical. Although each side had roughly the same number of ships, the English had a greater weight of shot. They had nearly 30 ships capable of firing 1,000 pounds of shot, the Dutch but one.[10]

On 1 June 1665, the English fleet was in Sole Bay, off Southwold, when it was reported that the Dutch were six miles away to the east-south-east. York weighed anchor and put to sea to meet them. Later that day, in the North Sea, the English and Dutch fleets first saw each other, but Obdam, despite having the advantage of an easterly wind, declined battle. However, in the early hours of 3 June the wind had come around to south-west which favoured the English. At this stage the fleets were about 14 miles north-north-east of the Suffolk port of Lowestoft. At dawn, 4:00 a.m., Myngs in the *Triumph* was to fire the first broadsides of the Battle of Lowestoft,[11] and with the leading division of the red squadron, cut across the bows of the Dutch ships to gain the weather gage.[12] Both sides then passed each other on opposite tacks but at such a distance that little damage was done. The English line was poorly formed with clumps of three or four ships together often firing into each other. At about 5:30 a.m., the Dutch tacked, and in response, the Duke of York intended to tack from the rear. Before he could raise the signal to do so, Prince Rupert impatiently tacked first, this apparently confused Lawson, leading the van of the red squadron, who failed to tack in turn. Thus a gap developed between the white squadron now sailing to the north-west and the red squadron still sailing to the south-east. To plug the gap Penn took the *Royal Charles* out of the line, rapidly followed by Sandwich's blue squadron. These ships then formed a second line to windward. Around 7:00 a.m., Obdam sought to take the initiative by breaking through to gain the wind but failed. The Duke of York then ordered his fleet to tack from the rear, which was successfully carried out. This was a remarkable achievement which was never to be repeated again in the era of the sailing ship. The English

---

7   The previous captain, John Stoakes, had died on 13 February 1665. The *Triumph* dated from James I's reign.

8   In general the Dutch ships were larger than they had been in the First Anglo-Dutch War.

9   Amsterdam, Maas, Noorderkwartier, Zeeland, and Friesland. They were all agencies of the States General.

10   Davies, *Pepys's Navy*, pp. 258–9.

11   The account of the Battle of Lowestoft: Davies, *Pepys's Navy*, pp. 258–61; Frank Fox, *The Four Days' Battle of 1666* (Barnsley: Seaforth Publishing 2009), pp. 83–101; Laird Clowes, *Royal Navy*, Vol. II, pp. 257–66.

12   Fox, *Four Days' Battle*, p. 85.

fleet was now on the same tack as the Dutch, allowing the former to fire at the latter at will. Therefore the Dutch were unable to put into practice their favoured tactic of closing with their opponents and boarding them.

Around 10:00 a.m., the battle began in earnest with both sides firing all their guns at each other with the cacophony of battle clearly audible in London.[13] Lawson whose division was leading the red squadron received a gunshot wound to his knee, which would later become gangrenous and lead to his demise. Confusion reigned in his division as the remainder of the red squadron kept position to the windward and thus virtually out of the action. Later William Berkeley, rear-admiral of the red, in the *Swiftsure,* would have the word coward attached to his name. As will be seen in the following year, 1666, the suicidal attack made by Berkeley at the Four Days' Battle may have been influenced by the sobriquet 'coward' dating from this time. The Duke of York himself was not immune from criticism as his ship, the *Royal Charles,* was in a similar position to Berkeley's. Sandwich, in the *Royal Prince,* became heavily engaged with Obdam's flagship, the *Eendracht,* supported by a powerful East Indiaman. At this point York sprang into action with the red squadron and managed to free Sandwich from his Dutch persecutors. Prince Rupert and Sandwich then launched their squadrons directly into the middle of the Dutch fleet.

At this juncture, the Duke of York ranged the *Royal Charles* alongside Obdam's *Eendracht* and a homicidal duel began. The Dutch made an unsuccessful attempt to board the royal flagship. Now the *Eendracht's* broadsides were so powerful that the *Royal Charles* was in danger of being sunk or having to surrender. Around noon, three of the Duke's courtiers were slain by a single chain-shot whilst standing in close proximity to him. They were Charles Berkeley, 1st Earl of Falmouth, Richard Boyle, a son of the Earl of Burlington,[14] and Lord Muskerry.[15] The Duke was spattered with blood and brains and received a laceration of the hand from a slither of skull. Gallows humour suggested that this facial coating of brains was: 'supplying his intellectual deficiencies.'[16] Charles Berkeley was the elder brother of the unfortunate 'cowardly' William of the *Swiftsure.*[17] Later the Duke would be greatly supportive of Falmouth's 20-year-old widow, born Mary Bagot, taking her under his protective wing and, such was his boundless libido, reputedly making her his mistress. Indeed, he even considered marriage to her after the death of Anne Hyde. Around 2:30 p.m., the *Eendracht* suddenly exploded with a colossal bang which could be heard in the Dutch homeland over 100 miles away. The most likely cause was either the faulty handling of powder in the magazine or the ignition of loose cartridges. One traditional Dutch story related that the black servant of Obdam, with the motive of revenge, deliberately ignited the powder with spectacular effect. Obdam did not live to suffer seeing the destruction of his ship, as he was swept off it by a cannonball shortly before the blast. There were to be only five survivors out of a crew of over 400 from the stricken flagship.

---

13   According to the poet John Dryden, 'the noise of the cannon from both navies reached our ears about the city, ----.'

14   Richard Boyle, son of the 1st Earl of Burlington and 2nd Earl of Cork.

15   As well as being surrounded by aristocratic courtiers, York had his dog aboard during the battle. Both John Narbrough and Cloudesley Shovell took dogs to sea with them: in their cases whippets or greyhounds.

16   Richard Ollard, *Cromwell's Earl* (London: Harper Collins 1994), p. 131.

17   The Earl of Falmouth was dissolute and reputed to have had 'criminal intercourse' with the Duchess of York. Later he denied this relationship.

The violent death of the unfortunate Obdam led to a breakdown in command and control of the Dutch fleet. Obdam's second-in-command, Egbert Cortenaer, had been severely wounded by a cannonball hitting him in the region of his hip, this leading to his later death. Jan Evertsen, from Zeeland, was the next in line for the command, but Cornelis Tromp's ships from Amsterdam would not accept orders from him. The Dutch fleet was in a state of utter chaos and many ships turned tail and fled towards their home ports. As the contemporary English sailor, Edward Barlow, put it so eloquently: 'the Dutch turned their arses and run.'[18] The English squadrons relentlessly followed them pouring a murderous fire into the smouldering hulks of their opponents in what had become a giant mêlée. Small clumps of Dutch ships were isolated and either forced to surrender or set alight by fire-ships. During this orgy of destruction, a most unsavoury incident took place much to the chagrin of Sandwich. The *Maarseveen,* the biggest ship in the Dutch fleet, had surrendered to him, when the *Dolphin* fireship, Captain William Gregory, torched her. Only around one hundred men survived the inferno. Sandwich aptly commented that the behaviour as 'not beseeming Christians.' In a later age Gregory would justly have found himself charged with war crimes.[19]

The Dutch fleet had received a crushing defeat, perhaps the worst in a long and distinguished naval history. However, through English oversight or perhaps good fortune, they escaped an even more cataclysmic defeat. On the night of 3–4 June, the English, following the instructions of one of York's courtiers, shortened their sails and did not follow up their undoubted success by closing on their Dutch opponents. The probable guilty party was one Henry Brouncker, a courtier, who persuaded the *Royal Charles'* captain, the able John Harman, and the ship's master, John Cox, that the sleeping York wished the sails to be shortened. The *Royal Charles* and the remainder of the English fleet left off the chase of the Dutch. By the time York awoke, around 4:00 a.m. on 4 June, and the pursuit was restarted in earnest, it was too late and some Dutch ships under Evertsen and Tromp escaped into the Texel at noon. A later Parliamentary enquiry investigated what had happened. One suggestion was that Brouncker, who was close to York and solicited women for him, had promised the Duke's wife to keep him out of harm's way. After York's near-death experience of earlier in the day, he liked to wear a metal skull cap covered in black velvet,[20] Brouncker took it upon himself to try to protect his master. Another theory believed that York had given an ambiguous order, something he was prone to do. In any event a significant number of Dutch ships had been allowed to escape.

As well as leading his division in Rupert's white squadron, Christopher Myngs, in the initial stages of the battle, had weathered the Dutch and fired the first shots. Later, at the point when Rupert and Sandwich had courageously charged into the centre of the Dutch fleet and the fighting was at its most ferocious, Myngs in the *Triumph,* had been prominent in the action. Robert Sansum, the junior flag officer in the white squadron, commanding the rear division, was killed during the day. Although Rupert and Myngs came from totally different ends of the social spectrum, they shared one major characteristic – in battle both

---

18   Fox, *Four Days' Battle*, p. 96; National Maritime Museum (NMM): JOD/4, Edward Barlow journal.

19   Davies, *Pepys's Navy*, p. 260. Sensibly, Gregory vanished after the battle, before a court-martial could take place, and was never heard of again.

20   Davies, *Pepys's Navy*, p. 152.

men were thrusters and threw caution to the winds. It was said about Rupert that a 'whiff of brimstone accompanied him wherever he went.'[21] Unfortunately, during the action Myngs was wounded in the leg. No doubt John Narbrough, in his 25th year, the lieutenant in the *Triumph,* gained useful battle experience of a fleet action. Cloudesley Shovell was, by his own words, in the West Indies with Myngs two years earlier. So it is likely that he followed him to the *Triumph:* making this his first experience of a major sea battle, aged 14 years. There would be many more in his long and distinguished naval career. On 17 June, it was reported that the *Triumph* needed to dock at Chatham for battle repairs. Ten days later, on 27 June, Myngs was knighted for his excellent service at the Battle of Lowestoft.[22] Clearly, his 'little local difficulty' in Jamaica six years earlier, had been forgotten by the generous and grateful Charles II.

The Battle of Lowestoft, fought on 3 June 1665, was and was seen at the time as a great English victory. It would be the last time the English had the advantage of the line of battle over the Dutch: from 1666 the latter would use the same method.[23] At Lowestoft, the Dutch had tried to use the tactic of charging in line abreast and attempting to board their English opponents. The Dutch had: lost 17 ships; with 5,000 casualties [including Obdam and two other flag officers]; nearly 3,000 prisoners were taken by York's fleet. In return the English had: lost a single ship; suffered around 600 casualties including 250 killed [Lawson who died from gangrene and the royalist captain, James Ley, Earl of Marlborough, killed by a cannonball amongst them];[24] perhaps as few as 200 taken prisoner. In Holland there were many recriminations: Jan Evertsen, who had fought well, was flung into the sea at Briel by a mob, and was lucky to escape drowning; three captains were sentenced to be shot; three more were publicly degraded; Cortenaer's captain was made to stand on a scaffold with a noose around his neck to witness the executions prior to being banished. The warm glow felt in England after the victory was soon dissipated with the spread of the dreaded bubonic plague which had taken hold of the country.

After the Battle of Lowestoft, both the Duke of York and Prince Rupert gave up their commands, leaving Edward Montagu, Earl of Sandwich in charge.[25] On 2 July, Myngs was appointed vice-admiral of the blue in Thomas Allin's squadron and around the same time, Sandwich took the fleet to the Texel and established that there was no likelihood of the Dutch being ready to come out for some weeks. Subsequently he took his ships, including Myngs' *Triumph*, to attempt the capture or destruction of a number of Dutch Smyrna and East India Company ships that had been forced to sail around the north of Ireland and Scotland to take refuge at Bergen, in Norway, in the aftermath of the Battle of Lowestoft. In early August, the recently knighted Sir Thomas Teddiman, with 14 ships, was delegated by Sandwich to make the assault on the merchant vessels. Frederick III of

---

21   Capp, *Cromwell's Navy*, p. 60.

22   Fox, *Four Days' Battle*, p. 101.

23   The line of battle would hinder the Dutch-favoured tactic of boarding.

24   Davies, *Pepys's Navy*, pp. 95–6. James Ley, 3rd Earl of Marlborough, captain of the *Old James* had foreseen his own death. A few months before he had written 'but with a Christian manly, brave resolution look to what is eternal.' 'Send us a happy resurrection.' He was buried in Westminster Abbey but without a monument as he had no money or issue.

25   Charles II was concerned for the safety of his brother and heir, York. Rupert declined to serve with Sandwich.

Denmark, who was also the sovereign of Norway, agreed not to hinder them for a share of the spoils. Unfortunately, from the English point of view, the message from the king had not reached the Governor of Bergen by the time of the attack [3 August], and Teddiman and his ships were driven off with heavy loss. Even by the low standards of the 17th century, the underhand arrangements between Frederick III and the English can only be described as disgraceful.[26] The Dutch merchant ships were in what was for them a supposedly safe refuge, a neutral port.[27]

During this time, Myngs continued to serve under Sandwich as vice-admiral of the blue, taking no part in the fiasco of Bergen, as he was in a more senior post than Teddiman. He remained with Sandwich and the main fleet whilst the action took place. Later, they rejoined Teddiman, off Flamborough Head, before returning to Sole Bay, Southwold. At the end of August, Sandwich and Myngs with the fleet sailed again and, on 3 September, three rich Dutch West Indiamen and their escorts were captured. The following day a further six merchantmen were added to the bag. On the voyage back to the buoy of the Nore, a council of flag officers decided, such was their greed, to take their share of the booty without waiting for the king's eagerly anticipated permission.[28] William Penn was particularly vociferous on the subject and stupidly Sandwich went along with it. Only George Ayscue and stout Christopher Myngs spoke out against the unlawful division. It is not difficult to understand Myngs' reluctance to help himself to the Dutch plunder. No doubt, he recalled his own problems of 1659, in Jamaica, when he had been in a similar position and burnt his fingers badly. Sandwich was reputed to have removed £5,000 for himself and most of the other admirals a proportionately lesser amount. Even the ordinary sailors had put their hands well and truly in the till and were selling cloves and nutmegs around the waterside. It is unlikely that Narbrough and Shovell were amongst them in view of Myngs' newly found strict attitude to the matter! Charles II, and his younger brother, the Duke of York, orchestrated by Sir William Coventry, were not pleased with the behaviour of their admirals, and Sandwich was packed off in semi-disgrace to Madrid as Ambassador.[29]

Although John Narbrough was with Myngs in the *Triumph*, as lieutenant, at the Battle of Lowestoft, he left him briefly in 1665 for the 70-gun *Royal James*[30] and then the 48-gun *Old James*.[31] However, that autumn Narbrough rejoined Myngs in the 52-gun *Fairfax*. On the balance of probabilities, it seems likely that Shovell stayed with Myngs for the whole summer.

After the return of the storm-battered fleet to the Nore in September, Sir William Coventry suggested that Myngs should take a squadron to Guinea to retake Michiel de Ruyter's conquests there. Nothing came of this proposal and during the winter months of late 1665 and early 1666, Myngs, in the *Fairfax*, was in command of the strong squadron in the English Channel, as the winter guard. *The London Gazette* recorded 'by sending out ships constantly to cruise about, he [Myngs] hath kept this coast very free from all the

---

26   The king was described by Sandwich as 'a blockhead'.
27   Davies, *Pepys's Navy*, p. 21; Fox, *Four Days' Battle*, p. 106; Laird Clowes, *Royal Navy*, Vol. II, p. 266.
28   The booty consisted of jewels, precious spices and silks.
29   Ollard, *Cromwell's Earl*, pp. 136–147; Fox, *Four Days' Battle*, p. 115.
30   Built in 1658 as the *Richard*, renamed the *Royal James* in 1660, and destroyed by the Dutch at Chatham in 1667.
31   Built in 1634 as the *James*, renamed *Old James* in 1660.

enemy's men of war'.[32] In an edition, a few weeks later, it was reported that 'his vigilance is such hardly anything can escape our frigates which come through the Channel.'[33] March 1666, found Myngs convoying the trade from Hamburg to the Thames.

For the summer campaign of 1666, Myngs had moved from the *Fairfax* to the larger, recently rebuilt, 82-gun, 1,029 tons, *Victory,* with 450 men aboard, and taking Narbrough with him as the lieutenant and probably Shovell too. In April, when the fleet started to assemble under the joint command of George Monck, Duke of Albemarle, and Prince Rupert,[34] Myngs was made vice-admiral of the red, a more important post in the senior squadron than before. Monck had a high opinion of Myngs' expertise as an experienced tarpaulin. He was a former royalist soldier who, unlike Myngs, knew little about managing a sailing ship in peaceful conditions, let alone in a battle. Monck's sailing master would have to interpret instructions such as 'wheel to the right', as if he were on a parade ground![35] His private life was somewhat irregular, even by the standards of the 17th century, for he had married a seamstress, Anne Clarges, the coarse daughter of his regimental farrier. Anne had ministered to his every need while he had been imprisoned in the Tower of London, and she was reputed to have had a problem with her personal hygiene – being known as 'Dirty Bessie.'[36] Prior, to the coming Four Days' Battle, Monck gave instructions that Bessie was not to be told in advance, until he had had the opportunity to break her in to the news by degrees. In this endeavour Monck was singularly unsuccessful, as 'Dirty Bessie' poured out a stream of foul-mouth curses against those responsible for the decision. No wonder he was keen to escape to sea! Whatever his eccentricities, Monck was a fine leader, a highly competent administrator, and the go-to man for catastrophes such as the Plague or the Fire of London.

On 27 May, the English fleet consisting of 80 ships, 4,460 guns and 21,085 men, collected in the Downs under the joint admirals, Monck and Rupert. Other ships were available but no crews could be found for them. The Dutch fleet that the English were soon to face had 85 ships, 4,581 guns with 21,144 men under Michiel de Ruyter, Cornelis Evertsen the elder, and the fiery, headstrong Cornelis Tromp. On paper the two fleets matched each other equally. However, the English ships were bigger and their largest cannon was a 42 pounder with its seven inch bore:[37] the Dutch ships were smaller, flat bottomed to get over the shoals surrounding their coast, and usually having only 24 pounder guns. If the 80-ship English fleet had been kept together with their greater fire-power, the advantage should have been theirs, although erroneously, Monck had a poor opinion of the Dutch. By nature a compulsive thruster in battle, Monck was said to love nothing better than the scuppers of his ships to be running freely with blood. A further factor would be that the Dutch had learnt by their mistakes at the Battle of Lowestoft, a year earlier, and started to use the line of battle

---

32   *The London Gazette*, No 18.

33   *The London Gazette*, No 39.

34   Charles II feared for the safety of his brother and heir, James, Duke of York and this is the reason he was overlooked for the command. An alternative, Edward Montagu, Earl of Sandwich, was in semi-disgrace as the ambassador at Madrid. Thus Monck and Rupert were the third and fourth choices. The king would like to have given the command to Rupert but, fearing the impetuosity of his cousin, brought in the steadying influence of Monck.

35   Fox, *Four Days' Battle*, p. 10.

36   Davies, *Pepys's Navy*, p. 97.

37   Cannon-of-seven.

for the first time. The English, at the time of Robert Blake, had first made this revolutionary battle formation standard in 1653.

Two days later, after due consideration, Charles II made a catastrophic strategic mistake: he divided his fleet.[38] Monck with the main body of ships was to be separated from Rupert and his small squadron of around 24 vessels. The rationale behind the king's decision was threefold. Firstly, the French had joined the Dutch cause in January 1666, and it was thought that François de Vendôme, Duc de Beaufort, with a fleet of 36 ships, was in the western approaches of the English Channel, having sailed from the Mediterranean. If these French ships were able to join de Ruyter's Dutch fleet, the English would be up against an over-whelming force. Secondly, there were concerns about Beaufort sailing around the north of Scotland to join de Ruyter. Thirdly, the king was concerned about a possible French invasion of Ireland by troops carried in Beaufort's ships. In order to counteract these possibilities, Rupert was to remain on the French coast for no longer than eight days before returning to England. He was forbidden to sail further south than the mouth of the Gironde. Although Charles II had carefully considered the situation, his fundamental error of dividing the fleet would cost the English their chance of winning the coming battle, the longest battle in British naval history – the Four Days' Battle, which would be fought from 1–4 June 1666.[39]

Despite the fact that Charles II had made the wrong decision in dividing his fleet, he had a lifelong love and interest in the sea and his navy. As in this case, he regularly decided on the disposition of his ships, often to the intense irritation of those who were nominally responsible for such matters. Charles had introduced yachting to the Dutch and reviewed the designs of his naval vessels. He named ships, sometimes after his latest mistress, and selected the officers to man them. Later in 1672, he would have his copper coins stamped with the image of Britannia supposedly modelled on his paramour, Frances Stuart, Duchess of Richmond. James, Duke of York, shared his brother's interest in the navy and was also an important influence in its development.[40]

On 29 May, Prince Rupert led his squadron down the English Channel in search of the Duc de Beaufort.[41] He was only too happy to have this independent command away from Monck, and the claustrophobic atmosphere of their joint flagship. Rupert took with him Christopher Myngs and Thomas Allin, originally the vice-admiral of the red and the admiral of the white respectively. It is likely that Myngs and Allin owed these senior posts to their restraint in not helping themselves to Dutch booty the previous autumn. In the newly constituted squadron, Myngs would sail as the vice-admiral in the *Victory,* having been selected for the post by Monck as 'a fit man for such an expedition', whilst Rupert was ashore. Initially, on his return, Rupert was concerned whether the *Victory,* a new three-decker, with untried sailing qualities, would be swift enough to keep up with the rest of his squadron of fast vessels. The loyal Allin, a skilled tarpaulin, would act as flag-captain and advisor to Rupert in the *Royal James.*

---

38   After the forthcoming battle, even the ordinary seamen were complaining that the fleet had been divided.

39   Account of the Four Days' Battle: Fox, *Four Days' Battle*, pp. 136–270; Laird Clowes, *Royal Navy*, Vol. II, pp. 267–278.

40   Davies, *Pepys's Navy*, p. 19.

41   Beaufort's ships were at Lisbon and would still be there during the coming Four Days' Battle.

Prior to an earlier action, an eyewitness of one of Rupert's squadrons reported: 'if hell be on earth, it is here.'[42] There is little doubt that when it came to action, be it on land or on sea, Rupert was certainly a swashbuckler of the first order and fearless in action. Myngs too, with his long experience of warfare in the West Indies, had something of the same ilk about him. The easterly wind which carried Rupert down the Channel, allowed de Ruyter to bring the Dutch fleet out of port to a position roughly half way between the French coast and the Downs. On 1 June Monck left the Downs and sailed in the direction of the Dutch. The four day battle would be fought in the expanse of water between the Thames Estuary and the Dutch coast.

Many historians have recorded that Monck was supremely confident as he sailed towards his Dutch foe with around 56 ships, 3,058 guns and 14,335 men under his command against a clearly superior enemy. This was far from the truth, as just prior to the engagement, he had sent a letter to the Earl of Arlington, hinting that he should not take on the Dutch unless he had a minimum of 70 ships to fight with, and he had constantly requested his numbers to be increased. Cryptically, Monck had indicated that he would attack the Dutch unless ordered otherwise and that order never came. Even so, he may still have underestimated the fighting capability of the opposition, and it was true that he was never happier than in a violent action with plenty of blood and thunder. One of his captains, Frescheville Holles, had even toasted his men in wine before the battle in which he would lose an arm.[43]

At a council of war, prior to the battle, de Ruyter warned his subordinate admirals and captains that, if necessary, he was empowered to hang cowards from amongst their number. There was to be no repetition of the scandalous behaviour of some of his captains at the Battle of Lowestoft. It was imperative that de Ruyter defeated the English, in order to allow a gap for the returning East India merchantmen to reach a Dutch port. The financial position of the state depended on this. Early in the morning of 1 June 1666, Monck with the wind in his favour attacked the Dutch off the North Foreland. The battle continued all day. William Berkeley in the *Swiftsure* made a suicidal run at the Dutch. When offered quarter by the enemy he answered: 'you dogs, you rogues, have ye the heart, so press on board.' The Dutch needed no second invitation and put a musket ball through his neck, this leading to his demise. Berkeley's rash behaviour may well have been related to his perceived poor performance a year earlier.

Later in the day, Monck received a most painful, not to say embarrassing, wound as part of his breeches were blown away, leaving a damaged buttock and thigh. It is difficult not to have sympathy for the poor man trying to command his fleet with his private parts exposed and also a very painful injury into the bargain. The satirist Andrew Marvell wrote about the incident and clearly enjoyed Monck's discomfiture:

> But most with story of his Hand or Thum,
> Conceale, as honour would, his Grace's Bum,
> When the rude bullet a large Collop tore
> Out of that Buttock, never turn'd before.

---

42   Capp, *Cromwell's Navy*, p. 60.

43   Sir William Batten, Surveyor of the Navy, described the boastful gentleman captain, Holles, as 'wind-fucker.' On another occasion, the foul-mouthed Batten commented: 'By God! I think the Devil shits Dutchmen.'

Fortune it seem'd would give him, by that lash,
Gentle correction for his Fight so rash.
But should the Rump perceive't they'd say that Mass
Had now reveng'd them upon Aumarle's Arse.[44]

Late that evening the enterprising John Harman, in the *Henry*, found himself isolated after a fleet pass. Making the most of their opportunity, three Dutch fireships attacked the *Henry*. In total panic, the chaplain said: 'What shall we do?' The exasperated boatswain cried: 'Jump overboard!' Whereupon the clergyman did so, and the ecclesiastical example was followed by no less than 50 men, who all followed him into the sea and drowned. Harman with firm leadership put an end to this mass hysteria and then had the misfortune of having his ankle fractured by a falling yard.[45] Somehow he extricated his ship from seemingly certain destruction, and cannon fire from the *Henry* also killed Cornelis Evertsen, the elder.

Action on day two, 2 June, began in the morning, as the English attacked with the southwesterly wind behind them. After the first day of fighting they now had 48 ships to the Dutch's seventy seven. At least seven passes of the two fleets took place during the day. Cornelis Tromp was isolated to the leeward of the Dutch fleet, and to his embarrassment had to be saved by his great rival de Ruyter. He too had his problems when his flagship, the *Zeven Provincien*, had a mast damaged, and de Ruyter allowed Aert van Nes to have temporary command of the Dutch fleet. The day ended with Monck and his stricken fleet retiring towards the Gunfleet. Casualties had been heavy with shed blood pouring from the scuppers, as if the very ships themselves were exsanguinating. In the *Royal Charles*, no less than 12 men with one member cut off, immediately after being bound up, went on deck once more to continue the fight.[46] Although laudanum might have been available,[47] the only analgesics were said to be haemorrhagic shock, loss of consciousness, and a merciful death.

Day three, 3 June, the anniversary of the Battle of Lowestoft, opened with the continued retreat of Monck and his battered fleet sailing towards the Gunfleet. He had placed a line of damaged ships in front, these protected from behind by his major surviving ships, with the Dutch snapping at their heels. At this stage the outlook for the English fleet was bleak and they looked to have been severely beaten. However, in the early afternoon, Prince Rupert, Christopher Myngs, Thomas Allin and their ships suddenly appeared – surely this would tip the balance back towards the English?[48] In order to join forces with Rupert, Monck inadvertently took his ships over the Galloper sand. Alas, George Ayscue's flagship, the *Royal Prince*, stuck fast and had to be surrendered to the Dutch. Poor Ayscue suffered the

---

44   Fox, *Four Days' Battle*, p. 274.
45   The universally respected Harman was knighted after the battle. His poorly healed fracture, coupled with recurring bouts of gout, meant that he was forced to command at sea from a chair on the poop.
46   Presumably their arms.
47   It was popularised in the 1660s.
48   Charles II's recall of Prince Rupert's squadron, on 30 May, was fortuitous as it was based on faulty intelligence that the Duc de Beaufort's ships had sailed to the north of Scotland, in order to effect a junction with the Dutch by that route. There was no proper understanding of the perilous situation that Monck found himself in. On 1 June, Rupert received the orders at St Helens and progressed in a leisurely manner to the Downs. Sailing to the north, two days later, Rupert was horrified to see Monck's ships retreating from the Dutch.

indignity of becoming the most senior English naval officer, to this day, ever to be captured in battle. Although he was taken to The Hague, the stories that he was paraded in public, painted up as a dog with a tail are pure propaganda.[49] De Ruyter resumed command of the Dutch fleet.

After the union of Monck's and Rupert's ships, the English had 52 to the Dutch's 69 ships. A council of war, attended by Myngs, was held, and a decision was made for Rupert to remain in the *Royal James* and to lead the van with the white squadron. He had never relished the thought of a joint command in the same flagship with Monck. Myngs, still in the *Victory* with Narbrough and probably Shovell as well, would stay with the van division under Rupert. Myngs was given custody of Captain Henry Teddiman, a cousin of Admiral Thomas Teddiman, who had been sacked from his post for cowardice during the battle. English hopes for the morrow were high: surely the aggressive Rupert aided and abetted by Myngs would turn things round.

The final day of the Four Days' Battle, opened with the wind at the south-south-west and the fleets about 20 miles to the east of the Galloper sand bank. Christopher Myngs, in the *Victory*, led his division in the van and raced to gain the wind. A year earlier, in the opening phase of the Battle of Lowestoft, he had been successful, but on this occasion he was beaten by the Dutch admiral, Aert van Nes who cut across the *Victory*'s bows. Myngs had been able to fire a few broadsides at the Dutch during the race for the wind, and then attempted to drive through the Dutch line. The enemy replied with heavy broadsides into the *Victory* and Myngs found his path blocked by Jan de Liefde's 66-gun *Ridderschap*. The *Victory* and the *Ridderschap* passed so close to each other that their yardarms were in danger of clashing. Both ships, at point-blank range, fired round after round of cannonballs, chain shot, case shot and musket balls. The seamen, particularly in the bows of both ships, fell like ninepins under the hail of fire. The *Ridderschap* was dismasted, whereupon Myngs made an unsuccessful attempt to burn her with a fireship. A contemporary naval ballad extolled the virtues of 'Stout Lawson and Minn ---- emptied their guns in their enemies' hearts.'[50]

At this juncture, Myngs was shot through both cheeks, probably by a musket ball and used two hands to hold his ruptured flesh together. He did not leave the deck and remained very much in command. The battered *Victory* struggled past several more Dutch opponents before Myngs was hit again by a second musket ball which penetrated his neck before ending up deep in his shoulder. This time, despite his reluctance to leave the deck, he was carried below for surgical attention.[51] John Narbrough, the lieutenant of the *Victory*, acceded to the command and took the semi-disabled ship away to the north. Several ships from the white squadron attempted to shield the *Victory* from further damage. Joseph Jordan, in particular, 'gave ye enemy noe small encouragement.' Whilst moving away to the north and out of trouble, the *Victory*'s huge, three ton, nine and a half feet long, brass cannon-of-seven

---

49   Ayscue was imprisoned in Louvestein Castle which was normally reserved for prominent political prisoners. His interrogation by the Dutch proved to be something of a failure as no one could understand his Lincolnshire burr!
50   Sir John Lawson had died the previous year from a wound inflicted at the Battle of Lowestoft.
51   A junior officer in the fleet, Richard Hals, commenting on the losses sustained in the battle wrote: 'whereof I must needs lament one. Sir Exgster Mynns, hee dies so much like a man, that he lyes more the subject of envy than pitty.' [Frances Verney, *Memoirs of the Verney Family*, Vol. IV (London: Longmans Green and Co 1892), p. 297]. The sentiment was correct, but Myngs did not die until six days after the battle.

did great damage to the *Ridderschap*.[52] Prince Rupert added to the misery of the latter by ordering two fireships to bear down on her. However, the *Ridderschap* was eventually towed back to the Netherlands.

Cornelis Tromp and van Nes, with no less than 25 ships, attempted to take the *Victory*, now under the command of Narbrough, as well as supporting ships. Narbrough manoeuvred repeatedly, turning this way and that, in order to get back to the safety of the main English fleet. However, the fleet was too close to the wind for him to succeed, but his able twisting and turning of the *Victory*, almost miraculously, kept her out of Dutch hands. Despite the mortal wounding of Christopher Myngs, the English had had the best of the opening exchanges of the day. After the first few passes, it was de Ruyter who had gained the wind and this factor became the main reason for his eventual success. In the afternoon he made the key attack of the day, which was about to be answered by Rupert, when the yards of the *Royal James* came tumbling down and his ship had to be towed out of the action. Without their dashing leader the other English ships declined to counter-attack. Monck's *Royal Charles*, too, had also been disabled and fog came down as the English retreated with the Dutch hard on their heels.

In the final analysis, the result of the Four Days' Battle was a clear-cut victory for Michiel de Ruyter and his Dutch fleet over a weaker English fleet. However, on days two and four, they had come close to defeat with no less than 1,500 men killed and a little less than 1,300 wounded in the whole action. The English casualties were also heavy with 1,000 dead, 1,450 wounded, and 1,800 taken prisoner, the latter including the inconsolable George Ayscue. A third of the senior English commanders were killed, wounded, or captured during the four days of battle. This was the largest number of officers ever lost by the Royal Navy in a single engagement. Such had been the violence of the action, that the sounds of cannon fire, during the battle, could clearly be heard as far away as Bedfordshire in central England.[53] After his unexpected defeat, poor George Monck, Duke of Albemarle, with his painful and embarrassing wound wished to slip ashore unnoticed. Instead he was greeted by *The London Gazette*, the sole official journal: 'The Duke had all his tackle taken off by chain shot, and his breeches to the skin were shot off, ----.'[54] After the result of the Four Days' Battle became known, Samuel Pepys cheered himself up in characteristic fashion by keeping little Mrs Tooker in his chamber all afternoon: 'did what I would with her.'[55]

We left Christopher Myngs having reluctantly been taken below to have his wounds attended to, and with John Narbrough in command of the *Victory*. Narbrough's entry for 4 June was succinct in the extreme. 'We fought their fleet: Sir Christopher was wounded. Wind ENE.' Certainly Narbrough and probably Shovell witnessed their gallant patron's mortal wounding. The *Victory*, carrying the injured Myngs, returned to the Gunfleet with the remainder of the English fleet and the next day, 6 June, Narbrough recorded 'Sir Chris sent to London.' Myngs returned to his home in Goodman's Fields, Whitechapel,

---

52 The *Victory* had 20 cannon-of-seven, 6 24-pounders, 26 culverins and 28 demi-culverins as armament. Only the *Royal Prince* carried a greater number of the powerful cannon-of-seven.

53 Davies, *Pepys's Navy*, p. 36.

54 Whether his testicles had been shot off is a matter of conjecture. He fathered no more children after 1666. Monck died, in 1670, from heart failure, propped upright with all his officers around him like a Roman general.

55 Relative of his official messenger.

the haunt of poor tarpaulin naval officers, in a sorry state. Initially, there were high hopes that he might recover from his facial, neck and shoulder wounds, inflicted by musket balls. However, four days later on the 10th, the gallant Christopher Myngs died in his forty-first year, probably from sepsis. In his journal Narbrough wrote as an obvious later interpolation, 'Sir Christopher Myngs died.'[56] Twenty eight men were killed and a further 87 were wounded serving in the *Victory* during the Four Days' Battle. This was second, in number of casualties, only to John Harman's *Henry*, with over 100 killed and more than half that number wounded. The dead included the 50 men drowned with the panicked chaplain.

Christopher Myngs' funeral took place in the evening of 13 June, at St Mary Matfelon Church,[57] on the Whitechapel Road, London. The funeral was attended by Sir William Coventry, the able and influential secretary to the Duke of York, and Samuel Pepys. Apart from Coventry, who was an important figure in the Royal Navy and role model to Pepys, there were no 'persons of quality' at the funeral. Afterwards, Coventry and Pepys were about to drive away in their carriage, when they were approached by about 'a dozen able, witty, proper men' who came to the side of the coach with tears in their eyes. One of them, speaking on behalf of the others said to Coventry:

> We are here a Dozen of us that have long known and loved and served our dead commander, Sir Chr. Mings, and have now done the last office of laying him in the ground. We would be glad we had any other to offer after him, and in revenge of him – all we have is our lives. If you will please to get his Royal Highness to give us a Fireshipp among us all, here is a Dozen of us, out of all which choose you one to be commander, and the rest of us, whoever he is, will serve him, and, if possible, do that shall show our memory of our dead commander and our revenge.[58]

Coventry and Pepys could barely refrain from weeping themselves. It is likely that the offer was accepted. Myngs' low-key funeral was a little different from some of the gentlemen commanders' who had fallen in the battle. For example, the embalmed corpse of William Berkeley, who had only served at sea for five years before becoming an admiral, was returned by the Dutch and buried in Westminster Abbey.[59] However, they subjected his body to the indignity of display in a sugar chest prior to its return. Myngs left a pregnant widow who would receive a pension, and a son, Christopher, and a daughter by his first marriage, Mary.[60] Christopher would become a distinguished naval officer in his own right and would later serve under his father's protégé, Cloudesley Shovell.

56   British Library (BL): ADD MS 88980, Narbrough journal, 10 June 1666.

57   St Mary Matfelon [commonly called St Mary's Church, Whitechapel] was knocked down in 1673 and then rebuilt. The executioner of Charles I was buried here, as was Richard Parker, one of the leading mutineers at the Nore, in 1797. Enemy action, on 29 December 1940, destroyed the church and it was not rebuilt after the war. It is now the seedy, East London, Altab Ali Park, named after an unfortunate Bangladeshi who was the victim of a racial murder near here, in 1978. Nothing in the park or its vicinity indicates that Sir Christopher Myngs was buried here.

58   *Pepys' Diary*, 13 June 1666. Quoted in Claire Tomalin, *Samuel Pepys The Unequalled Self* (London: Viking 2002), p. 186.

59   Davies, *Pepys's Navy*, p. 168; Berkeley was a lieutenant at 22 years, a captain at 23 years and a vice-admiral at 26 years!

60   A monument to Mary's memory is in St Nicholas' church, Salthouse, Norfolk.

Samuel Pepys, an excellent judge of naval personnel, has left us his own view of Myngs:

> Sir Christopher Myngs was a very stout man, and a man of great parts, and a most excellent tongue among ordinary men; as Sir William Coventry says could have been a most useful man at such a pinch of time as this----. He brought his family into a way of being great; but dying at this time his memory and name will be quite forgot in a few months as if he had never been, nor any of his name to be the better by it; he having not had time to will any estate but is dead poor rather rich.[61]

Perhaps, Pepys had forgotten the treasure Myngs had appropriated in the West Indies seven years before. He may have wept at Myngs' funeral, but it did not take long for Pepys to recover his spirits. Afterwards, he travelled to Deptford to visit Mrs Bagwell, the wife of the master carpenter there, and went into her house and 'did what I would'– pleasured her. At this point poor Pepys had a dreadful shock: it was not that the husband had returned unexpectedly and in any case he had encouraged the arrangement, in exchange for work. It was very much worse than that – the servant had died of the plague that very morning. Pepys was not reassured to be told that Mrs Bagwell had whitewashed the downstairs walls, and he rapidly took his leave not to return for quite some time![62]

Christopher Myngs acted the part of an Elizabethan buccaneer with consummate skill, and his courage and humane care of his men were renowned throughout the navy. It was highly unlikely that either John Narbrough or Cloudesley Shovell attended their patron Myngs' funeral. The former had been given a commission to command the 42-gun *Assurance* with 150 men aboard, on 10 June, the very day of Myngs' demise. This was a reward for Narbrough's skilful handling of the *Victory* after his admiral and benefactor had become incapacitated and on the day of the funeral, Narbrough wrote in his journal: 'I made way for fitting.' It is most likely, that Shovell followed Narbrough from the *Victory* to the *Assurance* although there is no documentary proof. What is certain is that Shovell was with Narbrough, the following year, 1667, in the West Indies.[63] In the early years of their naval careers, both Narbrough and Shovell owed a great deal to their first patron and fellow Norfolk mariner, Sir Christopher Myngs. In the case of Shovell, John Narbrough now became his guide and influential supporter in the place of the dead man.

The Four Days' Battle had ended on 4 June 1666 and with remarkable speed the battered English ships were repaired, manned and sent back to sea. Just 51 days later, on 25 July, they were ready to take part in the Saint James' Day Fight against the might of the Dutch Fleet. The battle took place in the widest part of the Thames estuary between Orfordness and the North Foreland, roughly on the same site as the action of 4 June. The English remained under the joint command of George Monck and Prince Rupert in the *Royal Charles*, with 87 ships, 4,854 guns and 23,142 men. Once more, the Dutch were under the able command of the great Michiel de Ruyter with 72 major ships, 4,645 guns and 22,234 men. John Narbrough, in his first independent command as captain of the *Assurance*, with Cloudesley Shovell as his servant, was part of the English van under Thomas Allin in the white squadron. Charles

---

61   Tomalin, *Samuel Pepys*, p. 186.
62   Tomalin, *Samuel Pepys*, p. 187.
63   HMC: Finch MS, Vol. IV, pp. 387–8.

II and his brother, the Duke of York, accompanied by the redoubtable Samuel Pepys, aptly retired to St James' Park, in London, to listen to the thunderous gunfire from the forthcoming sea battle.

The battle opened around 9:00 a.m., the wind from the north giving the weather gage to the English and the two fleets formed up in parallel lines, facing east. The English line, covering five or six miles, was an excellent one, unlike that of the Dutch, which had a gap between de Ruyter in the centre and Cornelis Tromp in the rear. Allin's van, including Narbrough's *Assurance*,[64] with kettledrums pounding, engaged the Dutch van under Jan Evertsen and in the centre the joint admirals took on de Ruyter himself. Characteristically, Tromp broke through the English line ahead of their rear and engaged in his own private battle with Jeremy Smyth's squadron, much to de Ruyter's irritation. One English chaplain, Thomas Dockray, received high praise indeed, for his performance in the battle: 'prayed like a Christian and fought like a Turk.' He would become a doctor of Divinity and senior chaplain in the navy. The English van, under Allin, gained a rapid superiority over their Dutch opponents who, in a short space of time, lost three important flag officers. Jan Evertsen was mortally wounded by shot cutting off both his legs; Tjerck Hiddes de Vries was hideously wounded by a shot into his leg which extended up to his abdomen and which would lead to his demise; Rudolf Coenders was fortunate in comparison, being killed outright. The battle was sharpest in the centre where de Ruyter's flagship, the *Zeven Provincien*, was eventually dismasted, and there was a confused mêlée in the rear. The Dutch had lost around 20 ships, with 4,000 men killed and 3,000 wounded, in addition to the dead flag officers recorded earlier. The English lost one major ship, few men, and no flag officers. The English victory was a truly remarkable one so soon after their defeat in the preceding month.[65]

John Narbrough's performance in the battle had been excellent and he recorded in his journal:

> Fair weather: little wind at N.E.: smooth water this morning: we stood with ye Dutch fleet and had them to leeward of us: so we stood with their van: and our van bore downe upon ye enemy and we fought them from nine of the clocke till about three of the clock. In the afternoon they run and we pursued them: the next morning: we fought them upon the pursuit.[66]

In the margin he recorded that they had taken two ships.

No doubt spurred on by their stunning victory so soon after their abject defeat of early June, and with temporary mastery of the seas, the English fleet crossed to the Dutch coast. Having anchored in the Schooneveld,[67] the decision was made to attack the islands of Vlieland and Terschelling,[68] and also the large fleet of merchantmen in their vicinity. Following a council of war, Robert Holmes, a swaggering protégé of Rupert's, was entrusted with a small

---

64   The *Assurance* was in Allin's division in the centre of the van.
65   Fox, *Four Days' Battle*, pp. 287–96.
66   Kent County Archives (KCA): Marsham MS U1515.03, Narbrough journal, 25 July 1666.
67   Schooneveld is a narrow basin at the mouth of the Scheldt River, near the island of Walcheren, off the coast of the Netherlands. It was a favourite anchorage of the Dutch fleet.
68   West Friesland islands.

squadron of nine men of war, five fireships and seven ketches plus 300 men to make the amphibious assault.[69] Narbrough, still in the *Assurance,* was an integral part of Holmes' squadron and would play his part in the action. On 8 August, Holmes' squadron parted company with the rest of the fleet. The following day they sailed into Terschelling road in order to destroy the merchantmen. Two Dutch guard ships were neutralized, and Holmes ordered William Jennings to go in with the ships' boats to burn the 160 merchantmen. Inclement weather had precluded an earlier attempt on the island of Vlieland.

Narbrough took part in this spectacular conflagration and described the scene in his journal: 'went up to the Dutch fleet; and burned: 140: sail all richly laden: outward bound to all ports: this we did by one of ye clocke in ye afternoon.' The next day, the 10th, men were landed on Terschelling and the town and its storehouses were torched. Narbrough entered into his journal: 'this morning we landed with eight hundred men: Sir Robert Holmes general: attacked Schelling Island: and went and burned the town without loss of one man: and then marched to our boats and went aboard and set sails and went out.'[70]

A vast amount of damage had been done to both shipping and stores. The total value was in the range £850,000–£1,000,000, and the assault on the Dutch islands and shipping became known as 'Sir Robert Holmes, his bonfire.'[71] The Dutch considered the Fire of London, which occurred the next month, as divine retribution for Holmes' conflagration. Whether Shovell, who was probably Narbough's servant at the time, went ashore with him is uncertain, although even from the relative safety in the *Assurance*, it must have been a truly spectacular sight. The *Assurance* returned to Southwold with the rest of the fleet. The only other incident of note in Narbrough's journal at this time, was that his ship's master had got drunk and Narbrough had hit him on the head with his hand![72] Drunkenness in the Stuart Navy was all too common. Prince Rupert was recorded as saying: 'God damn me, if they will turn out every man that be drunk, he must out all the commander[s] in the fleet. What is the matter if [he] be drunk, so when he comes to fight he doth his work.'[73]

On 13 August, the Duc de Beaufort arrived at La Rochelle, but it was too late in the year for a French attempt on Ireland. The English fleet moved into the English Channel to stop a junction between the Dutch and French fleets.[74] The weather was so bad that nothing came of it. On 5 September, Charles II ordered the irreplaceable Monck to return to London to deal with the crisis of the Fire of London. The following day the old man 'with tears in his eyes' left the fleet – never to return.

---

69   The ketch had two masts and was square-rigged on the main mast. They were used as advice boats [for carrying messages] or for protection against fireships.

70   KCA: Marsham MS: U1515.03, Narbrough journal, 10 August 1666.

71   Fox, *Four Days' Battle*, pp. 296–303.

72   KCA: Marsham MS: U1515.03, Narbrough journal, 30 September 1666.

73   John Powell, *The Rupert and Monck letter book of 1666* (London: Navy Records Society 1969), p. 261.

74   The junction never took place. The Dutch, fearing that Rupert was to the west of them, returned to port. Beaufort sensibly retired to Brest. The long-expected fleet of Dutch East Indiamen eventually reached home via the north of Scotland.

4

John Narbrough in the Caribbean: Martinique, Cayenne and Surinam 1667–1668

In the spring of 1667, John Narbrough, commanding the 42-gun *Assurance,* was included in a small squadron under Sir John Harman, which was to sail to the West Indies, where the Dutch and French had been interfering with the interests of Charles II. The island of Saint Christopher [better known as Saint Kitts] had been shared between the French and English but, when the French entered the war in 1666, they drove the English planters out. Surinam, rich from sugar production, had been under English control since 1650, but early in 1667, the Dutch admiral Abraham Crijnssen, appropriated the place. By his own written word, it is certain that Cloudesley Shovell served in the West Indies with Narbrough in 1667.[1] Shovell was now in his 17th year, a tall, well-built young man, having had a birthday the preceding November, and this would be his second and final visit to the Caribbean. Perhaps he was fortunate in his long, 45-year naval career not to have to visit again this most sickly of areas, where many an English sailor had left his bones.[2]

Harman's squadron left Plymouth on 28 April 1667, stopping briefly at Madeira on the way, before reaching Barbados on 10 June. Whilst Harman and Narbrough were approaching Barbados, back in Europe, the Dutch under Michiel de Ruyter, were beginning their audacious attack on the Medway and the port of Sheerness. Sheerness was briefly captured and the Dutch humiliated the English by burning several large men-of-war and capturing the pride of the fleet, the *Royal Charles,*[3] before carrying her back to the Netherlands. This perfectly executed operation expedited the end of the Second Anglo-Dutch War. There is little doubt that Harman, Narbrough and Shovell were only too delighted not to have been a party to this, the nadir of English fortunes in the war. The following month, the official end of the Second Anglo-Dutch War came on 21 July with the Treaty of Breda: not that Harman and his men were aware of it at the time.

Harman realised that he had insufficient resources to retake Saint Christopher Island, but hearing that the French admiral, Joseph-Antoine de la Barre, was at Martinique decided

---

1   HMC: Finch MS, Vol. IV, pp. 387–388.

2   David Marley, *Wars of the Americas: A Chronology of Armed Conflict in the New World* (Santa Barbara: ABC–CLIO 2008), pp. 161–5.

3   Part of the stern decoration is now displayed in the Rijksmuseum in Amsterdam.

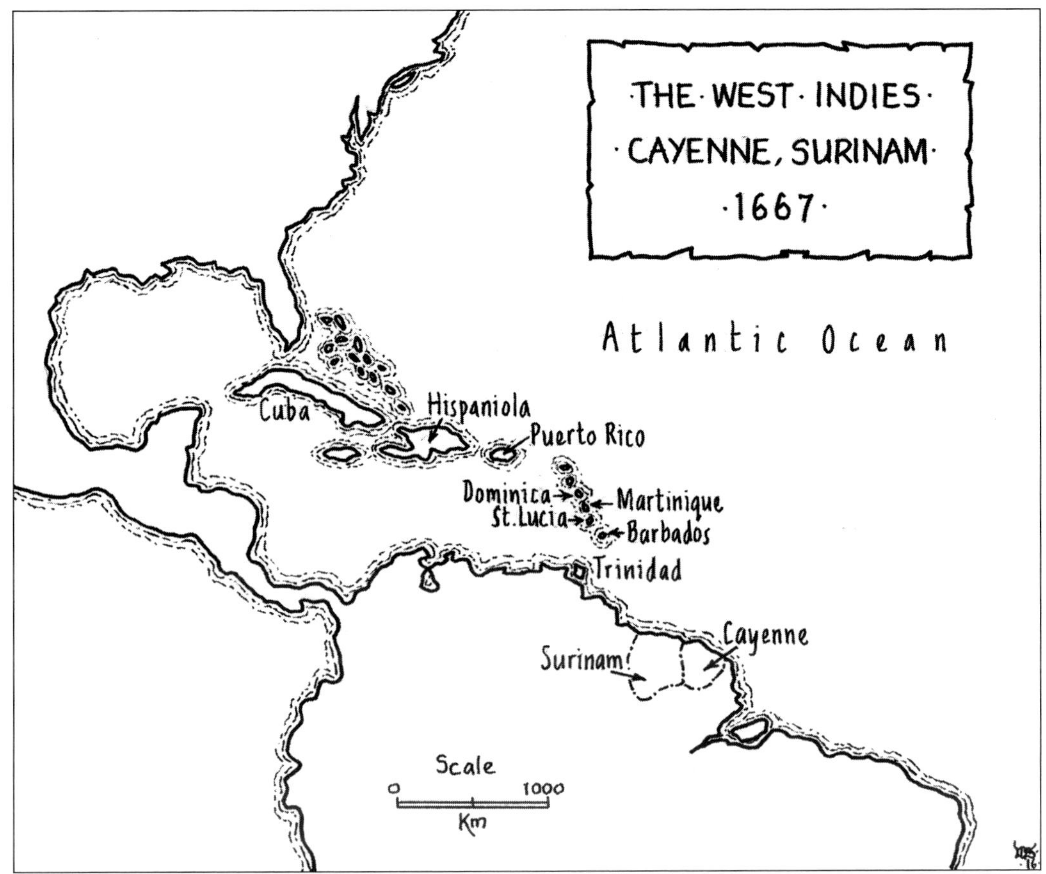

Map 6   The West Indies, Cayenne, Surinam 1667.

that he might be able to deal with him. La Barre was anchored under the powerful batteries of guns of Fort St Pierre with seven moderately sized and 14 smaller men-of-war plus three fireships.[4] Against this superior force Harman, in the 68-gun *Lion*, had nine men-of-war, two ketches and two fireships. On 19 June, Harman arrived off Martinique and proceeded to attack the French. He continued his intermittent attacks over the next few days without being able to bring them to a general action. Information had been received by Harman to the effect that the French were short of gunpowder and he deliberately stimulated them to expend as much as possible. At 4:00 a.m. on the first day, Narbrough took his ship into the range of the French and for his trouble had 400 guns concentrate on his ship, leading to a further depletion of the enemy's powder. The following day [20th], Narbrough bravely took the *Assurance* within a pistol shot of De la Barre's flagship, the 38-gun *Lis Couronnée*, and 'fought him about an hour.' Narbrough reported five men killed, 18 wounded, and the

---

4   The men-of-war varied in size from 24–32 guns.

Assurance's rigging and masts were damaged. He withdrew and his crew repaired the sails, rigging and masts as best they could under the circumstances.[5]

By 24 June, the English had managed to silence the powerful batteries of Fort St Pierre. On the 26th, Narbrough wrote in his journal: 'we all stood in and fired upon them. With our fire ships we burned their admiral [De la Barre] and six ships more.' The ships were burnt down to the waterline and to add to the confusion, the French fireship, the *Purcelle*, was set on fire by its own crew who, in a panic, swam ashore. Harman had lost no ships and recorded a spectacular victory against the odds. 1667 had been an appalling year for Charles II's navy, and this little victory in far-away Martinique was the best the English could offer all year.[6] Prior to the action, Harman had been lame, probably from a combination of the badly fractured ankle that he had suffered at the Four Days' Battle and gout. During the battle itself, Harman skipped about like a much younger, injury-free man, only to take to his bed immediately afterwards. Clearly there was bad feeling between the two sides as the French declined a prisoner exchange. There is little doubt that John Narbrough had been very forward in the action.[7]

From his couch, the victorious Harman led his damaged squadron away from Martinique towards the island of Nevis. A council of war briefly considered the possibility of a further attempt on Saint Christopher's garrison but, the available forces were not considered to be sufficient for a reasonable chance of success. Having refitted his squadron, consisting of the *Lion, Bonaventure, Jersey, Assistance, Assurance, Norwich, Willoughby, Roe*: Harman took aboard his ships troops under the command of Sir Harry Willoughby. A plan was formulated to make an amphibious assault on Cayenne [now French Guiana], which was held by the French and then to remove the Dutch from Surinam.[8] Both places were on the north-east coast of mainland South America – the Spanish Main. All those associated with the expedition were apparently still ignorant of the fact that peace had been proclaimed in Europe.

Willoughby drew up the plan of attack on Cayenne using the 500 men of his own regiment, under Lieutenant-Colonel Philip Warner, and a second foot regiment of 350 men under Colonel Samuel Barry. First ashore would be the 'Forlone Hope' under Major Richard Stevens, followed by three companies of seamen each consisting of 'sixty choice and well-armed mariners', at a distance of 100 yards, led by John Narbrough or Norborrow as he was described in one official despatch.[9] Narbrough held the post of senior captain, having drawn lots with two other naval captains. From the available evidence, Cloudesley Shovell would certainly have taken an active part in the coming fighting. Willoughby arranged to land his regiment behind the seamen and would come to the assistance of the others if required.

On the voyage from Nevis, Harman's squadron became becalmed for eight days, and towards the end of this time a serious shortage of water led to sickness amongst the

---

5   Marley, *Wars of the Americas*, pp. 167–8; KCA: Marsham MS U1515.03, Narbrough journal, 20 June 1667.

6   Frank Fox in *The Four Days' Battle of 1666* has described the action as the Royal Navy's only major success of 1667.

7   KCA: Marsham MS U1515.03, Narbrough journal, 28 June 1667.

8   In modern times spelt Suriname.

9   *CSP America and West Indies*, Vol. 5, July 1667, pp. 478–90. The Forlorn[e] Hope were the first wave of soldiers attacking a breach in defences during a siege. The commander was often a junior officer seeking promotion, but knowing that casualties were likely to be high. By extension it came to mean any soldiers in a dangerous position.

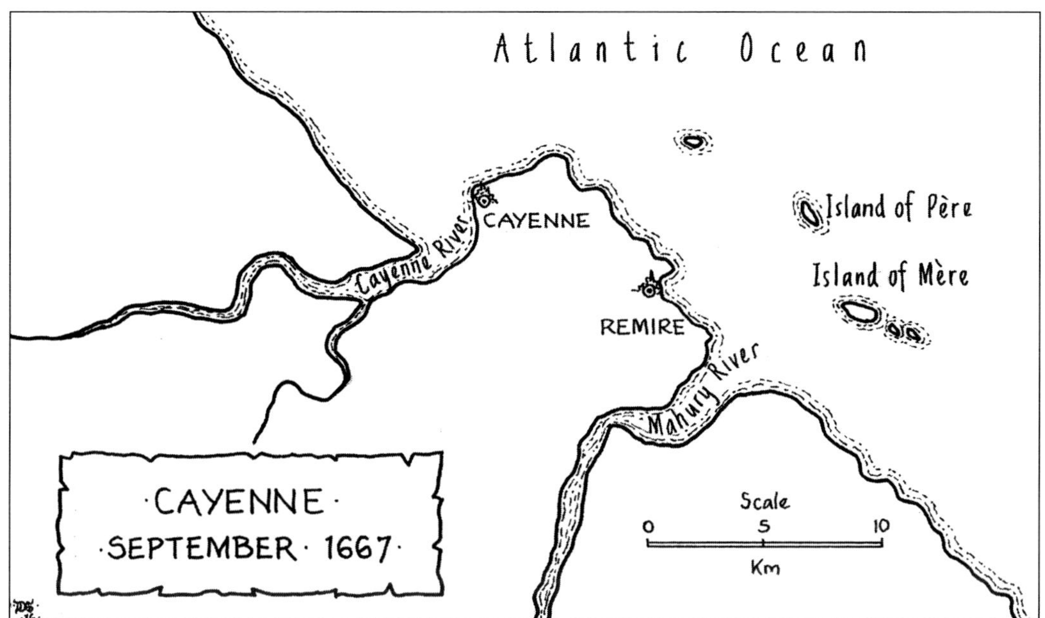

Map 7 Cayenne September 1667.

unfortunate soldiers. 12 September, saw the squadron six leagues off Cayenne and they were soon spotted by the French. Initially, the Governor Le Febvre de Lézy, thought that they were reinforcements sent from Martinique, despite the fact that he had been warned, 24 hours earlier by a brigantine, that Harman's squadron was on the way. Having discovered that they were English men-of-war, de Lézy organised a reception committee of 300–400 armed men at Rémire. On the 13th, Harman began to disembark soldiers and sailors into boats off the Island of Père and then by design moved his ships to the north-west off Romana, which was closer to Cayenne, to allow the soldiers an unopposed landing. De Lézy followed this movement and shifted the bulk of his men to Romana. Subsequently the English returned to their original plan and their forces went ashore relatively unopposed at Rémire.

Narbrough landed at 7:00 a.m. with about 40 men and was promptly shot at by the French defenders. However, the French were charged, with 20 of them being killed, before the remainder ran away. Narbrough did not give chase as he did not know the lie of the land and managed to capture a single prisoner in combat himself. By the evening the English had landed 900 men, the Governor, de Lézy, had fled, and the town was in Willoughby's hands. The leader of the 'Forlone Hope', had been wounded in no less than seven different places. Unfortunately, the English soldiers came across a supply of strong liquor, to which they helped themselves liberally, despite the best efforts of their officers to stop them. The town was torched, and the following day, the 14th, the English marched on the fort and captured it. Narbrough recorded, 'we cruelly plundered the French' and by the next day all Cayenne was in English hands, and the guns from the fort were transported to the ships. In all, about 36 guns and around 150 black slaves were brought off, prior to the departure of the English on the 29th. In his journal Narbrough summed up the situation: 'we burned and destroyed all the island.' The houses were highly combustible and a wall of fire soon separated the seaman on the beach from the town. The Governor, Le Febvre de Lézy, had behaved badly towards his men by escaping in a brigantine from the river with all his plate, leaving them to get what terms they could.[10]

Twenty five years later, Cloudesley Shovell gave his own account of the sacking of Cayenne and the division of booty:

> As to what you writte a bout the dividents of officers, seamen and souldiers in the West Indies, I can informe your Lordship that in 1667 we tooke the island of Keyan from the French, Sir John Herman commander at sea and Lieut-General Willoby at land. I was then with Sir John Narbrough and remember the dividment was made before we left the island. The things divided were negros, coppers and other brass or copper instrements belonging to the milles and sugar houses, also sugger, tobacco, mallasses and what else the iland affored for marchantdise. There was but a little pow(d)er theire, and that was I think given to the buckenners. The great guns was secured for the King, and magazeens of provision or licquer was never brought into the dividend but disposed for the good of the men as the cheife officers thought fit. But goods taken a bord ships in the road or harbower which fell into our hands by reason of takeing the place ware divided. There may be other things which I doe not well remember but the furniture of houses and pocket plunder remained with takers, for I well remember the people of the iland had hid their goods in the woods and carried some of them sum distance from the town. We followed them in partys and sum private men got great booteys both of silver and gold and remained with what they tooke, and had sum incorragement for the negros and other divideable bootey that they brought in.
>
> I know not directly every officer's shear but I think the Admirall and general a shore had a third or halfe between them. I was one of the seven that had a good negro and Sir John Narbrough had eight negros; but he was then captain of the Assurance. He had also sum coppers but I know not whether he had them in shear of wheither he stole them. This to the best of my knowledge is what happened theire but dividents have been variously made, for their never was a settelled prop(r)tion.[11]

From these comments concerning the taking of Cayenne and the division of plunder, it is clear that Cloudesley Shovell was actually present. His comments on the possible honesty of John Narbrough are enlightening. The earlier experiences of their late mentor Christopher Myngs would surely have meant no latitude in the division of booty and the king's share. One of the few criticisms of Shovell's character was that his covetousness knew no bounds. Some years later, a black slave was worth £20 or 3,287 lbs of sugar. Probably Shovell sold his slave.

Harman's squadron, with the re-embarked soldiers, left Cayenne on 29 September 1667 and sailed to the north-west along the coast of South America. On 4 October, they reached

---

10   Marley, *Wars of the Americas*, pp. 167–8; Dyer, *Narbrough*, pp. 41–9; KCA: Marsham MS U1515.03, Narbrough journal, 29 September 1667.
11   HMC: Finch MS, Vol. IV, pp. 387–8.

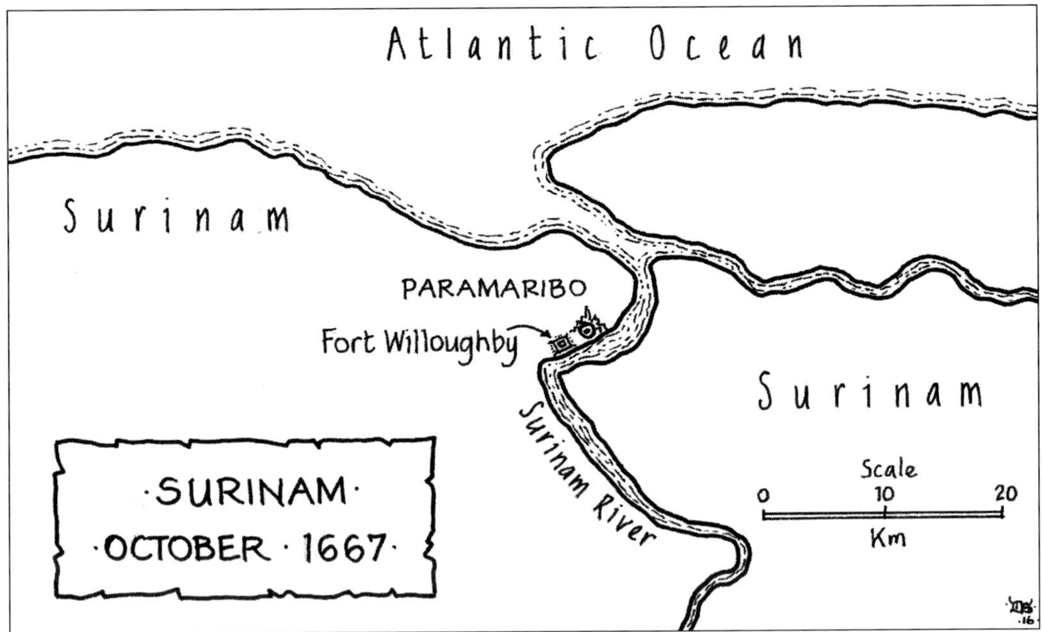

Map 8 Surinam October 1667.

the Surinam River and, sailing down it, anchored off the capital, Paramaribo. An unsuccessful attempt was made to persuade the Governor, Maurits de Rame, to surrender the fort with its garrison of 250 men, within half an hour's time. The following day, Lieutenant-General Harry Willoughby's men were landed about half a mile below Fort Zeelandia [Fort Willoughby],[12] and approached it via a wood and a sugar plantation. The fort proved to be a formidable strongpoint that would be difficult to take without assault ladders, as the walls were 18 feet high. Willoughby's plan of action was to bombard the fort with the men-of-war from the sea and combine this with an assault on it by his soldiers. After darkness, to make matters even more unpleasant for the beleaguered garrison, the wells, their sole water supply, were stopped up. Surprisingly the wells were to be found outside the fort at about a musket shot's distance.

On 7 October, Harman's squadron attacked the Fort Zeelandia from the Surinam River. Narbrough described the scene:

> The Bonaventure anchored first in a good birth I [the *Assurance*] stood within her and anchored. So the rest anchored with the ketches. The fort fired at us and we at them about 2 o'clock they killed Captain Hammond and Captain Willoughby and wounded me with a small shot through my thigh.[13]

---

12   Originally known as Fort Willoughby, the Dutch, on taking Surinam in early 1667, changed the name to Fort Zeelandia. In more recent times the Fort has been used for the incarceration of political prisoners and it was the site of the infamous 1982 murders.

13   KCA: Marsham MS U1515.03, Narbrough journal, 7 October 1667.

William Hammond was the captain of the *Bonaventure* and had made a name for himself as part of the landing party at Terschelling the previous year. William Willoughby had commanded the *Portsmouth* ketch. The fact that Narbrough was wounded by a musket ball shows just how close to the fort the *Assurance* lay. Residual effects of the musket ball through his thigh would trouble him for the rest of his life as did a recurrent fever, almost certainly malaria, which occurred from this time. Cloudesley Shovell would also suffer from a similar complaint. A medical report from 1668 concluded 'that a musket ball passing through the large muscle, bruising bone, tearing the tendons and causing persistent pain and numbness, caused the wound.'[14] Clearly, Narbrough suffered damage to a branch of a large nerve in the thigh, such as the femoral or sciatic as was demonstrated by the numbness. He was indeed fortunate not to have had a fracture of his femur or rupture of the femoral artery or vein. Both Tollemache, at Camaret Bay in 1694, and Hesse Darmstadt at Barcelona in 1705, would discover to their cost how leg wounds of this type were often fatal.

Eventually Fort Zeelandia was assaulted with minimal English casualties. The Dutch governor, Maurits de Rame, accused the English of barbarism, as he said that they had ignored a flag of truce whilst entering the fort using pieces of wood knocked off it during the naval bombardment. Of the garrison of around 250 men, 56 were wounded or killed. Surinam was in English hands once more, but not for long as a fortnight later a fleet arrived from the Netherlands with news that under the terms of the Treaty of Breda, Surinam was returned to the Dutch.

Narbrough's wound did not appear to have curtailed his activities as on 19 October he recorded in his journal that he went up to the fort. The entries for the 29th and 30th were:

> The admiral [Harman] ordered me to remove to the Bonaventure. I removed my things this day and muster men move with me to the Bonaventure. This day I received my Commission from Sir John Harman admiral of this expedition.
>
> This day I delivered the Asssurance to Captain Ball and I went aboard the Bonaventure to command. I mustered the men and had 180 aboard.[15]

The *Bonaventure* of 42-guns was a slightly larger ship than the *Asssurance* and represented a small promotion for Narbrough. It is likely that Shovell moved with him. On 1 November, Narbrough set sail for Barbados. On the way, he recorded 'we had a small contest about dividing the negroes.'[16] The 15th saw their arrival at Barbados where the soldiers, 45 prisoners and 25 black slaves were disembarked. On 28 November, Lord William Willoughby, the Governor of Barbados, father of Lieutenant-General Harry Willoughby, sent his son in the *Bonaventure* back to Surinam in order to bring off the inhabitants and their moveable possessions. This had been made necessary by the Treaty of Breda, giving Surinam back to the Dutch, of which the English had previously been unaware.

From this time until the *Bonaventure* sailed for England, in July 1668, Narbrough and his ship travelled all over the Caribbean. Amongst the many places visited were St Lucia, Antigua, Montserrat, Dominica, Guadeloupe, Nevis and periodically back to base

---

14   Dyer, *Narbrough*, pp. 55–6.
15   KCA: Marsham MS U1515.03, Narbrough journal, 29 October 1667.
16   KCA: Marsham MS UI515.03, Narbrough journal, 4 November 1667.

at Barbados. Early in June 1668, Narbrough acquainted Harman with the fact that the *Bonaventure* had the worm. The next month, on 23 July, the *Bonaventure* left Barbados for the last time. Prematurely, the day before, Narbrough wrote: 'To day I take leave of these shores.' In the company of the *Crome, Norwich* and some merchant ships, the *Bonaventure* sailed for England. After only three days of sailing, Narbrough put his men on half their water allowance, for fear of a long passage with the slow sailing merchant vessels. On the 29th, the senior captain, Poole, ordered Narbrough to accompany the six merchant vessels whilst he pushed ahead for England. Narbrough handed Poole, a package that he had been given by Colonel Simon Lambert for Charles II.[17] The relief in Narbrough's entry for 19 September is almost palpable: 'we saw ye Island of Scilly up north of us about 4 miles.' All the bread in the *Bonaventure* had been eaten and the crew were surviving on pease. In six days' time, there would have been no provisions left at all. Eventually, in October, the *Bonaventure* reached the Chatham River and Narbrough went to London: 'I came to London to Mr Mings house and being Sunday my brother Loads went to Norfolk.'[18] On 6 November John Narbrough went to Whitehall and 'kissed his royal highnesses hand.' This was the Duke of York.[19]

17 Lambert had fallen out with Lord William Willoughby and had refused to return the King's letter and commission. Perhaps the papers related to this little difficulty.

18 Mr Mings was almost certainly a relative of Sir Christopher Myngs: a further demonstration of the close ties between the Myngs and Narbrough families. John Narbrough's favourite sister had married a man called Loades. Thus he was John Narbrough's brother-in-law. The son of the marriage, Edmund Loades, would drown as flag captain of the *Association,* with Cloudesley Shovell, in 1707.

19 Marley, *Wars of the Americas,* p. 168; Dyer, *Narbrough,* pp. 49–56; Davies, *Pepys's Navy,* p. 237; KCA: Marsham MS U1515.03, Narbrough journal, 6 November 1668.

5

John Narbrough's voyage through the Strait of Magellan to Valdivia 1669–1671

Following the Second Anglo-Dutch War, Charles II was desperate to refill his coffers and he looked enviously at the Spanish exploitation of South America. Francisco Pizarro had conquered Peru some 130 years earlier, and the Spanish rapidly expanded their sphere of influence from Panama in the north, to present day Chile in the south. The silver mines of Potosi, now in Bolivia, brought enormous wealth to Spain. It was shipped back to Spain via the Isthmus of Panama and then carried home in the plate fleet. In 1688, it was this very Spanish silver that would lead to John Narbrough's premature demise.

In May 1669, Narbrough was ordered to prepare an expedition for a voyage to South America, as Charles II wanted to see if it was possible to trade with the Spanish on the west coast and to assess the feasibility of developing settlements, similar to those in North America, on the south-east coast. The original intention was for Narbrough to sail north as far as California. The King as a private venture would send goods such as glasses, scissors, knives, pins, cloth, tobacco and pipes for bartering purposes.[1]

During the summer of 1669, Narbrough fitted out the 300 tons ship, the *Sweepstakes*,[2] for the coming expedition. During the voyage which would last for almost two years, Narbrough would keep a detailed journal often with drawings of harbour layouts and animals and birds that he saw, detailed in the margins. Although Samuel Pepys described Narbrough's drawings as 'rude', meaning those of an amateur artist, they are still informative. Amongst the crew of 80 were Greenvile Collins, the renowned hydrographer and the future author of the '*Coasting Pilot*', and John Wood who would later find fame as an Arctic explorer.[3] Almost certainly Myngs and Narbrough's 18-year-old protégé Cloudesley Shovell sailed

---

1   The account of Narbrough's voyage to the South Seas is principally based on: KCA: Marsham MS U1515.03, Narbrough journal, 1669–71; Dyer, *Narbrough*, pp. 57–91; Scott Polar Research Institute (SPRI): MS SP 1636, William Chambers journal of the *Batchelor* 1669–70.
2   The *Sweepstakes* was built at Yarmouth in 1666, 109' by 28.5', 376 tons, with 42 guns in 1669. It is likely that some of the guns were removed for the voyage.
3   John Narbrough, *An Account of Several Late Voyages and Discoveries to the South and North* (Tennessee: General Books 2009, original publication 1694), p. 14. In Narbrough's journal in Marsham MS U1515.03, the entry for 30 July 1669 stated '114 men'. Thirty four men left the *Sweepstakes* prior to sailing, presumably to reduce the size of the crew before such a long voyage with limited food and water.

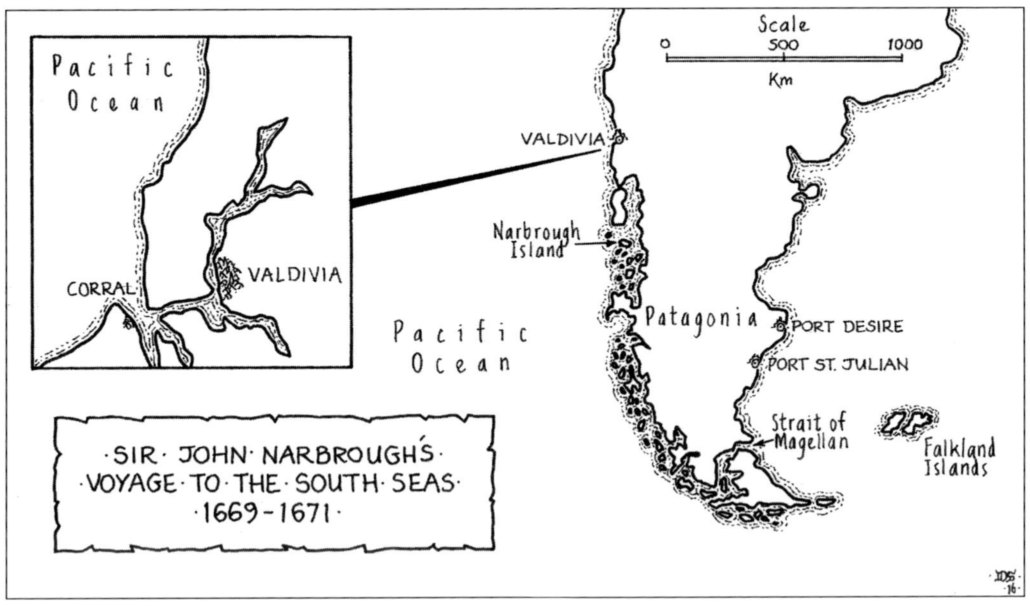

Map 9 Sir John Narbrough's Voyage to the South Seas 1669-1671.

with the expedition. It is known that Shovell was in the West Indies with Narbrough in 1667 and, as will be seen at the end of this chapter, he was documented as being part of the crew of the *Sweepstakes* for an abortive voyage to the West Indies in the autumn of 1671. In addition, John Macky who was active in Shovell's lifetime has recorded his presence on the voyage to Valdivia.[4] The lieutenants of the *Sweepstakes* were Nathaniel Peckett and Thomas Armiger, another Norfolk man and related to Christopher Myngs. In Narbrough's journal, little mention by name is made of ordinary sailors unless they died! This may explain why Shovell does not feature in the manuscript.[5]

At the end of August, Narbrough took his leave of Charles II and his brother, the Duke of York. Eventually, the *Sweepstakes* sailed from the Downs, on 29 September 1669, accompanied by the *Batchelor Pink* of 70 tons. The latter ship, with 18 men under the command of Humfrey Fleming, had been a last minute addition to the expedition. Their first port of call was Madeira where they were able to take on water and provisions before, a few days later, sailing on to the south-west. Soon, the two ships crossed the Tropic of Cancer and Narbrough recorded in his journal:

> Saturday October 23rd – this day I crossed the Tropic of Cancer, all my men in good health, I praise the Almighty God for it; many of my men that had been with

4   John Macky, *Memoirs of the Secret Services of John Macky Esq* (London: Spring Macky 1733), p. 122. John Macky stated that Shovell was with Narbrough on the voyage through the Strait of Magellan into the South Seas in an account of his secret services published in 1733. He was a Scottish spy who had been active in the reigns of William III, Anne and George I.
5   KCA: Marsham MS U1515.03, Narbrough journal, 1669–71.

me in the Indies formerly were let blood; for I take bleeding in those hot climates to be a great preserver of health, diverting Calentures; ----.[6, 7]

Narbrough's views on the treatment of scurvy were advanced for his era, but blood-letting by the surgeon for malarial fever was pointless.

The Cape Verde Islands, 350 miles off the coast of West Africa, were reached at the end of October and further victualling took place. The Portuguese fleet was in Porto Praya, the capital, and Narbrough was hard pressed to avoid a serious incident, when their sailors stole the hats of the English seamen. It must be remembered that there was a Portuguese Queen of England, Catherine of Braganza. For the first time, here at Porto Praya, Narbrough informed his crew what their destination was to be. Humfrey Fleming of the *Batchelor Pink* was given strict instructions that he must stay in company with the *Sweepstakes*. In case of accidental separation, detailed arrangements were made for meeting places, on the coast of South America, with messages to be left for each other. At the beginning of November, the two ships sailed on to the south-west and at times the *Sweepstakes* would tow the smaller vessel. Early in the new year, on 2 January, Narbrough recorded: 'my men are all in good health: God be praised being: 87: in number the same as I came out with from England ----.' He spoke too soon as two days later, John Mahon, an 18-year-old from Suffolk, died.[8]

On the anniversary of the execution of Charles I, 30 January, 21 years earlier, Narbrough judged that they were off the mouth of the River Plate, with a strong current driving them southwards. The two ships were surrounded by sea birds, some of which were shot for meat, and also by whales. When it came to food and drink, Narbrough made certain that there was no preferential treatment for himself and his officers:

> Today the Cooper found two buts of Beer had leaked out: this day all of us drank water only, for it was ever my order that the meanest boy in the ship should have the same allowance with myself; so that in general we all drank of the same cask and eat one sort of Provision, as long as they lasted. I never permitted any Officer to have a better piece of Meat than what fell to his lot; but one blinded with a Cloth serv'd every man, as they were call'd to touch and take, by which means we never had any Difference upon that score.[9]

Christopher Myngs had trained Narbrough to look after his men in an exemplary fashion. Both men would be role models for the young Cloudesley Shovell, in getting the very best out of their men, with due diligence for their welfare. In their time, Myngs, Narbrough and Shovell were all popular captains who never had any difficulty in manning their ships. This was partly due to their success in battle and in collecting prize money, but mainly to the affection that they inspired in their men.

In February 1670, during one of their periodic losses of contact with the *Batchelor Pink*, Narbrough discussed with his officers whether they should wait for the pink, or go for

---

6   A calenture was an old Spanish term meaning temporary delirium or fever.
7   Dyer, *Narbrough*, p. 60.
8   KCA: Marsham MS U1515.03, Narbrough journal, 4 January 1670.
9   Dyer, *Narbrough*, pp. 66–7.

the Strait of Magellan by themselves as the weather conditions were currently favourable. Understandably, there was considerable apprehension of tackling the dreaded Strait, as a lone vessel, for fear of being wrecked. According to the journal of Nathaniel Peckett, on the night of 19 February,[10] final contact was lost with the *Batchelor Pink* which would eventually find its way back to England. Peckett accused the pink of deserting them with a false report of the *Sweepstakes* having sunk.[11] This story appears to be a gross calumny as William Chambers, lieutenant of the *Batchelor Pink*, recorded that they lost sight of the *Sweepstakes*, a day later, the 20th, in a thick fog:

Feb 20th 1670.
Very thick and hazy with wett fog this morning, between 7 and 8 of the clock we had sight of the Sweepstakes – bearing off us SE by S which was on our weather bow dist. From us some three miles, ---- but wee could not get to him and it being thick wee lost sight of him, then we being near our Lat. Of Cape Blanco.[12]

The next day, the 21st, Chambers went on: 'it being very thick and foggy wee keeping good looking out if we could see her but could not.----.' Two days later the *Batchelor Pink* was off Port Desire [Puerto Deseado],[13] but there was no sign of the *Sweepstakes* and Fleming decided to make for Port St Julian [Puerto San Julian]. Over the next few weeks the *Batchelor Pink* made valiant efforts to find the harbour, but without success and believed it was not in the latitude that they had expected it to be in. Desperate for water and food they went into the next possible landing site before sailing for England. In summary, fog and inaccurate navigation led to the departure of the pink rather than cowardice.[14]

Two days after losing contact with the *Batchelor Pink*, land was seen and Narbrough went ashore for the first time in Patagonia. The land resembled Newmarket Heath and there was evidence of human habitation with graves and the remains of old fires.[15] Men were sent to the hills to look out to sea, in a vain attempt, to see the *Batchelor Pink*. Narbrough's greyhound killed several animals which provided them with welcome fresh meat. In addition, he found: 'thefe Herbs with the Peafe-leaves, make a good Sallad to refrefh fuch as were inclining to the Scurvy; for want of which frefli Trade feveral of my Men were inclining to the Scurvy.' The *Sweepstakes* set sail again and, on 4 March 1670, Port Desire was reached, several days after the *Batchelor Pink* had looked in there. Forty men stepped ashore and 400 seals were clubbed to death and salted for food. A stake and board were placed in the ground with a message for the *Batchelor Pink* if its crew should land there.[16]

---

10   Narbrough also gives the date as 19 February at 10:00 p.m. in Marsham MS U1515.03, Narbrough journal, 1669–71. Perhaps, in view of the resulting controversy, the *Batchelor Pink* could see the *Sweepstakes* whilst the reverse was not true.

11   British Library (BL): Sloane MS 819, Nathaniel Peckett journal, 1669–71.

12   Near Puerto Deseado which was originally called Port Desire and is on the eastern coast of Patagonia. SPRI: MS SP 1636, Chambers journal, 20 February 1670.

13   Port Desire was originally named, in 1586, by Thomas Cavendish after his ship.

14   SPRI: MS SP 1636, Chambers journal, 2 April 1670.

15   Perhaps Narbrough had been horse-racing with Charles II on Newmarket Heath.

16   KCA: Marsham MS U1515.03, Narbrough journal, 4 March 1670.

In early April, Narbrough took the *Sweepstakes* down the eastern coast of Patagonia to Port St Julian. There was no sign of the *Batchelor Pink* and it was at this stage that Narbrough finally gave up any hope of seeing the ship again. The crew were apprehensive at continuing the voyage as a lone vessel, in case they ran aground, and the dangerous Strait of Magellan was still ahead of them. Narbrough collected his men together and told them of the riches of the land and that Francis Drake had circumnavigated the world in one ship. Perhaps tongue in cheek, he described Drake as an ordinary navigator! It is extremely doubtful that the great Elizabethan seaman would have approved of the description. By the end of May, the southern hemisphere winter was upon them and the weather began to deteriorate. Narbrough made the decision to stay in Port St Julian until the spring, before attempting the formidable Strait of Magellan.

In their new winter quarters, the crew of the *Sweepstakes* occasionally made contact with the local natives, Mapuche Indians, and various small trinkets were handed out as presents. One of Narbrough's men described them as tawny-coloured, medium-sized savages, wearing short skins and some of them carrying bows and arrows. Unfortunately no gold was apparent about their persons and a bracelet that was examined consisted only of sea shells. Narbrough was impressed by the surrounding countryside with its plains and grassy meadows. He felt that the land could sustain cattle and would also allow grain to be grown. Whilst at Port St Julian, Narbrough drew and painted in his journal, an extremely accurate map of the harbour. In the margins of the map, Narbrough illustrated the animals and birds that he had seen: penguins, seals, deer, guanacos,[17] ostriches, kites, wild dogs, hares, foxes. He had done the same thing at Port Desire.[18]

The weather was now bitterly cold with hard frosts and snow. The health of the crew deteriorated and in August one man died of the flux,[19] followed a few days later by another suffering from scurvy. Ten men were reported to be ill with scurvy despite the fact that they were able to go ashore and eat fresh food. Some men became lame with the bitter cold and the circulation in their legs had been affected: 'their legs were as black as a black Hat in spots, the cold having chilled their blood.' The sails of the *Sweepstakes* were examined and found to have been damaged by rats. Narbrough had them repaired as best they could. To make matters worse, in September, the *Sweepstakes* was in danger of being driven ashore. However, the weather gradually started to improve and on 16 September, Narbrough took the *Sweepstakes* to sea and sailed to the north and Port Desire, to replenish his stocks of seal and penguin. There he found that the Mapuche Indians had built a model of the *Sweepstakes* from the branches of bushes and the soil. The crew feasted themselves on penguin eggs which were tasty and in size larger than a duck's. On 12 October 1670, John Narbrough wrote in his journal: 'I wait only the almighties pleasure to sail the first fair winds for the Straits of Magalen.'[20]

The Almighty's pleasure came three days later, and Narbrough took the *Sweepstakes* out of the bay of Port Desire and sailed to the south for the Strait of Magellan. Ferdinand Magellan, the Portuguese explorer, was the first European to pass through the Strait in 1520

---

17   A wild Andean mammal similar to a llama.
18   BL: ADD MS 88980, Narbrough journal, 1669–71.
19   Dysentery.
20   Strait of Magellan.

and hence its name. Francis Drake was the first Englishman to enter the South Seas [Pacific Ocean], in 1578, via the Strait, during his circumnavigation of the world. By 25 October the *Sweepstakes* was in the Strait and for the next month Narbrough made a careful exploration of both the shore of Patagonia and also that of Tierra del Fuego. He named the numerous islands, bays and capes after the King, Charles II, and his court, some of which names have survived to this day. Narbrough managed to make contact with the Mapuche Indians, but greatly to his disappointment there was no sign of any gold. He described the Indians as having: 'no hair on their bodies nor faces, nor anything to cover their privy parts.'

After his month of exploration in the Strait of Magellan, which was recorded in minute detail in his journal, Narbrough finally reached the South Seas on 19 November 1670. This would be the only occasion that either Narbrough or Cloudesley Shovell would sail in what we now call the Pacific Ocean. The *Sweepstakes* turned to the north and sailed along the coast of Chile with its myriad of small islands. Perhaps Narbrough was beginning to run out of suitable names to be given to islands that he came across during the voyage. For near latitude 44 degrees 50 minutes south, he discovered a densely, tree covered island, 12 miles from north to south and three miles from east to west. Immodestly, Narbrough wrote in his journal: 'I called it after my own Name Narbrough's Iſland; I took poſſeſſion of it for his Majeſty and his Heirs.'[21] There is also a Narborough Island [Fernandina] in the Galapagos group, although John Narbrough never travelled anywhere near it.

The Bay of Valdivia [Corral Bay], or Baldavia or Baldivia as Narbrough knew it, was reached on 15 December.[22] It was one and a half miles wide and three rivers emptied into it. Pedro de Valdivia had founded the city in the 16th century and it lay beside the river of the same name, nine miles from the bay. At the time of Narbrough's visit, Valdivia was administered by the Viceroyalty of Peru and was protected by the formidable array of 17 forts around Corral Bay. Valdivia was the southernmost outpost of the Spanish Empire. By this stage the *Sweepstakes* had run out of bread and needed to be resupplied. Don Carlos or Carolus [Carlos Enrique Clerq], a guide, supposedly familiar with the coast of Patagonia, was landed a mile south of Corral Bay, in his best clothes and with a bag full of trinkets. It was intended that he make contact with the Spanish settlement. That night he was to light a fire at the same spot, as a signal, and then to rejoin the *Sweepstakes*. No fire was lit and Narbrough would never see Don Carlos again. Reputedly, he was detained and eventually executed at Lima in 1682, on a charge of corresponding with the English in Jamaica.[23]

The next day, the 40-year-old Lieutenant Thomas Armiger took a boat along the shore in search of Don Carlos. Unexpectedly, Armiger's boat came into view of one of the Corral forts and he was immediately summoned ashore. He had little choice but to obey the Spanish, who were friendly and proceeded to wine and dine him. Armiger's health was drunk and he observed the plates that they had eaten off were made of silver. Both gold and silver were plentiful and not much esteemed. Four Spaniards joined Armiger on his return journey to the *Sweepstakes* and innocently suggested to Narbrough that they pilot his ship safely into

---

21   Isla Narbrough or Isla Ipun. Narbrough was fairly accurate with the position of the Island. It is actually 44 degrees and 36 minutes south and 74 degrees and 45 minutes west.

22   Probably the reason for Narbrough spelling the name of the city with a B was that the Spanish pronounced V as a B. Hence Baldivia. It was customary in the 17th century to use phonetic spelling.

23   Sir Clements Markham in Laird Clowes, *Royal Navy*, Vol. II, p. 539.

the harbour. Narbrough did not fall for this little subterfuge as he knew full well that once under the guns of a Corral fort, he was effectively a prisoner of the Spanish. Narbrough took the opportunity to question the Spaniards about their settlement and also their relationship with the Mapuche Indians. He learnt that the two sides were perpetually at war with each other, although trade was carried out with gold and other goods. The settlement was supplied each year by six ships from Lima. In their turn the Spaniards quizzed Narbrough about the purpose of his long voyage from England. Tactfully, if untruthfully, Narbrough replied that his ship was richly laden with merchandise and he was sailing to China, and all he required from Valdivia was water and wood. Graciously, the Spaniards assented to this.

On 19 December, Narbrough sent the Governor of Valdivia Madeira wine and glasses as a present in order to curry favour with the Spanish. In return, he received rum and bread. Narbrough was under no illusions as to the delicate situation he was in, and it was clear to him that the Spanish would not be open to future trade with England. The next day, Lieutenant Thomas Armiger took a boat with John Fortescue, gentleman, Henry Cooe, trumpeter, and Thomas Highway, linguist and went ashore under a flag of truce looking for water. Immediately they were detained, although they managed to get a letter off to Narbrough with a Spaniard and six Indians in a canoe:

> Myself [Armiger] and Mr Fortescue are kept here as prisoners, but for what cause I cannot tell; but they still pretend much friendship and say that if you will bring the ship into the Harbour you shall have all the accommodation that may be.[24]

Not for one moment was Narbrough fooled by the supposed friendship of the Spanish. He replied to Armiger:

> Lieutenant, take what notice you can of the fortifications of the fort, and what strength they have of people in it, and whether they are able to withstand a ship; and what quantities of provision they have in it; and whether Don Carlos is there; send me an account there of by John Wilkins, I will use all endeavours to have you off when I know the strength of the place.[25]

Narbrough also sent a stiff letter to the Spanish demanding the immediate return of his unfortunate men. He even risked going ashore himself, near to the spot where Don Carlos had been landed, without finding anything. Christmas must have been a miserable one for Narbrough and the crew of the *Sweepstakes*.

Narbrough was in a very difficult situation and must have agonised over whether to make an attempt to rescue his lieutenant and his other men. The garrison of the Corral forts numbered some 600 men and their guns effectively ranged over the whole harbour. Narbrough had already shown his courage in battle, but it must have been clear to him that any attack on a Corral fort would have led to the loss of the *Sweepstakes* and his crew. Although, Narbrough was criticised in some quarters for not trying to rescue his men, he

---

24 KCA: Marsham MS U1515.03, Narbrough journal, 20 December 1670.
25 Dyer, *Narbrough*, p. 86.

made the only sensible decision to sail away empty handed.[26] It is a gross calumny to hold this decision against him. What is much more difficult to understand, is why the authorities in England made no attempt to exchange the unfortunate captives. Thomas Armiger would live in Valdivia for another 16 years, marry a local Spanish woman, before being executed for treason. The Spanish had behaved badly in the affair and it has been suggested that this was related to the antics of English buccaneers in the Caribbean.

Shortly before Christmas 1670, Narbrough decided that it was no longer possible to continue up the western coast of South America and consequently decided to return to England. On 6 January 1671, the *Sweepstakes* entered the Strait of Magellan and by mid-February, Narbrough was back in his old haunts at Port Desire. His return journey through the Strait made him the first Englishman to accomplish a passage from west to east. This feat alone should allow his name never to be forgotten in the annals of English exploration. Soon the *Sweepstakes* sailed into the Atlantic Ocean and the Azores were reached in May, where Narbrough, a man before his time, sent on shore for oranges and lemons as some of his men were suffering from scurvy in their mouths and legs. By this time, the crew of the *Sweepstakes* had been reduced to 69 in number. The Downs were reached on 13 June and Narbrough was ordered to Whitehall, to report to Charles II and the Duke of York. He discussed the voyage with the royal brothers and they examined his charts. In July, the *Sweepstakes* slipped away for Deptford where their journey had begun nearly two years before and the crew were paid off. The *Batchelor Pink* had managed to sail safely back to England, thinking the *Sweepstakes* had been lost. Her captain Humfrey Fleming was never employed again.

Overall, Narbrough's voyage into the Pacific Ocean cannot be described as a great success. However, firstly, he had demonstrated that the Spanish and the Mapuche Indians were unlikely to permit trade on the west coast of South America. Secondly, Narbrough was able to provide Charles II with information about the climate and natural resources on the east coast of South America, so that an informed decision could be made about setting up new colonies there. Thirdly, his accurate charts of the coastline of Patagonia, and in particular that of the Strait of Magellan, would be of inestimable value to future mariners in those waters. With great prescience, Narbrough dedicated one of his charts to the influential Samuel Pepys. The two men were always close, unlike Pepys with Narbrough's protégé Cloudesley Shovell.

In October 1671, Charles II required urgent business to be conducted in the West Indies, and Narbrough in the *Sweepstakes* plus another vessel, were told off for the venture. In the event, the voyage came to nothing as by the time the ships were ready the need was over. The importance of this minor event was that Cloudesley Shovell was definitely part of the crew for the aborted voyage.[27]

---

26   James Burney, *A Chronological History of Voyages and Discoveries in the South Sea or Pacific Ocean* (London: Luke Hansard and Sons 1817), p. 374. James Burney [1750–1821] was an English rear-admiral who accompanied Captain James Cook on his last two voyages.

27   The National Archives (TNA): ADM 33/121, pay book *Sweepstakes*, discharge of Claudious Shovell 9 January 1672. John Narbrough was discharged on 4 January.

6

The Third Anglo-Dutch War 1672–1673

Soon after the Treaty of Breda ended the Second Anglo-Dutch War, England, the Netherlands and Sweden signed a Triple Alliance with a view to limiting the all-consuming power of Louis XIV of France. Irritated by this, Louis broke up the Alliance by detaching England from it. He did so by bribing Charles II with money and promises of territory in the Netherlands and that an Englishman would command a combined fleet. Thus, in 1670, Charles signed the secret Treaty of Dover with the French. The Dutch went out of their way to avoid giving offence. However, in the early spring of 1672, Robert Holmes attacked the homecoming Dutch convoy from Smyrna and Lisbon which led to England and France declaring war on the Dutch. The war would be fought both on land and by sea. A French army, under Louis XIV in person, attacked the Dutch in their low-lying land and it was only the masterly use by Michiel de Ruyter and his fleet of the shoals off his country's coastline that saved the Netherlands.[1]

John Narbrough was discharged from the *Sweepstakes* in January 1672 and was appointed to the 100-gun *Prince* or *Royal Prince,* as first lieutenant, under Captain John Cox. He was soon followed by Cloudesley Shovell who became a midshipman in the same vessel.[2] During February, Narbrough stayed for several nights with a John Myngs in London who is thought to have been the brother of Christopher Myngs.[3] Narbrough would now be in a key position for the coming battle as the Duke of York had selected the *Prince* to be his flagship. In March and April Narbrough supervised the fitting out of the vessel. The Third Anglo-Dutch War began in March 1672 and would continue until February 1674.

At the end of April, de Ruyter and the Dutch fleet attempted, unsuccessfully, to surprise or bottle up the English fleet, in the Thames, before they could join the French. Despite the fact that his victualling was still incomplete, York sailed for the Isle of Wight and met Jean d'Estrées with his French squadron of 33 ships. D'Estrées, in the 74-gun *St Philippe,* was a former army general, ignorant of naval matters and an uninspiring leader. Matters

---

1   Herbert Richmond, *The Navy as an Instrument of Policy 1558–1727* (Cambridge: Cambridge University Press 1953), pp. 168–71; Laird Clowes, *Royal Navy,* Vol. II, pp. 298–9.

2   TNA: ADM 33/121, pay book *Sweepstakes*; TNA: ADM 33/103, pay book *Prince,* ticket no 55, 22 January 1672; Pepysian Library (PL), Magdalene College, Cambridge: Pepysian MS 2555, Narbrough journal, *Prince,* 7 January 1672.

3   PL: Pepysian MS 2555, Narbrough journal, *Prince,* 12–13 February 1672.

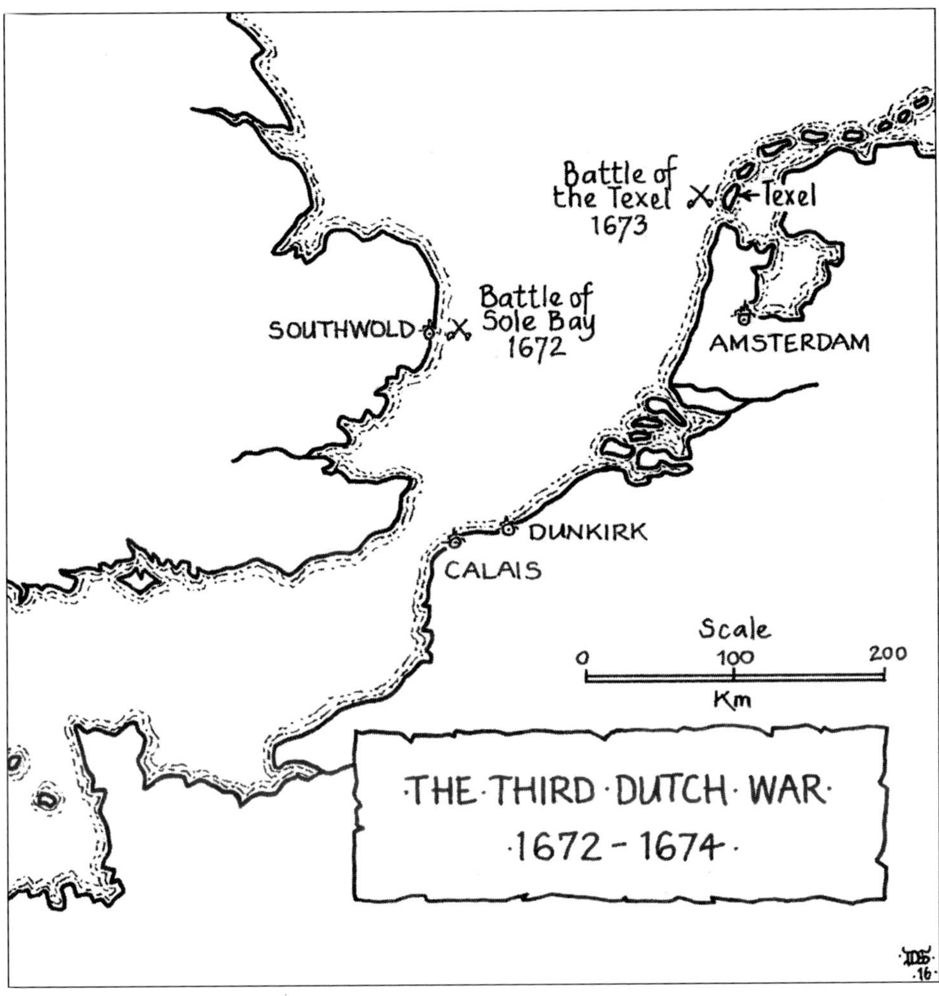

Map 10 The Third Dutch War 1672-1674.

were not helped by the fact that the English did not trust their new allies and held them in contempt as seamen. In this somewhat sulphurous atmosphere, the combined Anglo-French fleet sailed for the Gunfleet where they believed the Dutch fleet to be. Then the wily de Ruyter cunningly tried to lure York and d'Estrées on to the shoals of his own coast. By this time the English were short of water and sailed for Southwold. Narbrough recorded in his journal for 23 May:

We weighed with all the fleet and stores into Sole Bay and anchored in 8½ fathom water, the better to ride smooth, to take in our provisions. We rode about two miles from the shore side; the church of Southwold bore W.N.W. of us. This day many gentlemen of the fleet went ashore and many people of the shore came aboard our fleet.

The *Prince* and the remainder of the red squadron lay two miles off Southwold with the blue squadron under Edward Montagu, Earl of Sandwich, to the north off the small village of Covehithe.[4] Jean d'Estrées' French ships formed the white squadron and were positioned to the south off the remains of the medieval port of Dunwich and towards Aldeburgh.[5] Initially, the English were concerned about a sudden Dutch attack which would pin them on their own coast. On 26 May Narbrough confirmed their apprehensiveness in his journal: 'we rode fast unmoored keeping a good watch for I expect the enemy will be with us in the morning if the wind hang easterly.' However, on the 27th, at a council of war in the *Prince*, York believed reports that the Dutch had returned to their own coast. The one voice of dissent was that of Montagu who emphasised the dangers of being trapped on a lee shore. His sensible advice was ignored as York thought that he was unduly apprehensive and the English fleet momentarily dropped its collective guard. The decision probably cost Montagu his life.[6]

The sea off Southwold was flat as a mill-pond and, in the early hours of the 28th, Narbrough, acting on the orders of the captain of the *Prince*, John Cox, had the *Prince* heeled over and careened. A worse moment could not have been picked for, at 3:30 a.m., guns were heard from the east and a French frigate came towards them with her cannons firing a warning of danger. Astern of this ship, at a distance of nine miles, was the Dutch fleet. The English were caught totally unprepared with many men still ashore in Southwold. Narbrough informed John Cox and the Duke of York of the proximity of the Dutch. In a leisurely manner, York came to the quarterdeck of the *Prince* and gave instructions for sailing. At 5:30 a.m. on 28 May, they got under way and the Battle of Sole Bay was about to begin.[7] Most of the fighting would take place nine to 12 miles from the shore.

The Anglo-French fleet had 74 major ships and the Dutch 62, with the former's ships heavier and better armed. With the wind between east and east-south-east, the Dutch bore down on the Anglo-French fleet from the east-north-east. De Ruyter had divided his ships into two divisions of line abreast with frigates/fireships in front, followed by his more powerful vessels. Irritatingly for him he had the added encumbrance of Cornelis de Witt, as plenipotentiary, in the *Zeven Provincien*.[8] Amongst the subordinate admirals was Jan de Liefde, the slayer of Christopher Myngs. In the Anglo-French fleet confusion reigned with the French, believing themselves to be in the van and expecting to lead the line, getting off on the port tack and sailing to the south. The English contingent, consisting of the red and blue squadrons, sailed on the starboard tack to the north. The fault lay with York for not

---

4   The Duke of York was admiral of the red and commander-in-chief. The Anglo-French fleet was organised in the now traditional three squadron formation – red, white and blue.

5   D'Estrées actually hoisted the flag of the admiral of the white.

6   Richmond, *Instrument of Policy*, pp. 172–4; Laird Clowes, *Royal Navy*, Vol. II, p. 302; PL: Pepysian MS 2555, Narbrough journal, *Prince*, 26–27 May 1672.

7   Principal sources for the Battle of Sole Bay: PL: Pepysian MS 2555, Narbrough journal, *Prince*; Roger Anderson, *Journals and Narratives of the Third Dutch War* (London: Navy Records Society 1946), pp. 13–22; Dyer, *Narbrough*, pp. 95–113; Laird Clowes, *Royal Navy*, Vol. II, pp. 302–9.

8   Cornelis de Witt had accompanied de Ruyter in the Medway assault, in 1667. At the Battle of Sole Bay, de Witt sat in a chair, on the deck of the *Zeven Provincien*, dressed as a magistrate and surrounded by his 12 halberdiers, many of whom were killed in the action. Later in 1672, he and his brother, Johan, were assassinated in The Hague and their bodies mutilated. It is said that their extremities were cooked and eaten by the mob.

giving clear orders to the French other than to keep close to the wind. Hence the French were going in one direction and the English in the other! Certainly not an auspicious opening to the encounter.[9]

Montagu's worst fears were realised with the easterly wind favouring the Dutch. The flood tide meant that his ship, the huge 100-gun three decker, *Royal James*, faced north and he reacted quickly by cutting his cables and sailing to meet the Dutch right under Willem van Ghent. De Ruyter concentrated on the red squadron, in the centre, off Southwold, and Adrien Banckert, commanding the Dutch left, isolated d'Estrées and the French close to Dunwich. The French were unable to join the English but the allegation that Louis XIV had given instructions for them to stay out of harm's way was probably false. It is true that morale in the French squadron was not good as d'Estrées was feuding with his second-in-command, Abraham Duquesne,[10] the eventual conqueror of the incomparable Michiel de Ruyter.[11]

Montagu was first into action, at 7:00 a.m., with York, Narbrough and Shovell joining in about an hour later. York's *Prince* was directly opposed by de Ruyter's favourite flagship, the 80-gun *Zeven Provincien*, backed by his seconds and others. This made some seven ships against the isolated *Prince* and amongst them was Aert van Nes in the *Eendracht*. The light winds meant that the rest of the English red squadron was becalmed and unable to assist their hard-pressed chief. As the action was fought at a musket shot's distance, it was feared that the Dutch would put into practice their favourite tactic of boarding, but the rapidity of fire by the *Prince*'s gunners precluded this. York in his second major action at sea was calm, constantly moving around his ship, encouraging his men and calling for the *Prince* to be luffed closer to the enemy. Narbrough waxed lyrical on the subject in a much quoted extract from his journal:

> I do absolutely believe no Prince upon the whole earth can compare with his Royal Highness in gallant resolution in fighting his enemy, and with so great conduct and knowledge in navigation as never any General understood before him. He is better acquainted in these seas than many masters which are now in his fleet; he is General, Soldier, Pilot, Master, Seaman; to say all, he is everything that a man can be, and most pleasant when the great shots are thundering around his ears.[12]

No doubt Narbrough expected York to read these heady words of praise and hoped that they might improve his prospects of early promotion. It is fair to say that York's experience at sea, unlike his cousin, Prince Rupert's, was strictly limited and he depended very much on the advice of his professional seamen, such as William Penn at the Battle of Lowestoft. This is not to gainsay his calm bravery when cannonballs were striking down his retinue during the current action.

---

9   Anderson, *Journals and Narratives*, p. 14.
10   Unlike d'Estrées, he was an experienced and able seaman, but with a filthy temper. He was jealous of his commander-in-chief.
11   Laird Clowes, *Royal Navy*, Vol. II, pp. 301–3; Anderson, *Journals and Narratives*, pp. 17–8.
12   PL: Pepysian MS 2555, Narbrough journal, *Prince*, 28 May 1672.

Between 9 and 10:00 a.m., the captain of the *Prince*, the newly knighted Sir John Cox, was killed by a cannonball whilst in close proximity to York on the poop deck. Thus the command devolved on John Narbrough, who endeavoured to sail the *Prince* to the windward of the Dutch. Over the next few hours the damage to the *Prince* worsened with masts and rigging cut down by enemy shot. The main top mast fell on to the deck and the jumble of damaged rope and wood prevented the upper deck's cannons from being used. The intensity of the enemy's fire stopped the English seamen from effecting repairs to the rigging and sails. Narbrough's journal gave a flavour of the atmosphere:

> our great guns plying all this time as fast as our seamen could load and fire at the enemy's men of war and fireships; the enemy shooting as fast as us, killing and wounding our men very briskly and slapping the ship's sides and rigging.[13]

To make matters even more unpleasant, the Dutch towed two fireships towards the solitary, unsupported *Prince*. When Narbrough became aware of the danger, he ordered two ship's boats to tow the *Prince* away to the north and respite in the company of other English ships. York, realising that his flagship was so damaged that he could not lead his fleet from it, took his standard in a boat to the 90-gun *St Michael*, commanded by Sir Robert Holmes of bonfire fame. Once York's standard came down, the Dutch seemed to lose interest in the *Prince*. Between noon and 1:00 p.m., Narbrough got his ship on to the other tack and sailed in a southerly direction towards the town of Lowestoft. By this stage, the wind had come round to the east-north-east and Narbrough fired intermittently at the Dutch. Confusion reigned with smoke obliterating a clear vision of the land, making it difficult to judge where they were.

Between 3–4:00 p.m., the *Prince* passed the burnt-out flagship of Edward Montagu, Earl of Sandwich, which was still smouldering. Montagu had been undone by fireships which had torched the *Royal James*.[14] He was fortunate to escape the inferno but was drowned when the overladen boat in which he was doing so capsized. His corpse was later washed up on the shore and recognised by the George and Star on his chest;[15] subsequently he was buried in Westminster Abbey with great ceremony. There was a certain irony in the manner of Montagu's demise as he had opposed the outlawing of the fireship when both the English and Dutch were prepared to do so.[16] This was the implement of war feared above all others by the 17th century mariner. However, to be fair to Montagu, he was a fine sailor, leader, diplomat and a great loss to his country.

Narbrough tried to find York who had been forced to make a second hazardous trip in an open boat to the 96-gun *London*, this being necessary because the *St Michael* had become disabled. The *Prince* was joined by 30 other ships including that of Narbrough's former superior in the West Indies, John Harman, in the 80-gun *Royal Charles* and also by John Kempthorne in the 96-gun *St Andrew*. In the late evening, de Ruyter and the Dutch set

---

13   PL: Pepysian MS 2555, Narbrough journal, *Prince*, 28 May 1672.

14   One of the few survivors of the *Royal James* was its captain, Richard Haddock, who had been wounded in the foot. With some justification, he blamed Joseph Jordan for not coming to their assistance.

15   Order of the Garter.

16   Davies, *Pepys's Navy*, p. 61.

their sails and stood to the south-east and the safety of their own coasts. Further contact was made with the Dutch on the 29th, but fog prevented the resumption of hostilities. On 1 June, the Anglo-French fleet returned to Sole Bay to lick its wounds.[17]

The Battle of Sole Bay was indecisive with both sides losing ships, but the inferior Dutch force had come out of it in a better position, having done enough damage to the Anglo-French fleet to prevent any action on their own coast for the foreseeable future. De Ruyter had lost two major ships, 600 men killed [including the flag officer Willem van Ghent] and around 1,000 wounded. According to Narbrough, the English had lost one ship, the *Royal James* with 737 men killed [including Edward Montagu and several senior captains] and roughly the same number of wounded. In the *Prince* 150 seaman were killed and approximately 250 wounded out of a crew of nine hundred. The heavy casualties, in Narbrough's ship, reflected the intense fighting she had taken part in. French casualties were around 450 killed and wounded which belies allegations that they did not come to fight.[18] Subsequently, de Ruyter claimed that he had never before been present in so hard-fought and obstinate an engagement.

From Sole Bay, the Anglo-French fleet made for the Gunfleet which was reached on 3 June. Repairs were undertaken on the damaged ships and on the 18th of the month, the Duke of York, who had by this time returned to the *Prince*, entertained his brother, Charles II, and his queen, Catherine of Braganza, aboard his flagship. Narbrough described the colourful scene:

> At seven o'clock the King and Queen came aboard the Prince and several of the nobility. His Royal Highness received them with a bountiful entertainment having all the colours and pendants flying at the yard arms, the Standard at the top mast head, the Anchor-standard at the fore-topmast head, and the Union flag at the mizzen top mast head.[19]

That night the queen slept alone in the *Prince* and the king retired to his own yacht. Sadly, history does not relate which, if any, of Charles' numerous mistresses joined him!

Later in June, the English actually transported troops across the North Sea, but the cunning de Ruyter's watch from amongst the shoals off the Dutch coast precluded a landing. During the rest of the summer, Narbrough and Shovell remained in the *Prince* with the Duke of York. In mid-September the time came to lay up the larger ships to protect them from the winter storms. Narbrough and Shovell were not to be spared a winter at sea, as the former received a commission to command the 52-gun *Fairfax* and the latter came as master's mate.[20] The *Fairfax* joined Edward Spragge in an expedition into the North Sea where little was achieved apart from interfering with the profitable Dutch herring fleet. In late November Narbrough was ordered to take the *Fairfax* to the Downs to escort

---

17 PL: Pepysian MS 2555, Narbrough journal, *Prince*, 1 June 1672.

18 According to Laird Clowes, *Royal Navy*, Vol. II, p. 300, there was no love lost between the English and French. After the battle, English prisoners told their Dutch captors that they would rather be fighting the French.

19 PL: Pepysian MS 2555, Narbrough journal, *Prince*, 18 June 1672.

20 TNA: ADM 33/91, pay book *Fairfax*, ticket no 1076, 17 September 1672. The master, a warrant officer, was appointed by the Navy Board and was responsible for the navigation of the ship. The master's mate was his assistant.

100 merchant ships out to the Mediterranean. Further merchantmen were picked up at Plymouth and, early in the new year of 1673, they all sailed through the western approaches of the English Channel. Cloudesley Shovell continued to serve in the *Fairfax* as master's mate and he would be intimately involved with the navigation of the ship. As will unfold shortly, poor navigation would nearly lead to its loss.[21]

By now the number of merchantmen under convoy had been reduced to eighty-five. Various ships left Narbrough's care for Oporto, Lisbon and Cadiz as they sailed down past the Iberian Peninsula. At the end of January, Martin Westcombe, the consul at Cadiz, sent a tartan to inform Narbrough of the presence of seven Dutch warships on the coast.[22] This was a worrying turn of events and, at a council of war, it was decided to send the Smyrna and Scanderoon ships straight on to their destinations.[23] The remainder of Narbrough's ships got down to the mouth of the Strait of Gibraltar and into Tangier Road in early February.

Their stay in Tangier appeared to have been a convivial one as the elderly Governor, John Middleton, 1st Earl of Middleton, gave a ball at which all the ladies of the city and other persons of quality attended. It sounded a much more refined affair than the bawdy house that the immoral Arthur Herbert, later Earl of Torrington, used to keep there in the early 1680s. Narbrough and all the other sea officers attended the ball, but no doubt Shovell had to make do with the delights of the city. For the first time he would see the contentious mole at Tangier, which a decade later would cause him such grief.

Narbrough's respite in Tangier was all too short for, in mid-February, they returned across the mouth of the Straits and sailed to the north and Cadiz. Martin Westcombe informed them that the seven Dutch ships had recently sailed from Cadiz under their own colours. Previously, they had been in Spanish service and displayed that nation's flags. Early in March, Narbrough sailed for home with the 20 returning merchantmen, but inclement weather forced him back to Cadiz again. Consul Westcombe and the merchants persuaded him that it would be prudent, in view of the possible Dutch presence, to wait for Robert Robinson's ships to come round from Malaga before making another attempt to sail. This delayed their departure until early April, and by the middle of the month, Robinson was truculently threatening to sail directly for England alone. Narbrough discovered that the root of the problem was the petty jealousy of Robinson in whom should lead their combined fleet of ships.[24] Sensibly Narbrough got around this particular problem by alternating the lead of the 86 ships between himself and this irritating captain.[25]

Earlier, it has been stated that Narbrough was a popular and just captain who took great care of the welfare of his men. However, he could act the part of the disciplinarian when necessary. At about this time he had the gunner and carpenter of the *Thomas and Edward*

---

21   PL: Pepysian MS 2556, Narbrough journal, *Fairfax*, 22 May 1673.

22   A tartan or tartane was a small coastal or fishing vessel. It had a large lateen sail, fore-sail and bowsprit and they were used in the Mediterranean for 300 years.

23   Smyrna is now Izmir and Scanderoon is Iskenderun. Both are situated at the north-eastern end of the Mediterranean.

24   Robert Robinson was a prickly character who, unlike John Narbrough, had still not commanded a 1st or 2nd rate ship. Despite this he would receive a knighthood.

25   PL: Pepysian MS 2556, Narbrough journal, *Fairfax*, 21 April 1673.

fireship ducked at the yardarm of the *Fairfax* for bringing a black man aboard.[26] Whether this was for financial or sexual purposes is not clear. At Lagos Bay, Narbrough had put another man in irons for staying ashore.[27]

Narbrough and his fleet of merchantmen sailed through the Atlantic Ocean looking for the western approaches to the English Channel. Here a near disaster took place amongst the rocks of the Isles of Scilly. Narbrough and his master's mate, Cloudesley Shovell, would not be the first nor indeed the last English sailors to suffer in these treacherous waters.

In May 1673, Narbrough wrote in his journal:

> I feared the wind to be northerly and that it would blow so I could not fetch Plymouth [and this] caused me to keep so northerly a course tonight, reckoning we were to the eastward of Scilly Islands.[28]

Quite possibly, this entry was added at a later date, as an alibi for his faulty navigation.[29] Narbrough would have known that his journal was likely to be inspected. The following day, 22 May, he continued:

> Hazy, cloudy weather this morning at 1 oclock and rain; the wind at S.W., a fine small gale. We steered E. b N. with a short sail keeping ships ahead of us to the northward of us. Between 1 and 2 oclock this morning it blew a fresh gale and rained. Very hazy weather. I sailed after the rate of 6 leagues a watch. At 2 o'clock this morning we saw false fires to the eastward of me; we answered them again with false fires and a musket. At a quarter of an hour past 2 o'clock this morning we saw a breach of rocks near by us on our larboard side; several vessels ahead of us and on our larboard side did not see it. I caused the ship to be put a-stay, setting our after sails, and 2 guns to be fired, and to show as many lights as we could, that the fleet might take notice of it and look out. I saw that the ship did stay, and it fell little wind, and the tide set the ship within the breach to the northward; we also saw the breach of several other rocks ahead. I immediately let go the best bower anchor and brought the ship up and immediately rode fast until day-light, that we might see about us where we rode.[30]

The ships ahead of the *Fairfax* remained in the vicinity, whilst those astern tacked when they heard the guns go off and stood away. To his great surprise and indeed horror, Narbrough found that:

---

26 A naval form of punishment instituted by the French in the early 17th century. A rope was fastened below the man's arms and under his breech. He was then run up the yard arm and dropped violently into the sea. The process could be repeated several times and a variant was to drag the man under the keel of the ship–so called 'keel-hauling'. However, in the English navy, there is no record of 'keel-hauling' between 1650 and 1690. Both processes were very unpleasant and could lead to death from drowning.

27 PL: Pepysian MS 2556, Narbrough journal, *Fairfax*, 22 April 1673. Lagos is a Portuguese town in the western Algarve.

28 PL: Pepysian MS 2556, Narbrough journal, *Fairfax*, 21 May 1673.

29 This was suspected by Roger Anderson who edited the *Journals and Narratives of the Third Dutch War*.

30 PL: Pepysian MS 2556, Narbrough journal, *Fairfax*, 22 May 1673.

After it was fair daylight, that I could see round about me, I saw that we were entangled with rocks called the Bishops and Clerks. The windmills on St Mary's Island I saw plain; they bore N.E. b E. from me. I was right before Broad Sound. I saw several breaches of rocks about a quarter of a mile within me, and but one rock without me, about 2 cables' length from me S.W. I saw it was clear of rocks to N.W'ward and the sea open, and the ships that were got within the breach, as I was, stood out that way. I caused a hawser to be passed out at the gun-room port forward and bent to the cable and roused it taut and veered out the cable, to cast the ship the right way. When the ship was cast and the sails full, we cut the cable and stood out N.W. into the sea, until I got off from the rocks out of danger. I lay by, to have all the fleet together. Not one vessel received any damage in the least, but all of them got clear from so dangerous a place of rocks.[31]

Narbrough attributed this near catastrophe to a number of factors: the indraught of a current that set into the estuary of the River Severn and St George's Channel; a flood tide; constantly changing course to bring in lagging ships; variable soundings. Later, one of the other captains, James Jennifer of the *Saudadoes*, wrote that Narbrough's compasses were found to be inaccurate. Also it was said that the day before, others, who thought that they were to the east of the Isles of Scilly, had overruled Narbrough. It was a miracle that no ships were lost on 22 May 1673, but it was more by luck than good judgement that a catastrophe of the first order had not taken place. Since Narbrough saw the windmills of St Mary's Island to the north-east by east, the *Fairfax* cannot have been amongst the Bishop and Clerks rocks, but further to the south, on the edge of the Western Rocks to the south-west of St Agnes Island.[32] The *Fairfax*'s master's mate, Cloudesley Shovell, was present at this incident but sadly did not learn from it. The master of the *Fairfax* was responsible for navigation and Shovell was his assistant. Thirty-four years later he would find himself in a similar predicament and did not come out of it alive. The reasons for Narbrough's near disaster will be studied further in a later chapter.

In late May, the fortunate fleet got into Plymouth and three days later arrived in the Downs. John Narbrough reported to Whitehall where he kissed the hands of Charles II and the Duke of York. No doubt he was only too happy to be safely home again.[33]

Whilst Narbrough had been away, major events had taken place in England. The Test Act of March 1673 had come into force precluding Roman Catholics and Nonconformists from holding civil or military/naval offices. The Duke of York fell foul of the act and lost the post of Lord High Admiral. Although the Test Act was a factor in Prince Rupert's succeeding to the command of the fleet, fears about the safety of York, after the near-misses of Sole Bay, would probably have meant a change in command. Rupert's instructions were to defeat the Dutch fleet and land troops on the coast of the Netherlands in support of Louis XIV.

The first move of the new campaign season came from de Ruyter who planned to stop the junction of the English and French fleets by filling hulks with stones and sinking them

---

31   PL: Pepysian MS 2556, Narbrough journal, *Fairfax*, 22 May 1673.
32   An alternative explanation is that the outer western rocks, to the south-west of St Agnes Island, were originally called the Bishop and Clerks rocks.
33   PL: Pepysian MS 2556, Narbrough journal, *Fairfax*, 9 June 1673.

to block the exit channels of the Thames. However, this came to nothing as, in early May, de Ruyter found Rupert waiting for him. In the middle of the month, Rupert's ships joined the French ships of d'Estrées off Rye. On 28 May and 4 June the first and second Battles of Schooneveld were fought between the Anglo-French and Dutch fleets. Narbrough's *Fairfax* was not back from convoy duties in time for either battle. Thus neither Narbrough nor Shovell would see action in these two inconclusive engagements fought close to the Dutch coast and its dangerous shoals. Narbrough was expected to be in the junior flag position, that of rear-admiral of the blue squadron. However, his late return from the Straits meant that the aristocratic Thomas Butler, Earl of Ossory, was appointed on 18 May, in his place. This was just four days before the *Fairfax* had so narrowly escaped from being wrecked on the rocks of Scilly. In some quarters it has been suggested that Narbough's near disaster was caused by his hurrying home so that he did not miss out on becoming a flag. There does not seem to be any evidence for this.

At the end of June, it must have been galling for Narbrough to be appointed senior captain to the very same Ossory, in the 90-gun, *St Michael*.[34] However, if Narbrough had been appointed rear-admiral of the blue, petty jealousies might have arisen: '---- for, though he was a good seaman, yet there were many others in the fleet that were of better merit, and longer service; and the offence that must have been given to others, had he enjoyed it, was taken off by putting a person of so great quality as my Lord Ossory into the place.'[35] In the event, despite their very different backgrounds, Narbrough and Ossory got on remarkably well. Soon Cloudesley Shovell would join his patron in the *St Michael*.[36]

July saw Rupert's fleet at the Gunfleet and the *Greyhound* with Frederick Schomberg, commander of the land forces in the Netherlands, aboard was fired at on the orders of the Prince for failing to salute. The captain of the vessel was then put in irons for flying the St George flag at the main top mast head. At times Prince Rupert could be a very prickly character when it came to salutes. In September, he fired at a Danish ship bringing in the corpse of the Duke of Richmond for failing to salute properly.[37] Later in the July, Narbrough who had a strong constitution had a rare bout of sickness of unknown origin. Perhaps it was a reoccurrence of his malarial fever or even sea-sickness. In late July and early August 1673, Rupert took the combined fleet over to the Dutch coast. De Ruyter was also under pressure from the Amsterdam merchants to safeguard their home-coming merchant fleets. However, it was not until 11 August that the final encounter of the Third Anglo-Dutch War, the Battle of Texel or as the Dutch know it, the Battle of Kijkduin, took place.[38] It would be fought just off the Texel channel.[39]

34   PL: Pepysian MS 2556, Narbrough journal, *St Michael*, 1 July 1673.

35   Anderson, *Journals and Narratives*, p. 375.

36   TNA: ADM 33/104, pay book *St Michael*, ticket 1398, 1 July 1673.

37   Charles Stuart, Duke of Richmond had been sent to Denmark as ambassador in 1671 and had died there the following year. His third wife was a mistress of Charles II and apparently continued in the role after her marriage. Charles II informed Richmond of this fact whilst inebriated!

38   Principal sources for the Battle of the Texel: PL: Pepysian MS 2556, Narbrough journal, *St Michael*; Anderson, *Journals and Narratives*, pp. 48–56; Davies, *Pepys's Navy*, pp. 262–8; Dyer, *Narbrough*, pp. 127–37; Laird Clowes, *Royal Navy*, Vol. II, pp. 317–22.

39   The Island of Texel is the largest of the Frisian Islands and lies just off the coast of the Netherlands. Narbrough gave the distance of the battle from Texel as between three and nine leagues. One league equals approximately three

The Anglo-French fleet consisted of 86 major ships against the Dutch's 60: approximately a 3 to 2 superiority. In guns 5,386 to 3,667.[40] As was now the custom, the Anglo-French fleet was organized into three squadrons: the white squadron [French], in the van, was commanded again by Jean d'Estrées; the red squadron, in the centre, by Rupert; the blue squadron, in the rear, by Edward Spragge. The Dutch had: Adrien Banckert with the Zeeland ships in the van; de Ruyter, in the centre, with a largely Rotterdam contingent; the recalled Cornelis Tromp in the rear with the Amsterdam vessels. Ossory and his senior captain, Narbrough, in the *St Michael*, were in Spragge's blue squadron which had John Kempthorne, in the *St Andrew*, as vice-admiral. Spragge, a protégé of Prince Rupert, was a fiery Irishman who had reputedly been a slave in Algiers at an earlier stage in his career. He had been personally insulted, by Cornelis Tromp, after the Saint James' Day Fight, with the insinuation that Spragge's wife would make a better leader of a squadron than her husband! Spragge took all this very seriously and was also a mortal enemy of the English admiral, Robert Holmes. Such was the character of the man who was about to lead Ossory and Narbrough into battle.

At dawn on 11 August, with the wind, a fine small gale, from the east-south-east, the Anglo-French fleet was sailing in their three-squadron formation in roughly a south-westerly direction on a smooth sea. De Ruyter's Dutch fleet were approaching, from the south-east, with the advantage of the wind and had skilfully placed themselves between the Allies and their own coast. Around 8:00 a.m., the Dutch bore down upon the Allies with Banckert taking on d'Estrées' white squadron, de Ruyter making for Rupert's red squadron and leaving Tromp to have a private battle with his great enemy, Spragge, with his blue squadron. De Ruyter used the same tactics that he had employed at Sole Bay: bottling up the French, with a small number of ships, whilst he dealt with the other two squadrons.

Edward Spragge went to the lengths of ordering his blue squadron to back their sails, theoretically in order to keep them close together. They hove to and during the battle drifted to leeward.[41] In reality, Spragge wanted to make certain that he could continue his vendetta against Cornelis Tromp in person, and seemed supremely uninterested in maintaining contact with his commander-in-chief in the red squadron. Spragge was reported to have said that he would kill Tromp or die in the attempt. He had set up his blue squadron with Ossory in the *St Michael* ahead, himself in the *Prince* in the centre, and Kempthorne in the *St Andrew* at the rear.

For over three hours, Spragge's *Prince* engaged Tromp's famous *Gouden Leeuw* in their very personal duel and was worsted. The remainder of the blue squadron joined in a general engagement against Tromp's vessels, which lasted from 8:00 a.m. to noon, with both sides sailing to the south before turning in a north-westerly direction. Narbrough noted that the Dutch shooting was superior to that of the English, in speed and accuracy, and that Tromp had 26 ships to Spragge's 27 in the blue squadron. Ossory's division fired broadsides against the Amsterdam ships of Jan de Haan and the *St Michael* suffered considerable damage to her rigging. No sooner had Narbrough sent men to repair the rigging than it would be damaged all over again. Kempthorne, the vice-admiral of the blue, in the *St Andrew* at the

miles.

40   Anderson, *Journals and Narratives*, p. 47.
41   Heave to: by turning across the wind leaving the headsail backed in order to come to a stop.

extreme rear, lost two of his masts and was forced to anchor to leeward. His Dutch opponent had been Isaac Sweers, in the *Olifant*, who had certainly got much the better of him.

The *Prince* was severely damaged and Spragge was forced to shift his flag to the *St George* in order to continue the fight. Ossory placed the *St Michael* and the other ships of his division between the *Gouden Leeuw* and the *Prince* to shield Spragge's transfer. A little later, Ossory sent Narbrough across to the *St George*, by boat, to suggest to Spragge that they board the *Gouden Leeuw*. It was agreed that the *St Michael*'s crew should undertake this and that the *St George* would support them. Narbrough recorded:

> I immediately went on board the St. George and delivered my Lord's message to Sir Edward Spragge on the quarter-deck, there being Sir Edward Spragge and Captain Darcy and several officers on the place by.[42] Sir Edward Spragge answered me he would bear down upon the enemy as soon as possible he could, and that he would second my Lord in boarding, and that there would be no great danger in doing it.[43]

Nothing came of the plan as Tromp bore away and the expected support from Spragge did not materialise. Narbrough would never have the chance to speak to Spragge again.

Between 1–2:00 p.m., the *St George* became disabled and Spragge felt obliged to change ships once again, this time to the *Royal Charles*. Unfortunately a cannonball went straight through the *St George* and holed the boat that was transferring Spragge. The crew rowed back frantically, trying to regain the *St George*, but the boat sank before they were near enough for a rope to be thrown to it. Spragge was reported drowned, although he was later found with his head and shoulders above water, having taken such a firm hold on the side of the boat in death, that they could hardly disengage the corpse. He probably succumbed to hypothermia, in the cold North Sea, rather than actual drowning. The crew of Narbrough's *St Michael* witnessed their admiral's demise, although at the time, they did not realise that it was his boat.

The death of Edward Spragge meant that effective leadership of the blue squadron was lost and Tromp moved towards the hapless *Prince*. Fireships bore down and one was even attached to her before a brave member of the crew cut the ship free. Around noon, the wind had swung around to the south-west to give the English the weather gage. Ossory, with the able support of John Narbrough, took the *St Michael* close to the stricken *Prince* and kept fireships in position to deter Tromp who was again moving in for the kill. Tromp himself was forced to change flagships, from the *Gouden Leeuw* to the *Komeetster*, always a risky journey in a small boat.

At the beginning of the battle, Rupert's red squadron found itself in the alarming situation of being isolated with the white squadron vanishing ahead and the blue squadron astern. From around 8:00 a.m. until midday, his squadron steered to the north-west, all the time in a moving action, against de Ruyter's ships. More fireships were expended in this period of the action than at any other time in the Dutch wars. In the early afternoon, Rupert sailed northwards to support the blue squadron whilst at the same time de Ruyter moved to

---

42   Captain Thomas Darcy of the *Prince*.
43   PL: Pepysian MS 2556, Narbrough journal, *St Michael*, 11 August 1673.

assist Tromp. There was a most unusual sight, witnessed by Narbrough in person, of both squadrons sailing side by side but not firing at each other. It is very likely that both were short of ammunition. Between 4–5:00 p.m., the red rejoined the blue squadron and Rupert successfully stopped de Ruyter from despatching Spragge's original flagship, the *Prince*. Then two frigates, supported by Ossory, took the *Prince* in tow. Narbrough felt that the blue squadron had got the better of the Dutch before Rupert's arrival. But Tromp, with greater justification, believed that his ships would have overwhelmed the blue squadron if Rupert had not appeared on the scene.

Controversy surrounded the behaviour of Jean d'Estrées' white squadron [French] who made great efforts to gain the wind of the Dutch, as an object in itself, with a view to fighting the next day, but did not do much more. The French rear-admiral, the elderly Marquis Damien de Martel, reported that he had been keen to fight, but that he had been stopped from doing so by d'Estrées. De Ruyter's aim was to isolate the French so that he would have more ships for action against the red and blue squadrons. Banckert required very few ships to achieve his goal of locking up the French and was able to send the remainder to help de Ruyter in the centre.[44] This allowed odds against the English of 4 to 3 instead of 3 to 2. Eventually it would become 4 to 3 in his favour. The final indignity came at 5:00 p.m., when d'Estrées ignored Rupert's signal to follow in his wake. He claimed not to have understood the signal, but aggravated matters further by tactlessly stating that he would not have followed the order even if he had done so. It is not difficult to understand why some of the English contingent felt that d'Estrées may have been ordered by Louis XIV to stay out of the battle.

The action was effectively over by 8:00 p.m., when Rupert and the English fleet withdrew to the north-west to take care of their damaged ships and the Dutch turned eastward. Both sides claimed victory, although the Dutch had the stronger case as the English were returning to their own ports and the possibility of a landing on the Dutch coast had gone. The loss of officers was heavy on both sides. Amongst the Dutch fallen was Jan de Liefde whose ship had been responsible for the death of Christopher Myngs, at the Four Days' Battle, seven years earlier. No major ships were lost by either side. The Anglo-French fleet returned to Southwold on 22 August and Narbrough took the *St Michiel* into Chatham in early September. The *St Michiel* had suffered 60 dead and 130 wounded during the battle. Few Englishmen had come out of the Battle of Texel with much credit. Lord Ossory was promoted to vice-admiral of the red and finally, on 19 September, John Narbrough reached flag rank, as rear-admiral of the red. In addition he was knighted on 30 September 1673; it was long overdue. Although the Third Anglo-Dutch War would drag on until February 1674 with the signing of the Treaty of Westminster, in reality it ended at the Battle of Texel.

---

44   Banckert had only around 10–12 ships, the other Dutch squadrons each had over 30 ships.

Christopher Myngs, by Peter Lely. He led the English line at the Battle of Lowestoft and was mortally wounded during the Four Days' Battle of 1666. (Courtesy of the National Maritime Museum)

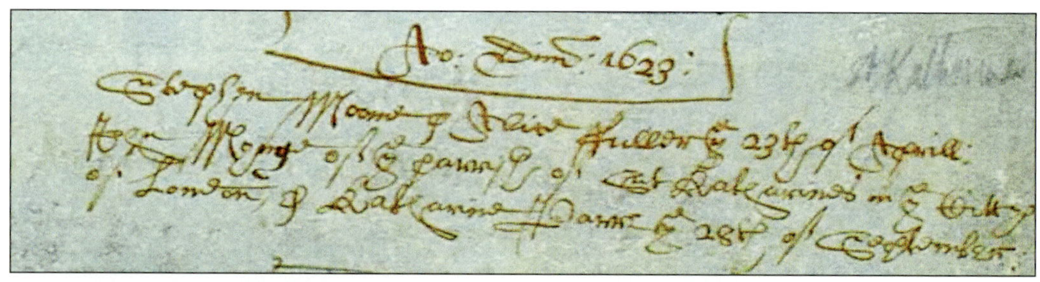

Marriage entry for Christopher Myngs' parents in the Salthouse Parish Register. (Courtesy of the incumbent of Salthouse and the Norfolk Record Office)

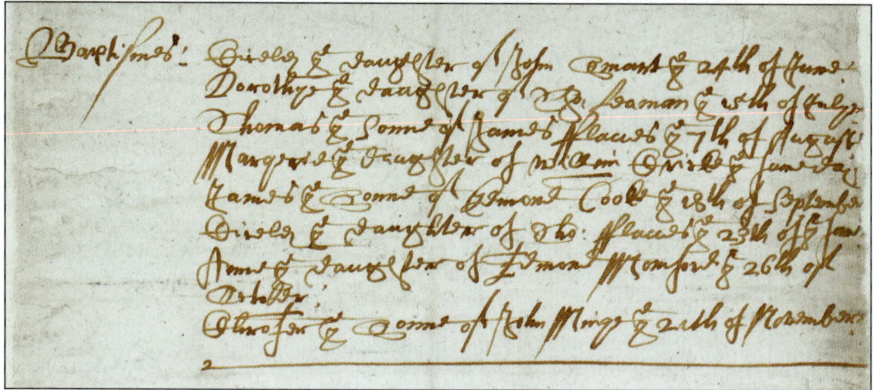

Baptismal entries for Christopher Myngs. Firstly, the remains of the original baptismal entry from the Salthouse Parish Register. Secondly, the Archdeacon's contemporary copy. (Courtesy of the incumbent of Salthouse and the Norfolk Record Office)

Cloudesley Shovell, miniature, 18th century English School. (Courtesy of a Private Collection)

Cloudesley Shovell, miniature, early 18th century English School. (Courtesy of a Private Collection)

Possibly Anne Shovell, mother of Cloudesley Shovell, early 18th century English School. (Courtesy of a Private Collection)

The young Cloudesley Shovell. (Courtesy of the Guildhall Museum, Rochester)

Elizabeth Hill, later the second wife of John Narbrough and after his death she married Cloudesley Shovell. Portrait by Simon Pietersz Verelst. Circa 1678. (Courtesy of a Private Collection)

Elizabeth D'Aeth, the eldest daughter of Sir John Narbrough. Portrait, early 18th century English school. (Courtesy of a Private Collection)

James Narbrough, son of Sir John who drowned with his stepfather, Cloudesley Shovell,
in the disaster of 22 October 1707. Portrait, late 17th century English school.
(Courtesy of John Narbrough Hughes-D'Aeth)

Cloudesley Shovell by Michael Dahl. (Courtesy of a Private Collection)

Elizabeth Shovell, née Hill, married firstly to John Narbrough and secondly to Cloudesley Shovell. Portrait by Michael Dahl. (Courtesy of the 8th Earl of Romney)

Cloudesley Shovell by Michael Dahl.
(Courtesy of the Guildhall Museum, Rochester)

Robert Marsham, 2nd Baron Romney, a grandson of Cloudesley Shovell who suggested that his grandfather had been murdered on the beach of Porthellick Cove for the sake of an emerald ring. Portrait by Frans van der Mijn. (Courtesy of the 8th Earl of Romney)

Drawing of Elizabeth Narbrough's tomb in Wembury Church. She was Sir John's first wife. (Courtesy of the National Maritime Museum)

Cloudesley Shovell's tomb in Westminster Abbey. (Courtesy of a Private Collection)

Memorial to John and James Narbrough, the sons of Sir John. They were buried in Old Town Church, St Mary's, Isles of Scilly. (Courtesy of a Private Collection)

Tomb of Sir John Narbrough in St Clement's Church, Knowlton, Kent. (Courtesy of a Private Collection)

James Greeve's tomb by the south transept of St Margaret's Church, Cley-next-the-Sea. (Courtesy of a Private Collection)

George Monck, 1st Duke of Albemarle, by the workshop of Peter Lely. Joint command with Prince Rupert at the Four Days' Battle and the 'go-to man' in a crisis. (Courtesy of the Rijksmuseum)

Prince Rupert, after Anthony van Dyck. The swashbuckling cousin of Charles II who held joint command for part of the Four Days' Battle and sole command at the Battle of Texel. It was said that 'a whiff of brimstone accompanied him wherever he went.' (Courtesy of the Rijksmuseum)

John Harman, by Peter Lely. Both John Narbrough and Cloudesley Shovell were in the highly respected John Harman's squadron to the West Indies in 1667. (Courtesy of the National Maritime Museum)

William Coventry, after Mary Beale, secretary to the Duke of York and something of a role model for Samuel Pepys. He attended Christopher Myngs' funeral. (Courtesy of the Houses of Parliament Collection)

Jacob van Wassenaer, Lord of Obdam by Abraham Evertsz van Westerveld. Commanded the Dutch fleet at the Battle of Lowestoft where he was killed. (Courtesy of the Rijksmuseum)

Michiel de Ruyter, by Ferdinand Bol. 'The Dutch Nelson'. (Courtesy of the Rijksmuseum)

Jan de Liefde, by Bartholomeus van der Helst. The slayer of Christopher Myngs. (Courtesy of the Rijksmuseum)

Cornelis Tromp, by Abraham Evertsz van Westerweld. The aggressive Dutch admiral in Roman costume. (Courtesy of the Rijksmuseum)

Arthur Herbert, Earl of Torrington, the circle of John Closterman. One of only two known portraits of the immoral, foul-mouthed admiral who led William of Orange's invasion fleet; he commanded the English fleet at the Battles of Bantry Bay and Beachy Head. Surprisingly, he got on well with Cloudesley Shovell. (Courtesy of a Private Collection)

John Leake, attributed to Godfrey Kneller. He served under Cloudesley Shovell at the Battle of Malaga when the two men fell out. (Courtesy of a Private Collection)

Edward Russell, Earl of Orford, by Godfrey Kneller. Short-tempered, but able admiral who commanded the Anglo/Dutch fleet at the Battle of Barfleur. There was great mutual respect between Russell and Cloudesley Shovell. (Courtesy of the National Maritime Museum)

George Rooke, by Michael Dahl. Cloudesley Shovell's aristocratic contemporary and rival. (Courtesy of the National Maritime Museum)

Matt Aylmer, by Jonathan Richardson. Handsome, aristocratic friend of Cloudesley Shovell. (Courtesy of the National Maritime Museum)

John Norris, by Godfrey Kneller. Protégé and trusted friend of Cloudesley Shovell. (Courtesy of the National Maritime Museum)

Charles II, by Peter Lely circa 1675. Charles took a close interest in his Navy and was too generous to hold a grudge against Cloudesley Shovell who had been granted a gold medal of a value not warranted by a second-lieutenant. (Courtesy of the National Portrait Gallery)

James II, by an unknown artist circa 1690. James fell out with Cloudesley Shovell over the former king's Catholicism. (Courtesy of the National Portrait Gallery)

William of Orange, in the manner of William Wissing. Squadrons under Cloudesley Shovell regularly escorted William to and from the Netherlands. (Courtesy of the Rijksmuseum)

Queen Mary, miniature by an anonymous artist circa 1695. Informed her husband, William: 'they tell me that Shovell is the best officer of his age.' (Courtesy of the Rijksmuseum)

Samuel Pepys, by John Hayls 1666. The influential Secretary to the Admiralty was an admirer of Myngs and Narbrough but took against Shovell. (Courtesy of the National Portrait Gallery)

Earl of Peterborough, by Godfrey Kneller. Charles Mordaunt, 3rd Earl of Peterborough had joint command of the fleet with Cloudesley Shovell at the Siege of Barcelona in 1705. (Courtesy of the National Portrait Gallery)

Queen Anne, early 18th century English School. (Courtesy of the Guildhall Museum, Rochester)

Stafford Fairborne, early 18th century English School. He served with Shovell as a subordinate admiral at the Siege of Barcelona. (Courtesy of the Guildhall Museum, Rochester)

Battle of Leghorn (Livorno) in 1653, by Reinier Nooms. Christopher Myngs was lieutenant or master of the *Elizabeth*, in Johan van Galen's defeat of Richard Badiley off Livorno. (Courtesy of the Rijksmuseum)

Episode from the Four Days' Battle [1666], attributed to Willem van de Velde the elder. Christopher Myngs in the *Victory* was mortally wounded on the fourth day of the battle. (Courtesy of the Rijksmuseum)

'Holmes's Bonfire'; the burning of Dutch Merchant Ships between Terschelling and Vlieland, 9 (19) August 1666, by Willem van de Velde the elder. John Narbrough commented: 'went up to the Dutch fleet and burned 140.' (Courtesy of the Royal Collection Trust)

The Attack on the French Ships at Martinique 26 June (6 July) 1667, by Willem van de Velde the younger. John Narbrough was prominent in this action against the French at Martinique. (Courtesy the Royal Collection Trust)

Narbrough's journal, Port St Julian. John Narbrough's depiction of the harbour of St Julian and the fauna of the surrounding area. (Courtesy of the British Library)

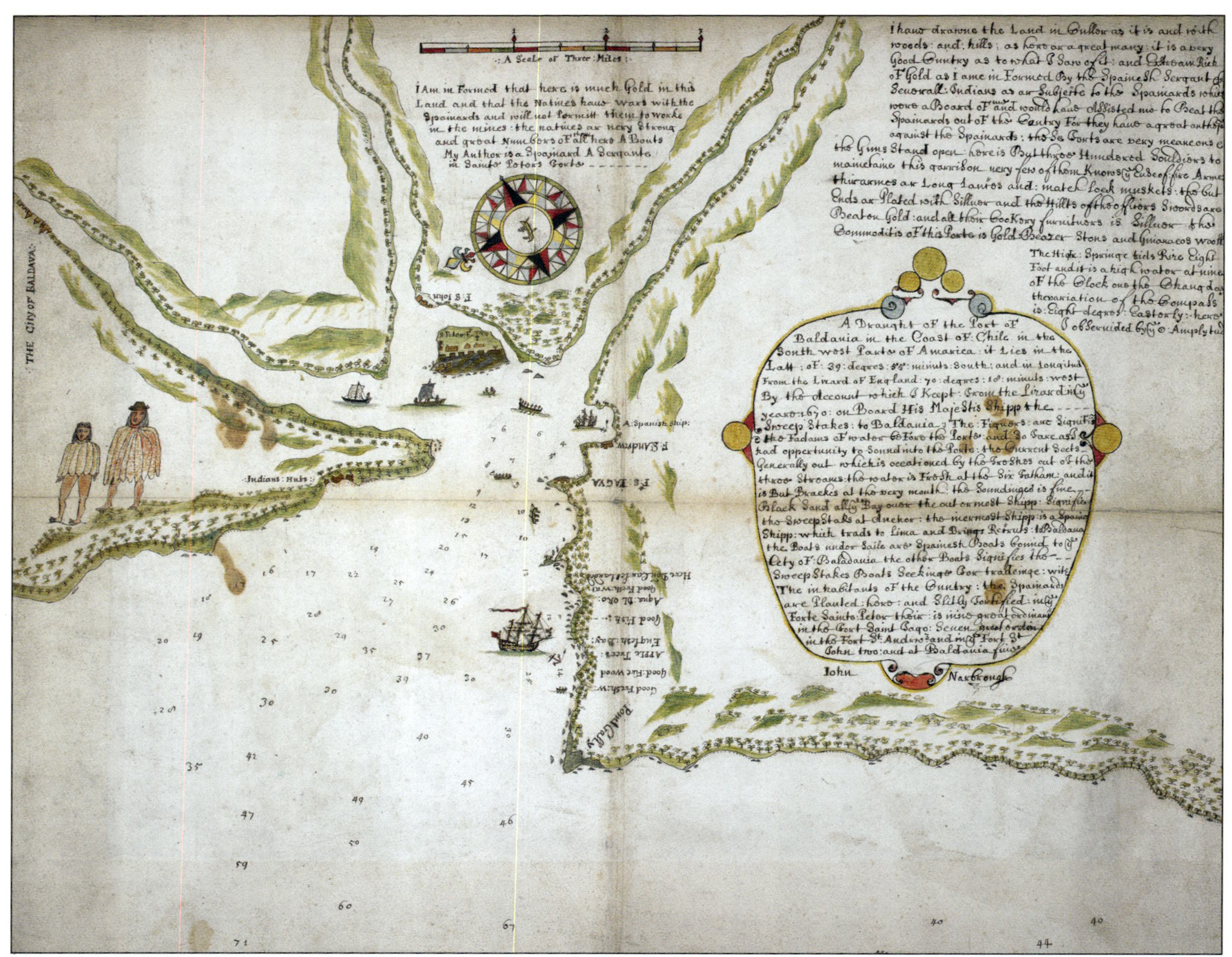

Narbrough's journal, Valdivia [Baldivia]. John Narbrough's illustration of the Bay of Valdivia [Corral Bay] where five of his crew were taken by the Spanish. (Courtesy of the British Library)

An action of the Barbary Wars by Peter Monamy. In the 1670s–80s, John Narbrough and Cloudesley Shovell were regularly in action against the ships of the Barbary regencies. (Courtesy of a Private Collection)

Battle of Sole Bay [1672], by Willem van de Velde the younger. This picture shows De Ruyter's *Zeven Provincien* opposing York's *Royal Prince*, in which John Narbrough was the first lieutenant and Cloudesley Shovell a midshipman. (Courtesy the Rijksmuseum)

Battle of Texel [1673], by Willem van de Velde the younger. In the action John Narbrough was Lord Ossory's senior captain in the *St Michael* and Cloudesley Shovell was part of the crew. (Courtesy of the Rijksmuseum)

The Attack on Shipping in Tripoli 14 (24) January 1676, by Willem van de Velde the elder. In this action, under the overall command of John Narbrough, Cloudesley Shovell came to national attention. (Courtesy of the Royal Collection Trust)

Duncannon Fort, by Thomas Phillips, circa 1690. In July 1691, Cloudesley Shovell took Duncannon Castle (Fort) in Southern Ireland. (Courtesy of the British Library)

Battle of Bantry Bay [1689], by Adriaen van Diest. Cloudesley Shovell was very forward in the action and knighted soon afterwards by William III. (Courtesy of the National Maritime Museum)

Bombardment of the Port of Dunkirk by an English squadron under Cloudesley Shovell; Anglo-Flemish school, late17th century.
(Courtesy of Sotheby's, London)

Battle of Barfleur [1692], by Ludolf Backhuizen. Cloudesley Shovell made the key move of the battle by breaking the French line.
(Courtesy of the National Maritime Museum)

Battle of La Hogue, 1692, by Adriaen van Diest. Injury precluded Cloudesley Shovell from having an even greater share of the glory. (Courtesy of the National Maritime Museum)

Battle of Malaga [1704], print circa 1710. Cloudesley Shovell commanded the van of the English fleet. (Courtesy of a Private Collection)

A View of Toulon in France, watercolour by Edward Dummer in 1685. The failure to take Toulon in August 1707 indirectly led to Cloudesley Shovell's death. (Courtesy of the British Library)

May Place, Crayford, the country home of Cloudesley Shovell, 18th century print.
(Courtesy of a Private Collection)

The *Royal Prince*, later *Royal William*, by Jan Karel Donatus van Beecq. The Duke of York's flagship at the Battle of Sole Bay: both John Narbrough and Cloudesley Shovell were part of the crew.
(Courtesy of the National Maritime Museum)

'Sam I would just like to mention – the Servant has died of the plague this very morning!' On the evening of his funeral the spirit of Christopher Myngs watches over Samuel Pepys and Mrs Bagwell. (Courtesy of John Osborne)

A very rare five guineas piece made from gold brought back from Vigo by Cloudesley Shovell in 1702. Valued in 2015 at around £325,000. (Courtesy of St James's Auctions Ltd)

Plantation in Surinam 1707, by Dirk Valkenburg. John Narbrough was seriously wounded in the thigh during the attack on Surinam. (Courtesy of the Rijksmuseum)

7

Barbary Corsairs and the Burning of the Tripoli Ships 1673–1682

The Barbary corsairs were based in the three North African regencies of Algiers, Tunis and Tripoli. All three had been founded in the 16th century and were part of the Ottoman Empire. In practice, they were ruled by local agas, beys, and deys who paid scant attention to the Ottoman Sultan and acted independently. Another corsair base, Sallee, was on the west coast of Morocco and thus outside the Strait of Gibraltar. Although by 1670, they were under the control of the Emperor of Morocco, a fair measure of piratical activity was allowed, in exchange for a share of the booty. The corsairs of Algiers acted principally around the western Mediterranean in the vicinity of Italy, Sicily, Corsica and Sardinia. They had the largest corsair fleet of around 20–40 ships, some with up to 60 guns. The corsairs of Tunis and Tripoli concentrated on the eastern Mediterranean and in the waters surrounding Sicily. Sallee pirates were to be found on the coasts of the Iberian Peninsula and in the Canary Isles. Occasionally, the Barbary corsairs went further afield and sailed to the north of Cape Finisterre. In 1631, the whole population of a village in county Cork was taken and, in 1654, they paid an unwelcome visit to St Michael's Mount in Cornwall. From Britain's point of view, it was the interference with their merchant shipping in the Mediterranean that became more than a minor irritation. Valuable cargoes were seized and the unfortunate crews sold as slaves or sent to the galleys. Over the years treaties with the various Barbary States had been signed and an elaborate system of passes for English merchant ships set up to protect them from the voracious pirates. It was into this unpredictable and violent world that John Narbrough and Cloudesley Shovell were about to step.[1]

Narbrough's fine performance at the Battle of Texel had been widely recognised and the following September, Prince Rupert gave him a commission to command the 62-gun *Henrietta*.[2] One of his first actions was to lobby for Shovell to be made a lieutenant under him. In a letter to Narbrough, Samuel Pepys, the influential Secretary to the Admiralty, 'promises to speak for Clowdisley Shovell to be lieutenant of the Henrietta.'[3] Pepys' support

---

1   Davies, *Pepys's Navy*, pp. 214–6.
2   PL: Pepysian MS 2556, Narbrough journal, *St Michael*, 12 September 1673.
3   Joseph Tanner, *A Descriptive Catalogue of the Naval Manuscripts in the Pepysian Library*, Vol. II (London: Navy Records Society 1904), p. 66.

must have done the trick, for on the same day, 23 September, Shovell became the Second-Lieutenant of the *Henrietta*.[4] Clearly, the 22-year-old Shovell owed his first commission as an officer to Narbrough, his North Norfolk neighbour and patron, but there was a certain irony in the crucial support of Pepys. Shortly, as will be recounted later in this chapter, we will see a permanent antipathy develop between Pepys and the young Shovell. Pepys had a very high opinion of Narbrough and looked upon him as one of the most able naval men of the day, but his opinion of Shovell was quite different. The *Henrietta*, with her new captain and second-lieutenant, spent the autumn of 1673 protecting shipping in the Channel before retiring to the River Thames. They would also spend the summer of 1674 in the Channel and its ports.

In the autumn of 1674, Narbrough still in the *Henrietta* with the rank of commodore, was sent out to the Mediterranean with a small squadron to deal with trouble that was brewing up in Algiers. Edward Spragge had concluded a treaty with the instigators in 1671 and the articles laid down in it had not been honoured. When a peace treaty was proclaimed, it was normal to have a general redemption of slaves and as this had not happened the Algerians had become impatient. They insisted that money for the redemption and ships must be provided at once. As soon as this dispute had been settled, Narbrough was to sail on to Tunis and Tripoli to ratify further peace treaties with those regencies.[5]

In late November, Narbrough's squadron put into Lisbon to collect money for the redemption of the slaves and arrived off Algiers early the following month. Algiers was a beautiful city with its chalk white houses, famous lighthouse and vineyards. Despite the fact that Christmas was nearly upon them, apples, oranges, lemons and vegetables of all types were plentiful. No doubt the fruit and vegetables kept the scurvy at bay following the voyage out. Aided by Samuel Martin, the resident consul at Algiers, Narbrough negotiated with the Dey, Ismail Pasha, the release of 189 English captives in exchange for over 50,000 pieces of eight.[6] Generously, the crews of Narbrough's small squadron clubbed together to pay for the release of captives taken on foreign ships. Cloudesley Shovell played his part in the negotiations and was rewarded with a welcome bounty of 100 pieces of eight.[7]

While Narbrough's squadron was en route to Algiers, Pepys had written to him to the effect that the merchants trading with the eastern Mediterranean, had complained of two of their ships being forcibly taken into Tripoli. The two ships, the *Hunter* and the *Martin*, were carrying cargos worth £30,000 or in today's money around £4,000,000. No wonder they were angry, as the Dey, Mustafa Pehlevan, argued that since their change of government there had been no communication with Charles II and he was uncertain whether the treaty was in force or not. This was disingenuous in the extreme, but many of the Barbary States depended on the capture of merchantmen for their livelihoods. Pepys instructed Narbrough to have the treaty ratified again and for the merchant ships to be returned with

---

4   TNA: ADM 33/98, pay book *Henrietta*, ticket no 680, 23 September 1673.

5   Tanner, *Naval Manuscripts*, Vol. IV, p. 68; Dyer, *Narbrough*, p. 143.

6   A piece of eight was worth one Spanish dollar or eight reales or royals. Spanish dollars were the world currency at the time.

7   Bodleian Library, Oxford (Bod Lib): Rawlinson MS, A 215, f. 117, copy of an account of charges for the release of English captives; Tanner, *Naval Manuscripts*, Vol. II, pp. 362, 366; Robert Playfair, *The Scourge of Christendom*, (London: Smith, Elder and Co 1884), p. 117.

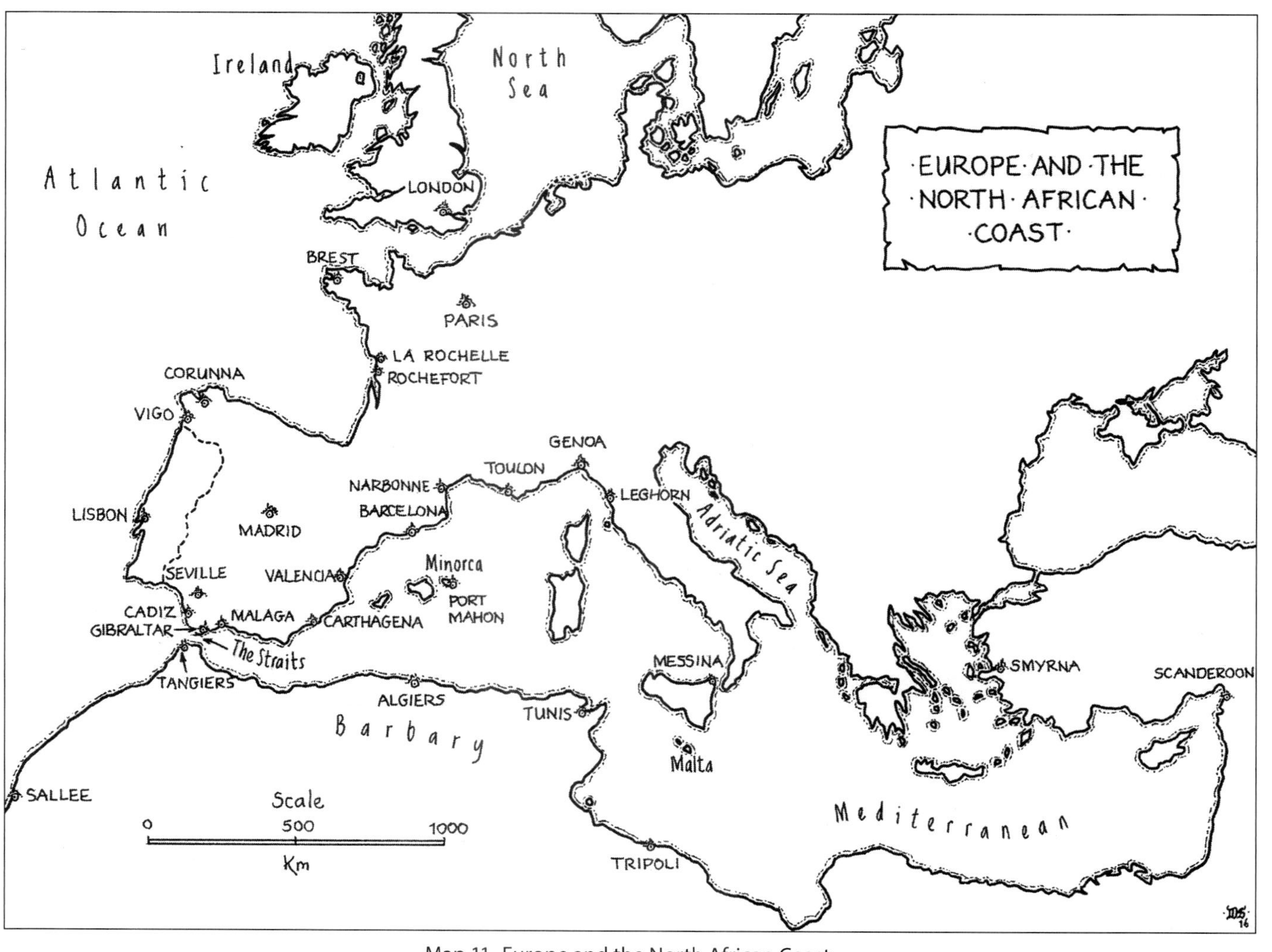

Map 11 Europe and the North African Coast.

their cargoes intact. Narbrough was rebuffed by the Dey and proceeded to blockade Tripoli for the best part of the next year. In addition he destroyed all the Dey's ships that he came into contact with.[8]

Narbrough required a base to operate from and chose Leghorn on the north-west coast of Italy. Grand Duke Cosmo III of Tuscany proved to be erratic in his relations with England and Narbrough, with the approval of Charles II, switched his squadron to Malta, a much closer spot to use.[9] In May 1675, the Dey of Tripoli died and the English authorities thought that this was a suitable moment in which to soften their demands. The return of the cargoes from the *Hunter* and the *Martin* were not deemed to be essential, but all the slaves were to be released and a few suitable heads were to roll. Unfortunately, the new Dey, Ibrahim Misrli-Oglu, had commanded the corsairs' ships that had captured the English merchantmen and, quite understandably, he was less than enthusiastic about the last condition! So the blockade continued with Charles II suggesting that the entry into Tripoli harbour be blocked by sinking a ship or two in the channel leading into it.[10]

The ironwork of Narbrough's flagship, the *Henrietta*, was becoming rusty due, it was thought, to her recent sheathing.[11] Samuel Pepys arranged for the *Harwich* and other vessels to come out to the Mediterranean to strengthen Narbrough's small squadron. During an autumnal fog, four of the largest corsair galleys escaped from Tripoli and they could not be caught. Harshly, Charles II ordered Narbrough to court-martial the captain he felt was responsible.[12] But the end result of the blockade was to allow English merchantmen to trade with the eastern Mediterranean in relative peace. It was not until December that Narbrough was able to exchange ships with Henry Killigrew who had brought the *Harwich* out from England in a rather dilatory fashion. There were suspicions that he had been conducting his own lucrative business on the way.[13] Killigrew, the son of a former chaplain to the Duke of York, was an interesting character who probably owed a number of prestigious commands to his affair with Charles II's former mistress, the Duchess of Cleveland.[14]

In January 1676, Narbrough struck the decisive blow of the war with Tripoli. Shovell, having transferred to the *Harwich* with his patron, was sent ashore to further negotiate with the Dey.[15] He delivered his instructions with great spirit, but was sent away with an inconclusive answer. Once more, Narbrough ordered his young second-lieutenant to return and confront the Dey. Perhaps because of his youth, the Dey was even more unpleasant if

---

8   Tanner, *Naval Manuscripts*, Vol. II, p. 403.

9   Narbrough used Malta as a base in 1675–6.

10   Tanner, *Naval Manuscripts*, Vol. III, pp. 37–8, 63 and Vol. IV, pp. 173, 181, 185; Dyer, *Narbrough*, pp. 143–7.

11   Sheathing was done to strengthen ships and to protect them against the worm, Teredo navalis, a species of saltwater clam. In 1671, lead sheathing had been experimented with in a number of ships including the *Henrietta*. The experiment was a failure as the lead eroded iron work by electrolytic action and particularly affected the rudder. In addition, the lead covering the hull could be washed so thin that the worm was able to get at the wood of the hull.

12   Tanner, *Naval Manuscripts*, Vol. III, p. 129; Dyer, *Narbrough*, pp. 150–1.

13   A 'good voyage'. Private trade.

14   Born Barbara Villiers, she was a promiscuous courtesan who gave the king no less than five illegitimate children. According to the diarist John Evelyn, she was the 'curse of the nation.'

15   It is difficult not to feel sorry for William Long, the first-lieutenant of the *Harwich*, who had been overlooked by Narbrough. Later, he asked for a share of the gratuity as he had volunteered for the boat action and had been told to stay behind. He received nothing. Patronage was everything in the 17th century navy.

not contemptuous of Shovell. Shovell bore the tirade with apparent equanimity although inwardly seething with anger. Whilst being transported ashore in a boat, he had made a careful note of the dispositions of the Dey's ships anchored close to the walls of Tripoli castle and on returning to the *Harwich,* Shovell told Narbrough that he thought that an attack on the Dey's ships was feasible. On the night of 14 January 1676, Cloudesley Shovell would come to national prominence by leading a boat action against the four ships in Tripoli harbour. Narbrough's account of the action was later published in *The London Gazette*:

> I hoped to have made an honourable and lasting peace, but the Dey and Government of Tripoli refusing to make restitution for the injuries done to his Majesty and his subjects, I, seeing four of the Tripoli ships of war of considerable force in the Port of Tripoli, preparing to go out on a cruise, I then having the fireships with me with fireworks, I fitted out a fire-boat accordingly out of them; commanding that all the boats of my Squadron being 12 in number should be mann'd, arm'd and fitted with fireworks: Also I ordered a considerable Officer to be commander in every boat and my Lieutenant Cloudesley Shovell to be commander in chief of them all, I, being resolved by God's permission that night to attack the Enemies ships in their Port, gave directions requisite for such a design.
>
> About 12 of the clock in the night, my boats resolvedly entered the Port, seized the guard-boat, boarded the ships, fired them and utterly destroyed them all; some Turks and Moors slain, the rest fled to save themselves. These four ships lay under the deep castle walls, which were all in the Port, excepting a Tunis merchant ship, which I ordered should not be meddled with, so escaped firing. This action was performed in less than an hours time without sustaining the least damage on our part, more than the expense of some ammunition, fire-works and fire-boat which effectually were bestowed as designed, to the great astonishment of the Turks, that endeavoured to impede our design by plying several great and innumerable small shot at our boats and men, which were within pistol shot of the Dey's own castle and palace. Such was the wonderful mercy of Almighty God towards us, that not one man of ours was killed, wounded or touched, nor a boat in any ways disabled, but all returned in safety, bringing the guard boat, two Moors and the Turkish colours of the two ships in triumph along with them, to my ship. Our men employed in the boats in this particular action were 157, they all behaving themselves as becometh Englishmen. And for a present reward of their good service I caused the next day 1956 Pieces of eight to be distributed amongst them.[16]

The names of the Tripoli ships that were burnt were: *White Crown'd Eagle* 50-guns; *Looking Glass* 34-guns; *Sancta Chiaro* 24-guns; French *Petach* 20-guns. Firstly the guard-ship was brought out with one Pedreroe and two Moors in her. Then the four corsair vessels, drawn up right under the Dey's castle walls, were torched.

---

16   *The London Gazette supplement*, A 1080, 21 July 1676; Dyer, *Narbrough*, pp. 151–3; NMM: RMT MS, MAT 40, quoting Sir John Narbrough, *A particular Narrative of the Burning in the Port of Tripoli Four men of War belonging to those Corsairs 14 Jan 1675/6 (1676)*.

Twelve boats with 157 men, led by the *Harwich*'s second-lieutenant, Cloudesley Shovell, took part in this highly successful naval boat action. He was supported by another Norfolk man, James Greeve, who acted as the second-in-command.[17] Rarely, in the annals of English naval history, can so many of the enemy's ships have been destroyed by fire at so slight a cost. Only ammunition and inflammable material had been expended and with no English casualties at all. The favourable outcome of this little enterprise owed a great deal to surprise, the hours of darkness and the resolution of Shovell and his men. Of the 1,956 pieces of eight distributed by Narbrough, from his own pocket, Shovell received 80 and Greeve 32. On returning to England, Narbrough had the greatest of difficulty in extracting this reward money from the English authorities.[18]

Rather surprisingly, the Dey at Tripoli did not give in to English demands but continued the conflict. Ten days after the boat-burning episode, Narbrough continued to persuade the Dey to come to terms with the cannon:

> The 26th of January I fired about One hundred shot into the City of Tripoli amongst the inhabitants; the first and third of February I took and destroyed five corn-boats on the coast to the eastward of Tripoli twenty leagues, and landed and burnt a stack of wood and timber which was for building their new ships, and some small masts and yards and some bags of bread brought off and two guns spiked up which could not be got off, beginning to blow and likely to be bad weather, so I was constrained to leave them and repair on board and leave the coast.[19]

Two months later, Narbrough chased a further four Tripoline ships into their harbour and managed to kill 600 of their men in the process. This was the final straw for the Dey who sent out asking for terms of peace. Narbrough was only too pleased to agree a quick settlement as the plague had broken out in his base at Malta.

Under the terms of peace, signed on 5 March 1676, all the English slaves plus foreign Christians, including some knights of Malta, were to be freed and goods worth 80,000 dollars were given to Charles II. Narbrough was all set to leave Tripoli when a revolution broke out there. The old Dey had died and Narbrough, fully understanding the instability of the local politics, insisted that the treaty be ratified by the new Dey, Ibrahim Djelebi Dey Annebli. Under the threat of a further bombardment this was eventually done.[20] Meanwhile, news of Narbrough's earlier boat burning exploits had reached London and, in early April, Samuel Pepys wrote to Narbrough:

17   Clearly this little action was the highlight of James Greeve's life. Close to the south transept of Cley-next-the-Sea church can be seen Greeve's table tomb and its inscription tells of his exploits at Tripoli in January 1676. He was made captain of the Algerian ship, the *Orange Tree*, and like Shovell was given a gold medal by Charles II.

18   Bod Lib: Rawlinson MS, A 214, f. 21b, copy of orders etc from the Commissioners of the Admiralty with respect to management of the fleet.

19   *The London Gazette supplement*, A 1080, 21 July 1676; Dyer, *Narbrough*, p. 154.

20   Bod Lib: Rawlinson MS, A 215, ff. 117, 123, list of Englishmen delivered from captivity at Tripoli by John Narbrough; BL: Sloane MS, 2755, f. 48; Dyer, *Narbrough*, pp. 154–7.

The King and Lords have commanded me to signify to you the extraordinary content they take in the effects of that action of yours, and what they observe to your upmost advantage in reference to your conduct therein, perfected with all the acceptable circumstances that can attend any attempt of that kind – namely, the being effectual, speedy, and not chargeable to his Majesty in his treasure nor to his subjects in their lives – his Majesty's esteem of which service to your particular benefit I doubt not but you will live to understand by better proofs than my bare telling it you, as also will Lieutenant Shovell (with whose management his Majesty and my Lords are most particularly satisfied) and the rest of the officers and boats companies when they shall return home.[21]

This was high praise indeed for both Narbrough and Shovell. It is interesting that Pepys placed his majesty's purse before his majesty's subjects' lives.

On the way home, Narbrough stopped off briefly at Algiers where the corsairs had brought in an English ship, the *Leopard* and helped themselves to the cargo worth a massive £150,000, in today's terms £23,000,000. The Algerians were prepared to release the crew and ship, but not the valuable cargo. Narbrough could not get them to budge and sailed away to Cadiz. Here he received instructions, from London, to return to Algiers and demand restitution. Bravely, Narbrough ignored his instructions and sailed for England in order to brief Charles II and his advisors directly. He reached Plymouth, in mid-September 1676, and his apparent disobedience of instructions was approved by his Monarch and their Lordships.[22]

Charles II showed his delight at the successful conclusion of the war with Tripoli with the award of medals. The commanders of the men-of-war were each to have one worth £60 and those of the lesser vessels cheaper medals. Unfortunately Shovell, the lowly second-lieutenant, had persuaded his sovereign to give him one worth fully £100 and this would lead to repercussions.[23] Early in the new year of 1677, the Admiralty journal commented on the subject:

It being observed to his Majesty that whereas his Majesty had been pleased to promise a medal in reward to each of the commanders of the boats employed in the late action under Sir John Narbrough against Tripoli, his Majesty's direction was become necessary to be expressly delivered touching the value of the said medals, for that Lieutenant Shovell had obtained a medal from his Majesty upon account of that service above the value of any hitherto given by his Majesty for any other service, and it being upon inquiry found that the same did arise by the said Lieutenant Shovell applying to his Majesty for the same by hands unacquainted with the practice of the Navy in like cases; His Majesty was pleased to declare his being surprised in the matter and to signify his being dissatisfied therewith, and

---

21 Tanner, *Naval Manuscripts*, Vol. III, p. 179.

22 Was Narbrough so keen to return to England for romantic reasons? See account below. Playfair, *Scourge of Christendom*, pp. 121–2; Tanner, *Naval Manuscripts*, Vol. IV, p. 352.

23 Tanner, *Naval Manuscripts*, Vol. IV, pp. 333, 373, 398, 437. The whereabouts of the medal is unknown. In the period 1686–9, Shovell kept a strong-box with his future father-in-law, John Hill, and in it was a gold medal and chain. Although it was only valued at £70: was this the medal?

to order that from henceforth no medals nor rewards be granted but at the public Board of Admiralty.[24]

Clearly Shovell's medal had caused quite a stir and was one of the reasons that his relationship with the influential Samuel Pepys deteriorated markedly. The medal saga continued into the New Year of 1677. Eventually, for their parts in the Tripoli action, Narbrough and James Greeve would receive medals worth £100 and £30 respectively. Charles II was far too generous a man to ask Shovell to return his medal and did not hold a grudge.

Narbrough and Shovell spent the early part of 1677 in England. John Narbrough took the opportunity to marry, for the first time, at the relatively late age of 36 years. He had been corresponding with his future wife, Elizabeth Calmady, aged 19 years, from the Mediterranean.[25] She was the daughter of Josias Calmady [1619–83], who owned the Langdon Court estate at Wembury in Devonshire and he was the Member of Parliament for Okehampton. Josias was the surviving son of Sir Shilston Calmady [1585–1645] who had been killed in the English Civil War. The family had several estates in Devonshire and they had been domiciled in the county since the 14th century. On 9 April 1677, the marriage took place in the picturesque St Werburgh's Church, overlooking Wembury beach with views over the Yealm Estuary.

Narbrough had little time to enjoy a honeymoon with his youthful bride as Samuel Pepys was soon enquiring: 'how soon the state of his new affairs would allow him to be looking after the carrying out of his old.' The Algerians were up to their old tricks in capturing further English merchant ships. In April 1677, Narbrough was given a commission to command, the 60-gun *Plymouth,* and he took Shovell with him as his first-lieutenant. There was a considerable delay in putting together a small squadron of nine ships to deal with the recalcitrant Algerians. In addition, Narbrough was ordered to renew any treaties with the Barbary States where there had been a change of government. In order to boost his status with the Algerians, Narbrough was given the rank of admiral. His strategy was to irritate and put pressure on them by placing his squadron around the mouth of the Strait of Gibraltar and to take any corsair vessels slipping home from the Atlantic.[26]

During 1677, Narbrough complained to Samuel Pepys concerning the capabilities of the lieutenants under his command. Narbrough's comments had fallen on fertile ground as Pepys was of a similar view. Pepys drafted a document compelling prospective lieutenants to serve a minimum of a year as a midshipman and then face an examination in front of a panel of senior captains. After due deliberation of the Navy Board and various former flag officers, the proposal was ratified at a meeting of the Admiralty Commission, in the presence of Charles II, on 7 December of the same year. The first examination took place in January 1678 and did much to further the cause of a truly professional navy.[27]

In September 1677, the captain of the *Sapphire*, Thomas Harman, was mortally wounded in action against the 22-gun corsair vessel, the *Orange Tree,* which was forced into port, at

<hr>

24   Tanner, *Naval Manuscripts*, Vol. IV, p. 398.
25   *DNB*, Narbrough [Laughton, Davies]. Elizabeth was baptised at Wembury on 25 March 1658.
26   Tanner, *Naval Manuscripts*, Vol. IV, pp. 450, 454.
27   Davies, *Pepys's Navy*, p. 92; Tanner, *Naval Manuscripts*, Vol. IV, pp. 493–4, 535–6, 543–5.

Sallee, with 100 casualties.[28] Harman's misfortune would give Shovell, aged 26 years, his first independent command as he received a commission from Narbrough, on 11 September 1677, to take command of the 32-gun *Sapphire*.[29] He would serve in her for the best part of the next two years and would gain valuable experience against formidable opponents. Having taken as many corsair ships as he could lay hands on, Narbrough sailed once more for Algiers, which he reached at the end of November. No agreement could be made with the Algerians and bad weather forced Narbrough to return to the mouth of the Straits with his small squadron. Over the next few months he valiantly attempted the impossible task of policing the Mediterranean from end to end. Matters were made even more difficult for Narbrough by impatient merchant navy captains sailing by themselves rather than waiting for escort vessels to protect a large group of them.[30] Narbrough was permitted to sell non-Christian slaves and he was also allowed to hang captured renegades.

As 1677 came to a close, Cloudesley Shovell wrote in his journal: 'God send us a happy and successful Yeare ensuing.'[31] Narbrough was to use Tangier as his initial summer base and he continued to harry the Algerians from there. In November 1678, yet again Narbrough appeared before Algiers and attempted a close blockade of the city. In this he was singularly unsuccessful with five corsair vessels slipping past him. Realising that his presence was serving no useful purpose, he sailed away to the excellent harbour at Port Mahon, in Minorca. Early in 1679, fears of war with France became acute and the Admiralty Board decided to recall most of Narbrough's squadron, leaving Vice-Admiral Arthur Herbert with a minimal number of ships, at Tangier, to make a nuisance of themselves around the mouth of the Straits. Narbrough was to return to England, thus putting an end to his extremely close association with his protégé Cloudesley Shovell.

Before returning to England, Narbrough wrote from Port Mahon to Henry Sheeres, the engineer building the mole at Tangier: 'His grace the Duke is in good health, continually coming in boats to and fro this harbour, in a short time will make a tarpauling sailor, fiting for a voyage of discovery, Cloudisly is one of his graces great favourites.'[32] The Duke was likely to have been Henry FitzRoy, 1st Duke of Grafton, the son of Charles II and his most notorious mistress, Barbara Villiers, later Duchess of Cleveland. The 15-year-old Grafton, had been sent to sea with Sir John Berry and was intermittently in the Mediterranean between 1675 and 1680. If there is doubt about the identity of the duke, there is none about 'Cloudisly.'

On 4 March 1679, Shovell, in the *Sapphire*, and his contemporary and great rival, the aristocratic George Rooke, in the *Nonsuch*, forced the ship of Treguee, son of the Dey of Algiers [Ismail Pasha], ashore where it was burnt by its own crew. Rooke described this action in a letter to Samuel Pepys:

---

28 Thomas Harman was no relation of Sir John Harman. Sir John's own son, James, was to be killed in 1678 fighting the Algerian ship, the *White Horse*.

29 TNA: ADM 51/857, Shovell journal, *Sapphire*. The 5th rate *Sapphire* had been built at Harwich in 1675. 364 tons, 106 by 27 feet.

30 In Narbrough's era, the term 'convoy' referred to the escort ships rather than the merchantmen that they were expected to protect.

31 TNA: ADM 51/857, Shovell journal, *Sapphire*.

32 BL: ADD MS 19872, f. 40, letter from John Narbrough to Henry Sheeres, 12 February 1679.

Nonsuch, in the bay of Cadiz April ye 26 79. Hond Sr This is the first opportunity has presented to advise you that on ye 4th March last past, cruising wh the Saphire off Cape-Faucon wee met wh an Algier man of war, wch at three a clocke we chast ashre about 3l to ye WtWd of Cape Fegalo.[33] The Turks sett her a fire and left her. I am informed by some ---- wch Captn Shovells boate took up, that she was the King of Algiers Shyppe built on a Portugues Carvell. She had the sunne in her sterne and was mounted wth 22 gunns and 10 Pettreroes, the same shyppe wch took the Quaker Kch. I have been since the 28th of the last month wth ye Vice Admirll by whose order I am now here excepting the l'res shall come by this port either for him or Tangier,[34] we looke daily for Sir John Narborough who I do imagine this Levant wch now blows may putt through. I have nought else at present but the Tender of my most humble service wch ends from, ----.

G. Rooke.[35]

Before returning to England Narbrough made one final attempt to bring the Algerians to heel. At the end of March 1679, he sailed to Algiers and a variety of officers endeavoured to get a treaty agreed upon. No doubt in disgust, Narbrough sailed away and it was later said that if only he had waited one more day, he would have had his treaty.[36] Shovell was not with Narbrough for the final negotiations as, in April, Vice-Admiral Herbert had moved him from the *Sapphire* into the *Phoenix*. Herbert had come out to be Narbrough's vice-admiral early in 1678. One of Narbough's final acts in the Mediterranean was to return Shovell to the *Sapphire*.

Finally, on 12 May 1679, Narbrough left Tangier for home. He felt that he had weakened the Algerians by reducing their ship numbers from 32 to 19 and that his vice-admiral, Arthur Herbert, with a reduced number of vessels, could still keep them in check.[37] Narbrough reached Plymouth Sound on 9 June, only to discover that his young wife, Elizabeth, had died on New Year's Day 1678, all of 18 months before. Eight days later, he wrote to Samuel Pepys: 'these are with the tender of my most humble service and most cordial respects, earnestly requesting your Honours pardon for my not paying my due respects at my arrival in England nor since, which I pray excuse on him who is heartily sorrowful and greatly afflicted (The Almighty God is great).'[38] It is surprising that the awful news had not reached Narbrough in the Mediterranean despite the primitive means of communication in the 17th century. After all he had romanced Elizabeth, by letter, from the Mediterranean, prior to their marriage. Perhaps the most likely explanation is that the news was deliberately kept from him by the Calmady family to spare his feelings, whilst on the King's service, so far from home. Elizabeth's father, Josias, was not a well man, being scorbutic and also

33   Cape Fegalo is part of Algeria.

34   Arthur Herbert was the Vice-Admiral.

35   Bod Lib: Rawlinson MS, A 181, f. 90, letter from George Rooke to Samuel Pepys, 26 April 1679; George Duckett, *Naval Commissioners* (published by the author 1889), pp. 112–3; Henry Teonge, *Diary of 1675–79* (London: Charles Knight 1825), p. 243.

36   Dyer, *Narbrough*, pp. 186–7.

37   BL: ADD MS 19872, f. 43, letter from John Narbrough to Henry Sheeres, 10 March 1679.

38   Dyer, *Narbrough*, pp. 192–3; Duckett, *Naval Commissioners*, p. 98.

suffering from the dropsy. To make matters even worse, Elizabeth had been pregnant when she died and if the child had lived it would have inherited the Langdon Court estate. It is clear that John Narbrough was deeply affected by his young wife's premature demise from what sounds like pulmonary tuberculosis. In 1681, he commissioned a drawing, on vellum, of her memorial in St Werburgh's Church, Wembury. Both the memorial and the drawing can be seen to this day.[39]

Lady Elizabeth Narbough's monument at Wembury is made of black and coloured marble surmounted by a kneeling figure of her:

> Here lyeth the body of Dame Elizab; Narbrough the truly loving and Truly beloved wife of Sir John Narbrough Knt One of his majesties flagge Officers at Sea. The said Dame Elizab; was daughter of Josias Calmady Esq and Elizab; his wife married with the said Sir John of the nineth day of April 1677. She was virtuous Pious Charitable Religious Sweet and loving Lady mightily afflicted with a cough and bigge with child departed this Mortall life the first day of January 167/8 To the great griefe of Sir John her husband and her relatives friends and all that knew her. Aged 20 years Elizabeth Lady Narbrough.[40]

The outspoken, volcanic tempered, Arthur Herbert was now the commander-in-chief in the Mediterranean and initially he used Tangier as his principal base. Whilst there, Herbert, very much the womaniser, kept a dissolute house on shore where he would drink with his captains such as Shovell, George Byng, George Rooke, Thomas Hopsonn, Matt Aylmer, Francis Wheeler and others.[41] According to Pepys, the captains were 'waiting his [Herbert's] rising and going to bed, combing his periwig, putting on his coat, as the King is served.' Also 'his mistresses visited and attended one after another as the King's are.' Wheeler was said to have been a particular creature of Herbert's. Pepys had also heard of a drunken surgeon being stripped during a night of debauchery on Herbert's orders. Rumours that Herbert took prostitutes to sea with him are probably not true, but he was certainly immoral. Tangier, at the time, was said to be a den of sexual perversions and 'popery'. Samuel Pepys, a leading detractor of his, commented: 'of all the worst men living, Herbert is the only man that I do not know to have any one virtue to compound all his vices.'[42] Others have seen Herbert's captains in a different light comparing them with Horatio Nelson's 'Band of Brothers.' Sir Julian Corbett described them as 'a school of Mediterranean officers.'[43]

The more puritanical Narbrough wisely insisted on his captains sleeping in their own ships. However, Herbert considered that the facilities at Tangier were poor: the lack of covered storehouses and fresh water cisterns; the threat of attack by the Moors. In 1680, Herbert made Gibraltar his main base as it had its own mole and was well placed to deal with

---

39 NMM: RMT MS, MAT 23, original drawing which John Narbrough carried on his person.

40 This may mean in her twentieth year. As she had been baptised on 25 March 1658, it was most likely that she was still 19 years old, unless she died on her birthday.

41 Herbert's exclusive group of favourites was resented by those outside it. In 1681, this led to a serious falling out between Herbert and his senior captain, Edward Russell, later Earl of Orford. Davies, *Pepys's Navy*, p. 90.

42 Edwin Chappell (ed), *The Tangier Papers of Samuel Pepys* (London: Navy Records Society 1936), p. 224.

43 Julian Corbett, *England in the Mediterranean 1603-1713*, Vol. II (London: Longman 1904), pp. 134–5.

the Algerian corsairs. He was one of the first to recognise the importance of Gibraltar and it would be two of his protégés, Rooke and Shovell, who would capture it from the Spanish in 1704. With his aristocratic background, Herbert came from very different origins than both the humble Narbrough and Shovell. In character he was foul-mouthed and highly sexed, and it was surprising that Shovell, who was neither a heavy drinker nor a womaniser, would get on so well with him.

Herbert kept Shovell in the *Sapphire* and, on 29 October 1679, she was heavily engaged with a 34-gun Algerian ship between Apes Hill and Cape Tres Forcas.[44] Herbert was obviously impressed by Shovell's leadership as, early the following month, he wrote to Samuel Pepys, the Secretary to the Admiralty:

> Captain Shovell has on many occasions and particularly in his last behaved himself with so much courage and conduct that I think it my duty warmly to recommend him to their [? Honours] as a man as well qualified as any man in England to serve the King in his station wherefore I humbly desire if their honours design any 5th rate to be employed in this war it may be the Saphire and Captain Shovell in her or rather a good sailing fourth rate for I am sure he will do service if it to be done; I should think that the James Galley or the Dragon very fit ships for this war which I am sure would be good service with Captain Shovell in her.[45]

In the 17th century navy patronage was everything and Shovell had moved seamlessly from Narbrough's to Herbert's. In 1681, Shovell would indeed have the command of the versatile *James Galley.*

During 1679–80, Tangier was under one of the periodic attacks by the Moors and Herbert used his ships to support the Deputy Governor, Sir Palmas Fairborne, there. At the beginning of November 1679, Herbert sent Shovell ashore to assist with the defence of the place by overseeing the digging and manning of trenches by English sailors. On 8 November, Shovell was wounded whilst repulsing the Moors. The nature of the wound is uncertain, but it cannot have been serious as he was only briefly out of action. Later that month on the 30th, Shovell was off the Islands of Majorca and Minorca when in stormy weather the *Sapphire* collided with the *Mary*:

> At four o'clock in ye morning, ye Rr Adml (Comg ye Mary) fired one gun, and showed some lights, wch at first I not distinguishing, but believing them to be his poop lights, thought it to be ye signall for allowing his course, but as I drew nearer, I perceived there were more lights ---- whereupon I ordered ye helm to be put a Port ---- at wch time ---- a horrible gust of wind and raine, unfortunately we came on board ye Mary.[46]

---

44   Cape Tres Forcas is a headland on the Mediterranean coast of Morocco.

45   Yale University Library (YUL): fb. 96, ff. 97–8, Herbert letter book, letter to the Secretary to the Admiralty, 2 November 1679.

46   Report written by Shovell for Herbert, in the *Plymouth*, at Port Mahon, on 5 December 1679. Private collection.

Herbert did not appear to hold 'a horrible gust of wind and raine' against Shovell and the accident was soon forgotten. Reputedly, Herbert's knowledge of sailing a ship was somewhat limited. He would say: 'haul up that whichum there', with a jest to disguise his not knowing the name for it.[47] Peace with the Moors eventually came in December 1680, allowing Herbert to go on the offensive against the Algerians. Earlier that year, Herbert briefly moved Shovell from the *Sapphire* into the 42-gun *Nonsuch* before, in the autumn of 1680, he was returned to his original ship. In April 1681, Shovell by then back in the *Sapphire*, took the 22-gun Algerian ship, the *Golden Rose of Algiers*. Herbert described the action briefly in his letter book:

> A letter from Captain Shovell bearing the date 12th of April I find he hath brought into Cadiz the Golden Rose of Algier a ship of 22 guns. I do not yet know how many men; it seems that he met her the day after I sent him out of Tangier road as you will find by his letter to me of which I send you his inclosed copy by which you will find that Capt Shovell's discretion in not charging when it was little wind and the Turk so considerable a distance from him was the occasion of drawing him nearer and consequently of Captain Shovell performing this service which he has done with great prudence and valour; He is a man that I never knew slip any occasion of advancing the king's service and his own reputation.[48]

High praise indeed from his commander-in-chief. In a letter to Sir Lionel Jenkins, the principal Secretary of State, in London, Herbert reinforced his high opinion of the Captain of the *Sapphire*: 'Captain Shovell in the chase [*Golden Rose of Algiers*] showed all the prudence and in the fight all the valour that becomes an experienced and brave Commander and indeed is a man to be admired for his behaviour on all occasions.'[49]

Soon after his successful action against the *Golden Rose of Algiers*, Herbert gave Shovell the command of the *James Galley*. In 1671, a full-blown galley, the *Margaret*, had been built in Italy for the Royal Navy to use in the Mediterranean. This had proved to be an expensive mistake and was difficult to man. However, Charles II instigated the production of two galley frigates, based on a French design, the *Charles* and the *James*, for use against the Barbary corsairs. The *James Galley* had only 30 guns as much of her lower deck was taken up with oarsmen. Although the galley frigates allowed the English navy to fight the corsairs with like-for-like ships they proved to be a disappointment with a maximum speed of only three knots. In addition, unsurprisingly, manning by oarsman was difficult to achieve.[50]

In September 1681, Shovell still in the *James Galley,* accompanied by his former ship, the *Sapphire,* with Anthony Hastings as captain, took the 32-gun Algerian ship, the *Half Moon*. Shovell has left an account of the action:

47   David West, *Admiral Russell and the Rise of British Naval Supremacy* (Forres, Scotland: Librario 2005), p. 248; Chappell (ed), *Tangier Papers*, p. 225.
48   YUL: fb. 96, f. 170, Herbert letter book.
49   YUL: fb. 96, f. 168, Herbert letter book, letter to Lionel Jenkins, Principal Secretary of State, 15 April 1681.
50   Davies, *Pepys's Navy*, pp. 54, 62.

A narrative of Captain Shovell's command of his Majesties frigate the James Galley touching the taking the Halfe Moone of Algier ----. September ye 9th about 10 in ye morning the Saphire and we cruising in company we saw a ship which we immediately chased ye wind being then at E n E or NE where it continued all day he hailed us in several languages we answered him we were French men; he told us they were ye halfe Moon of Algiers and had been from thence about 10 weeks we asked for Sally men and told him we suspected he was of Sally commanded his boat aboard which he refused to do in such like discourse we held him till we were alongside his larboard side which was the weather side. I was resolved to board him athwart ye hawse by Reason there went such a sea that I was confident by that means of bringing his bowsprit and foremast by the board but he suspecting my design put his helm a [port] and made his starboard side the weather side whereupon I fired all my guns into him the Saphire being a quarter of mile astern of us soon took this advantage and before the Turk could trim his sail run him aboard on the starboard side abaff the Foxshrouds. It was then half an hourer past 8 upon which as before I endeavoured to be thwart his hause and twice missed the third time I had him aboard so that his bowsprit was amongst ye main shrouds but which the fresh way we had we brought his ship a little about ye foxbraces being shott we could not back ye head sailes so that we were cleare of him again and fell astern occasioned by the loss of her bowsprit and foremast.[51] This was about 10 a clock. I now having the algeir to deal with all alone with all his masts standing steering away before the wind was resolved to be once more thwart his hause. Considering that my guns being but 6 pounders it was not likely I could do much good in shooting their masts by the board accordingly with all his sails full I steerd thwart his hause in which attempt we broke two of ye main shrowds also ye main chains and two mizzen shrouds and ye mizzen chains and shrouds ye [? gunnel] down to the deck but we broke his bowsprit, head and catswater, knee and cheeks of his head so that he had a smooth stern quite below the waters edge. we lay thus thwart his hause about half an hour and then being intangled with his rigging fell alongst his side – with our head to his stern where we lay about half an hour. When ye rigging broke we swung clear again. I then layed him abord on ye starboard bow where we lay to keep him from securing his masts which I expected to fall any moment for the knee of his head being gone ye collar of his main stay came back on ye deck so that both main and foremast were equally in danger and at a quarter after one his foremast came by the board. Soon after his main mast and mizzen mast. I then laid my sailes aback and called to them. They told me they yielded the ship whereupon we immediately fell to work to secure ye masts and mend ye boat that she might swim which was not done before day light at which time we went on board and took possession. She is ye halfe moon of algier carrying 32 guns and come out of Port with 246 men where of 39 xptians of which 20 English they had taken a small English vessel

---

51   Hawse [hause]: the part of a ship's bows through which the anchor cables pass.

bound to Bermoodus with 7 English men and a woman which they took on board and sank ye vessel.[52] The captains name is Jonas Raife a Turk his lieutenant an English renegade which I caused to be hanged at my yard arm. The damage we have received is 18 men killed and 32 wounded and both main and foremast spoiled – we took her 45 leagues SWN ½ N from Cape Spartel. There was killed aboard the Turk 93 Turkes and Moores and most of the living were wounded. They assure me that there is but two better ships in Algier which ye Canary and the White Horse.[53]

The taking of the *Half Moon* was a particularly bloody affair and as was customary the English renegade was summarily executed. The following month, December, Shovell in the *James Galley* took another ship, the *Flower Pot*. He had had a successful 1681 with the capture of three notable corsair vessels – the *Golden Rose*, the *Half Moon* and lastly the *Flower Pot*. Shovell's name may have come to national prominence with his actions at Tripoli in 1676, but his name remained in the English public's mind with accounts of his further deeds in the western Mediterranean and around the Strait of Gibraltar.

The war with Algiers had dragged into 1681 and, following instructions from home, Herbert found himself yet again seeking a peace treaty with these unpredictable people. He used Shovell as his principal envoy in the negotiations and, in April 1682, the Algerians finally agreed to a treaty. This proved to be a more stable one and lasted until 1816.

---

52 xptians means Christians.
53 HMC: Finch MS, Vol. II, pp. 120–1; Historical Manuscripts Commission (HMC): Dartmouth MS, Vol. I, p. 68.

8

Cloudesley Shovell's Iberian Challenges and Transport of the Queen of Portugal to Lisbon 1683–1688

In late June 1683, Arthur Herbert returned to England leaving Cloudesley Shovell with a small squadron initially based on Lisbon and then at Gibraltar. Herbert had concluded a peace, at Algiers, leaving only Sallee as a potential troublemaker. Unfortunately, the same month as Herbert's departure, Shovell found himself in a dilemma. On 23 June, at Cadiz, he had escorted a group of merchantmen into port. The Spanish admiral, Conde de Aguilar [Acquila] demanded that Shovell's ship, the *James Galley*, fire its guns in salute to him or technically to the Royal Standard. Bravely, Shovell declined on the grounds that Charles II's orders would not allow him to do so. The Spaniards with their overwhelmingly superior number of ships replied that if he failed to salute he would be sunk. Not only would Shovell lose his life and ship, but the merchantmen's cargoes would be stolen or destroyed. Whatever criticisms may be laid at Shovell's door lack of courage was not one of them. What should he do? In the end he made the only sensible decision open to him of firing his guns in salute.

Shovell tried to get Sir Martin Westcombe, the influential English consul and agent, at Cadiz, to intercede with the Spanish on his behalf:

Papacin with three other ships of 70 guns apiece came this morning by day-light to anchor round me. Their chief sent me a message to salute their flag, or that they would compel me to it; and upon my denial Papachin fired a great gun at me shot and all, with near 100 small shott; and upon sending my boat aboard him to know his reason, he could give me no other than he complyd with his General's commands. I do not think myself able to fight ye Spanish Armada and therefore must be obliged to comply with their demands. I desire that you capitulate with their General yet he would give me Gun for Gun or give leave to some of his other ships to answer me Gun for Gun or I firing 5 guns he answering me with ye same now I return 3 again. If none of these propositions take and you think fit capitulate with him yet he give 5 guns for 7. They have fired again into an English ship near me which was hit under water and made her very leaky. Not else to trouble your honour.[1]

Shovell's final line in the letter, 'not else to trouble your honour', was a masterly understatement, considering his dire circumstances, with the Spanish Armada itching to send him to the bottom of the sea.

Westcombe did go and see Conde de Aguilar who insisted that the salute be made by 8:00 a.m. the next morning. The consul suggested that Shovell should quietly sail out of Cadiz, at night, in pretence that he was following his own admiral's orders. Additionally, Shovell was not to divulge to the Spanish authorities the secret information that Westcombe had been imparting. Privately, if cynically, the consul protested that 'if hee [Shovell] and all had bin lost by Maintaineinge our Kings honor, he had don his Deutye and left a famous Name behynde him.' In fact the *James Galley* was hemmed in, and there were the merchantmen to consider as well.[2]

Wisely, Shovell saluted the Spanish admiral's ship with the *James Galley* firing nine guns, but was only answered with an insulting three. Later, it transpired that the admiral was piqued that the *James Galley* was the only ship in port not to salute him. Shovell was allowed to leave Cadiz, knowing full well that news of his disgrace would reach England soon enough.

Shovell was not the only English captain to have saluting difficulties with the Spanish fleet. The following month, his friend, Matthew Aylmer in the *Tiger Prize* met the Spanish fleet in open seas near the Strait of Gibraltar.[3] Forewarned by Shovell, he made 'a run for it', but as his ship was foul and some of the Spanish ships were clean, he was soon caught.[4] Aylmer's Lieutenant, one E. Stagings put up a spirited defence in front of the Spanish admiral: 'there was no need to salute unless assured that it be returned gun for gun. If my captain salute you it might be his ruin. Do not take advantage of a young gentleman's fortune.' The admiral replied: 'if it were not for the respect for his Majesty of Great Britain he would have sent for the Commander and hanged him for doing what he did. Salute or be sunk.' Aylmer, like Shovell had no choice but to comply. He fired 13 guns and in reply received an insulting three, two more than the admiral thought necessary! Plaintively, Aylmer asked his superiors what he should have done. No answer was forthcoming.[5]

Later, on oath at an enquiry, before Judge Advocate Will Morgan, Shovell stated:

> Each of themselves [Spanish ships] that we could not cast our ship without being aboard of one of them and ye Guns in ye Towne made ready to fire at us. I finding his majesty's ships and subjects in such unavoidable danger of being destroyed

---

1   Bod Lib: Rawlinson MS, A 190, ff. 248, 250, 257, correspondence between Cloudesley Shovell and Martin Westcombe plus the latter's comments on the saluting, July–August 1683.
2   PL: Pepysian MS 2877, proclamation by the king concerning colours to be worn on ships; Bod Lib: Rawlinson A 190, ff. 248, 250, 257; All Souls College, Oxford (ASC): MS 240, f. 466, three letters from Cloudesley Shovell, 1683; J. David Davies, *Gentlemen and Tarpaulins* (Oxford: Clarendon Press 1991), p. 64.
3   One of Aylmer's sons, Edward, would later drown with Shovell, in the *Association*, as the Fifth Lieutenant.
4   Some of the Spanish ships had recently been careened and were thus faster through the water than Aylmer's *Tiger Prize*.
5   PL: Pepysian MS 2877, f. 213, Aylmer and saluting.

without saluting, I thought 'twas better to redeem ship and lives with a salute that [than] to ruine ye whole.[6]

Shovell was supported by his officers in a statement to the Judge Advocate, their number included Christopher Myngs, the son of his first patron. Clearly, Shovell was reciprocating what the father had done for his own career.[7]

The timing of Shovell's and Aylmer's saluting incidents could not have been worse as that summer the expedition under George Legge, 1st Baron Dartmouth, set off for Tangier with instructions from Charles II to extricate him from his expensive colony of Tangier. This had been part of his wife, Catherine of Braganza's dowry in 1662, but it had become an encumbrance on his finances. Travelling with Dartmouth was the still influential Samuel Pepys.[8] The party would remain in Tangier from 17 September until 1 December 1683. According to Pepys, Dartmouth intended to try Shovell and Aylmer for their behaviour. Pepys described the two young men as poltroons and compared their actions unfavourably with a French commander who had refused to salute, in similar circumstances, and had gone to the bottom with all hands. Despite his own similar background, Pepys brought up Shovell's relatively humble origins:

> And it is plain here led him to it in another nation's port, and may be a good argument of the use of having gentlemen employed who can better judge of what is fitting in that kind, he being in everything else spoken of as a man of valour and knowledge in his trade and a good man.[9]

Pepys' argument did not stand up to scrutiny as Aylmer was an Irish aristocrat, and he had behaved in an identical manner to Shovell over the saluting. Possibly, Pepys had not recovered from Shovell persuading, an overgenerous, Charles II to award him a gold medal, worth £100, after the ship-burning exploits, at Tripoli, in 1676.

The recall of Arthur Herbert from the Mediterranean, at the end of June 1683, was a godsend to Shovell and Aylmer in avoiding punishment for the saluting fiasco. Shovell's agonising suspense ended on receiving a letter from John Brisbane, the Secretary to the Admiralty, dated 27 August:

> What I have to say in answer to yours of the 13th July is, that upon Admiral Herbert's arrival in England he did acquaint the Lords of the Admiralty with what happened between you and the Spanish ships at Cadiz, and they laid it before his Majesty, who I doubt not will come to some resolutions thereon in few days. In the meantime all I can advise you is his Majesty thinks there is wrong done him, and he is not dissatisfied with you.[10]

---

6   PL: Pepysian MS 2877, f. 205, Shovell's statement on oath.
7   PL: Pepysian MS 2877, f. 205, Shovell's officers' statements on oath.
8   Samuel Pepys had resigned as Secretary to the Admiralty in 1679. He would be re-instated in 1684.
9   Chappell (ed), *Tangier Papers*, p. 167. Pepys was the son of a London tailor.
10   HMC: Dartmouth MS, Vol. I, p. 89; J. David Davies, 'James II, William of Orange and the Admirals', in Eveline Cruikshanks (ed), *By Force or Default? The Revolution of 1688–1689* (Edinburgh: John Donald 1989), p. 83. John

By the time Shovell received this letter Dartmouth and Pepys were breathing heavily down his neck at Tangier. Charles II was concerned about lack of respect for England, but did not blame poor Shovell.

In England the Lords of the Admiralty, held an enquiry into the affair with the Spanish Ambassador giving his nation's view. The result was that Charles II's ships, in the seas, south of Cape Finisterre, were not to salute Spanish ships and that in the ports of Spain, under some circumstances, salutes might be given provided that there was an equal return. Amongst the signatories to this document was Arthur Herbert, who had protected his young protégés from approbation and possibly worse.[11]

Nowadays, it seems extraordinary that so much time and energy could be expended on saluting. Already we have seen Prince Rupert fire at an English ship and throw its captain into irons for failing to salute him. In 1676, Captain Joseph Harris had been sentenced to death for striking his colours to a Spanish warship and was reprieved only when the muskets were at his head.[12] Undoubtedly, memories of incidents such as these were at the forefront of Shovell's and Aylmer's minds whilst the enquiry was underway.

As a result of the peace treaty with Algiers, in 1682, Arthur Herbert had been recalled to England as it was felt that a lesser naval presence was required in the Mediterranean and around the Straits. In addition, the outspoken Herbert might be obstructive to the outward-bound Dartmouth expedition, whose aim was discretely to abandon the costly port at Tangier. Poor Shovell, the new commodore, with a few frigates under his command was unlikely to be so difficult. Shovell's instructions, from the departing Herbert, was to endeavour to destroy the ships of the still active Sallee.[13] However, the arrival of Dartmouth effectively put Shovell under his command.

Dartmouth's remit was to evacuate Tangier because of its expense and to find plausible reasons for doing so. Despite showing his goodwill towards them, Dartmouth soon fell foul of Shovell and the other naval officers over the mole at Tangier. The contract for the mole or breakwater had been signed 20 years before, but its construction was constantly being interrupted by inclement weather. In the late 1670's John Narbrough's frigates had been careened there. However, Arthur Herbert had taken against Tangier and in 1680, had moved his base to Gibraltar. By 1683, the mole was an enormous structure consisting of three million cubic feet of concrete and 500 yards in length. It would prove difficult to dismantle.

The naval officers on station were expected to declare that Tangier was unsuitable as a base against the Barbary regencies and to dam the mole into the bargain. It was true that it was suitable for use against Algiers and Sallee, but too distant from Tunis and Tripoli to be practicable. In any event, a peace treaty had been signed with Algiers the year before. Two naval officers, John Berry and William Booth, who were a part of Dartmouth's mission were instructed to haul Shovell and his frigate captains into line. Immediately, they had trouble with Shovell, Aylmer and Francis Wheeler who resented Herbert's recall and believed Tangier to be a useful base for the higher rates and small merchantmen. Samuel Pepys who witnessed these events recorded:

Brisbane was the Secretary to the Admiralty 1680–84, the year he died. He was replaced by Samuel Pepys.

11   PL: Pepysian MS 2877, ff. 199–234, Herbert's opinion, 1 December 1683.
12   Davies, *Gentlemen and Tarpaulins*, p. 64.
13   KCA: Marsham MS U1515.011, Herbert's instructions on departure, 29 June 1683.

> It is pretty to see that no kindness obliges these rogues. I have shown my Lord [Dartmouth], to his surprise, instances in Shovel, Wheeler, and Matt Elmer (to all of whom, especially the last, as being Herbert's creatures, he hath thought fit to be very kind since his being here,) their making a difficulty to sign the paper prepared by my Lord's orders for the sea captains to sign, about the condition of the harbour of Tangier, and the impractableness of making it a good one. Though they have been prevailed with by Booth to sign this, yet they did declare to Booth their satisfaction in the harbour when they signed it, and will be ready to do the like when they come to England. This is your men of honour and gentlemen! At least the two latter.[14]

Shovell, whose relatively humble origins precluded him from being described by Pepys as a gentleman, was initially not prepared to perjure himself to help Dartmouth and Berry. The most obstinate of the captains was reputed to be Shovell and possibly the atmosphere was made more toxic by the presence of Berry, who had been calling for Shovell's court-martial over the saluting affair. One man who was compliant was George Rooke, Shovell's great contemporary and rival. However, Shovell and his fellow captains were no match for the wily skills of Samuel Pepys who framed a series of cunning questions for them. The captains were forced to admit that careening under the mole was difficult with the swell, and they had to admit that Herbert had taken the hulk used for repairing ships across to Gibraltar as being an easier place to work. It was also admitted that the proximity of the Atlantic Ocean with its great waves would damage the mole, and that the water supply at Tangier was meagre and foul.[15]

Perhaps Herbert, if he had still been on station, would not have been quite so obstructive as he had no liking for Tangier as a base. Finally, in mid-October, Dartmouth received the signed report damming the mole. Among the signatories were Berry, the heavily drinking John Ashby, the womanising Henry Killigrew, the treacherous William Booth,[16] the Irish aristocratic Aylmer brothers, George and Matt, Shovell, the compliant Rooke, Wheeler, and Anthony Hastings,[17] the vicious 'valet de chambre' of Herbert. Pepys had done his work skilfully. The mole was doomed and Henry Sheeres, the military engineer, who had built it, was forced to blow it up.[18] No doubt Samuel Pepys got a certain amount of schadenfreude, from Sheeres having to destroy his own handiwork as earlier the two had been friends, until the latter made advances to Pepys' wife, Elisabeth.

By early December 1683, Dartmouth's work was done, with his having accomplished an orderly withdrawal from Tangier. Commodore Shovell with his small squadron had sailed with Dartmouth and intending to stay on station to deal with the pirates of Sallee. In late

---

14 Chappell (ed), *Tangier Papers*, p. 59.
15 HMC: Dartmouth MS, Vol. III, pp. 40–3.
16 Later Booth would give his allegiance to William III, was knighted and became a commissioner of the navy. All the time his sympathies were with James II, whose agent he became.
17 In 1680, the then Lieutenant Anthony Hastings was acquitted of murdering a seaman with the court accepting his plea of self-defence. By chance Arthur Herbert was the president of the court! Quoted by Davies, *Pepys's Navy*, p. 160.
18 Corbett, *Mediterranean*, Vol. II, pp. 132–7.

February 1684, he recorded in his journal of the *James Galley*: 'we saluted Lord Dartmouth and so took our leave of him and this evening anchored in Cadiz by whom we found ye Bonadventure and Tyger Prize.'[19] Once again, Shovell had his independent command back in his own hands.

From February 1684 until his return to England in 1686, Shovell and his small squadron of frigates were principally based on Lisbon.[20] From this port they endeavoured to patrol the Straits and harry the ships of Sallee. In August 1684, Shovell was off Sallee and there was an exchange of letters with the Emperor of Morocco.[21] The Emperor acknowledged that Shovell had taken several of their ships with mainly Mohammedan crew members and could do what he liked with them including throwing them in the sea! Insolently, he continued that he was pleased that the English had left Tangier, threatened to send ships to England and considered Shovell's behaviour a poor way to make peace. Shovell replied: 'your Majesty tells that we may threw them overboard if we please; All this we very well know; but we are Christians and they bear the form of men which is reason enough for us not to do it.' He also pointed out to the Emperor that England had left Tangier of its own volition; played down the possibility of Sallee building ships of sufficient size to sail to England; was prepared to exchange his slaves for English captives; would take peace proposals to Charles II.[22]

Shovell, a devout Anglican, showed a compassionate side to his character, although it was more than likely that the Mohammedans would have ended up being sold in a slave market. Compassion was sadly lacking in the 17th century Barbary regencies. A few years later, following a bombing assault on Algiers, the French Consul was fired away at the mouth of a cannon. In retaliation the French shot four captured Turks and sent them on shore on a raft as a warning. The Algerians in turn cut off the nose and ears of the Father Vicaire and then fired him from a gun. In their turn, the French strangled four Turkish captains and also sent them on shore on a raft. It is not surprising that the North African coast in this era was called Barbary.[23]

In February 1685, Shovell was back off Sallee where he took one of their richest merchant ships and drove another under the walls of the fort. The following month he took his small squadron of six to seven ships through the Straits and into the Mediterranean. Here he visited Leghorn, Messina and his old haunt of Malta. On 23 April, Saint George's Day 1685, Shovell wrote in his journal: 'Today ye King's Coronation Day we fired all our guns twice also all our small arms.'[24] Of course, the new king was the former Duke of York, now crowned James II. Shovell had served in James' ship, *Royal Prince*, at the Battle of Sole Bay in 1672 and his early career had been promoted by him. At this stage Shovell undoubtedly felt nothing but warmth for his new Sovereign. As we shall soon see, James' behaviour and

19   TNA: ADM 51/489, Shovell journal, *James Galley*, February 1684.

20   KCA: Marsham MS UI515.011, Shovell's journal and also his storebook for the *James Galley* indicates that Lisbon was his main base from March 1684–August 1686.

21   Ismael Ibn Sharif [ruled 1672–1727]. Known as the 'bloodthirsty'. On one occasion he had the walls of his city decorated with 10,000 heads of his enemies. It is easy to understand that he had no conscience about his captured sailors being drowned.

22   Simon Ockley, *An Account of South West Barbary* (London: J. Bowyer and M. Clements 1713), pp. 142–8.

23   Playfair, *Scourge of Christendom*, p. 156.

24   TNA: ADM 51/489, Shovell journal, *James Galley*, 23 April 1685.

Catholicism would lead to mutual antipathy and a permanent rift developing between the two men.

In August 1685, Shovell visited the Canary Islands and left gold, silver, silk and seven Moors in the hands of a merchant in Tenerife. The Moors were to be sold for him and the money forwarded to Cadiz or directly to John Narbrough back in London. Narbrough appeared to have been playing the part of a personal banker for his former protégé. Debts Narbrough held for Shovell included Lord Charles Mordaunt for 50 guineas in 1680, George Rooke for £200 in 1681, and John Ashby for £390. Even the young Christopher Myngs who was serving in the *James Galley* with Shovell was lent money throughout the 1680s. Not only the officers borrowed money as several men serving in the *Sapphire* and *James Galley* received loans using their tickets as collateral. In all the debts amounted to a massive £2,000.[25]

In the late autumn of 1686, Shovell's independent command, based on Lisbon and in the Atlantic Ocean off Sallee, came to an end as he sailed the *James Galley* back to England, arriving at Deptford in early December. Two days later the crew were paid off. Captain Henry Priestman succeeded Shovell in command of the Straits squadron.

Shovell was to spend the greater part of 1687 in the 70-gun *Anne*. During the second half of the year, he sailed for Lisbon and then on to the Mediterranean. Henry FitzRoy, 1st Duke of Grafton, the Vice-Admiral of England, was to escort Maria Sophia, one of the 17 children of Philip William of Neuberg, Elector Palatine, by his second wife, out to Lisbon for her marriage to Pedro II of Portugal. The royal party sailed in the *Anne* with Shovell and Grafton. It will be recalled that Shovell and the young Grafton, earlier in the Mediterranean, had got on well together, in the time of John Narbrough's command. Additionally, Shovell and Grafton were to renew the peace treaties with Algiers, Tunis and Tripoli. Samuel Pepys sent Shovell books with the details of the current treaties for him to study.

By the end of May, the *Anne* had taken on supplies and had sailed for the Downs. During June, Shovell was in correspondence with Samuel Pepys and the Navy Office over Sir Robert Gordon's new pump which was being tested in the *Anne*. Water on the decks of ships drained into scuppers and then to the exterior. Water collecting in the hold was extracted by a number of chain pumps. Each consisted of a loop with saucers passing in a tube from the hold to the gundeck where it was turned manually by a wheel. Fluid collected in this manner was discharged through a horizontal tube to the side of the hull. Shovell was singularly unimpressed by Gordon's pump and reported that it had broken. Gordon, in person, asked to be allowed to repair his pump and also that it be kept secret from the French. The pump was supposed to require fewer men to operate it than the standard one. A further experimental pump designed by Sir Samuel Morland was found to be more effective than Gordon's.[26] The excitement over Gordon's defective pump paled into insignificance compared with the furore over the return of the *James* and *Mary* from the West Indies with its cargo of treasure that would indirectly lead to the death of John Narbrough the following year. This will be covered in detail in a later chapter.

---

25   KCA: Marsham MS U1515.011, Shovell account book. In 2017 this was equivalent to £306,700.

26   Davies, *Pepys's Navy*, p. 74; Simon Harris, *Sir Cloudesley Shovell Stuart Admiral* (Staplehurst: Spellmount 2001), p. 96.

In early July, Roger Strickland joined Shovell in the *Anne*, with four frigates at the Gunfleet, and they sailed together for the Maes to collect Maria Sophia, soon to be the new Queen of Portugal. At the beginning of August, Shovell informed Pepys of their safe arrival in the Tagus after a journey of nine days: 'yesterday at about three in the afternoon we got up the river, and anchored before the King's palace and at about six this evening the King [Pedro II] came on board and after staying about half an hour he returned with his Queen to his palace, we are now discharging ourselves of the Queen's retinue of baggage.'[27] Grafton had an audience with King Pedro II, although Shovell did not appear to have been invited to the palace. The Duke 'much desired to stay till the Kings marriage is consummated. To be done next week with great solemnity.'[28]

From Lisbon, the *Anne* set sail for Gibraltar which was reached in early September. It was then on to Algiers where the local inhabitants were not sticking to the current peace treaty. Grafton used Shovell to deliver the English demands to the local government. A particular irritation was that the Sallee corsairs were allowed to sell their prizes at Algiers which was contrary to the articles of peace. A number of English captives from the Sallee boats, were freed. From Algiers they left for Tunis, which was reached in late October, and here Grafton and Shovell were pleasantly surprised to find that the peace treaty was being adhered to. The next port of call was Tripoli where they found all manner of complaint against the government. Shovell recorded in a letter to Pepys:

I find the Government very fickle for they generally have two to three King's every year, they all pretend great friendship with the English and say they resolve to keep the peace with us, they are mightily fallen off from their pirating for from ten ships they had when we made peace with them, they have but four, one of twenty four guns and another of upwards of forty.[29]

From Tripoli the English squadron sailed to Malta, Messina in Sicily and finally to Leghorn. In mid-January 1688, the *Anne* departed for home via Gibraltar. Early in March, it was off Falmouth and on the 19th, Shovell reported to Pepys that they had reached the Downs. It had been a most satisfactory voyage. Maria Sophia had been safely carried to Lisbon and the Barbary regencies had been reminded of their treaty obligations. 1688 was to be a momentous year for the English crown and Shovell would have his part to play in the Glorious Revolution.

27   KCA: Marsham MS U1515.012, Shovell to Samuel Pepys, 2 August 1687.
28   KCA: Marsham MS U1515.012, Shovell to Samuel Pepys, 10 August 1687.
29   KCA: Marsham MS U1515.012, Shovell to Samuel Pepys, 29 October 1687.

9

Sir John Narbrough: Commissioner of the Navy, Sunken Treasure and his Demise 1679–1688

On 29 April 1680, John Narbrough received a commission to join the Navy Board, a position he would hold until his death.[1] On the restoration of the monarchy in 1660, Charles II, had reorganised the administration of the Navy. The four principal officers of the Navy Board, Treasurer, Controller, Surveyor and Clerk of the Acts were restored. In addition a number of extra-commissioners were appointed. The Board was responsible for building, repairing and the setting out of ships. Also it paid, clothed and provided food for the crews. Thus Narbrough had found a niche in naval administration and would not go to sea again until his final voyage in 1687–8. Above the Navy Board was the Lord High Admiral, James, Duke of York, who had lost his position, in June 1673, when the Test Act was passed precluding Catholics from holding public office. Charles II hoped to run the navy himself with an Admiralty Commission as 'window dressing.' In the initial years of Narbrough's time at the Navy Board, the Admiralty Commission of 1679–84 was damned for its incompetence. When the Duke of York acceded to the throne, in 1685, as James II, he and the faithful Pepys effectively suspended the Navy Board. In its place was a special commission of five members 'without portfolio', who were charged with spending £400,000 a year for three years on the repair of the fleet.[2] Narbrough kept his place as one of these new commissioners. The Navy Board had occupied a large house near the junction of Crutched Friars and Seething Lane. This building was burnt down in 1673 and the Board was forced into temporary quarters until 1684, when the Christopher Wren designed building was opened on the same site.[3]

On 20 June 1681, at Wanstead, Essex, the widower John Narbrough was married for a second time to the 21-year-old Elizabeth Hill. She was the daughter of a wealthy businessman and probably a former merchant navy captain, John Hill, and his wife Elizabeth, née Kingsman. Their daughter, Elizabeth had been born at Shadwell, Middlesex, on 7 December 1659. Narbrough used his new bride's dowry, prize money and the rewards of 'good voyages' to buy the Knowlton estate, near Deal, in Kent. Five thousand pounds of the dowry went towards the estate. In addition, the Manors of Northcote, Southcote and

---

1   Bod Lib: Rawlinson MS, A 216, f. 145, copies of commissions etc from the library of Samuel Pepys.
2   £400,000 in 1680 is equivalent to £58,400,000 in 2017.
3   Davies, *Pepys's Navy*, pp. 25–8.

Sandowne, also in Kent, were purchased. 'Good voyages' were ones used by captains of men-of-war for private trading. In 1673, it had been decreed that captains could receive 1% interest on any bullion that they carried. Narbrough and others, in the Mediterranean, had made the most of these lucrative possibilities.[4] Knowlton was situated close to the major 17th century anchorage in the Downs. The newly-wed Narbroughs also kept a town house in the parish of St Olave, Hart Street, close to the Navy Office.

Elizabeth and John Narbrough's marriage was a happy one despite the fact that he was nearly twice the age of his young bride. The appearance of children, year on year, is indicative of Narbrough's desk rather than sea job! Five children were born to the union, although two of them would die in infancy. They were: Elizabeth, born 1682 [died 1721]; Ann, born 1683 and died the same year; John, born 1684 [died 1707]; James, born 1685 [died 1707]; Isaac, born 1687 and also died the same year. All the children were baptised at St Olave's and have memorials in St Clement's Church, Knowlton. Elizabeth, the eldest daughter, was married to Thomas D'Aeth,[5] on 23 January 1701, at St Dionis, Backchurch, London and had issue.[6] John Narbrough's present-day descendants come down from this line. In 1716, Thomas D'Aeth was created a baronet. Both the young Narbroughs, John and James, drowned in 1707, as a result of the wrecking of the *Association* on the Gilstone.[7] It is worth recalling that both Samuel Pepys and his wife Elisabeth were buried in St Olave Church, which was seriously damaged by the Luftwaffe in World War II.

Narbrough had been made a commissioner of the navy in view of his great experience as a mariner both in the major actions of the Dutch wars and also in the lesser actions against the Barbary pirates. In addition, he was recognised as an accomplished navigator with a voyage of exploration to the Pacific Ocean on his curriculum vitae. Narbrough had the added advantage of being on good terms with both Charles II and his brother, James, Duke of York. During Narbrough's seven active years as a commissioner, England was largely at peace with the major continental powers. However, the merchant fleet had to be protected against French privateers and the Barbary pirates. Trading areas as far away as America and the East Indies needed to be constantly patrolled. Narbrough and his fellow commissioners were responsible for building the ships, maintaining them and seeing that their crews were clothed and fed.

We saw earlier the problems Narbrough had faced with the lead sheathing of the *Henrietta* in the Mediterranean. In 1670, a company that had been formed by the English soldier and politician, Sir Philip Howard who, with Francis Watson, began experimenting with lead sheathing on ships. This was an attempt to strengthen the hulls and also protect them against the damaging worm. Samuel Pepys was impressed by Howard and thought him handsome and courteous as well. Lead was applied in 1671 to the *Phoenix* and then the experiment was extended to several other ships such as the *Dreadnought*, *James Galley*, *Mary* and, as we have seen previously, the *Henrietta*. On the *James Galley* Narbrough had found the rudder loose: 'so they unhung it and hoisted it upon deck, where they found the Pinckle Iron quite

---

4   Davies, *Pepys's Navy*, p. 105.
5   Pronounced Death.
6   St Dionis was a Christopher Wren designed church which was demolished in 1878.
7   Robert Marsham-Townshend, 'The Death of Sir John Narbrough', *Notes and Queries* (London: John Francis 29 December 1888), p. 502.

consumed and eaten by the salt of the lead or some other matter, which corrodes from the lead that eats the iron and nayles.' Charles II was greatly in favour of sheathing and went in person, in 1673, to Sheerness, to see the *Phoenix* careened. Narbrough, with his practical experience of sheathing, was vehemently against the practice and not afraid to voice opposition on the matter to his sovereign. It was not only the electrolytic effect on the iron in the rudders, but also that the removal of shells fastened to hulls split the underlying lead. The whole matter came to a head in 1682, with Narbrough much to the fore, and lead sheathing was dropped.[8] It was not until 1758 that George Anson began experimenting with more effective copper sheathing which became standard in 1783.[9]

It seems likely that Narbrough suggested to Charles II that his former shipmate, Greenvile Collins, should use one of the King's yachts, the *Merlin*, to survey the English coastline and eventually, in 1693, his *Great Britain's Coasting Pilot* was published. This proved to be much more accurate than anything that had gone before. During his time as a commissioner, Narbrough undoubtedly prepared a manuscript which James Lightbody later published, with a few additions of his own, as *The Mariners Jewel*, in 1695. This was a pocket dictionary for use by officers, seamen, boatswain, carpenters, pursers and stewards. It contained an alphabetical list of naval terms, a pay table, a compendium of boatswains' and pursers' stores and information concerning the division of prizes.

Narbrough complained to Pepys, one of his admirers whose ear he had, about the excessive number of yachts in commission and how little they were deployed. He suggested that they might be used to give practical training to the Christ's Hospital boys.[10] In 1673, Pepys had instigated a mathematical school within Christ's Hospital in order to improve navigation. Unfortunately, the school was not a success, leaving a disappointed Pepys.[11] For many years Narbrough had been in favour of commanding officers depositing copies of their journals with the Secretary to the Admiralty. He thought that the experiences of men in uncharted seas would be of benefit to their successors. Many captains had parted with their journals on a voluntary basis, but it is likely that Narbrough had persuaded the new King, James II, to make the practice compulsory in 1686.[12]

Narbrough's duties as a commissioner involved the Victualling Department, a veritable goldmine even for an honest man, where he had succeeded Sir Anthony Deane. He was responsible for provisions, stores, and balancing the accounts. During Narbrough's time at the Navy Office, the Board was in conflict with the Treasury. The Treasury demanded to know how money was being spent and the Board answered that it was only accountable to the Admiralty and not to the Treasury. Despite pressure being exerted on it, the Board serenely carried on with its uncommunicative policy much to the irritation of the Treasury. It is clear that the commissioners were not being profligate as by 1686, the Naval Debt had been reduced to £172,000 from £1,250,000 20 years earlier.[13]

8   Davies, *Pepys's Navy*, p. 72; Dyer, *Narbrough*, p. 196.
9   West, *Admiral Russell*, p. 330.
10   Dyer, *Narbrough*, p. 197; Tanner, *Naval Manuscripts*, Vol. IV, p. lviii.
11   Davies, *Pepys's Navy*, p. 145.
12   Dyer, *Narbrough*, p. 198.
13   Dyer, *Narbrough*, pp. 199–202.

New members of the Navy Board were said to have deferred to Narbrough when warfare at sea was on the agenda. When Sir Samuel Morland, diplomat, academic and mathematician, was asked by Pepys, in 1687, to quiz the commissioners about the introduction of new naval gun-carriages, he reported:

> I went to see what the Commissioners had done ---- relating to the new gun carriages, etc, but met none but Sir John Narbrough who told me your orders expres't a trial of shooting like that to be made at Portsmouth, which was impracticable at Deptford; because shooting with powder only was no tryall; and shooting with bullets too dangerous. And therefore his opinion, which he did believe would be the opinion of the whole Board, was that to each new carriage should be the addition of a windlass, and also the false truck at the end of the carriages, and that all other things as eye-bolts, tackles, etc., should be left as they are in the old carriages, till such time as a full trial be made of the new way both at sea and in a fight, and then what shall prove to be useless in the whole way may be wholly left on and layd aside.[14]

In 1683, Narbrough was approached by the 32-year-old William Phips, a Boston sea captain and adventurer. Phips was a huge, sunburned man and physically intimidating. He was looking for a ship to take him to the Caribbean in search of the Spanish plate ship, *Nuestra Senora de la Concepcion*, which had sunk, in 1641, after striking a coral reef to the north of Hispaniola.[15] Phips did not know its name other than it was an Almiranta with bullion and plate in abundance. Both Charles II and Narbrough were impressed by Phips' larger than life personality despite the fact that he had no personal knowledge of the wreck site. The previous year, the King had funded an expedition to find the same sunken ship. That expedition claimed to have had 'Spanish directions', to locate the site of the wreck, from the former pilot of the *Concepcion* and it had been unsuccessful. Indeed, it has been said that Narbrough had been dreaming about finding the ship since his days in the West Indies. He had heard stories from soldiers at Jamaica telling of the sunken Spanish plate.[16]

Charles II lent Phips, the *Golden Rose of Algier*, a ship that had recently been captured from the Algerian corsairs.[17] She was quite a large ship, capable of looking after herself, with a crew of 100 men and 18 guns. In September 1683, the *Rose* sailed for Boston via Limerick to collect provisions. In Boston, the crew went on the rampage fuelled by an excess of alcohol. Phips arrived and successfully ordered the crew aboard and commented: 'he did not care a turd for the Governor' and invited the constables to kiss his arse. The *Rose* sailed for New Providence, in the Bahamas, where Phips hoped to salvage silver from a local wreck site in order to finance his search for the *Concepcion*. Although details are sparse, Phips

---

14   Dyer, *Narbrough*, pp. 204–5.
15   Today, Haiti and the Dominican Republic.
16   According to Peter Earle, in his excellent book, *The Wreck of the Almiranta* (London: Macmillan 1979), p. 120: 'Narbrough had first gone to the West Indies in 1657, when he was seventeen, ----.' However, Myngs went home to England from the West Indies in 1657. It is more than likely that Narbrough was in the West Indies with Myngs, but possibly the date is wrong. The other possibility is that Narbrough was serving under another captain in 1657.
17   Captured in 1681 by Cloudesley Shovell.

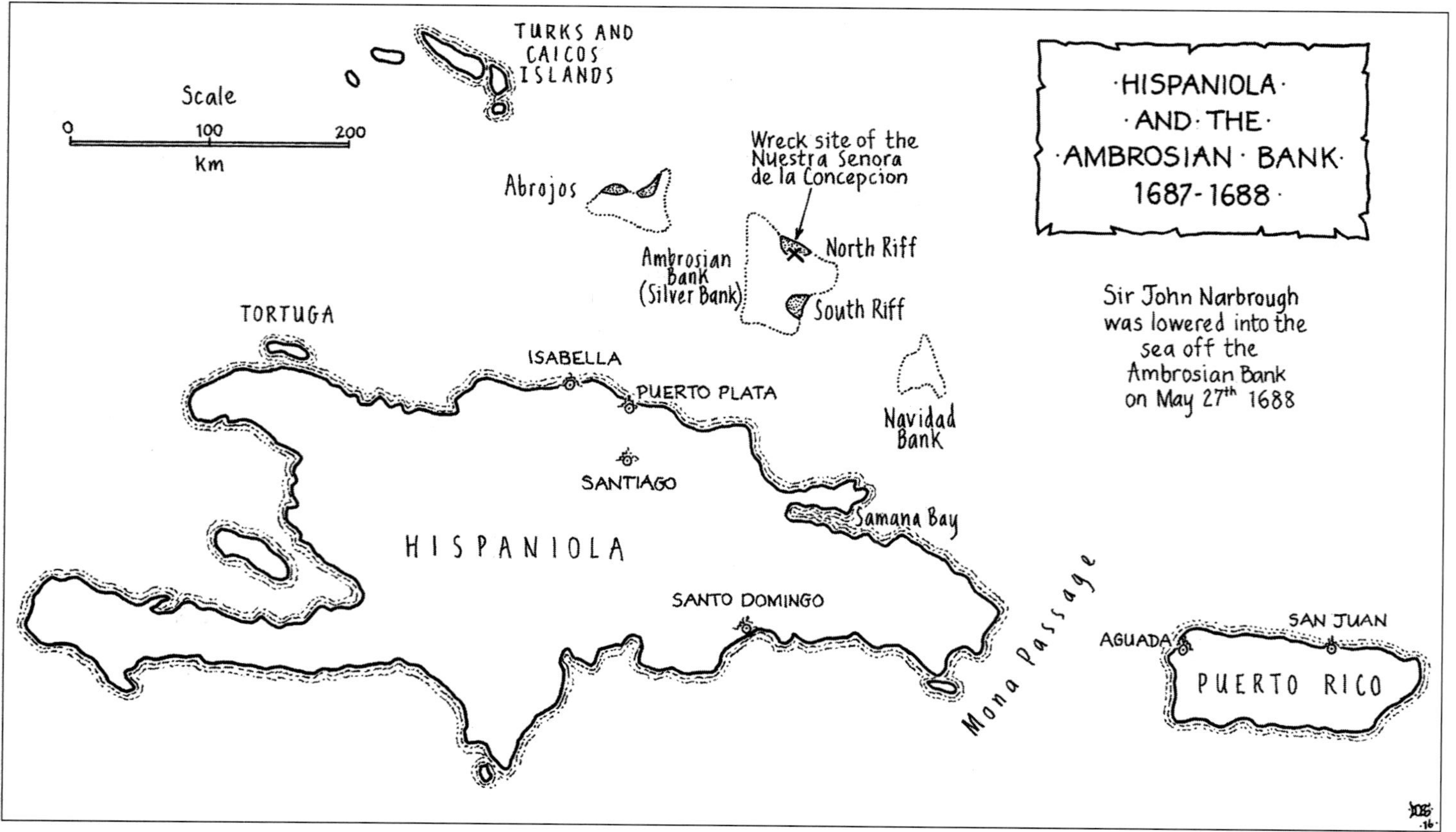

Map 12 Hispaniola and the Ambrosian Bank 1687-1688.

gained very little from the site and was not helped by an outbreak of smallpox in his ship. It was not until late 1684 that he was able to sail to the vicinity of the Ambrosian Bank [Silver Bank], north of Hispaniola, where he hoped to find the remnants of the *Concepcion*. Phips was unsuccessful and returned to England in 1686 to find a new king on the throne who was keen to find out the conditions under which he, Phips, had been lent the *Rose*. The profit from the voyage even failed to cover the maintenance costs of the ship.[18]

William Phips may have had a disappointing three years, but he had not given up on finding the *Concepcion*. In late March 1686, he approached Christopher Monck, 2nd Duke of Albemarle and John Narbrough.[19] Albemarle, as we shall call him, to avoid confusion with his distinguished father, had been profligate with his inherited fortune and was much out of favour at the new court. In 1683, he had sold his London home, Clarendon House, to a consortium of investors who demolished it and built on its site, Albemarle, Bond and Dover Streets. In addition Albemarle was a sick man; he had alcohol-induced liver disease and was chronically jaundiced. He jumped at the idea of easy money and the kudos that might come from a successful expedition. Narbrough was also keen on the project, although with different motives from the dissolute, alcoholic duke. He had been involved with the two earlier attempts to find the *Concepcion* and had been fascinated by the thought of salvaging her for 30 years. Narbrough was a wealthy man in his own right and had also married a rich wife. He did not need the money and invested only a modest one-eighth share in the new enterprise.

Phips was instructed to find a suitable ship and came up with the *Bridgewater*, of 200 tons and 23 guns, which was for sale. Narbrough, in person, surveyed her and found that she was in a satisfactory condition for a purchase price of £860. The name was changed to the *James and Mary* in honour of the new king and queen. It was decided to buy a sloop to accompany the *James and Mary* and Phips suggested the 40-ton *Henry* whose owner agreed to credit the purchase price of £230 to the partnership in exchange for an eighth share.[20] Four further speculators were added to the partnership including Anthony Cary, the 5th Viscount Falkland, the Treasurer of the Navy from 1681–89, who undoubtedly knew Narbrough well. Clearly they were attracted by the lure of financial gain and by association with the grand ducal name of Albemarle.

Albemarle received a warrant from James II 'to search for, seize and take up all such wrecks as shall by him or them found in ye seas to ye windward of ye north side of Hispaniola or about the islands or shoales of Bahama near the Gulf of Florida in America.' The royal warrant was in exchange for one tenth of the profits to go to the king. Narbrough and one of the other partners did not think that this was a watertight arrangement and Albemarle proceeded to have it confirmed under the Great Seal, but this was not achieved until six months after the expedition had sailed.[21] The partners agreed to fit out and provision the

18   Earle, *Wreck of the Almiranta*, pp. 118–158.

19   Albemarle's mother was 'Dirty Bessie' whom we met earlier in this account. In 1681, Albemarle was credited with arranging the first recorded boxing match in England, this between his butler and a butcher. The butcher was the victor.

20   Sloop comes from the Dutch sloep and is a sailing boat with a single mast and fore-and-aft rig. Much information can be found in the *Journal of the Henry* in the Kent County Archives U 1515.010, 1686–87.

21   Earle, *Wreck of the Almiranta*, p. 164; TNA: ADM 2/1741, James II's warrant.

ships and Phips was instructed to keep books showing all the transactions of the voyage. He was obliged to put up a surety of £20,000 to carry out the agreement and not to swindle the partners. In return his share was to be one sixteenth of the treasure, but only after the King's one tenth part had been taken and also the expenses of the voyage settled.[22] This arrangement was not overgenerous to Phips. A small cargo of cloth, pottery, hardware and alcohol, to the value of £500, was to be taken on the expedition in order to barter with the Spanish in Hispaniola.

The purchase price of the two ships made up approximately half the initial cost of £3,210. The ships needed to be in a good state of repair and freshly rigged before departure in order to avoid colonial dockyards and thus preserve the secrecy of the expedition. Particular attention was placed on anchors, cables and chains as there would be no one to support them on the reef. The beer for the expedition was supplied by the aptly named Mr Whitbread.[23] Of course, Phips took diving equipment with him in the form of diving tubs, dredges,[24] rakes and grapples in addition to the standard lifting gear to be found on ships. The joint crews consisted of about 70 men with William Phips commanding the *James and Mary* and a Francis Rogers as captain of the *Henry*. Surprisingly, Phips only took four divers with him. Judging by their names, such as John Pasqua, they may have been American Indians. At the time 'fish' was the term used for diving operations. In the final analysis, the six men, including Narbrough, with one-eighth shares, paid out £400 and Albemarle £800. Finally, the two ships sailed from the Downs for the Caribbean on 12 September 1686. No doubt Albemarle, Narbrough and their partners prayed to God and hoped for the best.

At the beginning of November 1686, the *James and Mary* and *Henry* arrived independently at Barbados. Having watered and taken on provisions, they sailed for the Mona Passage between Hispaniola and Puerto Rico and, on 28 November, anchored in Samana Bay on the east coast of Hispaniola. From here Phips took the two vessels to Puerto Plata on the north coast of the island. Contact was made with the Spanish who sent a small party of men from Santiago, thirty miles away to the south, to find out their business. Naturally, the real purpose of their voyage was not alluded to. In early January 1687, Phips sent the *Henry* out of harbour to make a preliminary search for the *Concepcion* on the Ambrosian Bank. On 18 January, Francis Rogers in the *Henry* came across the east end of the reef. This reef is now known as the North Riff and forms the northern edge of the Ambrosian Bank. It is 40 miles long, running south-east to north-west between 20°30' and 20° north. Rogers began to search the bank and to his utter amazement, on 20 January, he found the wreck site. To be more precise, it was William Covill, the second mate of the *James and Mary*, now with Rogers, who went in a canoe with two divers to search the north side of the reef and made the actual discovery:

> Bringing us happy and joyfull news of ye cannew's finding ye wrecke, their being in her Mr Coule [Covill], Francis and Jonas, ye 2 dieverrs. For which blessing wee returne infinite praise and thanks to Almighty God. Our boate carried [away] with her a chaine and grapnel, a new buoy rope, a new buoy, and severall wooden buoyes,

22   Earle, *Wreck of the Almiranta*, p. 165.
23   This cannot have been the famous London firm of Whitbread brewers which was not formed until 1742.
24   A device for bringing up objects from the seabed by scooping or dragging.

and 2 longe oares, to fix upon ye wrecke that wee might better find her when we came on ye banke next. She lyes in ye midst of reife betweene 3 large boylers that ye tops of them are dry att low water.[25] In some places upon her there's 7 fathoms, which is the largest depth, 6 and 5, ye shoallest [shallowest]. Most of her timber is consum'd away, and soe over growne with curlle [coral] that had itt not been for her guns shee would scarce ever been founde, itt being at least 45 years since shee was lost and ye richest ship that ever went out of ye West Indies.[26]

Forty five years and 80 days after the *Nuestra Senora de la Concepcion* had been wrecked, Covill and his divers had at last found her.

Phips did not act precipitously, but had both the *James and Mary* and the *Henry* careened and revictualled before sailing to the wreck site. With William Covill acting as their pilot, the *James and Mary* arrived at the wreck site on 21 February 1687. The ship: 'came to anchor, ye wreck bearing of us north-east a half east, about four or five miles, the reefe making like to a halfe moone.'[27] The next morning Phips visited the site with his four divers. Francis Rogers was ordered to bring the *Henry* as close as he dared and eventually he anchored about two miles south-west of the remains of the *Concepcion*. This was about halfway between the *James and Mary* and the reef. Both ships were anchored with great care to stop them driving on to the coral reef.

The ships' crews and divers were now to undertake a season of hard labour on the reef. Each day, the ship's pinnace and longboat took out a party of crew and divers to work on the wreck, until they returned for sustenance late in the afternoon. Sundays were sacrosanct and no work was carried out. The men were able to work on the wreck for 40 days out of the 58 that the *James and Mary* was on the coral reef. The divers stayed underwater for as long as they were able to hold their breaths and they used crow-bars and pickaxes to break up the coral surrounding the silver treasure.[28] The crews in the boats, on the surface, helped clear the site of debris using long-handled rakes and dredges. The divers filled baskets with silver coins or bits of plate which were hauled to the surface. Each evening Phips sat down to calculate how much treasure had been salvaged. It was clear that the whole process was going to take many months and Phips was limited by the amount of food and water he had in his ships. What should he do?

Towards the end of the first week, two sails appeared on the horizon and there were fears that they might be rampaging French corsairs from Tortuga.[29] In reality, they turned out to be two small vessels, owned by men who had been with Phips in the *Rose*, on the earlier voyage, and they too were looking for the *Concepcion*. They were Abraham Adderley of Jamaica and William Davis of Bermuda and Phips came to an agreement with the two men to assist with the bringing up of the treasure. Thus with an increased number of divers the salvage work could be carried out considerably faster. Coins were no longer counted but

---

25   Three large boylers refers to clumps of coral.
26   Earle, *Wreck of the Almiranta*, pp. 173–4.
27   Earle, *Wreck of the Almiranta*, p. 181.
28   The treasure consisted of coins, bullion [silver or gold before coining] and plate [silver or gold utensils]. In fact very little gold in these or any other form was found on the site.
29   An island to the north-west of Hispaniola.

weighed. One of the main storerooms of the *Concepcion* was discovered and whole chests of silver could be pulled to the surface. In most cases the wood of the chest had rotted away, but the silver had become bound together in great clumps.

Early in March, Phips persuaded William Davis to take his sloop right into the reef and anchor her directly over the wreck site. An attempt was made to use a Bermuda tub to extend the time a diver could remain underwater. The Bermuda tub had been invented earlier in the 17th century and consisted of a large open ended wine cask which was weighted at the open end. The tub was dropped into the water trapping air inside it and the divers could go into it periodically to refill their lungs. A man could stay under water for up to 45 minutes, but the tub was only practical to depths of about 11 fathoms [66 feet] as at greater depths the air became unacceptably compressed. The tub used by Phips' men was a large one with a seat which allowed the divers to take a quick swig of brandy, from a bottle, in order to refresh themselves. Unfortunately, the tub was only used for a single day as the sloop was damaged on the reef.

By mid-April 1687, Phips calculated that he had over 25 tons of silver, seven guns and a small amount of gold. He realised that this was worth a huge sum of money which might attract the attention of French corsairs and he was also running short of food and water. Phips made the sensible decision to return to England with his vast and profitable hoard of treasure. On 19 April, the *James and Mary* with the *Henry* sailed for the Turks Islands to take in food and water. From these islands, on 2 May, they left for home, reaching the Downs on 6 June 1687 after a nine months round voyage which would give William Phips lasting fame.

The news of the success of Phips' expedition rapidly spread throughout the kingdom. On 9 June, the Spanish ambassador, Don Pedro Ronquillo sent a memorial claiming the silver and cannon for the King of Spain. He was of the quaint opinion: 'that his master might let his money lie as long at the bottom of the sea as he pleased.'[30] Neither an ounce of silver nor a single cannon was returned to Spain. The very same day as the ambassador's complaint was sent to the king, Cloudesley Shovell returned to the story again, when he reported to the Navy Office that he had been ordered by James II to secure the *James and Mary* in the Thames. Shovell ordered his lieutenant in the *Anne*, to go aboard the *James and Mary*, to see that no gold or silver was removed and Second-Lieutenant Francis Wivell and 17 men did so. Off Grays, Albemarle with Narbrough, aboard a yacht, came to inspect the ship. As a nervous Shovell reported to Pepys: 'they came but did not offer to meddle in anything. I strictly commanded Phips that nothing is carried from her.'[31] Clearly, James II was keen on having his full share of the booty without any of it slipping away through unauthorised channels. He must have been reproaching himself for not having financed Phips' expedition in the way his brother had the previous one. Surely, Shovell must have felt a twinge of embarrassment at having 'to keep an eye' on Narbrough, his former patron and friend. Wivell cannot have been that vigilant as it was said that casks of wine were broached and the crew drank the health of their fortunate employers. One experienced naval officer, Richard Haddock, the captain of Montagu's ill-fated *Royal James*, at Sole Bay, must have

---

30   Gavin De Beer, *Sir Hans Sloane and the British Museum* (London: Oxford University Press 1953), p. 29; Earle, *Wreck of the Almiranta*, p. 194.

31   Harris, *Cloudesley Shovell*, p. 96.

been kicking himself. He had bought in a £100 share, but had foolishly sold it before Phips' return![32]

Albemarle was generous in that the crews of the *James and Mary* and the *Henry* were given £8,000 after the king had received his share. Rogers and Covill were reputed to have got £1,000 each. James II's royalty was £20,872. The shares worked out as: Albemarle £43,534; Narbrough £21,766;[33] Falkland £21,766; Sir James Hayes £21,766; Isaac Foxcroft £21,766; Francis Nicholson £21,766; John Smith's compensation £13,287. Smith, the owner of the *Henry*, had been in Flanders at the time of the return of the *James and Mary*. Initially, he was to get nothing as it was claimed that there had been irregularities in his original accounts. A subsequent court case, at which both Albemarle and Narbrough gave evidence, was followed by a settlement. As Peter Earle has commented: 'Nevertheless, it does look as though Smith was a victim of a very nasty piece of sharp practice by his aristocratic and well-connected partners.'[34] If this is the case, it is a stain on Narbrough's otherwise irreproachable reputation. In total the value of the treasure was around £210,000.[35] To put it into context, Phips brought home almost as much treasure as did the famous pirate, Sir Henry Morgan after his three most prominent raids, on Spanish treasure, at Portobelo, Maracaibo and Panama. Moreover Phips did this, without the loss of a man, at a cost of £3,200. No wonder there was national excitement. Phips was rewarded with a knighthood and was granted the post of Provost-Marshal of his native New England. Later, he became the first Governor of the Province of Massachusetts Bay from 1692–4.

Almost immediately, arrangements were made for a further voyage to the wreck of the *Concepcion*. James II met Albemarle, Narbrough and the other partners at Windsor Castle, and a new agreement was drawn up. The King would provide a frigate and would 'discourage' other predators from going to the site. In exchange he would receive one fifth of the treasure with a value of up to £150,000 and thereafter a third.[36] Quite understandably, the Spanish ambassador, Don Pedro Ronquillo, was not a happy man: 'His Majesty cannot give patents for fishing up things that belong to the Spaniards.' Implausibly, James II excused himself by arguing that it was just a general agreement not one applying to any specific wreck.[37] Albemarle and his partners were besieged by greedy compatriots wanting to join in the adventure for financial gain. The unfortunate John Smith's share was sold partly to Thomas Neale with Albemarle taking up the remainder. Neale was the Master of the Mint and a useful man to have onside. Thus under the new contractual arrangements shares were allocated: Albemarle nine thirty-seconds; Narbrough one eighth; Falkland one eighth; James Hayes one eighth; Francis Nicholson one eighth; Isaac Foxcroft one eighth; Thomas Neale three thirty-seconds.

The ships for the expedition were rapidly made ready. Narbrough was to take the 50-gun *Foresight* with Edward Stanley as his captain.[38] Stanley had had experience of the waters

---

32   Dyer, *Narbrough*, pp. 216–18.

33   About £3,406,000 in 2017.

34   Earle, *Wreck of the Almiranta*, p. 200.

35   About £32,860,000 in 2017.

36   Bod Lib: Rawlinson MS, A 189, ff. 370, 373, agreement between James II and Albemarle, 14 June 1687.

37   Earle, *Wreck of the Almiranta*, p. 202.

38   Earle, *Wreck of the Almiranta*, p. 203; TNA: ADM 52/35/2, Edward Stanley journal, *Foresight*, 1687–88.

around Hispaniola as he had been part of a previous expedition, which had failed to find the *Concepcion*. The newly knighted Sir William Phips, with all the diving gear, was to be in the oddly named merchantman *Good Luck and a Boy*. The *James and Mary* and the *Henry* were also refitted in order to return to their old haunts and a further ship, the *Princess,* was to complete Narbrough's small squadron. It has been estimated that the cost of the expedition was £16,000, all of five times the expense of the first one. To complicate matters, the sick Albemarle would accompany them as he was sailing to Jamaica to take up the post of Governor.

Such was the lure of further treasure that all the ships of the squadron were ready to sail for the Caribbean by the middle of July 1687. Unfortunately, Albemarle gave a sumptuous, goodbye banquet where he indulged himself to excess and fell dangerously ill from his liver complaint. This led to a delay, until 3 September, before Narbrough and Phips were able to sail from the Downs. No doubt Narbrough spent some time at nearby Knowlton with his wife and young children. They would never see him again. The six week delay had serious consequences as there were rumours of ships being fitted out by all the maritime nations of Europe who were keen to obtain a share of the treasure from the wreck for themselves. Amongst them was Charles, Viscount Mordaunt,[39] who had obtained a patent from the Prince of Orange to fit out a heavily armed expedition of his own. At this juncture, a William Constable petitioned James II to act as his agent, in the collection of the one tenth of the salvaged treasure, due to the King from his subjects, after their illicit removal of silver from the wreck site following Phips' original expedition. James II readily agreed. Over a month later, the chronically sick Albemarle followed in the wake of Narbrough and Phips onboard the 50-gun *Assistance*.

In the middle of October, Narbrough was forced into an unscheduled visit to Madeira to take on further supplies. The weather had been poor with contrary winds which had forced Phips, with all the diving gear, back to Plymouth. To make matters even worse Narbrough had lost contact with the *James and Mary*. He sailed on to Barbados, reaching the island on 16 November and here he had to await the arrival of Albemarle: 'in hopes of kissing your Grace's hand.' By this stage Narbrough must have been a very frustrated man as he knew that the wreck site was alive with would be salvagers and more were coming from Europe. Whilst awaiting Albemarle, he took on board 600 gallons of rum in place of the customary brandy. Soon the Admiralty ordered all ships on the Jamaica station to use rum instead of brandy. When Albemarle arrived, in the *Assistance,* he was greeted by a salute from all the ships in the vicinity and from the forts.[40] Having seen Albemarle on his way to Jamaica, Narbrough set sail for Samana Bay on the East Coast of Hispaniola. He anchored the *Foresight,* in the Bay, on 5 December and two days later Phips joined him from England. Also in the Bay were numerous sloops who were revictualling before returning to salvage yet more treasure from the *Concepcion*. The sloops also reported that there were no less than 25 ships currently working on the site. Narbrough's heart must have sunk further at this not unexpected news.

---

39   Charles Mordaunt, from 1697 3rd Earl of Peterborough [1658–1735]. A bitter opponent of James II.
40   TNA: ADM 52/35/2, Stanley journal, *Foresight*, 26 November 1687.

By 15 December, Lieutenant John Hubbard of the *Foresight* reported: 'At noone saw the ships and sloops riding at the wrack ---- At 3 anchored ---- Saw the boats at the wreck plaine. They bore of us N by E 4 miles off.'[41] Most of the illicit ships took one swift look at the 50-gun *Foresight,* weighed anchor and vanished into the sunset with their haul of silver. A few who had found little treasure remained to discuss their situation with Narbrough. One small vessel was actually anchored over the site of the *Concepcion* and was using a diving-tub. It was clear that Phips' attempt to keep the wreck's location secret had spectacularly failed. A boy who had been with Abraham Adderley earlier in the year was forced to show some of the Bermudans the site of the wreck. Narbrough recorded: 'the Burmudoes men which Sir William Phips left behind him discovered ye wreck into all these parts.'[42] It was clear that local fortune hunters had been plundering the wreck for the best part of five months without interference.

On arrival on the North Riff of the Ambrosian Bank, Narbrough ordered Stanley and Hubbard to go in the *Foresight's* boats to take possession of the wreck site. The few ships present made no trouble and only a little silver was found in them. Narbrough employed some of the sloops and their divers to work for him. Stanley's own divers went down on the *Concepcion*, but she had been stripped bare. All the accessible silver had already been taken by the colonial vultures.

The Governors of Jamaica and Bermuda had been endeavouring to collect the King's entitlement, of one tenth of the treasure, from the returning ships, with mixed success. When Albemarle arrived, to become the new Governor of Jamaica, he informed the local authorities that they should have been collecting a half rather than a tenth share for the King. James II had gone to the Admiralty Court, in London, and a decision had been made that he should receive half the treasure as his legal due. Many colonial adventurers had already paid their tenth share and were simply not prepared to pay any more. In addition, some of them had already, surreptitiously, parted with their ill-gotten gains. The arrival of William Constable, in the West Indies, to recover the King's dues complicated matters further. He and his agents were also unsuccessful and his backers had little return on their investment. Narbrough thought that the colonial adventurers, in their sloops, had collected around £250,000 worth of bullion and plate, which was more than Phips had found in his successful voyage earlier in the year. As the Spanish ambassador believed that the *Concepcion's* cargo was worth £1,000,000, potentially there was another £500,000 or so still embedded in the coral of the North Riff.

Narbrough set his men to work with a will. He was not short of labour as his squadron provided around 400 men and there were 200 divers, some from England and the remainder hired from the sloops.[43] As an incentive the divers were allowed to keep a quarter of everything they salvaged. Initially, they worked on the part of the *Concepcion* from the base of the main mast to the bow. The divers hacked away at the coral with pickaxes and chunks of coral were raised to be smashed with hammers to get at the encased silver. Relatively little was found and Lieutenant John Hubbard recorded on 17 February 1688: 'The best days

41   National Maritime Museum (NMM): ADM/L/F/198, Lieutenant John Hubbard journal, *Foresight,* 15 December 1687.
42   National Maritime Museum (NMM): LBK/1, John Narbrough letter book 1687–88, 14 April 1688.
43   NMM: LBK/1, Narbrough letter book, f. 19.

worke since our being at the wrack.'[44] They had raised 275 lbs of silver instead of their daily average of less than 50 lbs. In Phips' first successful expedition they had found 2,750 lbs in a single day. After two months on site Narbrough had finished clearing the fore-part of the ship as far as the residual base planks of the hull.

On 15 February, Narbrough received the dreaded news that Lord Charles Mordaunt had arrived in Samana Bay with his Dutch squadron. The Dutch ships could outgun Narbrough's less powerful vessels and so he immediately informed Albemarle, in Jamaica, of his situation and requested the frigates *Falcon* and *Assistance* to come to his aid. Narbrough wrote: 'I hope ye ships are on there [sic] way unto me or will be speedily dispatch'd ---- to secure ye wreck. Otherwise, it will be a loose-ing voyage to your Grace and ye gentlemen concerned.' When one of the Dutch ships appeared at the wreck site, Narbrough had the *Foresight* cleared for action. On 22 February, Mordaunt, in person, arrived in the 48-gun *North Holland* and quietly observed the scene for the next two days. Then Mordaunt asked permission for his officers to view the wreck. In a relaxed atmosphere, Edward Stanley took the men over the site in a boat. The sea was rough and little could be seen beneath the surface. A few days later, Mordaunt took his ships back to Samana Bay and was reportedly still in the vicinity of Hispaniola during the following month of May. Soon after Mordaunt's departure, Albemarle's reinforcements arrived on the Ambrosian Bank. What was the purpose of Mordaunt's visit to the wreck site? It has been suggested that he was sounding out Narbrough's loyalty to James II. The two men had served together earlier in the Mediterranean,[45] but surprisingly, there is no evidence that there was a meeting of the two off the Ambrosian Bank. Perhaps Mordaunt realised that there was so little treasure aboard the *Foresight* that it was not worth fighting over.

Narbrough resumed work on the wreck and concentrated on the yet untouched stern. He believed that: 'there is more treasure in ye wreck than what hath binn taken up.'[46] The problem was to get at the aft plate stores as the stern was deeply encased in coral. Narbrough had 60 divers working at a time with pickaxes whilst the boats' crews above hauled up the chunks of solid coral. Three cannons were seen and also the ship's cargo of indigo. On 15 March Narbrough wrote: 'Most here take it for a good signe to have stowed silver under indigo.'[47] Soon work came to a virtual standstill as the coral was rock hard and pickaxes were unable to cope with the situation. A forty-foot spar, with an iron crow-bar attached to its distal end, was used by the crew of the boats, but was no more effective than the divers' pickaxes. Grappling lines attached to the coral were hauled upon by the longboat's tackle with the result that lines broke. It was decided that underwater explosives must be used to get into the aft plate departments.

On 9 April, a calm day, Phips attempted to blast his way into the stern of the *Concepcion*. A 40-foot fuse was led down through hollow cane tubing to an explosive charge of gunpowder placed in a waterproof chest. The fuse was lit by Phips in the longboat above the wreck. Fortunately, the cane split at 20 feet and water rushed in: 'soe that ye powder

---

44   NMM: ADM/L/F/198, Hubbard journal, 17 February 1688.

45   In the campaign against Tripoli in 1675–6.

46   Earle, *Wreck of the Almiranta*, p. 213; NMM: LBK/1, Narbrough letter book, f. 16, 14 April 1688.

47   NMM: LBK/1, Narbrough letter book, f. 14, 15 March 1688. Indigo dye was being transported from Mexico to Spain. It is a colour between blue and violet in the spectrum.

in ye chest was damnafied.' Otherwise the longboat's crew and any divers who had not swum far enough away would have been killed. Gunpowder was not used again. The divers returned to work with their pickaxes, but without success. Lieutenant John Hubbard, on 20 April, commented: 'our divers doe not take up a pound weight of silver a day.'[48] Morale was sinking fast, when the crews were put on half-rations as victuals were getting low and the weather was inclement throughout their time on the reef. The men were becoming fractious as the purser of one of the ships bit off a great piece of the master's nose! In early May, Narbrough informed Falkland: 'Ye divers we carried out of England are most of them tired and cannot or will not hold ye work ---- saying there is no treasure remaining.'[49]

On 1 May, the men of the squadron started to die and by the 4th, Edward Stanley recorded that: 'wee have a sickley ship.'[50] Still Narbrough would not give up and any little find, such as a gold coin, spurred him on. He wrote in his letter book: 'Though we lye a great charge, I am unwilling to leave off till I have more reason to believe there is no more treasure of value. It would trouble me if treasure should be found by others after we leave it.'[51] He was only too well aware that the silver that had been salvaged would not cover the expenses of the expedition. On the 8th, Phips lost all hope and sailed away to return to his wife in New England. The remaining escort ships, with the exception of the *Foresight,* and most of the remaining sloops sailed away from the reef on the 20th. At last Narbrough accepted defeat for on 18 May, he had caught the febrile, infectious disease that was sweeping through the *Foresight.* Just what the disease was is not clear, although Typhus or Yellow Fever ['Yellow Jack'] were the most likely causes. On the 26th, Narbrough wrote to Albemarle, in Jamaica: 'We are finding very little silver on ye wreck and have used all our endeavours to gitt up ye rocks abaft, but find them too strong for us.'[52] Narbrough left two sloops on site to take possession of the wreck for James II. In his parlous, feverish, state he intended to return to England.

At 3:00 a.m. on 27 May 1688, Sir John Narbrough died. His final order was for the divers to recover one of the *Foresight*'s anchors which was lodged firmly in the coral. Edward Stanley and John Hubbard asked the surgeons if they could embalm his corpse, but they were unable to do so as the required ingredients were not available to them. The surgeons, from the *Foresight* and the sloops, did remove Narbrough's 'bowells' and placed them in a container for transport home to England.[53] At 5:00 p.m., the same day, Stanley reverently took Narbrough's mortal remains, in the pinnace and rowed towards the reef, where he lowered the body into the sea. The pinnace's flag was struck, the *Foresight* fired three volleys of musket shot and 40 cannons, with the remaining vessels joining in the salute to their dead admiral. Thus Narbrough was laid to rest near the wreck site he had tried so valiantly to salvage. Captain Edward Stanley took the *Foresight* home and reached the Gunfleet, on 24 July, where Narbrough's 'bowells' in their container were handed over, on

48   NMM: ADM/L/F/198, Hubbard journal, 20 April 1688.
49   Earle, *Wreck of the Almiranta*, p. 215.
50   Earle, *Wreck of the Almiranta*, p. 215.
51   NMM: LBK/1, Narbrough letter book, f. 19, 26 May 1688.
52   NMM: LBK/1, Narbrough letter book, f. 23, 26 May 1688.
53   'Bowells': in the 17th century, the term meant heart and other vital organs, but not the intestines as might be imagined nowadays from the term.

the instructions of his father-in-law, John Hill, to a Deal 'hoeker' for carriage to that port.[54] Deal was close to the Narbrough estate at Knowlton. As the container was handed over, Stanley fired a further salute to his dead admiral. Lady Elizabeth Narbrough was left bereft with three young children, aged six, three and two years, to bring up. Later, the remains would be interred in Saint Clement's Church, Knowlton, adjacent to Narbrough's country house, Knowlton Court. An altar tomb was constructed with the following inscription:

> Here lies the remains of Sr John Narbrough Knight / who departed this life the 27th of May 1688 / in the 49th Yeare of his Age[55] / Alsoe the body of Ann his daughter by Elizabeth his/second wife, who dyed the 6th of November 1683 / Alsoe the body of Isack their son, who died 8th of / March 1686/7.

Later, in the superstructure of Sir John's altar tomb was added an inscription in memory of his eldest daughter, Dame Elizabeth D'Aeth who died on 24 June 1721 and was buried at Knowlton. On the other side of the chancel an altar tomb was eventually set up, in the early 18th century, in memory of her two younger brothers, John and James who, as will be seen in a later chapter, drowned with Sir Cloudesley Shovell and were buried in the Isles of Scilly.[56] Under Sir John Narbrough's will, dated 26 August 1687, he left his four Kent estates, including Knowlton, to his son, John, and cash totalling £25,000 to his surviving children, Elizabeth, John and James, £100 to a sister and £50 to each of her children and those of his two deceased sisters. His jewels were left to his wife.

In early August, the officers of the Mint came aboard the *Foresight* to collect the treasure. It weighed 3,213 lb 10 oz with the silver valued at around £7,500, less than half the expenses of the voyage. James II naturally took his fifth share.[57] On 15 November, only a month before he fled his kingdom, James II acted generously: 'in gratitude for his memory and service and in token of his sincere attachment to him', he conferred a baronetcy on Narbrough's eldest son, John, a child of four years.[58] Pepys too felt that he had lost a valued friend. As late as 1704, Narbrough's widow, by now Lady Elizabeth Shovell, and her second husband were endeavouring, in an appeal to the House of Lords, to make the estate of the 2nd Duke of Albemarle pay its share of the expenses of Narbrough's final voyage. They were successful.[59] Albemarle had died, in Jamaica, on 6 October 1688, and he would have been well aware of the expedition's failure. He died childless and his body was buried, in Westminster Abbey, nine months later.

It would be 1978 before the wreck site of the *Concepcion* was successfully found again and the remaining treasure salvaged. When the divers of that later expedition were working on the North Riff, in search of the site, they saw on a daily basis a circling albatross where subsequently they found the wreck to be. Was this the spirit of Sir John Narbrough?[60]

---

54   'Hoeker' or hooker was a 17th century merchant vessel, of Dutch origin, with three masts.

55   It should have read '48th Yeare of his Age.' He was baptised on 11 October 1640.

56   Harris, *Cloudesley Shovell*, p. 386; NMM: RMT MS, MAT 17, monumental inscriptions of the Shovell, Narbrough and Shorting families; Marsham-Townshend, 'Death of Sir John Narbrough', p. 503.

57   NMM: ADM/L/F/198, Hubbard journal, 2 August 1688.

58   Dyer, *Narbrough*, p. 231.

59   House of Lords (H of L) MS 1704–06 NS, Vol. VI (London: HMSO 1900–21), pp. 59–60.

60   The principal source for the section on the *Nuestra Senora de la Concepcion*: Earle, *Wreck of the Almiranta*, pp. 118–238.

10

Cloudesley Shovell and the Glorious Revolution 1688

James II's reckless pursuit of Catholicism had undermined his standing in the Kingdom. In March 1687, Arthur Herbert had refused, on principle, to support the repeal of the Test Act which precluded Catholics from holding public office. There was considerable surprise that Herbert had taken this step apparently on the grounds of conscience.[1] As we have seen in an earlier chapter, he had a reputation for being foul-mouthed, immoral and lacking of principle. In addition, he resigned from his sinecure as Master of the Robes and Rear-Admiral of England, losing the former post's salary of £4,000 a year. As he had little other means of supporting himself, this must have been a significant sacrifice. A waggish poet at the time aptly put it: 'Murders and rapes his honor can digest – Boggles at nought but taking off the Test.'[2] At this juncture Herbert was approached by Edward Russell, on behalf of William Prince of Orange, and in the autumn of 1688 he would command William's invasion fleet. There was a certain irony in that it was Russell who had made the approach, as there was a mutual loathing between the two men going back to 1681, during their time in the Mediterranean.[3] William selected Herbert to lead his fleet in the belief of the support he enjoyed amongst the English naval captains.

Lacking sensibility, James II had endeavoured to bring his Catholic faith to the army and navy. The army was Protestant and the navy partially so. The majority of naval officers rejected Catholicism and when Catholic priests were introduced by James II into the navy, the seamen threatened to toss them overboard. A contemporary view was that: 'all

---

1   Edward Powley, *The English Navy in the Revolution of 1688* (Cambridge: Cambridge University Press 1928), p. 13; Davies, 'James II', pp. 89–90.

2   Galbraith Crump (ed), *Poems on Affairs of State*, Vol. IV (New Haven: Yale University Press 1968), p. 167.

3   The relationship between Herbert and Russell cannot always have been poor, judging from two letters written by the latter to the former in the 1680s. The first had coarse sexual content: Russell wrote; 'P[i]ercy Kirke can fuck several fair ladies and buggar Mrs Bramley.' [Private collection]. In the second: 'I hope you will have a bellyful of Greek maidenheads' and 'hee has great obligations to the Governour of Tangier alsoo [Kirke], you are a Couple of Civil Gentlemen, when I have a wife or a Daughter, I'le keep her out of either of yor Clutches pray take my advice as a friend: for ye future & live a Chast life as I doe; it will not only bee good for yor body in his butt yor sould in ye next world: by ye first ship yt comes out I'le send you Doct Olivers instructions to fortify you against a wicked life.' [Private collection].

the great seamen are averse to Popery and lovers of liberty.'[4] Foolishly, James II appointed Roger Strickland, a Roman Catholic, to command the fleet and this caused much resentment among the sea fraternity. Not until September 1688, did James II realise his error and George Legge, 1st Baron Dartmouth,[5] was appointed in his place with Strickland downgraded to second-in-command. On 3 October, Dartmouth took command of the fleet and it was he who was charged with stopping William of Orange and his fleet from invading England. Unfortunately for James, Dartmouth was not a strong character and relatively inexperienced in commanding a fleet.

For James II to retain the throne of England, Dartmouth's ships had to defeat the Dutch invasion fleet under Herbert, before any troops could be established ashore. James expected that the invasion would be effected in the Thames' Estuary, East Anglia or the north of England after a naval battle. Indeed, William wished to disembark his men to the north of the River Thames. However, Herbert favoured the alternative course of action with a landing to be made in the south of England via the English Channel. Where should Dartmouth position his ships? No port was ideal but he favoured the Gunfleet, off Harwich, unlike James II who wished his ships to be positioned off the Dutch coast. Despite the King's view, on 15 October, Dartmouth took the English fleet to the Gunfleet and from this point matters would start to unravel for him and his sovereign.

During the second half of October, with the fleet at the Gunfleet, there was a great deal of informal discussion between the captains of Dartmouth's ships. Clearly, Dartmouth was concerned about this as he wrote to James II on 17 October:

> I would be glad of more sea room and keep my commanders now they are in good order as much as may be aboard their own ships and not liable to be caballing one with another, which, lieing idle together they may be apt as Englishmen naturally do to fall into especially being in the way of dayley pamphlets and newes letters.[6]

On the 22nd, Dartmouth wrote again to the King:

> I must acquaint your Majestie that on Friday last I had some hints of dissatisfaction in some young men in the fleet, and hearing Mr Russell is gone for Holland (if it be so) makes me more jealous then of any interest Herbert can have here ----.[7] The Duke of Grafton was down here a little after my comeing tho' he would not let me know it. My Lord Berkeley.[8] I am told is very pert but I have taken him in next ship to me and shall know more of their tempers in a little time.[9]

---

4   Stephen Martin-Leake, *The Life of Sir John Leake Rear-Admiral of Great Britain,* Vol. I (London: Navy Records Society 1918), pp. 17–19.
5   Dartmouth's mother was a Washington and through her line he was related to George Washington.
6   Powley, *Revolution of 1688,* p. 67.
7   'Mr Russell': Edward Russell, later Earl of Orford. 'Herbert': Arthur Herbert.
8   John, 3rd Baron of Stratton.
9   Powley, *Revolution of 1688,* pp. 67–8.

Henry FitzRoy, 1st Duke of Grafton, the illegitimate son of Charles II and the Duchess of Cleveland had expected to be offered command of the fleet in 1688 and was offended by Dartmouth's appointment. He had also secretly visited William of Orange and was intent on mischief-making on his behalf. The fleet's rear-admiral, John Berry, even hatched a plot to kidnap Dartmouth aboard Anthony Hastings' ship and to give Grafton command of the fleet. The scheme came to nothing after Dartmouth was made aware of it.[10]

A pamphlet written by Herbert was almost certainly read in the fleet as a supplement to a circular letter from William: 'I am a true Englishman and your friend exhort you to join arms to the Prince for the common cause.'[11] Herbert suggested that the English fleet was being used as an instrument of 'Popish Slavery.'[12] The atmosphere at the Gunfleet was becoming extremely toxic as Herbert hated Dartmouth and had a large number of supporters amongst the officers who had served under him at Tangier earlier in the decade.[13] Matthew Aylmer and George Byng were active in the Orangist cause, having been recruited by the senior army officers, Piercy Kirke and the Duke of Ormonde. In particular, Kirke had been a womanising and drinking companion of Herbert's in Tangier during the former's service as Deputy Governor. Shovell too, was deemed by Pepys to be one of Herbert's creatures and was kept in Dartmouth's own red squadron, no doubt to keep a close eye on him.[14]

On 26 October and again on the 28, Dartmouth held councils of war at the Gunfleet to determine where the fleet should be based. Each council consisted of two parts. Firstly, there was a meeting of the elite flag officers/senior captains, this being followed by a full meeting with the addition of the remaining captains of the fleet. In practice the first council of the elite made a decision which was then endorsed by the rest of the council. An admiral with a dominant personality, such as Herbert or Russell, might force through a particular course of action, but Dartmouth was not of that ilk. It was at these fateful meetings on the 26th and 28th that a decision was made to support Dartmouth's view of using the Gunfleet as a safe base and only the eccentric William Jennens supported his king, by favouring sailing to the Dutch coast. There was a general concern that this course of action might lead to the driving of the major ships on to shoals, off the Dutch coast, by autumnal storms. This was a sound professional view and not necessarily anti-Jacobite. In any event, Jennens was not taken seriously as he had had such a chequered career in the navy: court-martialled twice, lying, embezzlement, drunkenness and immoral acts with both sexes.[15] It was hoped that whichever direction Herbert's fleet sailed in, whether it was up the coast of East Anglia or down the English Channel, he could be checked before his disembarkation of troops.

It is time to look at the awkward position that Shovell found himself in during the autumn of 1688. What was the attitude of Shovell towards James II at this juncture? Both his early patrons, Myngs and Narbrough, had been favourites of the then Duke of York and his own

10   Davies, 'James II', p. 85.
11   Powley, *Revolution of 1688*, p. 69.
12   Davies, 'James II', p. 85.
13   The feeling was mutual as Dartmouth was quoted on the subject of Herbert by Burnet: 'was universally hated by the seaman of any man that ever commanded at sea.'
14   'Herbert's creatures': Peter Le Fevre, 'Tangier, the Navy and Its Connection with the Glorious Revolution of *1688*', *Mariner's Mirror*, Vol. 73 (United Kingdom: Society for Nautical Research 1987), p. 189.
15   Davies, 'James II', p. 95.

career had been promoted by his future King. James had been the all-powerful Lord High Admiral from 1660–1673 in the formative years of Shovell's naval career. In the Dutch wars, James had been the commander-in-chief at the Battles of Lowestoft in 1665 and Sole Bay in 1672. Indeed, Shovell was actually serving in James' flagship, the *Prince*, at the latter battle. As late as 5 October 1688, James II had asked Dartmouth to 'let Shovell and Skelton know if this war continues they will soon be better mounted after the first brush shall be over.'[16] Clearly this meant promotion to a bigger and better ship. Shovell must have felt a certain loyalty towards the existing King. Any bond between the two men would be finally and irretrievably ruptured when, two years later, Shovell shot up the Royal Guards, in front of James, in Dublin Bay.

We have already seen that Shovell had a close relationship with Herbert in the period 1679–83 out in the Mediterranean, and that both men thought highly of each other. This was somewhat surprising as Herbert was a hard-living, womanising, foul-mouthed and heavy-drinking man. Shovell was quite the opposite, being faithful to his wife, drinking little alcohol and not using profane language. As we have seen earlier, Henry FitzRoy, 1st Duke of Grafton was also an intimate of Shovell's, again from their time together in the Mediterranean. Matt Aylmer was a friend of Shovell's and Edward Russell had been a close colleague. Shovell had been brought up an Anglican from his mother's knee and had no time for Catholicism or 'Popery' as he would have called it. Therefore, with these connections, it is not surprising that despite past loyalties to James II, Shovell went over to the cause of William of Orange.

In April 1688, Shovell had joined the 48-gun *Dover*, in which he would spend the next year, and then in following month he had waited at Tilbury on James II, the King with whom he would soon be at odds. That June, whilst in the Downs, Shovell and his crew were informed of the birth of a son to James II. The newborn child was the Prince of Wales, James Edward, afterwards known as the Old Pretender.[17] Lieutenant Francis Wivell who had transferred with Shovell, from the *Anne* to the *Dover* wrote: 'we hereing the Joyfull news of A Prince being Borne & Joy was demonstrated by firreing guns & Spread y Coulours.'[18] It would not be long before Shovell's warmth towards his king and the new prince would cool. In late June–early July, the *Dover* was sent, by Roger Strickland, on two cruises, off Orfordness and Sole Bay, to gain intelligence of Dutch movements. By 19 July, the *Dover* was back at the Nore and Wivell recorded: 'the King Came on Or Shipp & at night ye King went to London.'[19]

By 2 October Shovell, still in the *Dover*, had accompanied Strickland to the Nore, before going on to the Gunfleet and then back to the South Foreland on the 4th. On the 14th, Pepys wrote to Dartmouth stating that: 'his majesty approves your sending Shovell to the Gunfleet, and the cautions that you have given him.'[20] Just what were these cautions? Shovell was at the Gunfleet when, on 23 October, he wrote to Dartmouth his thanks for the ships put under his command and stating how he would use them to gain intelligence of the Dutch.

---

16 HMC: Dartmouth MS, App V, p. 144. Charles Skelton would drown in the *Coronation* disaster of 1691.
17 The child was born on 10 June and the news reached Shovell on the 11th.
18 NMM: RMT MS, MAT 26 (29), extract Francis Wivell, journals *of the Dover* 1679–1694.
19 NMM: RMT MS, MAT 26 (29), extract Francis Wivell, journals *of the Dover* 1679–1694.
20 HMC: Dartmouth MS, Appendix V, p. 161.

Unfortunately, Shovell's letter book between 23 October and 26 December 1688 had no entries and the log of the *Dover* for this period is not available in the National Archives. Did the lack of entries in his letter book indicate that he was concerned about putting anything down on paper at this critical juncture? It is likely that Shovell was present at the crucial councils of war, on 26 October and the 28th, when the fateful decision was made not to sail to the Dutch coast as James II and William Jennens would have liked. Undoubtedly he took part in the caballing that took place in the fleet during late October.

According to some sources, the Protestant commanders at the Gunfleet, including Shovell, had decided that it was better to avoid meeting the Dutch fleet under Herbert, rather than being put into the invidious position of declining to fight. This may have been a factor behind the decision to remain in the Gunfleet rather than sail to the Dutch coast. James II thought that two thirds of his captains would refuse to fight.[21] More conservatively, Edward Russell believed the number to be eight. On 13 November, he wrote to Herbert: 'captains were resolved to salute my Lord Dartmouth and come over to us the names Berry, Deane, Hastings, Delaval, Churchill, Aylmer, Shovell, Berkeley.'[22] If Russell was correct, this places Shovell at the centre of the conspiracy. Later, James felt the main motive behind the naval officers' behaviour in November 1688 was 'fear of losing their command.'[23] In the actuality, the eight naval officers did not defect to William of Orange and remained with Dartmouth's fleet until its final surrender at Spithead.

On 30 October Dartmouth received accurate intelligence that William of Orange's fleet, under Herbert, was preparing to sail and he attempted to get his own ships around the Gunfleet shoal to meet them.[24] On 1 November with the advantage of a brisk north-easterly gale, Herbert's 59 ships, including 32 ships of the line, sailed from Hellevoetsluis into the open sea. The 'Protestant wind', which allowed Herbert to sail down the English Channel, trapped Dartmouth's ships behind sandbanks in the Gunfleet until 3 November. By this time Herbert's fleet was off Dover. On 5 November William of Orange came ashore at Brixham, in Devonshire, with Dartmouth still struggling past Beachy Head.

At this juncture, Dartmouth held a council of war at which it was decided not to attack what he believed to be a greatly superior force, although in reality the two fleets were of a comparable size. Any suggestion that Dartmouth did not wish to fight Herbert is erroneous as there was a mutual antipathy between the two men. At this stage, storms forced Dartmouth and his ships back to the Downs where they remained until 16 November. On this day they sailed to the west once more, and by the 19th, actually saw the Dutch fleet in Torbay, before further storms drove them back up the Channel again to seek shelter at Spithead. In the first week of November, the *Dover* had been away from the main fleet cruising independently and thus Shovell was not part of the 5 November council that declined to take on Herbert's supposedly superior number of ships. However, he was back with Dartmouth at the Downs by 9 November and certainly took part in the drive up the

21   Davies, 'James II', p. 86.

22   Britisl Library (BL): Egerton MS 2621, f. 47, Edward Russell to Arthur Herbert, 13 November 1688.

23   James Clarke, *The Life of James II*, Vol. II (London: Longman 1816), pp. 233–4; Davies, 'James II', p. 92.

24   Richmond, *Instrument of Policy*, p. 196.

Channel to Torbay and then back to Spithead. Dartmouth's fleet remained at Spithead until it surrendered to William on 13 December.[25]

Between 20–22 November, Lieutenant George Byng, of the *Defiance*, a leading conspirator against James II, was allowed ashore at Gosport, supposedly to visit his relatives, but actually to make contact with William of Orange. After a hard ride by horse, dressed as a farmer, Byng made contact with Edward Russell and then William, at Sherborne, in Dorset. Here Byng assured William the support of Orangist officers in the fleet. Then he returned to the fleet carrying a letter from William for Dartmouth making it clear that he should now desert James II. The letter was smuggled into Dartmouth's privy by Matt Aylmer so that it could be studied in private. Initially, Dartmouth's response was cool, but he was furious to learn that James was planning to send the infant Prince of Wales to France. Dartmouth was concerned that if he assisted the removal of the infant Prince he might be guilty of treason.[26] That same day, Byng and Wolfran Cornwall were sent to watch a house in Portsmouth where the baby son of James was supposed to be, prior to being taken by Roger Strickland to France. Then Dartmouth sent Shovell, Matt Aylmer and Anthony Hastings, in their respective ships, to stop this unauthorised egress from the harbour. Despite the fact that the Prince's baggage had been put aboard the *Mary Yacht*, the baby was returned to London on the Duke of Powis' coach. Shovell, in the *Dover*, was not called into action.[27] On 9 December, the Queen [Mary of Modena] and her baby son left Whitehall for Gravesend, where they embarked on the *Isabella Yacht* for France. They were graciously received by Louis XIV and sumptuously housed.[28]

Finally, on 23 December, James II left England via Rochester and on Christmas Day he heard mass in France. He would never return to his throne or even set foot again in England. The immediate cause for the loss of his kingdom was naval: the loyal Dartmouth had failed to defeat Herbert's Dutch fleet, which allowed William of Orange to disembark troops in England. Naively, James was surprised that the seaman had placed religion before loyalty to their sovereign. Cloudesley Shovell would move seamlessly from one king to another. It was very much a Protestant wind in November 1688.

25 Davies, 'James II', p. 84.
26 Davies, 'James II', p. 86.
27 Powley, *Revolution of 1688*, pp. 137–8.
28 West, *Admiral Russell*, p. 101.

11

Action in Irish Waters 1689–1690

Following the Glorious Revolution, William of Orange, as William III, reigned jointly with his wife Mary, the elder daughter of James II. James had fled to France and was keen to regain his throne in England. He had the support of Louis XIV, partly as a brother catholic and also as a champion of the divine right of kings. Ireland could be used as a stepping stone by James to regain his English throne and would have the added attraction of distracting William from his conflict with the French king in the Spanish Netherlands. This was part of the Nine Years' War [1688–97] fought between Louis XIV and a grand alliance of William, the Holy Roman Emperor, Leopold I, Victor Amadeus II, Duke of Savoy and Charles II of Spain.[1] Whilst in France, James had sent money to build up an army to support his Lord Deputy in Ireland, the Earl of Tyrconnell. In March 1689, James II in person, entered southern Ireland with French forces before moving to Dublin. He hoped to gain rapid control over all Ireland before moving on to Scotland and England, but the Protestant enclaves in the north precluded this possibility. The Battle of Bantry Bay resulted from the landing of further troops and supplies in Southern Ireland for James. Cloudesley Shovell would have a major role in this first naval battle of the Nine Years' War.

Early 1689 saw Shovell, in the 48-gun *Dover*, frequently on the move in the service of William III.[2] He had transferred his loyalty effortlessly from one king to another. January found Shovell in the Channel Islands seeking to ascertain whether the French were occupying them or not. Two months later, Phineas Bowles replaced the redoubtable Samuel Pepys as Secretary to the Admiralty. Bowles and Shovell knew each other intimately from the former's time as secretary to Lord Dartmouth and then later to Arthur Herbert. Around this time Shovell was offered the command of the 70-gun *Kent* and he wrote to his friend, the new Secretary to the Admiralty,[3] stating that he had never refused a commission to a bigger ship before. Shovell wished to carry to the *Kent* his surgeon and 100–150 men, some of whom had been under his command for seven to 10 years. 'I humbly beg their honours pardon that I do not remove till I hear further and rather they give me leave to continue

---

1   Also known as the War of the Grand Alliance or the War of the League of Augsburg.

2   A convention of the Houses of Lords and Commons, on 13 February 1689, declared William and his wife Mary, King and Queen.

3   John Ehrman, *The Navy in the War of William III 1688–97* (Cambridge: Cambridge University Press 1953), pp. 289–93.

where I am than remove into the best ship in England without my men.'[4] Although it was usual for captains to take a number of crew with them on transfer to a new ship, 150 men plus the fact that some had served with him for 10 years, is indicative of Shovell's leadership skills and popularity with the common sailor. In the event Shovell did not join the *Kent* at that time.

Although Shovell did not join the *Kent*, he took command of the 70-gun *Edgar* on 27 March 1689, taking with him a number of men who were close to him. They included John Flaxman, a midshipman, Thomas Shovell, an able seaman, and John Jenkenson, another able seaman. Judging by their names, they were all related to him.[5] Thirteen years earlier, in his boat-burning exploits off Tripoli, Shovell had come to national attention. In his new ship, the *Edgar*, he would play one of the leading roles in the forthcoming Battle of Bantry Bay.

Louis XIV fitted out a fleet of 25 ships under Jean Gabaret at Brest. It carried James II and 5,000 men to Kinsale in Southern Ireland where they arrived on 12 March 1689 and went ashore to a rapturous welcome. Then Gabaret took his ships back to Brest without meeting any English ships. Catholic Ireland, with the exception of Ulster, was pro-James and anti-William who was slow to respond despite repeated warnings of the danger building up there. He was loath to send the English fleet to Ireland as he feared wrongly that the ships' captains might not be loyal to him. Eventually, on 11 March, the day before James landed in Ireland, William appointed Arthur Herbert, as admiral-of-the fleet and commander-in-chief in the Channel and Irish waters. He was to cruise between Ushant and the Irish coast to preclude the French sending troops to Ireland and Scotland.[6] It took some time for Herbert to get his fleet together as ships had to be collected from eastern and western ports with the usual supply difficulties. It was not until early April that Herbert was able to sail with his fleet from Spithead for the Irish coast. He spent most of the month of April off Cork and Kinsale before inclement weather forced him to seek shelter at Milford Haven at the end of the month.

Whilst Herbert and his ships were trapped at Milford Haven, Louis Francois de Rousselet, Comte de Châteaurenault, a short, stockily-built Breton noble,[7] with 25 ships sailed from Brest carrying around 1,500 troops, their arms, ammunition and money for James in Ireland. The French fleet was commanded in the van by Jean Gabaret in the 56-gun *Saint Michel*, in the centre by Châteaurenault in the 66-gun *Ardent* and in the rear by the experienced Job Forant in the 56-gun *Le Courageux*. Finally, Herbert sailed from Milford Haven on 27 April intending to lie off Brest, but the wind from the east made him alter course for Kinsale. On the 29th, the two fleets were made aware of the presence of each other and Châteaurenault with an easterly wind and knowing that Herbert was off Kinsale, his original destination, made the sensible decision to sail around Cape Clear to Bantry Bay. He anchored in the Bay on the 30th. Meanwhile Herbert's ships lay off Kinsale where they

---

4   KCA: Marsham MS U1515.012, Shovell to Phineas Bowles, 14 March 1689.

5   Flaxman was the surname of Cloudesley's stepfather: Jenkenson was the maiden name of Cloudesley's mother.

6   Peter Le Fevre, 'The battle of Bantry Bay, 1 May 1689', *The Irish Sword*, Vol. XVIII (Dublin: The Military History Society of Ireland 1990), pp. 2–3.

7   Shovell's contemporary Henry Killigrew had problems with the name and called him 'Chatternaw'.

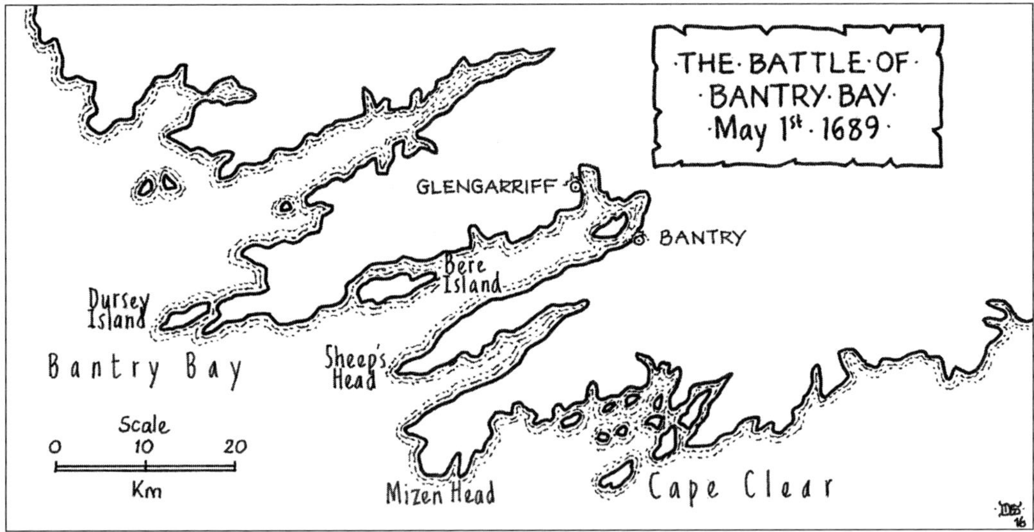

Map 13 The Battle of Bantry Bay May 1st 1689.

anticipated that the French landing would be. Eventually, on the 30th, they would follow the French to Bantry Bay and await the morrow for battle.

On 30 April, Châteaurenault took his ships into Bantry Bay on the south-west coast of Ireland; the bay was 22 miles from north-east to south-west; two miles wide at the head and six miles wide at the entrance; the town of Bantry lay at the head of the bay. Inside the Bay, the initial French anchorage was close to the Sheep's Head and some 12 miles south-west of Bantry. Châteaurenault began the laborious task of unloading the 1,500 troops and their supplies. Frigates and fireships were used to carry men and their rations to Balgoben on Bantry Creek, the final point of disembarkation.[8] One of the French passengers, John Stevens, an English Roman Catholic, was singularly unimpressed with what he saw: 'a miserable poor place, not worthy the name of a town, having not above seven or eight houses, the rest very mean cottages.'[9] Five hours after the start of the disembarkation, Châteaurenault's scouts reported that the English fleet had been seen and were lying off the bay. Hurriedly, around midnight, the remaining troops, in many cases much against their will, were deposited on the nearby rocks as Châteaurenault prepared his ships for battle.

1 May 1689, was a clear day with the wind from the east-north-east and gale force in strength. Herbert's fleet of around 22 ships lay some four miles from the Mizen Head, to the south of Bantry Bay, and he gave the signal to form the line of battle. Amongst the English captains were many who had or would later feature in Cloudesley Shovell's naval career. George Rooke, John Leake, Ralph Delaval and the Irish brothers, George and Matthew Aylmer were all participants in the coming battle. The English fleet sailed around the

---

8   Balgoben was at the head of Glengarriff Bay, just to the north of the town of Bantry. Some accounts gave Bantry itself as the point of disembarkation. See Edward Powley, *The Naval Side of King William's War* (London: John Baker 1972), pp. 156–7, note 8.

9   Le Fevre, 'The battle of Bantry Bay', p. 8.

Sheep's Head and the French were spotted at anchor close to the mouth of the bay. The number of French ships involved in the coming battle was estimated by their English opponents as between 28 and 33, superior in number to themselves. Herbert's ships sailed into the Bay with difficulty, tacking in line, as the wind was against them. Knowing that he had the advantage of the wind, Châteaurenault was not keen to fight prior to 11:00 a.m. with the turn of the insetting tide. The French ships hugged the rocky, south-eastern shore of the Bay and shielded their transports. They moved away from the English ships in the direction of the town of Bantry and it was 10:00 a.m. before the action began. Herbert raised the red flag under his crosstrees at the topmast head and the fight was soon to begin.[10]

The only way that Herbert's ships could advance up Bantry Bay was by persistent tacking as the wind was against them. John Ashby in the *Defiance* led the English van with Shovell's *Edgar*, next to Herbert's *Elizabeth* in the centre. The exact order of the English line is uncertain. The most probable point of contact between the two sides was well up the Bay close to Bantry where it is at its narrowest. Châteaurenault swung his ships into an orderly line. The *Defiance,* was soon in action against three French ships who came within pistol shot firing all the time. After nearly an hour of battering, the *Francois* which had been attacking the *Defiance,* collided with one of its seconds and Ashby, making the most of his opportunity, hammered away at them. Eventually, he was forced away to leeward to repair his damaged rigging before his masts fell down. Herbert, in the *Elizabeth,* engaged Châteaurenault's *Ardent,* with the result that the English ship's mainmast was shot away. Herbert was forced to break off the action until around noon when he re-engaged Châteaurenault.

At this juncture Herbert stood to the south in the direction of the sea so that his line of battle might be better kept and with the vain hope that he might gain the all-important advantage of the wind. In essence the battle was fought in an anticlockwise fashion around the narrow Bantry Bay. The French remained to windward and much of the English shot did not reach them. Ralph Sanderson's *Woolwich*, with damage to her masts and rigging and two guns split, was forced a little out of the line. George Aylmer in the *Portland* was mortally wounded although he lived long enough to make an oral will.

What of Cloudesley Shovell's role in this sharp engagement? We saw earlier that his ship, the *Edgar,* was positioned in the line of battle next to Herbert's *Elizabeth.* He was heavily engaged and although a contemporary biography recorded that the casualties in his ship exceeded those in all the other ships put together, this was not the case.[11] It is true that 13 men were killed and 42 more wounded serving in the *Edgar* that day, but Ashby's *Defiance* had 22 men killed with 40 wounded and Herbert's *Elizabeth* had 15 killed and 27 wounded. Records show that the *Edgar's* masts, sails and rigging had been seriously damaged. Masts and yards: foreyard shot through in the quarter; mainmast in three places; foremast in two places; mizzenmast in two places one quite through; crossjack yard shot in pieces; maintopmast disabled. Rigging and sails: standing and running rigging and sails much shattered; mainstay shot in two places. Hull: several shots under water and not withstanding any endeavours to stop the leaks, we can but just free her with one pump in fair weather. Guns: two lower and three upper guns split. Boats: longboat sunk.[12]

---

10   Le Fevre, 'The battle of Bantry Bay', p. 9.
11   Anon, *Secret Memoirs*, p. 19.
12   Le Fevre, 'The battle of Bantry Bay', p. 14.

One of the 42 men wounded in the *Edgar* during the battle was a midshipman, Stephen Martin. Late that afternoon, he had the misfortune to have his left thigh broken by a cannonball which also, before reaching him, had taken a man's legs off. He was carried below for the surgeon to attend to. Confusion reigned on the lower deck as there were so many casualties requiring attention at the same time. Martin was barely conscious from loss of blood and pain when he realised that the surgeon was about to amputate his injured leg. At this news Martin revived himself, refused to have his leg cut off, crying out that he would live or die with it on. The surgeon changed his mind and set the leg, but so badly that the agonizing procedure had to be repeated or the leg would have been completely useless. Martin had saved his limb but it was to be shorter than the other one, resulting in a limp for the rest of his life. Shovell was characteristically kind and supportive of the wounded young man. He offered to make him his lieutenant once he had recovered fully and provided a certificate of good standing as well. Martin, through affection, preferred to join John Leake who would later become his brother-in-law.[13] One of the other midshipmen in the *Edgar* was the youthful John Norris, a Shovell protégé, who would rise to be an admiral-of-the-fleet and whose future career would be intimately related to that of his current captain.[14]

John Leake, like Shovell, was another man to enhance his reputation in the battle. Although he was only in the *Firedrake*, classified as a fireship but in fact used as a bomb ketch, he managed to cause considerable damage to the French ship of Alain, Marquis de Coëtlogon, the *Diament*, which was set on fire with Leake's father's invention the 'cushee piece' or mortar. An explosion was triggered by the ignition of ammunition in the captain's cabin. From this time on, bomb ketches became a feature in every English fleet. Leake did not seem to be keen on this new weapon, possibly because his brother had lost his life in an accident with it. Leake's fine performance was brought to Herbert's attention and led to his promotion.[15]

At 5:00 p.m., Châteaurenault, having had the best of the afternoon's fighting, tacked away from the English fleet and sailed back into Bantry Bay. Herbert's ships stood off to sea and the six-hour Battle of Bantry Bay was over. Châteaurenault had had the superior force and the advantage of the wind and he might have comprehensively defeated the English at this point. Two factors were against him: firstly his fireships were unavailable as they were unloading troops; secondly he had a problem with his leading subordinates Gabaret and Forant. Both men were senior in service to Châteaurenault but did not have his aristocratic background. The near 70-year-old Gabaret had already safely carried the deposed James II to Ireland and no doubt wondered why he did not have the overall command. In any event, it was suggested that they had tacitly avoided pressing home the advantage. However, the French had achieved what they had set out to do and that was to deliver men and supplies to Bantry. Quietly they slipped away to France and arrived at Brest on 8 May.[16] Later in France, Châteaurenault was severely criticised for failing to turn a tactical victory into

---

13   They would marry sisters.

14   Clements Markham (ed), *Life of Captain Stephen Martin* (London: Navy Records Society 1895), pp. 8–9.

15   Martin-Leake, *John Leake*, Vol. I, pp. 22–3.

16   John Laughton (ed), *Memoirs Relating to Lord Torrington* (London: Camden Society 1889), p. 38; Laird Clowes, *Royal Navy*, Vol. II, p. 329.

overall superiority at sea. After the battle, in Dublin, James II somewhat reluctantly ordered the singing of the *Te Deum* and a firework display.

Herbert's fleet had been considerably mauled and made for the Isles of Scilly, looking for reinforcements and then it set sail for Portsmouth, arriving there on 12 May.[17] The English losses at Bantry Bay were 96 killed and 250 wounded.[18] The dead included George Aylmer, the brother of Matt, who was buried at sea – 'was this morning thrown overboard.' It was reported that the French had 40 killed and 93 wounded.[19] In England, Herbert's performance with the weaker fleet, was generally approved.[20] William III went in person to Portsmouth to meet those who had distinguished themselves in his cause. *The London Gazette* recorded the scene:

> Portsmouth, May 15th. Admiral Herbert, with the Chief Officers of the fleet, met His Majesty near the main Guard, and attended Him on Board the Elizabeth, where he splendidly entertained His Majesty at Dinner. The King was pleased, as a Mark of his great Satisfaction in the Conduct and good Services of Admiral Herbert, to declare His Royal Intention of Conferring upon him the Title and Dignity of an Earl of this Kingdom. And was likewise pleased to confer the Honor of Knighthood upon Capt. John Ashby of the Defiance and Capt. Clowdesley Shovell of the Edgar. And farther, to encourage the Seamen, His Majesty was Graciously pleased to bestow upon such of them as were in the late Engagement with the French, a Donative of 10s. a Man, which was distributed accordingly, amounting to 2600l. The Officers, and all the Seamen of the fleet, exprefs'd on this Occasion the greatest joy and loyalty that can be imagined, accompanied with loud Shouts and Huzza's, and with all the Demonstrations of a brave Resolution to employ their lives in their Majesties Service.[21]

Thus Cloudesley Shovell became a knight on 15 May 1689, in his 39th year. Arthur Herbert was made Earl of Torrington at the same ceremony aboard his flagship the *Elizabeth*.[22] There was no apparent reason for the awards and it has been suggested that in reality they were for services rendered during the Glorious Revolution.[23] At dinner William III asked Herbert: 'how he durst engage the French fleet with such disadvantage.' Herbert replied: 'he was forced to do it for his own security, or his seamen would have cast him overboard.' The new King was pleased by this comment.[24]

Following the Battle of Bantry Bay, war was officially declared between England and France. James II's troops swept from the south to the north of Ireland. The Protestants of Ulster retired into Londonderry and Enniskillen. In April 1689, a Jacobite army began the

17   Laughton, *Torrington*, p. 38; Richmond, *Instrument of Policy*, p. 204.
18   Powley, *King William's War*, p. 142.
19   Powley, *King William's War*, p. 141.
20   Richmond, *Instrument of Policy*, p. 204.
21   *The London Gazette*, No 2454, 16–20 May 1689.
22   Initially he was created Earl of Torbay and the title was later changed to Earl of Torrington.
23   *DNB*, Herbert [Laughton].
24   Le Fevre, 'The battle of Bantry Bay', p. 11.

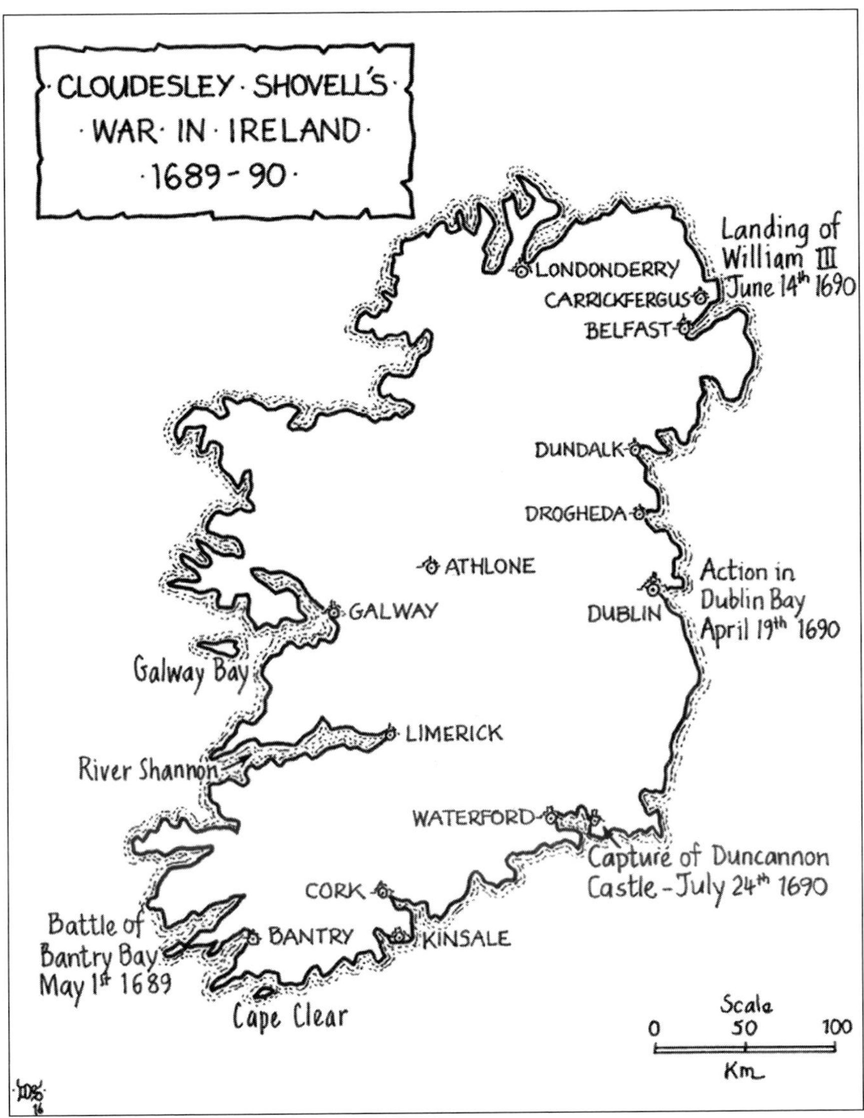

Map 14 Cloudesley Shovell's War in Ireland 1689-1690.

siege of Londonderry and by July the defenders were starving and on the point of surrendering. At this juncture, John Leake and George Rooke managed to get ships down the lough into the River Foyle to relieve them. The following month the Marshal Frederick Schomberg landed with William III's army in Antrim. However, there was to be no decision on land in 1689.

The French had missed a golden opportunity by failing to follow up their advantage gained at Bantry Bay. Anne Hilarion de Costentin, Comte de Tourville, with the Toulon squadron, passed through the Strait of Gibraltar in early July with the intention of joining the 20 ships at Brest. This possibility had been foreseen by the English who had sent Herbert with a fleet of over 40 vessels to stop this junction and Shovell was a part of it. However, Tourville managed to slip into Brest under cover of fog. In October 1689, Herbert removed Shovell from the *Edgar* and sent him to the 60-gun *Monck* which had been designated for service in the West Indies.[25] But the seriousness of the situation in Ireland soon aborted this voyage. The following December, Lord Berkeley of Stratton sailed with 26 ships to search for the French.[26] Berkeley sent Shovell, with a detached squadron, to the Irish coast to gain intelligence of French movements.

So 1689 came to a close: if it had been an inconclusive year for the war in Ireland, it had been a successful one for Cloudesley Shovell personally, with a knighthood for his valour in Bantry Bay and for his services to the Glorious Revolution.

Shovell would spend much of his time in 1690 in Irish waters commanding a squadron which was responsible for maintaining the supply route from England to the soldiers in Ireland. He remained in the *Monck* or as he knew it, the *Monk,* and was principally based at Hoylake [Highlake] and Milford Haven with regular excursions into the Irish Sea. In March, Shovell complained that he had only 15 ships as opposed to the France's forty.[27] During April, he took his squadron, consisting of seven major vessels, a fireship and four tenders, from Hoylake across to the Irish coast. Then on 19 April 1690, he went into Dublin Bay and a vigorous action took place in the presence of James II himself. This led to a final rupture of the relationship between the two men with subsequent mutual loathing. Shovell described the encounter to Major-General Piercy Kirke, an army commander in Ireland, and former boon companion of Arthur Herbert in Tangier:

> I make bold to trouble your honour with an account of my going into Dublin and what happened there ----. On ye 19th in the morning we stood into Dublin bay and saw a ship about a mile within ye Barr at a place called Polebege [Poolbeg] after we anchored in the bay I went aboard ye Monmouth yaucth [yacht] and at a little more than half flood ye wind which was northerly which made a smooth barr and having water enough I with ye yaucth,[28] two hoys, a ketch and ye pinnaces went over ye barr upon which ye ship run higher up about a mile and a half to a place called Salmon Pool: and there run aground within shot of Frenchman of 12 guns, and also an English ship or two filled with soldiers of ye Kings guards and kept firing at us: we followed him and gave him battle but he defended himself for above an hour and a halfe, then I made a sign for ye fireship to come in which when they saw coming in they forsook their ship and got ashore in their boats. We went aboard and got out an anchor and by heaving some of her things overboard we got her off; they filled this Frenchman of 12 guns full of men and also five or six other small ships and made a show of sayleing therefore I expected they would have attacked us but they never offered at us: the wind weared out of ye sea and in turning out one of our hoys about a mile and a half within ye barr: run aground so that we could not get her off before ye water fell away, therefore we lay

<hr>

25 Peter Le Fevre and Richard Harding (eds), *Precursors of Nelson* (London: Chatham 2000), p. 51.
26 John Berkeley, 3rd Baron Berkeley of Stratton [1663–97].
27 HMC: Finch MS, Vol. II, p. 273.
28 Alas today [2013] there is a power station at Poolbeg making it difficult to imagine the scene as Shovell saw it.

by her and took her guns and other things out ready to heave off next high water, at low water ye Hoy was dry round and many thousand people came upon ye sand also King James was there as were his guards, we lay in our boats armed to keep ye enemy from attempting the Hoy and two Protestants among many others that were running about ye sand at length came running to us and we took them in, likewise ye Guards to show their briskness came rideing near us, Among the rest a Frenchman came rideing to ye water and called us in English as well as he could speak a great many hard names and fired his pistols at us, we shott down his horse and rowed ashore ye Frenchman slipped his legs out of his boots and run away, but ye saylors went ashor and unrigged his horse. Ye ship we took was the Pelican ye biggest of ye scotch men of war taken last summer by ye French and she lay there in order to take in some of King James ill gotten goods which he forced from poor Protestants for his damned brass money.[29] In this ship was twenty guns and she had upward of forty men, two or three we found dead upon deck and one mortally wounded we also found a Spaniard and an Englishman which were forced aboard her – they inform us that twelve men were killed and several others wounded that went ashoar ----.

The Protestants that came to us are people of no intelligence and can tell us no more than what your Honour already know: they think there is two regiments besides ye Royall Regiment in Dublin: and two or three companies of French white coats are come to town: tis talked that King James will make one of his regiments his Royal Regiment which have so much displeased ye Irish: that they are ready to go together by ye ears and some have already killed about it: nothing else but my humble service to your honour.[30]

Shovell wrote a similar letter to James Southerne, who had replaced Phineas Bowles as the Secretary to the Admiralty. He had been directly responsible for the taking of the *Pelican* with its cargo of hides and tallow. Additionally Shovell had saved the hoy from the clutches of the French. His comments about 'King James ill gotten goods which he forced from poor Protestants' made quite clear Shovell's feelings for his former sovereign. As was recorded earlier in this account, the contempt Shovell held James II in was entirely reciprocated, as James was said to have conceived a mortal aversion to him. In turn, Shovell was reputed to have no more heeded James' threats than formerly he did his promises.[31] In some quarters Shovell was criticised for shooting the ex-King's guards in the royal presence – a charge that had been trumped up by James' friends.[32] Others saw Shovell's action in Dublin Bay in a different light: 'Cloudesley Shovell bravely fell upon the French ships in the sight of James II and he has retaken a scotch man of war taken last summer.'[33] The action was even celebrated in a ballad 'The Courageous Commander.'[34]

---

29   Lacking gold and silver in Ireland, as much had been sent to England for safe-keeping, James II had emergency brass money minted for him in Dublin.
30   KCA: Marsham MS U1515.012, Shovell to Piercy Kirke, around 26 April 1690.
31   Anon, *Secret Memoirs*, pp. 24–5.
32   Anon, *Secret Memoirs*, pp. 24–5.
33   Historical Manuscripts Commission (HMC): Portland MS, E. Harley to Sir Edward Harley, 26 April 1690.
34   Charles Firth, *Naval Songs and Ballads* (London: Navy Records Society 1908), pp. 106–7.

In this little conflict in Dublin Bay, Shovell had demonstrated considerable dash, courage and resolution. However, it has to be questioned why, as the squadron commander, he was hazarding his person in a small boat with the tide going out and in close proximity to the enemy. As commander-in-chief in the Mediterranean in 1707 he would put himself in danger in a similar manner on the River Var. In both cases it can be argued that he should have directed operations safely from his flagship, in the manner of his patron John Narbrough, during their boat-burning exploits of 1676. However, Shovell was renowned for always being forward in action and brave to a fault. In this respect he was similar to that other Norfolk sailor, Horatio Nelson, a century later.

After his adventures in Dublin Bay, Shovell returned to more prosaic duties. He patrolled the Irish Sea, sometimes sending ships through St George's Channel to Waterford and beyond. In May 1690, Shovell was taken ill whilst out cruising. The nature of this illness is unknown, although he was subject to malaria, gout and quinsies. Shovell's indisposition did not last long although it did stop him from writing reports for a few days. During the same month, Shovell appointed Edmund Loades to be the *Dover's* lieutenant. 'Mr Loades is a pretty seaman and has gone to sea from his childhood and about two years last has served as a midshipman and masters mate.'[35] Loades was the bachelor son of John Narbrough's favourite sister and he would drown, as Shovell's Flag Captain, with the rest of the crew of the *Association*, in October 1707. Nepotism was an integral part of the 17th century navy. In late May, Shovell's barge capsized on the entry to Hoylake and the lieutenant of the *Monck* was drowned. He was replaced by: 'Mr Robert Hancock who has served under my [Shovell's] command for nine years and is at present my chief mate ----.'[36] Hancock, as the captain of the *Eagle*, was another man to drown with Shovell in the Isles of Scilly.

In Ireland, the land campaign had gone badly for William's troops under Marshal Frederick Schomberg. William felt the time had come for him to lead his troops in person as it was essential that Ireland be dealt with so that he might concentrate on his main front in Flanders. By mid-June, an army of 27,000 men was collected at Hoylake, this to be carried across the Irish Sea in transport ships. A squadron of six ships under Shovell, in the *Monck*, was to provide protection for their journey to Carrickfergus. William had travelled to Hoylake with a commission, dated 3 June 1690, making Shovell Rear-Admiral of the Blue. This was his first commission to be a flag officer and he recorded 'humble and hearty thanks' in his letter book.[37] As early as January 1690, there had been plans to raise Shovell to flag rank, but there had been rumours that he was involved in a fleet plot against the new king. By May his name had been cleared and the new appointment went ahead.

On 10 June, William III came on board the *Mary Yacht* under the command of the experienced Greenvile Collins, of coastal chart fame. The next day the King, escorted by Shovell's squadron and with the troops in 250 transports, set off from Hoylake for Ireland. The journey was not an easy one with thick fog reducing visibility to two ships' lengths and for a time Shovell lost sight of the *Mary Yacht*.[38] Eventually four days later the fleet safely

---

35   KCA: Marsham MS U1515.012, Shovell to unknown recipient possibly the Commissioners of the Admiralty, May 1690.

36   KCA: Marsham MS U1515.012, Shovell letter as for the above.

37   KCA: Marsham MS U1515.012, Shovell letter book, *Monck* at Carrickfergus, 14 June 1690.

38   Powley, *King William's War*, p. 357.

reached Carrickfergus. That afternoon William was rowed ashore in Shovell's barge and travelled to Belfast where he met his land commanders.[39] Shovell spent four days revictualling his ships at Carrickfergus before waiting on William at Belfast. He received orders to rejoin the main fleet in England, under Arthur Herbert, now Earl of Torrington. Shovell sailed on 18 June, but did not reach Milford Haven until the 23rd because of a calm sea and lack of wind.[40]

Whilst Shovell had been active in the seas around Ireland, Edward Russell had been sent with a squadron of 30 ships, plus 400 merchant vessels and Princess Anna Maria, to Spain.[41] Russell reached Corunna in March and had returned to England by the end of April. Henry Killigrew with a squadron of 13 ships had been ordered to the Mediterranean in early March to defend the trade there and to shadow the Toulon squadron. Unfortunately, neither Shovell's ships nor Killigrew's would be available to Torrington in the major naval battle of 1690, off Beachy Head. This would have catastrophic consequences for Torrington in the coming battle. In May, the French Toulon squadron slipped past Killigrew and was able to join the Comte de Tourville with the principal French fleet at Brest, in time for the Battle of Beachy Head on 30 June. Killigrew returned from the Mediterranean in a dilatory fashion and did not reach Plymouth until a fortnight after the battle. At about the time that William III was landing at Carrickfergus, Tourville slipped out of Brest with the combined French fleet intent upon destroying an inferior English one, under Torrington, before it could be reinforced by Killigrew's and Shovell's ships.

On 21 June, Tourville and his fleet were reported to be off Falmouth and Torrington was ordered to put to sea. Torrington held a council of war and it was decided to try and get to the windward of the French and link up with Killigrew's and Shovell's squadrons if they were in the area. Failing this, Torrington would lead his fleet back up the English Channel, if necessary as far as the River Thames, in order to keep the fleet in being. If his missing squadrons had returned in time, Torrington would have had something like parity with the French and his 'fleet in being' would have precluded the possibility of a French invasion of England. Queen Mary, temporarily in charge in London in the absence of her husband, and her advisers were not happy with Torrington's strategy and gave him positive orders to attack. It is possible that one of the reasons behind the Queen's decision was the vulnerability of a fleet of merchantmen worth £700,000 who were west of the French fleet.

On 30 June 1690, off Beachy Head, the combined Anglo-Dutch fleet of 56 ships under Torrington swept down on Tourville's 68 ships. Torrington's fleet was severely mauled with 15 ships lost and the Dutch suffered particularly severely. The French had won a comprehensive victory with Torrington retiring back into the Downs. Surprisingly Tourville did not follow up his success with the total decimation of the English fleet. He contented himself with a threatening passage down the Channel and an attack on Teignmouth before returning to Brest. Torrington was blamed for the defeat and was clapped in the Tower of London to await court-martial. The diarist John Evelyn commented: 'the whole nation now exceedingly alarmed by the French fleet braving our coast even to the very Thames mouth;

---

39   Richmond, *Instrument of Policy*, p. 213; Philip Aubrey, *The Defeat of James Stuart's Armada* (Leicester: Leicester University Press 1979), p. 46.

40   KCA: Marsham MS U1515.012, Shovell letter book, 25 June 1690.

41   Princess Anna Maria of Neuburg had married King Charles II of Spain by proxy. It was his second marriage.

our fleet commanded by debauched young men, and likewise inferior in force, giving way to the enemy, to our exceeding reproach.[42] It was also said that: Torrington had: 'made us slaves to the French, knaves to the Dutch and cowards to the whole world.'[43]

What had happened to Killigrew's and Shovell's squadrons during the battle? As recorded earlier, Killigrew did not arrive back at Plymouth from the Mediterranean until a fortnight after the battle. Wisely, he retired into the Hamoaze and set up batteries to protect his ships from a possible French attack. Although some accounts record that Shovell acted as rear-admiral of the blue at the Battle of Beachy Head, this is incorrect.[44] Shovell, still in the *Monck*, had reached Milford Haven on 23 June and sailed on to Plymouth which he reached around 26 June. He had been ordered by Torrington to find the first secure harbour. In his letter book he recorded: 'this morning we went into Plymouth Sound which was not secure enough.'[45] Clearly, Shovell was not in a position to sail down the Channel with Tourville's fleet blocking the way and so during the Battle of Beachy Head, he was at Plymouth.

During the little over two weeks that he was at Plymouth, Shovell secured the post of commander of the *Pelican*, the ship that he had taken in Dublin Bay, for his protégé John Norris, the future admiral-of-the-fleet Sir John Norris. He described Norris as a 'very fit man for such a command for he is a diligent, sober and good officer.'[46] Shovell was ordered by William III to take his squadron to the west as there was intelligence that French frigates were being sent to St George's Channel to burn English transport vessels there. He sailed from Plymouth on 13 July, the day before Killigrew arrived there.[47] About this time, Queen Mary informed her husband: 'they tell me Shovell is the best officer of his age.'[48]

The Battle of Beachy Head had been disastrous for the naval interests of England, and more particularly so for Torrington who was largely blamed for the defeat. It was fortunate that on the very next day after the Battle of Beachy Head, 1 July, William III had won a major land victory at the Battle of the Boyne. This spelled defeat for James II in Ireland, with Dublin soon falling, and James himself fleeing from Kinsale. William reached Limerick but was checked there and so, in early September 1690, left for England; apart from the ports of the south-west, most of the Irish coast was then in his hands.

On 24 July 1690, Shovell participated in the taking of Duncannon Castle, a fortress on the south-west coast of Ireland whose guns commanded the entrance to the harbour of Waterford. On 27 July, in a letter to Major-General Piercy Kirke, an acquaintance from their Tangier days, he stated that he was off Waterford with 16 men-of-war. For the attack on Duncannon Castle, Shovell had transferred to the 32-gun *Experiment*, a shallower-draught

---

42   Esmond De Beer (ed), *The Diary of John Evelyn*, Vol. V (Oxford: Oxford University Press 1955), p. 928, entry for 6 July 1690.

43   West, *Admiral Russell*, p. 200; British Library (BL): Stowe MS, 305, f. 186.

44   Anonymous, *The Life and Glorious Actions of Sir Cloudesley Shovell* (London: D. Brown 1707), p. 3.

45   KCA: Marsham MS, U1515.012. Although the report is undated the entries in Shovell's letter book immediately before and after it bear the dates 25 June and 26 June respectively.

46   KCA: Marsham MS, U1515.012, Shovell to James Southerne, undated letter.

47   Although Sir John Laughton in the *Dictionary of National Biography* stated that Shovell and Killigrew, with their squadrons at Plymouth, to an extent controlled the movements of the French, it is unlikely that they were there together and thus the statement is suspect.

48   Eveline Cruikshanks, *The History of Parliament 1690–1715* (Woodbridge: Boydell and Brewer and online 2002), Shovell entry.

vessel than the *Monck*, for use in the Waterford River. The *Experiment*, with another frigate, the 16-gun *Greyhound* and all the boats of his squadron, were used in the assault on the castle. The castle's defenders fired upon them but agreed to surrender on the same terms that had been permitted earlier at Waterford. The next day, the governor of the castle, Colonel Michael Burke, 'Brute Burke', marched out at the head of 250 men leaving behind no less than 42 cannons. The sudden surrender of Duncannon Castle was the direct result of Shovell and his squadron.[49]

Following their success at Duncannon Castle, Shovell's squadron returned to Plymouth and then in the late summer, he and his ships were to be found on the west coast of Ireland at Limerick, where William III's siege failed, and Galway. In early September, Shovell was sent to Galway to deal with a French squadron under Marquis Charles-François Davy d'Amfreville. But, despite his best efforts, he was unable to find d'Amfreville who had returned to Brest. At around this time, Shovell wrote to Sir Robert Southwell, William III's principal secretary in Ireland, asking for a stronger squadron:

> I will take all opertunitys to putt his Majestie's commands in execution, but we can hope for small success if our enemy be stronger, for at sea, if the fleets be near equall, there must be great success to gaine a great victory; for by that time the one is beaten the other generally is wearey, Sir, we ought to make use of this opertunity, for since we have ships enough at sea, why not a squadron that will leave no doubt of a victory; for I believe nothing but necessity will obleage the French to give you such an opertunity as may prove.[50]

This was a view that Shovell held throughout his whole career and constantly repeated. His squadron was recalled from Irish waters and he reached the Downs on 10 October.[51] Shovell was met with orders to proceed to Plymouth and then to sail to the Soundings to ensure the safety of returning merchant vessels. Eventually, he returned once more to the Downs in the middle of January 1691.

After Beachy Head, Torrington was removed from command of the English fleet and following considerable debate, his place was taken by the joint commission of Richard Haddock, John Ashby, and Henry Killigrew. Initially, Queen Mary had told her husband, William, that she had heard Shovell was the best officer of the age, but this was not acted upon.[52] In September the fleet supported Marlborough in his successful efforts to take Kinsale and Cork, in the south-west of Ireland.[53] The year 1690 ended with William III in control of most of Ireland and the deposed James II back where he had started, in France.

---

49   Josiah Burchett, *A Complete History of the most remarkable transactions at sea* (London: J. Walthroe 1720), p. 432; Narcissus Luttrell, *A Brief Historical Relation of State Affairs from September 1678–April 1714*, Vol. II (Oxford: Oxford University Press 1857), p. 86; HMC: Finch MS, Vol. II, p. 387.

50   HMC: Finch MS, Vol. II, p. 453.

51   Burchett, *Transactions at Sea*, pp. 432–3; HMC: Finch MS, Vol. II, pp. 450–7.

52   Aubrey, *The Defeat*, p. 53.

53   John Churchill [1650–1722]. At the time he was the 1st Earl of Marlborough and later became the 1st Duke of Marlborough.

The final, sensational, event of 1690 was the trial of the unfortunate Arthur Herbert, Earl of Torrington. He was charged with 'keeping back and not engaging and coming into the fight and not relieving and assisting a known friend in need' – a potential capital offence. In December, Torrington was taken to the *Kent* frigate at Sheerness, where his court-martial was to be held. The president of the court was Ralph Delaval, who had been present at Beachy Head, and a number of other captains including John Leake were members. Supposedly the prisoner, Torrington sat next to Delaval during the trial! The Dutch contingent who bore the brunt of the battle, were vitriolic about Torrington's behaviour. Rear-Admiral Gilles Schey lost his temper and challenged an English captain to a duel for his negative comments about another of the Dutch admirals.[54] A rumour circulated that William III had given instructions that Torrington was to be executed as soon as he was found guilty. In London, for three days, the trial was talk of the town. Torrington was unanimously acquitted by his peers, and returned to London in his barge never to be employed at sea again. William was furious and refused to see him. It was an extraordinary way to treat a man who had come over early to his side and had commanded his invasion fleet.[55]

Cloudesley Shovell played no part in the trial, possibly because he was seen as 'one of Torrington's creatures.'[56] In any event he was away at sea. There is in existence a letter from Shovell to Torrington, which makes his views on the matter crystal clear. Extracts from the letter state: 'tis not unknown to your Lordship that both your loyalty and your courage are questioned.' 'Your retreat was absolutely necessary.' 'Nothing more rejoiced me than your Lordship declined fighting them.' 'It was my opinion that nothing more to your Lordships honour nor to our country's safety than keeping out of reach of them.'[57]

Let Shovell have the last word on the matter.

54 Le Fevre and Harding, *Precursors*, pp. 37–8.
55 Thomas Macaulay, *The History of England*, Vol. IV (London: Macmillan and Co 1914), pp. 1956–7; Martin-Leake, *John Leake*, Vol. I, pp. 38–42; Richmond, *Instrument of Policy*, pp. 220–1; Laird Clowes, *Royal Navy*, Vol. II, p. 344; HMC: Finch MS, Vol. II, pp. 382–3.
56 Chappell (ed), *Tangier Papers*, p. 59.
57 Huntington Library (HL), San Marino: MS SR 1–85, Shovell to Herbert, undated, 1690.

12

Hide and Seek at Sea and the Twin Battles of Barfleur and La Hogue 1691–1692

1691 was to be a sterile year at sea with the politically minded Edward Russell, in command of the Anglo-Dutch fleet, unable to find, let alone bring to action, the French fleet under Anne Hilarion de Costentin, Comte de Tourville. Louis XIV had instructed Tourville to avoid battle if he possibly could, but to keep the English Channel open for trade and to maintain the supply of his troops in Galway. That summer, one English success was the safe arrival from the Mediterranean of the Smyrna merchant fleet, under the handsome Irish aristocrat Matthew Aylmer.

Cloudesley Shovell's first duty of the New Year was to be a part of George Rooke's squadron which escorted William III back to the Netherlands. In mid-January 1691, the King embarked on his yacht at Gravesend and it was not until the fifth day that the Dutch coast was reached. Thick fog covered the shore and the impatient William set off in an open boat to find land. In freezing conditions, the King found his way barred by chunks of floating ice as water broke over the boat and its unfortunate occupants. He said: 'are you afraid to die with me?' and at this juncture an intrepid Dutch seaman dived into the sea and with difficulty reached the shore. Here he lit a fire and fired a musket to indicate that he was safe. Unsurprisingly, no one followed his example and William spent the rest of an unpleasant night in the open skiff. Next morning, once they were able to see clearly, they found that they were close to the island of Goree. A frozen King, covered in icicles waded ashore.[1]

Having safely escorted William III to the Netherlands, Shovell returned to England. Then in the following month, February, he received a commission to become Major of the First Marine Regiment. Seven months later, Shovell transferred to the Second Marine Regiment as Lieutenant-Colonel in place of an officer who had drowned in the *Coronation* disaster and would become its full Colonel in 1697.[2] All these posts were lucrative, undemanding

---

1   Macaulay, *History*, Vol. IV, pp. 1968–9.
2   On 3 September 1691, the *Coronation*, a 90-gun ship foundered off Rame Head near Plymouth with the loss of over 600 men.

sinecures. The marine posts, although strictly speaking naval, were to be his first and only military connection.[3]

On 10 March 1691, Shovell married Elizabeth Narbrough, née Hill, the widow of his former patron Sir John Narbrough who had died in the West Indies nearly three years earlier. The wedding took place in All Hallows Church, Staining, close to the present day Fenchurch Street railway station in the City of London. All that remains of the church is its stone tower. At the time of their marriage Shovell was 40-years-old and his bride nine years younger. It is unique in British naval history for the former cabin boy to marry his admiral's widow. However, it was to be a supremely happy marriage with Shovell remaining tender and faithful to his wife. Also he looked after the surviving Narbrough children, Elizabeth, John and James as if they were his own. A near contemporary source recorded:

> She [Elizabeth Shovell] proved as kind a wife as she had shewed herself an indulgent mistress carrying herself without either pride in general or contempt to that Gentleman in particular tho' formerly in her Service merited as much her embraces as he who was honoured with her early kindness or any person whatsoever, tho' he drew his extraction from a long and successive train of glorious ancestors.[4]

Although Elizabeth Shovell had married her former husband's lowly protégé, she had not really married beneath herself. By 1691, Shovell was a rear-admiral, had been knighted and was considered one of the outstanding naval officers of his generation. There were to be two daughters of the marriage, Elizabeth and Anne, but no son. Hence the name Shovell died out with Cloudesley's death in 1707.

Elizabeth's father, John Hill, had been made an extra commissioner of the navy shortly before the wedding and he would be joined at the Navy Board by his new son-in-law. Hill may well have started life as a merchant navy captain and he certainly made a fortune trading at Cadiz and in the Mediterranean. When he died in 1706, Hill left Shovell the enormous sum of one hundred thousand pounds.[5]

Edward Russell had succeeded the triumvirate of Richard Haddock, Henry Killigrew and John Ashby in command of the fleet but, unlike in 1690, there was to be no major engagement at sea. After their misfortunes at the Battle of Beachy Head, by the spring of 1691 the English fleet had been restored to full strength and would be superior in numbers to their French enemy. The combined Anglo-Dutch fleet would have 74 men of war to France's sixty nine. Russell was instructed to: keep the privateers at Dunkirk in check and thus cover the transport vessels sailing to the Dutch coast; prevent the maintenance of troops in Galway; position his main body of ships in the Soundings to deal with the French fleet and also protect the incoming Smyrna convoy which was valued at one and a half million pounds.

Russell and the English fleet, with Shovell in the 96-gun *London,* sailed from the Downs at the end of May 1691, and during the next three months a gigantic game of hide and seek was played by Russell's and Tourville's fleets. The setting for this recreation was off Brest, in the Soundings and around the coast of Ireland. The fleets did not meet, although

---

3   Lourenco Edye, *Historical Records of the Royal Marines,* Vol. I, 1664–1701 (London: Harrison 1893), pp. 361, 495.
4   Anon, *Secret Memoirs,* pp. 5, 78–9.
5   Dyer, *Narbrough,* p. 207. Around £14,020,000 in 2017 terms.

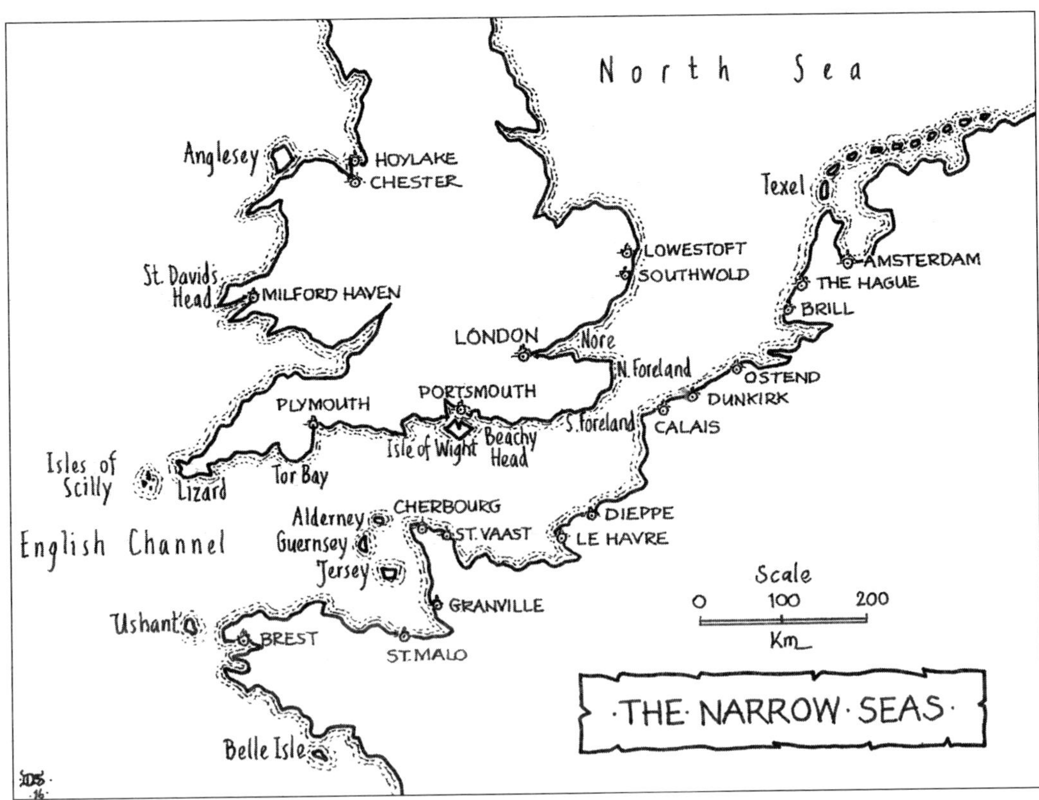

Map 15 The Narrow Seas.

on one occasion the French scouts were seen, but Tourville was able to slip away without fighting. In mid-June, Shovell, the rear-admiral of the blue, was sent by Russell to look into Brest in the smaller 52-gun *Montagu* with its shallower draught.[6] Pretending to be a French squadron returning with prizes, he flew white flags from some of his ships but not others.[7] A month later, on 20 July, Shovell reported back to Russell:

> About 8 this morning we were within a league of St Mathews Point,[8] when we espied a fleet of about fourty sayle comeing out of Brest, which to our great comfort proved to be Brittons all,[9] except three men of war of about 36 to 40 guns each, one of which men of war stood to leeward of me, and I wared my ship and missed him but half a shipp's length, fireing at him, shot downe his maine yard. He putt before the wind and got from us all by putting his ship amongst the rocks called the chickens, and notwithstanding I had three pilots on board I could not persuade

---

6   Charnock, *Biographia*, Vol. II, footnote p. 19 and Aubrey, *The Defeat*, p. 65 state that Shovell was in the *Plymouth*.
7   Le Fevre and Harding, *Precursors*, p. 54.
8   Pointe Saint-Mathieu is the tip of the northern promontory leading into Brest water.
9   Brittons: nationals of Britanny.

them to follow him, but they carried me through amongst the island neare the point of Comorett,[10] but 'twas too late, for he got up his maine yard and out sayled me much. By all I can learne from the pilots 'twas well I did not follow my inclination in pursueing him through those rocks; the breach was all over him and hardly water for a ship of that draught to passe. In the scuffle we have got five or six Brittons. The fleet was bound to Bordeaux and have nothing but stores; they all stood into Brest water. Some of our shipps were neare the castle, which is not such a bugbear as reported. What I have hitherto learned concerning their fleete is that they have beene at sea near forty days, and about a week since a ship of about 80 guns sailed from hence to joine them, and about two or three days agoe a water ship came from them, and one man says he left them forty leagues to the westward of Ushant, where, 'tis said here, they have beene, and in the Soundings ever since they have been out. What made those shipps soe bold was that the news here is that theire fleet has taken severall English men of war and marchant men, some of our shipps that stood in with French colours they tooke to be French men of war, and the shipps that had noe colours abroad they took to be prizes.[11]

The day after Shovell wrote his report, Russell sent it on to the Secretary of State, Daniel Finch 2nd Earl of Nottingham with some comments of his own:

I here send your lordship a copy of his letter to mee, which sufficiently shews how prudently hee has executed his orders, and I am sure hee will doe the like in any service he is employed on. I do not flatter him [Shovell] when I say in all respects I doe not know a better man.[12]

Like Myngs, Narbrough and Torrington, Russell had come to appreciate Shovell's great capabilities. In a final letter to Nottingham concerning these events, Russell wrote on 31 July stating that Shovell's squadron had gone into Brest: 'the drum was beat and the burghters took arms', as they thought that the ships had soldiers on board.[13] They were mistaken.

By mid-August the combined Anglo-Dutch fleet had been forced to go into Torbay for further supplies. At a council of war, attended by Shovell, a decision was made not to stay at sea later than 10 September.[14] When this view was communicated to Queen Mary who was acting in the absence of her husband, she suggested rather than ordered that an attack on the French fleet, now safely back at Brest, should be considered. A further council of war felt that it was too late in the year for such an undertaking.[15]

Early in September a south-easterly gale forced Russell to look for shelter at Plymouth. A part of his fleet narrowly missed running on to the Eddystone Reef and others had difficulty weathering Penlee Point. Some ships ran foul of each other trying to get into the Hamoaze.

---

10   Camaret Point is the southern promontory leading into Brest water. There are several islands off it.
11   HMC: Finch MS, Vol. III, pp. 170–1.
12   HMC: Finch MS, Vol. III, p. 170.
13   HMC: Finch MS, Vol. III, p. 190.
14   HMC: Finch MS, Vol. III, p. 219.
15   Laughton, *Torrington*, pp. 56–60.

Shovell's former ship, the 70-gun *Harwich*, in which he had come to national attention, was wrecked under Mount Edgcumbe. The 70-gun *Royal Oak* and the 70-gun *Northumberland* both grounded and were lucky to be refloated. In order to ride out the storm, Shovell, back in the 96-gun *London*, anchored off Rame Head together with the 90-gun *Duchess* and the 90-gun *Coronation*. On 3 September, Shovell witnessed from his poop deck, at three cables distance,[16] the dismasting and foundering of the *Coronation*. Her captain, Charles Skelton, with over 600 crew and marines, drowned before Shovell's eyes. It was the same Skelton that in October 1688 James II had asked Dartmouth to: 'let Shovell and Skelton know that if this war continues they will soon be better mounted after the first brush shall be over.' The *Coronation* had been Ralph Delaval's flagship at Beachy Head the year before. Russell speculated that the guns had broken loose or the lower deck gun ports had been forced open, leading to the ship capsizing. It must have been a harrowing sight even for a battle-hardened man like Shovell.[17]

In some quarters Russell was harshly censured for attempting to get into Plymouth in a storm rather than trying to ride it out at sea. He was not an easy man to give advice to and John Leake described him as: 'excessively proud and haughty; difficult to be pleased unless flattered; and implacable if offended.'[18] Shovell had known and worked happily with Russell from their time in the Mediterranean together. Their relationship can be summed up as one of mutual respect.

On 8 September, Russell sailed from Plymouth for Spithead leaving Shovell behind to await the repair of the damaged ships before joining him. On the day that Russell sailed, that is five days after the loss of the *Coronation*, Shovell petitioned the Secretary of State, Nottingham, for the post of Lieutenant-Colonel of the Second Marine Regiment in place of a man called Paston, who had drowned in the disaster. Not only that, but he also suggested that he should have the post over his great rival, George Rooke. 'I hear, my Lord, that tis designed that Rear Admiral Rooke shall have the leiut collonellship; he is a gentleman I have no objection against but humbley wish he had been a major before me or I may be a leiut colonel before him.'[19] The naked self-interest of Shovell was surprising, particularly in its inopportune timing. On 11 September, Nottingham wrote to Lord Sidney: 'Sir Cloudsly Shovell is a humble suitor for Mr Paston's place, and I must be so too for him ----.' In fact by the time of Nottingham's letter, William III had already signed Shovell's commission.[20] Shovell was not normally one to push himself forward quite so blatantly. Perhaps the additional expense of having married in the spring was uppermost in his mind. One of the few criticisms of his character was that his covetousness knew no bounds.

By the end of September, Shovell had reached Spithead where he sat as president of the court-martial of the gunner of the *Exeter* frigate. The unfortunate man was condemned to death and hanged.[21] Shovell often sat at courts-martial and had the reputation of pardoning

---

16 About 720 yards.
17 Laughton, *Torrington*, p. 62; Richard Larn and Peter McBride, *Sir Clowdisley Shovell's Disaster* (Plymouth: Historic Maritime Series 1985), p. 8; Laird Clowes, *Royal Navy*, Vol. II, pp. 345–6; HMC: Finch MS, Vol. III, p. 251.
18 Martin-Leake, *John Leake*, Vol. I, p. 43.
19 HMC: Finch MS, Vol. III, pp. 255–6.
20 HMC: Finch MS, Vol. III, p. 260.
21 Luttrell, *State Affairs*, Vol. II, p. 289.

crimes in others that he was never guilty of himself.[22] Following the court-martial Shovell took a squadron across to the Dutch coast to bring back William III to England. Shovell landed the King at Margate and then the royal coach overturned at Gravesend, fortunately without any damage to its royal passenger.[23]

On 29 September 1691, Shovell's half-sister, Anne Flaxman, was married to Thomas Shorting at Morston in north Norfolk. No doubt Shovell's mother, Anne, attended the wedding in the church where she would eventually be buried. Shorting was the Collector of Customs at nearby Cley-next-the-Sea. Judging by some of his letters to his half-sister and brother-in-law, Shovell was fond of them both and went out of his way to help them.[24] He could not attend the ceremony because of his commitments, mentioned earlier, as president of a court-martial and of sailing to fetch the king from the Netherlands.

Shovell's protective role in William III's return was to be his last official duty of 1691. This had been an undistinguished year for the fleets of both England and France, but at least Ireland had finally fallen to William, with the taking of Athlone and Limerick. 1692 would be a much more eventful year for the English navy and particularly so for Shovell himself.

Early in January 1692, Shovell was granted a coat of arms to commemorate his victories over the Barbary regencies and the French. The arms incorporated a lion, a sail, a fleur-de-lys and two crescents. The fleur-de-lys and crescents illustrated Shovell's victories over the French and the Barbary corsairs. A fortnight later, he was appointed rear-admiral of the red under Edward Russell, a more senior post than the one he had held in the previous year.[25] In March, Shovell escorted William III to the Netherlands and in the same month was writing to the Commissioners of the Admiralty concerning bounty money.[26]

Late in 1691, William III had decided that the principal effort of 1692 should be on land in Flanders, and that his fleet would support the military expedition and stop supplies from reaching Louis XIV's forces. Russell, Henri de Massue, Viscount Galway,[27] and the fiery Meinhardt Schomberg, Duke of Leinster, were instructed to prepare plans for offensive action against the key French port of Brest and also St Malo.[28] Fourteen thousand soldiers were to be encamped near Portsmouth to be ready for the expedition.[29] The English were not alone in planning offensive action as, across the Channel, the French had collected an invasion force of their own at Saint-Vaast-la-Hougue.[30] James II in person inspected the troops and their transport ships.[31] Initially it was thought that Louis XIV had designs on the Channel Islands and Richard Carter was sent with a small squadron to cruise off Guernsey.[32] Later, Ralph Delaval with an advance squadron of the main fleet, was sent to reinforce them.

22   Anon, *Secret Memoirs*, p. 129.

23   Luttrell, *State Affairs*, Vol. II, p. 296.

24   NMM: RMT MS, MAT 19, transcripts relating to the Shorting branch of the Shovell family.

25   Rear-admiral of the blue.

26   Luttrell, *State Affairs*, Vol. II, pp. 375, 383; HMC: Finch MS, Vol. IV, pp. 28–9, 38–9.

27   He became the Earl of Galway in 1697.

28   Richmond, *Instrument of Policy*, pp. 226–7.

29   William Aiken, *Conduct of the Earl of Nottingham* (New Haven: Yale University Press 1941), p. 92.

30   Known to the English at the time as La Hogue. Hence the Battle of La Hogue.

31   Laird Clowes, *Royal Navy*, Vol. II, p. 346.

32   Ehrman, *War of William III*, p. 393.

On 19 April, came the stunning news that a French invasion of the mainland of England, in Dorset, was intended rather than the Channel Islands and the intention was for it to be made before the junction of the Dutch and English fleets. A French vessel had run ashore on the Goodwin Sands with letters to Jacobites in England making clear Louis XIV's real intentions.[33] This dramatic news led to the suspension of troop movements and the collection of stores that had been intended for the attack on France. Russell, with the main fleet, was sent to the Flats of the Foreland to await further orders.[34] Shovell spent the months of March and April attending councils of flag officers to decide how to deal with the French challenge.

In March, Louis XIV signed orders for Tourville, giving him strict instructions to take the French fleet out of Brest, on 15 April 1692, and proceed to Saint-Vaast-la-Hougue. He was then to accompany the invasion force to England, even if he had intelligence of the enemy being at sea with a superior force, and if necessary attack them. These potentially suicidal orders were the foundation of the French defeat at the Battle of Barfleur, and the subsequent destruction of a large part of their fleet at Saint-Vaast-la-Hougue, known as the Battle of La Hogue [sic], a few days later. Two years earlier, Torrington had found himself faced with a similar predicament before Beachy Head. Later, Louis XIV, who knew little of naval matters, received the vanquished Tourville and was honest enough to admit his responsibility for the defeat. Louis XIV and his Secretary of State for the Navy, Louis Pontchartrain intended Tourville's fleet to protect the transports and troops as they crossed the Channel to Torbay before the critical juncture of the English and Dutch fleets.[35] With the addition of Victor-Marie d'Estrées' [son of Jean] ships from Toulon, the combined French fleet could protect the invasion force and then its supply and communications.[36] A successful French invasion of England from Saint-Vaast-la-Hougue would have had a certain irony for it was here that Edward III and the Black Prince had landed before the Crécy campaign in 1346.

Louis XIV's plans may have been influenced by erroneous Jacobite intelligence that morale was poor in the English fleet and some of the captains, such as John Ashby, Ralph Delaval, Richard Carter and even Edward Russell did not wish to fight. After his exploits in Dublin Bay, two years earlier, there was no question of Shovell's name being on the list. However, rumours had reached Queen Mary that the fleet might defect to her father, James II. On 15 May, at a council of flag officers, an address was signed and sent to the Queen reaffirming the loyalty of the fleet.[37] Unsurprisingly, Shovell was amongst the signatories, as one Jacobite emissary reported 'he was not a man to be spoken to.'[38]

Russell rightly judged that it was essential to join the Dutch and English fleets as soon as possible and this was effected at Rye, on 7 May. On the 15th, Shovell was amongst the flag officers who recommended that the fleet should not proceed west of St Helens until it

---

33   Ehrman, *War of William III*, p. 392.
34   TNA: ADM 1/4080, Admiralty correspondence, f. 123.
35   Louis, Marquis of Phélypeaux, Comte de Maurepas, Comte de Pontchartrain [1643–1727].
36   Richmond, *Instrument of Policy*, p. 228.
37   Anon, *Secret Memoirs*, pp. 41–3; Laird Clowes, *Royal Navy*, Vol. II, p. 347.
38   Charles Knight, *Popular History of England*, Vol. V (Boston: Estes and Lauriat 1874), p. 372.

was known for certain that: 'the French were on our coast and then fight them.'[39] What of the French fleet? As was recorded earlier, Tourville had been ordered to leave Brest with his fleet by 15 April. However, inclement weather precluded him from sailing until 2 May, when finally he managed to get to sea. Meanwhile d'Estrées, with the Toulon squadron of 18 ships had sailed from the Mediterranean to join Tourville's 44 ships at Brest. He too had been held up by contrary winds and his ships eventually reached Brest on 19 May, the very day of the Battle of Barfleur. Tourville would sorely miss d'Estrées' contingent and also a further unmanned, 26 ships in the ports of western France. These ships would be ready for sea by June.[40]

In Paris, Pontchartrain, the Secretary of State for the Navy, was getting decidedly cold feet after intelligence from the Netherlands indicated what a mess the French had got themselves into. On 9 May, he wrote to Marshal Bellefonds,[41] who commanded the troops at Saint-Vaast-la-Hougue, stating that the French king had delegated to him and James II the direction of the movements of Tourville and his fleet. Nothing was done until 18 May, when two boats put to sea with instructions to draw back should Tourville have no greater force than when he left Brest. One of the boats actually got alongside, the *Soleil Royal*, Tourville's flagship, on 19 May, just before the onset of the Battle of Barfleur. It was all too late and the die was cast.[42] On board one of the French ships, the chaplain told the crew to get down on their knees and to recite the 'Miserere' and 'Confiteor.'[43] This was followed by a welcome swig of brandy and then away to action stations.

Louis XIV's carelessness had put Tourville's fleet of 44 ships [11 carrying more than 80 guns] into the invidious position of facing Russell's numerically superior fleet of no less than 82 ships [24 with more than 80 guns]. Thus the French were outgunned by rather more than five to three and they had the lighter guns too.[44] By 18 May, Carter's and Delaval's ships had joined Russell and the fleet at St Helens. Information was received that the French were at sea and the combined Anglo-Dutch fleet sailed to meet them.[45] On 19 May 1692, the two fleets came into sight of one another when about 20 miles north-east of Cape Barfleur.[46] If the wind had been favourable, Tourville would have reached Saint-Vaast-la-Hougue with its troops and transports prior to meeting Russell's fleet. The 'Trafalgar of the seventeenth century', as it was described by Winston Churchill, was about to begin.[47]

This account of the twin Battles of Barfleur and La Hogue is largely based on the works of Allyn, Aubrey and Laughton.[48] The Anglo-Dutch fleet was organised with: the Dutch

39   HMC: Finch MS, Vol. IV, p. 158.

40   John Laughton, 'The Battle of La Hogue and Maritime War', *Quarterly Review*, Vol. CLXXVI (1893), p. 482.

41   Marshal Bernardin Gigault de Bellefonds [1630–94].

42   Laughton, 'La Hogue', p. 482.

43   'Miserere': 'Have mercy on me. O God'; a setting of Psalm 51. 'Confiteor': 'I confess'; it is a prayer said during the Penitential Act at the beginning of mass in the Roman Catholic Church.

44   Davies, *Pepys's Navy*, p. 277.

45   Ehrman, *War of William III*, p. 395.

46   Aubrey, *The Defeat*, p. 90; Laird Clowes, *Royal Navy*, Vol. II, p. 349 stated that when the French were sighted the Cape bore SW by S, about 21 miles.

47   West, *Admiral Russell*, p. 292.

48   Richard Allyn, *A narrative of the Victory obtained by the English over that of France in the year 1692* (London: J. Robinson 1744), pp. 1–58; Aubrey, *The Defeat*, pp. 77–148; Laughton, 'La Hogue', pp. 461–489.

in the van under Philip Almonde; the red squadron under Russell in the centre; the blue squadron under John Ashby in the rear. The French had: the white and blue squadron under Marquis d'Amfreville in the van; the white squadron under Tourville in the centre; the blue squadron under Jean Gabaret in the rear. As rear-admiral of the red, Shovell with his flag in the 100-gun *Royal William* was in the centre near to Russell also in a 100-gun ship, the *Britannia*. The *Royal William*, renamed in 1692, had formerly been called the *Prince* and was the ship in which Shovell had served with James II at the Battle of Sole Bay 20 years earlier. His captain was Thomas Jennings who would also command Shovell's ship, the *Neptune*, in the action at Camaret Bay in 1694.

At 3:00 a.m. on 19 May 1692, the English scouts who were to the westward of the main fleet saw a large body of French ships and made haste to inform Russell. The French were to the south-west of the English fleet with a fine gale from the south-west-by-west and the visibility was hazy.[49] Tourville, with the weather gage, was in a position to fight or quietly withdraw. He was probably unaware of the junction of the English and Dutch fleets and the foggy conditions made it difficult for him to judge the number of ships up against his French fleet. In addition, he had his sovereign's orders to attack the enemy despite being numerically inferior. With a heavy heart Tourville bravely bore down on the Anglo-Dutch fleet.

As day broke, Tourville, with the French fleet in line of battle, was seen approaching from the south-south-west and Russell's fleet responded by forming their own battle line. The English line was tolerable and took until 8:00 a.m. to fully form. The two lines of ships now extended from the north-north-east to the south-south-west, with the wind still to the south-west, but decreasing in strength. It was 11:00 a.m. before the battle began in earnest with Tourville's massive 106-gun *Soleil Royal* standing in for Russell's *Britannia*. As the *Soleil Royal* approached, Russell called upon his crew to give the French ship three cheers. Inhospitably, Tourville replied with a volley of musket shot from close range. Russell's counter was to give the *Soleil Royal* a full broadside and the first casualties of the battle occurred. Strictly speaking, the first casualty of the campaign was the unfortunate surgeon's mate of the *Deptford*, who was accidently killed whilst easing himself in the head [evacuating his bowels] during a birthday salute for Queen Mary on 30 April. Shot from a chase gun hit him at a delicate moment![50]

In the section written by Shovell in Richard Allyn's book, he recorded that he had never seen anyone come as close before opening fire. The red squadron were soon in the thick of the battle with Tourville's white squadron in the centre. It was as hot an engagement as the experienced Shovell had ever been involved in.[51] The van, consisting of the Dutch contingent of 26 ships, was attacked by the 14 ships of d'Amfreville's white and blue squadron and heavy fighting took place. At the beginning of the encounter, in the rear, Ashby's blue squadron was somewhat to the leeward of the remainder of the Anglo-Dutch fleet and consequently a part of Gabaret's contingent had no ships to fight and moved abreast of Shovell's division.

49   Allyn, *A narrative of the Victory*, pp. 25, 33.
50   Allyn, *A narrative of the Victory*, p. 10.
51   Allyn, *A narrative of the Victory*, pp. 33–4.

For around two hours the battle continued with the ever decreasing wind blowing from the south-west. The heaviest fighting was in the centre with Russell, aided by Shovell, in the thick of it. By 1:00 p.m., the *Britannia* had so beaten the *Soleil Royal* with shot that Tourville was forced to tack away. The wind shifted to the west-north-west and carried Tourville still further away from Russell. It was at this juncture that Shovell took his chance to make one of the critical moves of the battle. When the wind shifted to the west-north-west, Shovell, with six ships [including John Neville's *Kent*] plus his fireships, kept his luff [turned towards the wind] and weathered Tourville and his squadron. This manoeuvre broke the French line and separated their white and blue squadrons. Ashby, with part of his squadron, followed Shovell's example and at this point Shovell said: 'from that moment they [the French] began to run.'[52] Later he criticized Ashby's squadron for not attacking the disengaged side of the main body of the French fleet as he had done.[53]

It was now 4:00 p.m. on a very foggy afternoon; the wind had fallen away and the sea was calm. By this stage Shovell and some of the ships from his division had managed to interpose themselves on the French line of retreat. An hour later, the fog began to lift and a light breeze got up from the east. As the French attempted to fight their way through Shovell's division, the wind died away and the fog came down once more. Soon after 6:00 p.m. the tide started to drive both the English and French ships to the north-east. Tourville and Shovell both ordered their ships to anchor, which meant that the latter could only bring his stern guns to bear on the French. Unfortunately, the 90-gun *Sandwich* under Shovell's old friend, Anthony Hastings, was not held by her anchors and drove through the French and attracted a hail of shot. Poor Hastings, who had taken the *Half Moon* with Shovell in the Mediterranean 11 years before, was slain. Nearby, also drifting through the French line, Richard Carter, the rear-admiral of the blue, whose Jacobite sympathies were most suspected, was hit by shot which took off his leg. As he lay dying on the deck of his ship, the *Duke*, he ordered his captain to 'fight the ship as long as she will swim.'[54]

Shovell realised that Tourville's ships were in a vulnerable position and ordered his fireships to attack them. Tourville was able to escape by cutting his cables and being towed away. On the deck of the *Soleil Royal* the crew could barely turn their faces towards the flames so great was the heat. One of James II's illegitimate sons, Henry FitzJames, who was serving in the *Soleil Royal* bravely commented: 'I would sooner have my nose toasted than turn my back on the enemy.'[55] After the narrow failure of his fireships' attacks, Shovell was engaged by fresh French vessels and was forced to order the cutting of the cables of his own ships. As a consequence of this, they then drifted through a gap in the French line to safety. Tourville thought that this was a bad mistake as Shovell was blocking the French escape route to St Malo and Brest. However the English ships were in an exposed position and could expect the whole French fleet to fall upon them when the tide turned.

So night fell on 19 May and by a little after 10:00 p.m. all fighting ceased. Although at this stage of the battle the French had lost no ships, both sides had suffered damage to their

52   Allyn, *A narrative of the Victory*, p. 35.
53   Aubrey, *The Defeat*, pp. 99–100.
54   Laird Clowes, *Royal Navy*, Vol. II, pp. 352–3.
55   West, *Admiral Russell*, p. 279.

vessels and more importantly to their men. Most of the wounds were due to shot or splinters and one man serving in Delaval's division had half his face shot away. He survived for two days and sang for most of this time. Amongst the wounded was Shovell himself. The exact details of his condition are unclear. One report stated that he had a splinter wound of the thigh and another from Russell himself recorded: 'he is a little wounded in a fall, but will do very well again.'[56] Whatever the nature of the wound, having put in a stellar performance at the Battle of Barfleur, it would cost Shovell an even greater share of the glory in the aftermath.

At daybreak on 20 May, Shovell found the weather: 'mighty thick and foggy.'[57] Soon the French were spotted and he led the ensuing general chase. Neither side could make much headway against the flood tide and they anchored between Cape Barfleur and Cherbourg. As his ship, the *Royal William*, had suffered considerable damage the previous day, Shovell moved his flag to the 70-gun *Kent* under John Neville.

On the morning of 21 May, Shovell clearly saw the French at anchor in the Race of Alderney to the west of the Cherbourg Peninsula. When the flood tide came some of the French ships' anchors would not hold and they were forced to cut their cables and, as a consequence, were driven along the shore line to the east. Ashby and a Dutch contingent held fast and stayed in position to follow the remaining French ships once conditions improved. Some ships including those of Russell and Shovell cut their cables and followed in the wake of the French ships being driven along the shore to the east. Tourville, still in the *Soleil Royal*, realised that unless the wind changed direction he would be forced ashore. So he carried his flag to the *Ambitieux* before eventually going ashore himself. Tourville was proved correct and the *Soleil Royal*, *Admirable* and *Triomphant* were beached and stranded in Cherbourg Bay. The next day all three ships were destroyed by Delaval's men.

The remaining French ships being driven to the east outsailed the entire contingent except for Shovell in the *Kent* and two or three others. As the leading ship, Shovell kept close to those that were sometimes within shot, but he did not fire, in case it slowed him down. On the night of 21 May some of the French anchored close to the shore at Saint-Vaast-la-Hougue and others just off Tatihou Island. Shovell too, anchored in sight of the French ships with his boats out closely watching them. The next day, the 22nd, Russell and the bulk of the fleet joined Shovell at Saint-Vaast-la-Hougue. The surviving 12 French ships had got as close to the shore as possible and appeared to be preparing to defend themselves. A decision was made to attack the French the next day and Shovell was deservedly chosen by Russell to lead the coming action – the Battle of La Hogue.

Whilst Russell and Shovell were drawing up plans for a boat action at Saint-Vaast-la-Hougue and Tatihou Island, Ashby and the Dutch were chasing around 20 French ships who escaped through the dangerous Race of Alderney to safety in St Malo.

23 May came and, off Saint-Vaast-la-Hougue, Shovell was fully expecting to lead the coming boat action in person. However, he had fallen seriously ill overnight, probably suffering from an infection of his splinter wound in the thigh or from bruising from a fall. The injury had occurred during the battle on the 19th. On hearing of Shovell's indisposition,

---

56   Luttrell, *State Affairs*, Vol. II, p. 465; HMC: Finch MS, Vol. IV, pp. 176–8.
57   Allyn, *A narrative of the Victory*, p. 36.

George Rooke immediately put himself forward as a replacement: he was not going to miss a golden opportunity such as this. The French had hauled their ships so close to the shore, under cover of the forts, that only small craft could approach them. That night, Rooke took the ships' boats and fireships and the six outermost French ships in Saint-Vaast-la-Hougue and off Tatihou Island were torched. The soldiers who were part of the intended invasion force for England helped in the defence of the French vessels. The water was so shallow that cavalry was able to ride into the water and the riders were unceremoniously pulled off their horses by rough English sailors with their boat hooks, before being dispatched to eternity. The French sailors and also their soldiers fought poorly as they were thoroughly demoralised. The next day, the 24th, the English boats went in again and a further six French men-of-war were torched. In all, Tourville lost 16 ships, including the 12 at Saint-Vaast-la-Hougue and off Tatihou Island. No English ships were lost in the battle.

James II, Tourville and French ministers witnessed the destruction of this part of the French fleet at Saint-Vaast-la-Hougue. All hopes of an invasion of England and the regaining of James' crown had now vanished. Tactlessly, the obtuse James did not endear himself to his hosts by declaring: 'who but my brave English tars could do such a thing?' Later, he was said to be inconsolable when the magnitude of the defeat became apparent.[58]

Russell with his overwhelming force had won a great victory over Tourville's French, and in England bonfires were lit and the church bells pealed all day.[59] Shovell came out of the battle and subsequent chase of the French with nothing but credit. He had been the leading figure on 19 May when he broke the French line and he was also first in the chase down the eastern side of the Cherbourg Peninsula to Saint-Vaast-la-Hougue. Only injury prevented him from gaining even greater fame in the ensuing boat action. Clearly Russell recognised the value of Shovell's contribution to the defeat of the French and he wrote to the Secretary of State, Nottingham, on 23 May 1692:

> As to the behaviour of the officers in the red squadron (whom I mention because the stress of battle fell upon them) they did extremely well. Cloudesley Shovell lay upon my weather quarter, by which means he is pretty well mauled, but he will always be shewing the young gallant. He is a little hurt with a fall, but will do very well again; a better man the King has not in his service.[60]

Later, on 22 June, Russell wrote once more to Nottingham suggesting that Delaval be sent to command in the West Indies. 'I do not know anyone so proper as Sir Ralph Delaval, for he is diligent, except Shovell, who in my opinion ought not to be spared. The rest are not fit for that service.' In fact Russell was only too keen to see the back of Ralph Delaval, but Shovell was still basking in the glory of Barfleur.[61]

Russell had won a great victory over the French at sea which precluded any possibility of a French invasion on the mainland of England. Furthermore, his fleet was still intact and

---

58   Laird Clowes, *Royal Navy*, Vol. II, p. 355; Aubrey, *The Defeat*, p. 121; Anon, *Secret Memoirs* pp. 54–6.
59   The English lost no ships at the Battles of Barfleur and La Hogue. The casualties may have been of the order: English 2,000 dead and 3,000 wounded; French 1,700 dead or wounded. The figures are difficult to substantiate.
60   HMC: Finch MS, Vol. IV, pp. 176–8.
61   HMC: Finch MS, Vol. IV, p. 256.

14,000 men were at his disposal in England to act as a land force in an expedition against St Malo or Brest. On 23 May, Russell returned with most of his fleet to St Helens, leaving Ashby and a Dutch squadron on the coast of France. The intention was to stop the French ships which had escaped into St Malo from coming out and sailing to Brest, but Ashby and the Dutch were unsuccessful in this operation.[62]

Queen Mary, on receiving information that Russell and the fleet were on the way to St Helens, instructed Nottingham, the Secretary of State, to have them remain there. Thus they would be in an excellent position to attempt St Malo or Brest as her husband had instructed before leaving the country. Rightly suspecting that Russell would do nothing, Mary sent the Lords Rochester, Sidney and Portland to Portsmouth to discuss the matter with him.[63] Prior to meeting the noble lords on 28 May, Russell had good grounds for feeling ill-used as he had received off Saint-Vaast-la-Hougue, whilst savouring his victory, orders from the Queen, written prior to the battle, that criticized his proposals. Russell wrote to Nottingham stating that he would see out the remainder of the campaign and then go and hunt.[64] It can be seen that Russell had become morose and was not in a suitable frame of mind to attack anywhere.

When Russell and his flag officers met the lords, it was agreed that 60 men-of-war, without troops, would be sent to attack French shipping at Brest, but nothing was done.[65] Shovell would not have attended this meeting as he had gone ashore that same day to recuperate at Fareham from his wounded thigh. Queen Mary had sent 40 extra surgeons to Portsmouth and in London, at St Thomas' and St Bartholomew's Hospitals, room was cleared for the casualties. Then the Queen ordered Russell to attempt St Malo which he pretended to do.[66] Throughout the high summer of 1692, earnest debate took place between the Queen, her council, the land officers and Russell and his flag officers about the most appropriate course of action to follow up the successes of mid-May. In June–July, Russell did eventually take the fleet to sea with St Malo as his goal, but a combination of poor weather and reluctance of his pilots ended the attempt.[67]

Shovell appears to have made a rapid recovery from his wound as we find him joining the 90-gun *Duke* on 7 June and with five ships he followed Russell in his abortive attempt on St Malo. During the summer he played his part in the various councils of war and Nottingham reported that both the Dutch admiral, Almonde, and Shovell would have acted against Brest if they had been allowed to. He described them as brave men.[68] But by early August, it was clear that it was too late in the year for any major undertaking against St Malo or Brest involving the great ships of the English fleet. Shovell, who had returned to the *Kent*, was ordered to accompany the Duke of Leinster and his troops in transport ships to Nieuport and Ostend. His former ship, the *Royal William*, had been so damaged in the Battle of Barfleur that it could not be used again that season. The squadron and transports arrived off

62   Laird Clowes, *Royal Navy*, Vol. II, p. 357.
63   Aiken, *Nottingham*, p. 97.
64   HMC: Finch MS, Vol. IV, p. 191.
65   Aiken, *Nottingham*, p. 98.
66   Aiken, *Nottingham*, p. 98.
67   Aiken, *Nottingham*, p. 99.
68   Aiken, *Nottingham*, p. 104.

the ports on 22 August, and Leinster and his men were disembarked in order to reinforce William III.[69] Delaval had complained bitterly to Nottingham about Shovell: 'Shovell out of all course is appointed to go with the Duke of Leinster and you may be confident he will see the King as soon as possible and tell a story as he did last year.'[70] These carping comments reflected the fact that Shovell was his junior. Ironically, the following year, 1693, the two men plus the libidinous Henry Killigrew were to be cooped up together in the *Britannia* as joint commanders-in-chief of the fleet!

In the middle of September, Shovell's squadron with the Dutch artillery officer, William Meesters, took part in the bombing of Dunkirk. Shovell was singularly unimpressed with Meesters' plan to bomb the forts there. He had informed Nottingham: 'I wish the project may take its designed effect though I much doubt it.'[71] Over the next few years Shovell's view on the ideas of Meesters would not change, indeed they would harden; there is little doubt that Meesters was a complete charlatan. About this time, Shovell was taken ill with a fever and ague. Ague was a malarial fever which he had picked up either in the Mediterranean or even earlier during his time in the West Indies. Fortunately he made a full recovery. Then in October, he undertook his customary duty of returning William III from the Netherlands to England.

The following month, Elizabeth and Cloudesley Shovell were blessed with the birth of their first child, although she had already had five children by her first husband Sir John Narbrough, three of whom survived into adulthood. The new baby was born at their home in Prescot Street, Goodman's Fields on 2 November 1692. She was a daughter, named Elizabeth like her mother, and was christened on 22 November at St Mary Matfelon, Whitechapel. In the churchyard were the mortal remains of Sir Christopher Myngs, Shovell's first great patron. In 1708, Elizabeth would marry firstly Sir Robert Marsham and secondly in 1732, John, Lord Carmichael.[72] The poorer tarpaulin captains such as Myngs and Shovell had their homes just to the north of the River Thames in Goodman's Fields. Shortly, the Shovells would own a new home in Soho Square at its junction with Frith Street, it was a most select area close to where the late Duke of Monmouth had lived.

The autumn of 1692 saw a parliamentary enquiry into the alleged mismanagement of the fleet during the summer. Russell defended himself and the finger was pointed at Nottingham, but he too justified himself in the House of Lords. Greenwich Hospital, in its final form, sprang partly from the fate of casualties suffered at the Battle of Barfleur.[73] Russell looked upon Barfleur as the climax of his naval career. In later years, he gave the home farm on his estate at Chippenham the name 'La Hogue' and planted a grove of trees, some of which were still alive in the 1950s, to represent his tactical formation that day.[74] If Russell had been a fortnight later in concentrating his fleet, Tourville might well have landed a Franco-Irish army on English soil.[75]

---

69   HMC: Finch MS, Vol. IV, pp. 394, 408, 448.
70   HMC: Finch MS, Vol. IV, p. 372.
71   HMC: Finch MS, Vol. IV, p. 420.
72   Marsham-Townshend, 'Parentage of Cloudesley Shovell', p. 43.
73   Ehrman, *War of William III*, p. 399.
74   Ehrman, *War of William III*, p. 399.
75   Aubrey, *The Defeat*, p. 128.

Despite the plaudits all round, it is hard to escape the conclusion that naval affairs during the summer of 1692 were mismanaged. Barfleur and La Hogue were great victories, the greatest in English naval history up to that time,[76] but they were not followed up effectively. However, Shovell had had a year of unqualified success as a junior admiral. He would see rapid promotion in 1693, but not success, as the next chapter will unfold.

76 Aubrey, *The Defeat*, p. 124.

13

Two Disasters: the Smyrna Convoy and the Landing at Camaret Bay 1693–1694

The early stages of the Nine Years' War had not gone well at sea for the allies. Defeats at Bantry Bay and Beachy Head had been followed by success at Barfleur and La Hogue. However, the French losses at Barfleur and La Hogue had been no greater than Anglo-Dutch losses at Beachy Head. As we shall see shortly, the main event of 1693 was the destruction of a significant part of the rich Smyrna convoy owing to negligence. In the last years of the war, the French commissioned fewer ships and there were to be no further fleet actions. They would concentrate their resources on supporting their army in Catalonia and harrying Anglo-Dutch trade with their formidable force of privateers. The final years of the war would also see a continuation of the barbaric bombardment of French coastal towns from Dunkirk to Brest.

Edward Russell had commanded the fleet in 1692 and had rightly been given the credit for the defeat of the French in the twin battles of Barfleur and La Hogue. However, the prevailing view at the time was that he had not followed up his victory as successfully as he might have done and consequently he felt ill-used. Suggestions were made that in 1693, as there had been in 1690, a joint commission would be more appropriate than a single one. But the politically-minded Whig, Russell was not prepared to go to sea sharing the command with anyone else. In any event, he refused to serve if he had to take orders from the Tory Secretary of State, Daniel Finch, 2nd Earl of Nottingham.[1] Nottingham suggested a joint commission and William III chose Henry Killigrew, Ralph Delaval and Cloudesley Shovell. Although the three names had been put forward by the king in January 1693, it was to be mid-March before the command of the fleet was officially put into a joint commission.[2]

In April, serious discussions took place over the use of the fleet during the summer campaign season. Consideration was given to: firstly, an amphibious assault on the principal French naval base of Brest; secondly, a squadron for service in the Mediterranean; thirdly, the convoying of merchant ships to Turkey, Italy, Portugal, Spain and Virginia.

---

1   Luttrell, *State Affairs*, Vol. III, p. 18; Henry Horwitz, *Parliament, Policy and Politics in the Reign of William III* (Manchester: Manchester University Press 1977), p. 109; Anchitell Grey, *Debates of the House of Commons 1667–1694* (London: Henry and Cave 1763), p. 293.
2   Laird Clowes, *Royal Navy*, Vol. II, pp. 357–9.

William III was keen to have a squadron in the Mediterranean to further his war aims in that region and the European merchants had been pressing for a convoy to go there for nearly two years. So it was decided to use the Mediterranean squadron to convoy the merchant vessels and the attack on Brest would have to wait, although Queen Mary was still hankering after it in May. George Rooke, recently knighted for his services at the Battle of La Hogue, was to command the Mediterranean squadron and he had been appointed as early as February.[3] Twice he was ready to sail with the merchant vessels and each time his orders were cancelled.[4]

The Levant Company, which specialised in trade with the eastern Mediterranean, had been collecting together English, Dutch, German, Swedish and Danish ships to be escorted to the Mediterranean, in safety from the French. By this time no less than 400 ships, containing mainly woollen goods, were ready to sail and the merchants were becoming restive at the constant delays. The name that has become associated with the ill-fated convoy is that of Smyrna, now Izmir, on the west coast of Turkey. Here woollen goods were exchanged for oriental silks, yarn and grogram [coarse fabric stiffened with gum].

On 6 April, Shovell had been made an extra commissioner of the navy with a salary of £1,000. No doubt this was a welcome addition to his finances for a newly married man with a child. On the 29th, the joint admirals, Killigrew, Delaval and Shovell, went aboard their flagship, the 100-gun *Britannia,* at Deal. The day before, they had again discussed with the Cabinet Council possible action against Brest. At the end of the meeting, Shovell slipped back into the room for private words with Thomas Osborne, Marquis of Carmarthen. He was concerned that the Dutch would not attack without positive orders and he feared that if the English contingent held councils of war, nothing would be done. Clearly, he was thinking back to the inaction of the latter part of the summer of 1692. Carmarthen forwarded Shovell's views to the king.

By now the *Britannia* was at St Helens and Queen Mary sent a number of Lords of the Council to meet with the joint admirals, in order to decide what should be done with George Rooke's Straits squadron and its charges. The Queen's representatives included Carmarthen, Laurence Hyde Earl of Rochester, Thomas Herbert Earl of Pembroke and the Secretary of State, John Trenchard. On 14 May, the assembled lords met with the admirals in the *Britannia,* but no firm conclusions were made and it was resolved to meet again the following day. On the 15th, a council of war made up solely of naval officers again considered the Straits squadron. Apart from the admirals, George Rooke, Matt Aylmer and the captain of the *Britannia,* John Neville, were present. The key finding at this crucial meeting was that if the whereabouts of the Toulon squadron were not known, then the Straits squadron and the merchant ships should remain at St Helens until they were.[5] The Lords of the Council and Trenchard were made aware of these naval conclusions, but there appeared to have been a failure of communication in that Queen Mary and the Admiralty Commissioners either did not receive this information or took no notice of it.

Further orders were sent to the admirals on 20 May and were considered at a council of war two days later. In essence, the new instructions ordered the admirals to sail with the

3   H of L MS 1693–5 NS, Vol. I, p. 107.
4   Richmond, *Instrument of Policy,* pp. 238–45.
5   H of L MS 1693–5 NS, Vol. I, p. 231; BL: ADD MS 35898, f. 2, proceedings related to the Smyrna convoy of 1693.

main fleet and to accompany Rooke with the Straits squadron 'so far as you shall think it requisite.' They were then to order the course by which Rooke and his charges should steer for Cadiz, in relation to the Brest fleet and Toulon squadron. The assembled admirals and further naval officers, including the sick John Ashby who would die shortly from an alcohol-related illness, all attended the council of war. They looked upon these instructions as direct orders from the Admiralty Commissioners in the name of Queen Mary. The orders must be obeyed whatever their misgivings and despite the fact that their views of 15 May had been ignored. Hence they merely decided the various rendezvous in relation to different wind directions. If the wind was fair, the rendezvous would be 30 leagues [90 miles] west-south-west of Ushant.[6] Unfortunately, the wording of the conclusions was ambiguous, in that it did not make it clear whether this was purely a rendezvous, or the actual departure point of Rooke and the merchant ships. Lord Falkland was not slow to seize on this ambiguity at the subsequent enquiry.[7]

Eventually on 30 May, the main fleet, including Dutch ships under Philip Almonde, the Straits squadron and the merchant vessels sailed from St Helens.[8] The delay was caused by bad weather and the perennial problem of victualling. On 4 June, the rendezvous 30 leagues west-south-west of Ushant was reached and the admirals ordered the raising of the blue flag at the foretop masthead and the firing of five guns. This was the agreed signal for Rooke and the merchant vessels to depart from the main fleet for Cadiz and their other ports of destination. According to Rooke, as there was little wind, he decided to go across to the *Britannia* and enquire of the admirals what intelligence they had of the Brest fleet.[9] The admirals proceeded to call a council of war, which decided that they would accompany Rooke and his charges for a further 20 leagues and then proceed to a position 10 leagues north-west of Ushant.[10] They were mindful of the necessity of protecting the coast of England from French aggression and were also low on victuals. Rooke's assertion has the ring of truth about it, as subsequently the admirals were not specific in giving reasons for calling this particular council of war.

Clearly earnest debate took place at the 4 June council. Later, Delaval claimed that it was he who had instigated the meeting and proposed sailing a further 50 leagues with Rooke, or until there was firm intelligence of the whereabouts of the French fleet. His view was not supported by the Dutch and some of the other English naval officers. In the end Delaval said that he could not persuade the Dutch to sail more than 20 leagues further.[11] If the date of the letter, of 29 June, is accurate, it was written two days after disaster befell Rooke's ships. Hence he could not possibly have known about it.

6 June saw the separation of the main fleet from Rooke and his merchant vessels. Rooke stated that 'we lost sight of them at night.'[12] The admirals reported that: 'this evening we

---

6   H of L MS 1693–5 NS, Vol. I, p. 231; BL: ADD MS 35898, f. 3, proceedings related to the Smyrna convoy of 1693.
7   H of L MS 1693–5 NS, Vol. I, p. 232; BL: ADD MS 35898, ff. 4–5, proceedings related to the Smyrna convoy of 1693.
8   Today, the mass of merchant vessels would be described as a convoy. In the 17th century, it was the escort ships that were known as the convoy.
9   H of L MS 1693–5 NS, Vol. I, pp. 215–6.
10   H of L MS 1693–5 NS, Vol. I, p. 233.
11   BL: Egerton MS 2618, f. 178, Ralph Delaval to Mr G. Clarke, 29 June 1693.
12   H of L MS 1693–5 NS, Vol. I, p. 216.

parted with the Mediterranean fleet.' In any case, whether the departure was intended or accidental, Rooke's squadron and the merchant ships were sailing directly into the arms of the Brest fleet. In late April, Anne Hilarion de Costentin, Comte de Tourville had taken his fleet out of Brest, down the Iberian Peninsula, around Cape St Vincent to Lagos Bay. He had hoped to join the Brest fleet with the Toulon squadron off the Cape.[13] Rooke had 13 ships of 40–60 guns plus some smaller vessels under his command. In addition, the Dutch admiral, Philips van der Goes had a further eight ships to add to the protective force. Rooke's and van der Goes' ships were certainly a match for the Toulon squadron, but not for the Brest fleet or a combination of them.[14] Unfortunately, Rooke, van der Goes and the 400 merchantmen ran slap into Tourville's fleet near Lagos Bay on 27 June. Wisely Rooke retired and the merchant vessels scattered in all directions.[15] The Anglo-Dutch squadron lost four ships, three Dutch and one English. Forty merchantmen were taken, including four rich Smyrna ships and fifty more were destroyed. Just under a quarter of the merchantmen had been taken, but in view of the disparity in size of the opposing naval forces, it could have been very much worse.[16] The surviving merchantmen took refuge in any friendly port that they could find. Rooke returned to England via Kinsale, in his ship the 70-gun *Royal Oak*, with six other vessels and arrived at Torbay on 17 August.

Let us return to the main fleet which proceeded to its allotted position 10 leagues north-west of Ushant, unaware of the disaster that was to unfold far to the south of them. On 8 June, Shovell wrote to his new father-in-law, John Hill, stating that the Straits ships would sail close to the coast of Portugal, sending a frigate ahead to check whether the French were off Cadiz. He wrote in terms of arriving at the place of rendezvous, on 4 June, 30 leagues west-south-west of Ushant, and that Rooke had steered to the south-west. No mention was made of the extra 20 leagues or the final departure on 6 June. All this is strange: did Shovell not take the extra 20 leagues seriously or is it a simple factual error?[17] The same day, 8 June, the admirals wrote to Trenchard:

> The wind having blown hard from S. and S.S.E. we doubt not that in all probability he [Rooke] is out of the way of danger which might happen to him in these parts. We have not yet been able to gain any intelligence of the French fleet, but shall use all possible endeavours to that purpose.[18]

The admirals were to be proved catastrophically wrong on both counts. Rooke was not out of danger and no attempt had been made to look into Brest roads prior to the departure of Rooke.

On 14 June, the 70-gun *Warspite* and two brigantines were sent by the admirals to check out Brest and the surrounding waters. At this point the main English fleet was two or three leagues off Ushant and consideration was given to attacking the French fleet if it was there.

<hr>

13 Richmond, *Instrument of Policy*, pp. 238–45.
14 *DNB*, Rooke [Laughton].
15 Richmond, *Instrument of Policy*, pp. 238–45.
16 Martin-Leake, *John Leake*, Vol. I, pp. 60–1.
17 H of L MS 1693–5 NS, Vol. I, p. 237.
18 H of L MS 1693–5 NS, Vol. I, p. 130.

The *Warspite* returned on the 17th, with the news that Brest was empty apart from some fishing vessels. The unsuspecting admirals decided to look for the enemy off the Isles of Scilly and if they did not find them to return to Torbay to revictual.[19] At this stage, they showed no concern for Rooke's squadron. The question has to be asked why the *Warspite* was not sent to review Brest prior to the departure of Rooke and the Straits squadron plus merchant vessels?

Having found no sign of the French in the vicinity of the Isles of Scilly, the admirals took the fleet into Torbay. On arrival they were greeted by a letter from Trenchard stating that the French had plans to interrupt Rooke's squadron and the merchantmen. He instructed that everything possible must be done to retake them from the French if there had been a successful attack and there was no limit to the distance the main fleet might sail from England. No doubt the admirals were alarmed by this, to them, an unexpected development. Trenchard ordered the admirals to put to sea at once, but the taking on of victuals was slow and then followed by bad weather which forced the fleet back to port. At this juncture, on 14 July, the 4th rate *Lark[e]*, arrived at Torbay carrying Rooke's secretary, who told the shocked admirals of the disaster that had befallen Rooke's squadron and the merchantmen. From this time onwards the admirals were under continuous attack in their management of the fleet.[20]

During late July and August, the admirals took the fleet to sea to try and redeem themselves by intercepting the French on their return to Brest. They failed and in early September the admirals recommended that the fleet be laid up for the winter. Between 9 and 27 September, Killigrew, Delaval and Shovell were stuck in Portsmouth and, despite frequent requests to the Queen and the Admiralty, were not permitted to come to London to defend themselves. They were left in limbo. Finally, on the 27th, Queen Mary relented, although the admirals were instructed to report to the Admiralty and Trenchard.[21] They were questioned by the Privy Council and enquiries were set up by both the Houses of Commons and Lords.

The nub of the matter was Tourville's Brest fleet. If the Brest fleet had been in harbour it would have posed no threat to the Smyrna merchant convoy, provided they were to be accompanied past Brest by the main fleet. Rooke's squadron was capable of dealing with Victor-Marie d'Estrées' Toulon squadron. If the Brest fleet had been out of harbour, it posed a potential threat to the Smyrna convoy, unless its position was known and could be avoided. It seems inconceivable that the Cabinet Council, Admiralty Commissioners and the joint admirals could overlook this most basic of facts. But they did not. Nottingham had received an account of French preparations at Brest and Trenchard had been instructed to order the joint admirals to look into Brest with the main fleet and the Straits squadron to ascertain the whereabouts of the main French fleet. The Straits squadron was not to leave the protection of the main English fleet until this time.[22] But the orders had not been transmitted properly to the admirals by Trenchard. Clearly, the Second Secretary of State, Sir John Trenchard, should be held primarily responsible for the Smyrna convoy disaster. This fact is not widely known.

<hr>

19   H of L MS 1693–5 NS, Vol. I, pp. 130–1, 212–13.
20   H of L MS 1693–5 NS, Vol. I, p. 177.
21   H of L MS 1693–5 NS, Vol. I, pp. 179–80.
22   Aiken, *Nottingham*, p. 117.

Killigrew, Delaval and Shovell had all commanded squadrons on numerous occasions in the past. It is extraordinary that they did not take the precaution of looking into Brest water before sending the Straits squadron and the merchantmen on their way into Tourville's arms. In their defence the admirals argued that on 15 May, they had advised that if the whereabouts of the Toulon squadron were unknown, then the merchant ships should remain at St Helens. When they received the Admiralty's instructions on 20 May, they viewed them as a direct order to sail which overruled their own advice of 15 May. Much play was made of whether at their council of war on 22 May they had discussed looking into Brest or not. The admirals supported by the senior Dutch admiral said they had not as the matter had been fully aired on 15 May. Only Rooke thought that it had been discussed on the 22nd. The admirals' explanation for this oversight is still questionable, in that they had only spoken in terms of the Toulon squadron on 15 May and no mention had been made of the Brest fleet.

To complicate matters even further, reference must be made to the evidence of a certain William Rutter. He claimed to have told the admirals that he had seen the French fleet coming out of Brest water on 7 May. Killigrew was said to have threatened him with hanging and that Shovell was the only admiral to be interested in this information. Rutter's account was obviously a complete fabrication, but he was frequently produced at the House of Commons' enquiry to embarrass the admirals.[23] One of Samuel Pepys' former servants who had served aboard the *Britannia* had described the alleged mismanagement of the ship to him. There had been a fire in the Bay of Biscay, they had run aground and the admirals set a poor example by drinking until the early hours of the morning.[24] Certainly in the case of Shovell, this sounded like a gross calumny as he was renowned for not drinking to excess. However, it was the kind of gossip Pepys revelled in.

As a final plea to the Admiralty, the admirals contended: 'they had answered questions not with art but with truth and plainness of seamen.' They had acted by calling councils of war in response to express orders and had followed the unanimous advice of the flag officers. In addition, the admirals pointed out that the Dutch had approved of the actions of Philip Almonde and it was very hard that their self-same actions were considered a crime.[25] It is difficult to disagree with the logic of their view.

The House of Commons' debates and enquiry followed a speech made by William III, on 7 November, 1693 concerning the miscarriage of affairs at sea. 'For what relates to the latter (which has brought so great a disgrace upon the Nation) I have resented it extremely; and as I will take care that those who have not done their duty shall be punished, that our power at sea may be rightly managed for the future.'[26] On 13 November, a member of the Commons said that 'the fleet should have convoyed the Turkey fleet out of danger. They fiddled and danced at Torbay and must pay the music.' A number of motions were debated in the Commons: the most critical from the admirals' point of view was: 'that there has been a notorious and treacherous mismanagement in that affair' [i.e. the Smyrna convoy]. This was passed by 140–103. However, a further motion: 'that the admirals that commanded the fleet last Summer, by not gaining such intelligence before they left the Streights Squadron

---

23   H of L MS 1693–5 NS, Vol. I, pp. 98–9; Grey, *Debates*, pp. 311–75.
24   Aubrey, *The Defeat*, p. 161.
25   BL: ADD MS 35898, f. 39, proceedings related to the Smyrna convoy of 1693.
26   Grey, *Debates*, pp. 311–75.

are guilty of a high breach of Trust that was put in them to the great loss and dishonour of the Nation.' This was narrowly rejected by 185–175.[27]

In early January 1694, the House of Lords was a little kinder to the oppressed admirals. 'The Lords had resolved that the Admirals who had commanded the fleet last summer had done well in the execution of the orders they received.' However some Lords entered their protest.[28] Perhaps the best summing up of the position of the unfortunate admirals was made by William Blathwayt, the Secretary of State at War and a great favourite of William III. He said simply: 'they had been cut down after hanging.'[29] Another victim of the Smyrna convoy disaster was Nottingham who, in an age of endemic political corruption, was a man of unimpeachable integrity; he was made to resign as Secretary of State. This was largely through Whig pressure orchestrated by the Wharton brothers, Thomas and Goodwin, with that most political of naval men – Edward Russell. A scurrilous rhyme circulated in the city taverns. 'That the Turkey fleet was sold is true and not a sham; You may find it out by searching as far as Nottingham.'[30]

Nottingham has left a record of his opinion on Shovell:

> Then some attempted to blame the admirals (or rather two of them, Killigrew and Delaval), and great endeavours were used to separate Sir Cloudesley Shovel from joining them in defense of their conduct, for he was in great esteem, and very deservedly, with every faction in the fleet and with all seamen. But he could not be persuaded to do so dishonourable a proceeding but frankly owned to the committee that he had heartily concurred in every resolution which had been taken by them and declared further that, if he had had sole command of the fleet, everything which had been done he would and must have done and should have thought it his duty.[31]

Rooke came off remarkably lightly from the various enquiries and could justifiably claim to have been following the orders of the joint admirals. However, his management of the squadron had been casual, in that little attempt had been made to scout ahead in search of the French. At the time of the enquiries, Rooke was suffering from a painful attack of gout and on one occasion had to be carried in a chair.[32]

William III treated Killgrew and Delaval harshly and on 11 November Trenchard informed them that they could no longer act as commissioners of the admiralty.[33] A month later, the King, in order to show his dissatisfaction with the joint admirals, declared them discharged from all military and civil employment. Killigrew lost his marine regiment and Delaval his company of guards. Oddly, Shovell was not removed as an extra commissioner

---

27 Grey, *Debates*, pp. 311–75; Horwitz, *Parliament*, p. 125.
28 Grey, *Debates*, p. 375.
29 Gertrude Jacobsen, *William Blathwayt: A Late 17th Century English Administrator* (New Haven: Yale University Press 1932), p. 290.
30 Aiken, *Nottingham*, pp. 120–1.
31 Aiken, *Nottingham*, pp. 120–1.
32 H of L MS 1693–5 NS, Vol. I, p. 243.
33 *CSP Dom, William and Mary,* Vol. 4, 1693, p. 395.

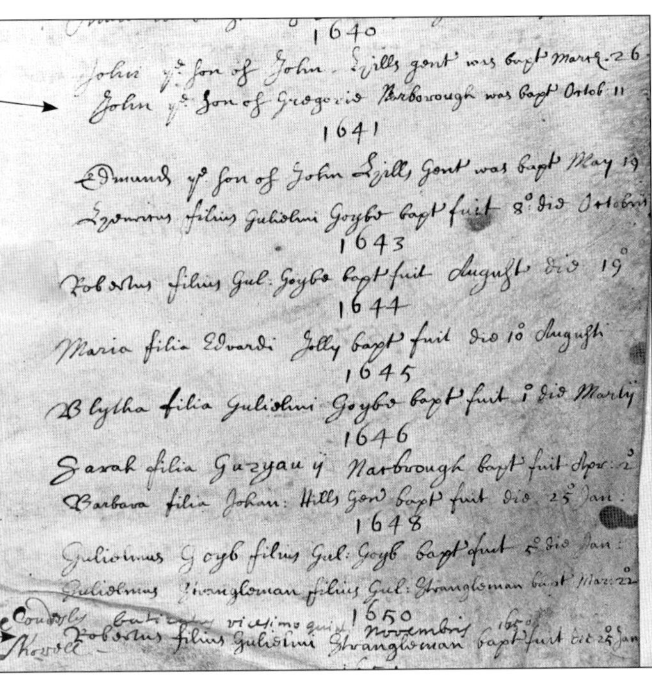

The font in All Saints Church, Cockthorpe
where both John Narbrough and
Cloudesley Shovell were baptised.
(Courtesy of a Private Collection)

St Mary Matfelon where Christopher Myngs and Cloudesley Jenkenson were buried. (Courtesy of the London Metropolitan Archives, City of London)

Knowlton Court, Kent, the country home of John Narbrough, 18th century print. Seen when it was still owned by the descendants of his daughter, Elizabeth D'Aeth. (Courtesy of a Private Collection)

Christopher Myngs. The 'admiral-buccaneer' who was repeatedly wounded in action. (Courtesy of a Private Collection)

Thomas Brooks, woodcut by an unknown artist, early to mid-17th century. The Puritan clergyman was a friend and supporter of Christopher Myngs whom he said 'had brains on both sides of his head.' (Courtesy of the National Portrait Gallery)

Thomas Tollemache [Talmash], commanded the landing forces at the disastrous attack on Camaret Bay in 1694. Brave but foolhardy, he was mortally wounded in the leg during the action and died later in England. (Courtesy of a Private Collection)

John Benbow, the bombing expert. (Courtesy of a Private Collection)

Thomas Herbert, 5th Earl of Pembroke. Briefly, Lord High Admiral before being replaced by Prince George of Denmark, the husband of Queen Anne. (Courtesy of a Private Collection)

George Byng, 1st Viscount Torrington led the surviving ships to safety after the *Association* was wrecked on 22 October 1707. (Courtesy of a Private Collection)

Prince George of Hesse Darmstadt. An able leader at the Sieges of Gibraltar [1704] and Barcelona [1705]. He had the great misfortune to exsanguinate following a musket ball rupturing his femoral artery during the latter siege. (Courtesy of a Private Collection)

Edward Montagu, 1st Earl of Sandwich was drowned during the Battle of Sole Bay in 1672. (Courtesy of a Private Collection)

Louis Alexandre, Count of Toulouse. A natural son of Louis XIV who nominally commanded the French at the Battle of Malaga in 1704. (Courtesy of a Private Collection)

Jean d'Estrées, print. The uninspiring commander of the French contingent at the Battles of Sole Bay [1672] and Texel [1673]. (Courtesy of the National Maritime Museum)

Victor Amadeus II, Duke of Savoy. Despite the protestations of Cloudesley Shovell, the Duke lost heart during the failed siege of Toulon. (Courtesy of a Private Collection)

Prince Eugene, mezzotint by John Smith after David Richter 1706. Eugene's irresolution was a major factor in the failure to take Toulon in 1707. (Courtesy of the National Portrait Gallery)

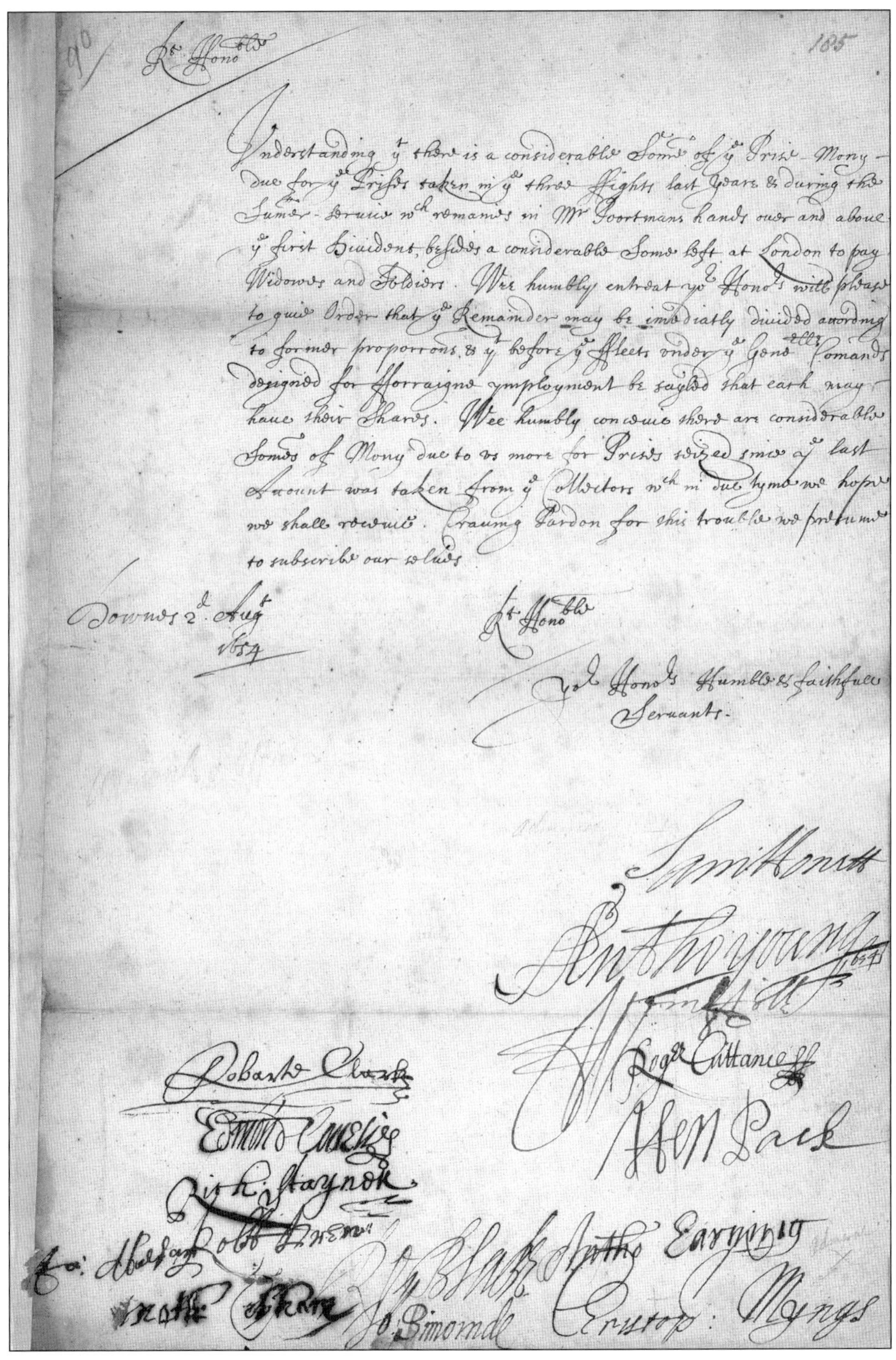

A rare document signed by Christopher Myngs in 1654. (Courtesy of the British Library)

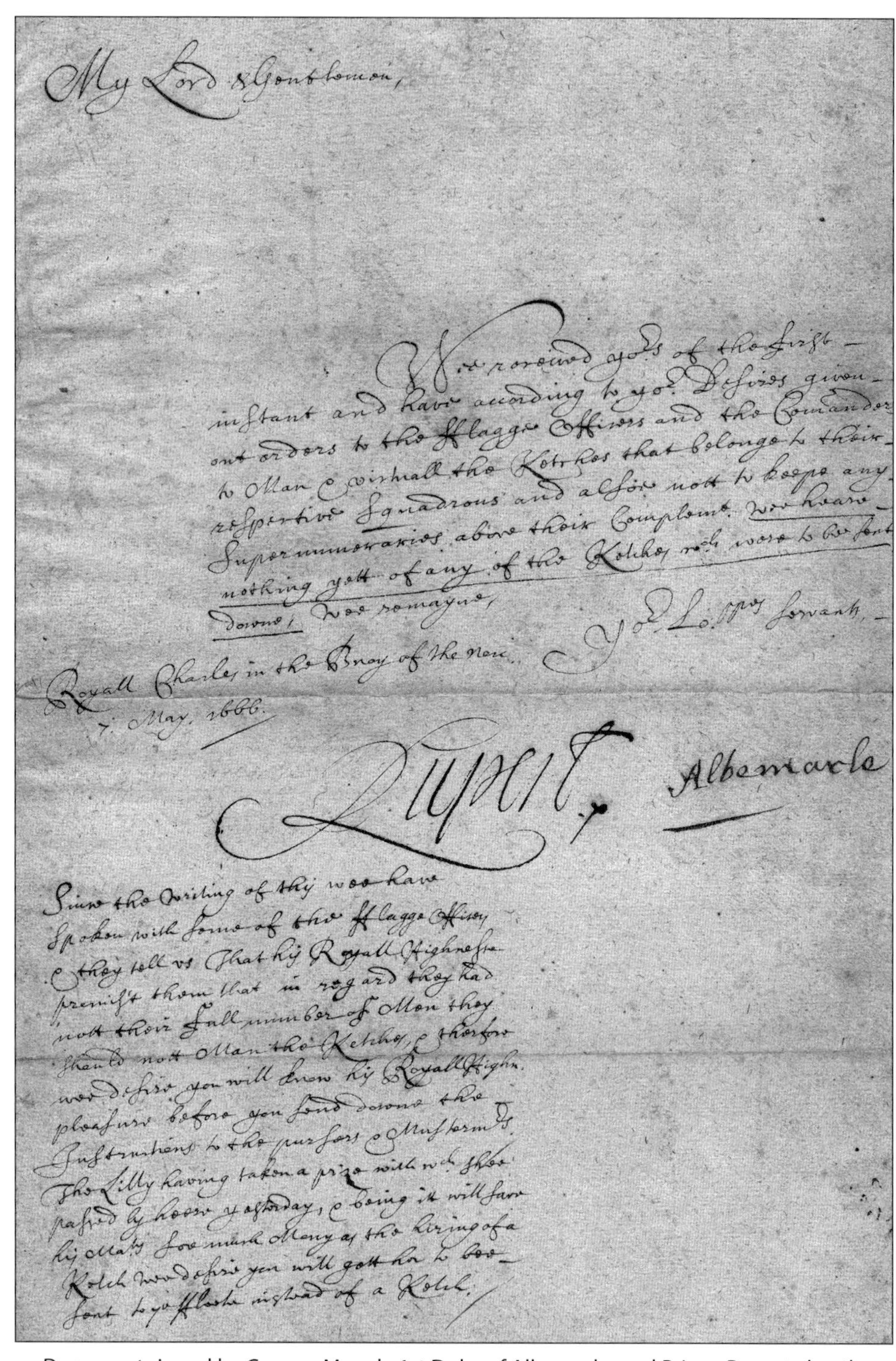

Document signed by George Monck, 1st Duke of Albemarle, and Prince Rupert shortly before the Four Days' Battle of 1666. (Courtesy of a Private Collection)

xi.

Narbrough's journal, with the entry of Christopher Myngs' death on 10 June 1666. (Courtesy of the British Library)

Rt Honble Sr

These are Certifieing yor Honor
of my Arriuall in the Hope where I am now
at Anchor; I do Sire there may be three Cable
Sent downe & an Anchor by the first opportunitie
I haue not more then what ye Shipp now Rideth
that I can trust too, In case the Shipp proceed
to Sea without goeing further It will be
Conuenient to haue a Supply of Store, which
will be wanting; I humbly take my leaue
& Remaine

Yor Honors Most humble Seruant
John Narbrough

On board his Maties Shipp Fairfax
in the Hope: June: 5: 1673

read & answered p 6

John Narbrough document. (Courtesy of a Private Collection)

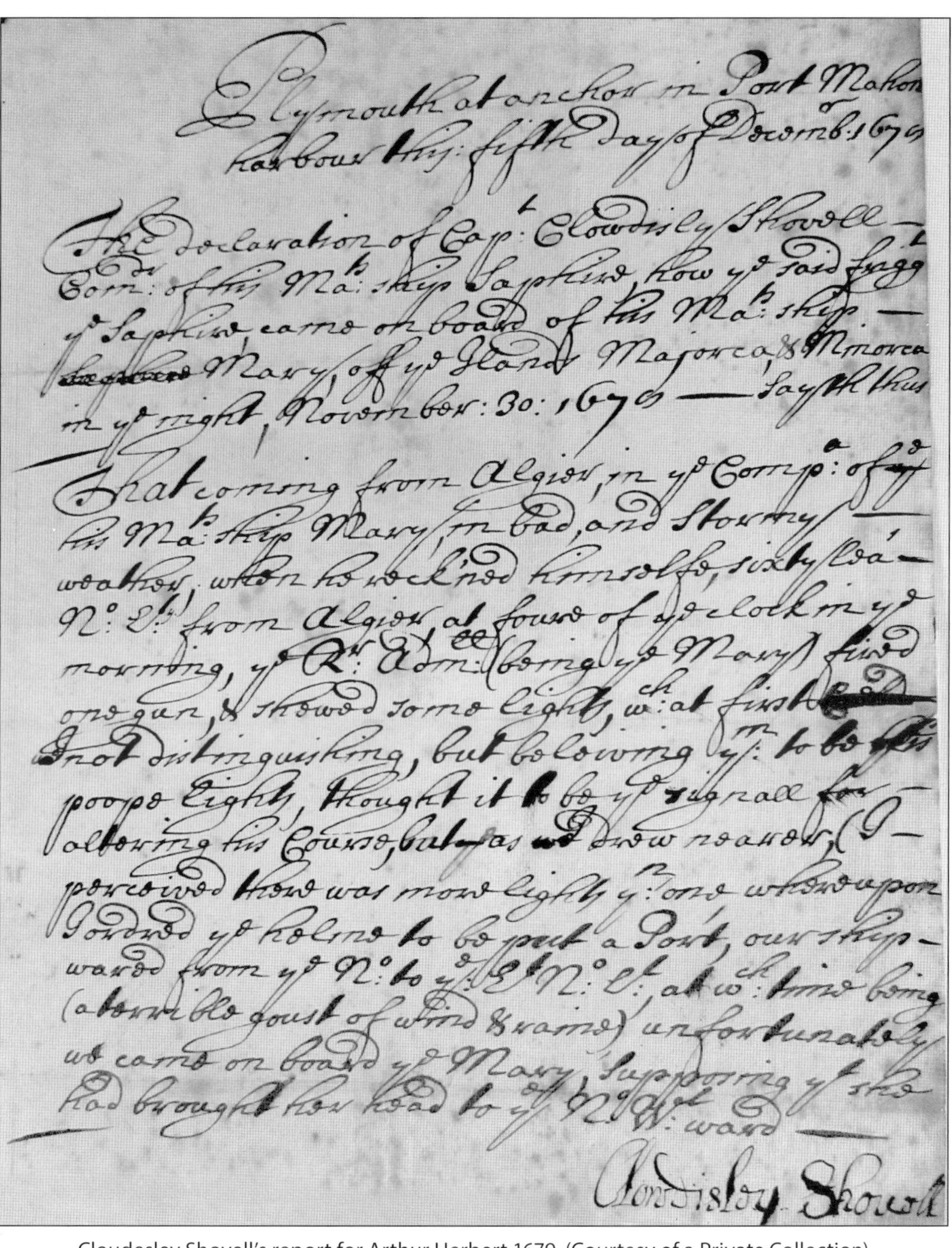

Cloudesley Shovell's report for Arthur Herbert 1679. (Courtesy of a Private Collection)

Coarse letter from Edward Russell to Arthur Herbert 1683. (Courtesy of a Private Collection)

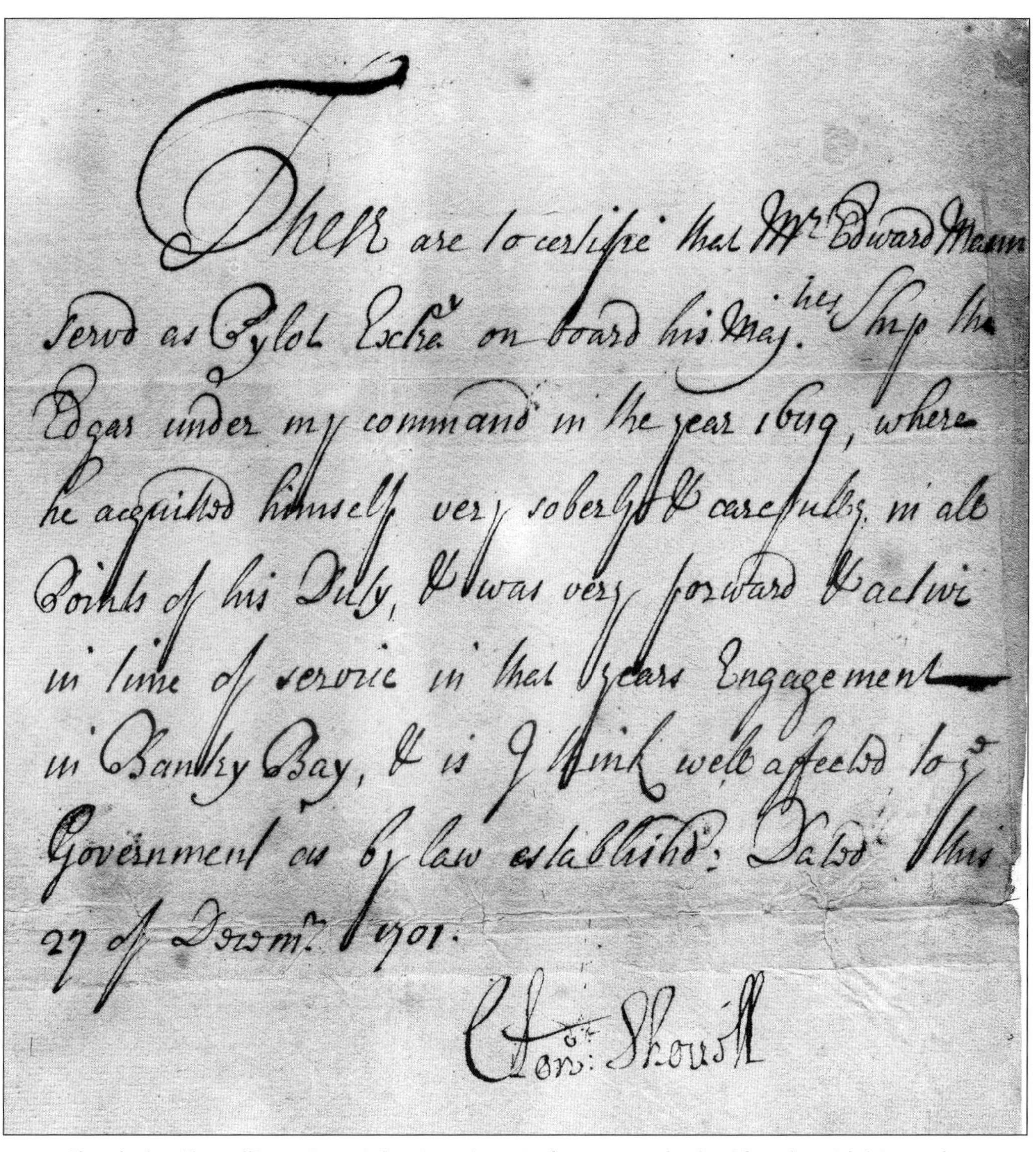

These are to certifie that Mr Edward Mann servd as Pylot Extra on board his Majhies Ship the Edgar under my command in the year 1689, where he acquitted himself very soberly & carefully in all Points of his Duty, & was very forward & active in time of service in that years Engagement in Bantry Bay, & is I think well affected to ye Government as by law establishd. Dated this 27 of Decmr 1701.

Clow: Shovell

Cloudesley Shovell's testimonial written in 1701 for a man who had fought with him at the Battle of Bantry Bay in 1689. (Courtesy of a Private Collection)

Brass money was used by the forces of James II, in Ireland from 1689–91, during the Nine Years' War. If the former king had been victorious it would have been replaced by silver coinage. Described by Cloudesley Shovell as 'damned brass money.' (Courtesy of a Private Collection)

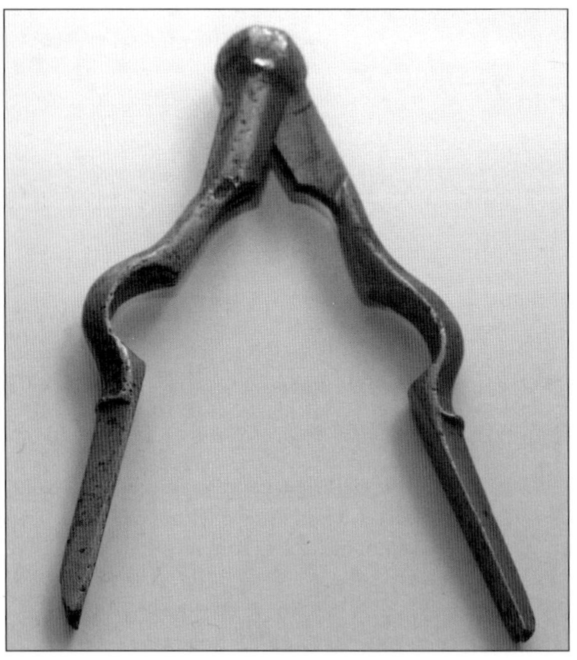

Navigational dividers from the wreck of the *Association*. (Courtesy of a Private Collection)

Pewter medicinal syringe from the wreck of the *Association*. There is a similar one in the *Mary Rose* Collection at Portsmouth. (Courtesy of a Private Collection)

Cloudeley Shovell's strongbox. (Courtesy of a Private Collection)

Pewter chamber pot salvaged from the wreck of the *Association*. (Courtesy of the Isles of Scilly Museum)

Gold coin salvaged from Cloudesley Shovell's flagship, the *Association*, which was wrecked on the Gilstone 22 October 1707. (Courtesy of a Private Collection)

Onion bottle from the *Eagle*, part of Shovell's fleet, which was also wrecked on 22 October 1707. (Courtesy of a Private Collection)

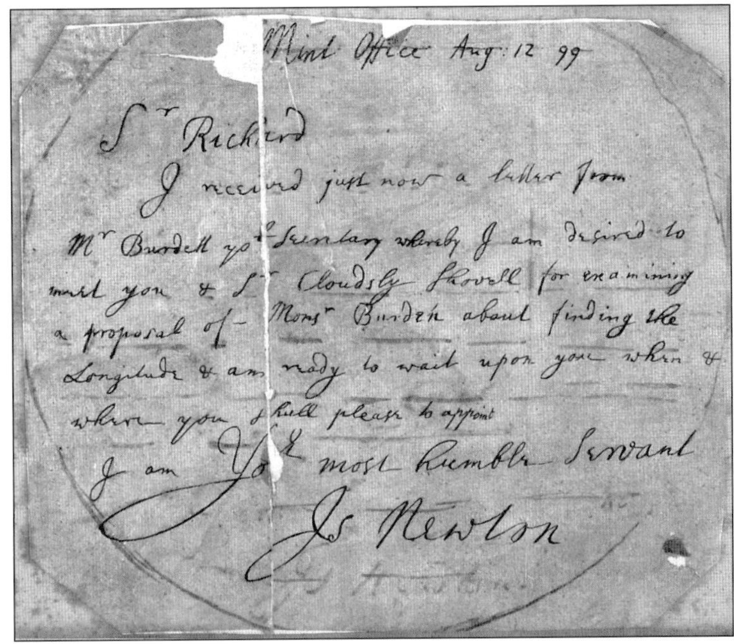

Note written in 1699 by Sir Isaac Newton that discusses a possible meeting with Cloudesley Shovell to discuss longitude. (Courtesy of Mullock's Auctions Ltd of Shropshire)

St Michael model. Both John Narbrough and Cloudesley Shovell served in the ship at the Battle of Texel. (Courtesy of the National Maritime Museum)

Battle of Scheveningen [1653], print maker Salomon Savery. Christopher Myngs, in the *Elizabeth*, played his part in the bloodiest battle of the First Dutch War. (Courtesy of the Rijksmuseum)

xx

St Francisco de Campeche: a naval battle by John Ogilby 1671. In February 1663, Christopher Myngs was wounded in the face and both thighs in Campeche. (Courtesy of the British Library)

Battle of Lowestoft [1665], brush/pen possibly by Jan Abrahamsz Beerstraten. Christopher Myngs in the *Triumph* fired the first shots of the battle and was knighted afterwards. (Courtesy of the Rijksmuseum)

Battle of La Hogue [1692], print by William Woolett after Benjamin West 1781. Cloudesley Shovell was unable to lead the boat action in person as the result of a splinter wound to his thigh or a fall. (Courtesy of the Rijksmuseum)

Siege of Barcelona 1705, print by Sieuwert van de Meulen. At the siege, Cloudesley Shovell had the joint command at sea with the diminutive and arrogant Charles Mordaunt, 3rd Earl of Peterborough. (Courtesy of the Rijksmuseum)

of the navy and it was said that he would be employed again at sea. The clear inference is that Killigrew and Delaval were being separated from Shovell in the magnitude of their punishment.[34]

Neither Killigrew nor Delaval would serve at sea again and their naval careers were over. Shovell's was not, although it had suffered a temporary setback. In the straightforward, honest manner that underwrote his character, he refused to distance himself from Killigrew and Delaval. According to Campbell, at the bar of the House of Commons, he defended his colleagues as well as himself: 'giving so clear and plain account of the matter, that it satisfied all people who were capable of being satisfied of the innocence of the commanders, I mean in a point of treachery.'[35] In fact in 1693, there is little evidence that Jacobitism was active in the fleet, although there was suspicion, that as Tories, Killigrew and Delaval were sympathetic towards James II.[36] Shovell, a Whig, was known to loathe the former King and his religion. It is unlikely that Shovell would have been amused by a piece of contemporary Dutch wit, with a picture of Shovell aboard ship, with his hands tied behind his back and one end of the cord held by each of his colleagues. This was to insinuate that Shovell would have prevented the disaster if Killigrew and Delaval had not hindered him.[37] Shovell with his ancestral roots in the Low Countries, always got on well with the Dutch and their showing him in a favourable light is not surprising.

The Smyrna convoy disaster was a catastrophe of the first order. In the City of London it was looked upon as the severest blow since the Great Fire, over 27 years earlier. Everyone from the Secretaries of State, the Admiralty Commissioners and the Admirals, both English and Dutch, had inexplicably blocked out of their collective minds that Tourville's French fleet was anywhere save Brest. This fact coupled with administrative and clerical incompetence led to the fate that befell Rooke's Straits squadron and their merchant vessel charges. As was stated earlier in this chapter, a great measure of the blame lay at the door of Sir John Trenchard. The King, the Levant Company and the other merchants had every reason to be livid.

In November 1693, Killigrew, Delaval and Shovell had been refused permission to come and kiss the King's hand.[38] On 8 March 1694, Edward Russell took Shovell to meet William III and he was allowed to kiss his hand. 'Tis said he will be employed at sea this summer.' He had been forgiven.[39]

It was possible that the controversy over the Smyrna convoy had saved Shovell's life. In the winter of 1693–4, Francis Wheeler was sent to escort merchant vessels to the Mediterranean and his ship, the brand new 80-gun *Sussex*, foundered in a storm trying to pass through the Strait of Gibraltar in mid-February 1694. Wheeler and most of the crew had drowned. Initially, Shovell had been chosen for the command.[40] Two months later, there was a report that Shovell had fought a duel with the commander of the *Hampton Court*, the vain John

34   *CSP Dom, William and Mary*, Vol. 4, 1693, pp. 426–7.
35   Campbell, *British Admirals*, Vol. IV, p. 245.
36   Historical Manuscripts Commission (HMC): Buccleuch MS, Vol. II, Part I (London: HMSO 1903), p. 396.
37   Campbell, *British Admirals*, Vol. IV, p. 245.
38   BL: ADD MS 35855, f. 28, John Trenchard letter book.
39   Luttrell, *State Affairs*, Vol. III, p. 280.
40   Ehrman, *War of William III*, p. 504; Burchett, *Transactions at Sea*, p. 204.

Graydon, and had been slightly wounded.[41] Whether the duel actually took place or not, and if it did, what the cause of it was is unknown. Possibly it related to the doomed Smyrna convoy, in which both men had played a part. In 1702, as will be seen in a later chapter, Shovell and Graydon worked amicably together to bring the treasure home from Vigo.

In the autumn of 1693, William III, on his return from Flanders and in the aftermath of the Smyrna convoy disaster, appointed Edward Russell as commander-in-chief of the fleet for the campaign season of 1694. In April, Shovell was appointed vice-admiral of the red in that fleet. Undoubtedly, he owed his position to the influence and strong support of Russell who recalled his fine performance at the Battle of Barfleur. Shovell was to serve in the 90-gun *Neptune* with Thomas Jennings as commander for most of 1694. Plans had been drawn up to send a strong fleet to the Mediterranean to bolster the ailing King of Spain, Charles II, and to prevent the French Toulon squadron from joining the ships at Brest. Additionally an attempt was to be made on Brest itself.

At the beginning of May 1694, Russell took most of the Anglo-Dutch fleet to sea, leaving Shovell with a squadron at Portsmouth to embark 6,000 troops for the attempt on Brest. The army commander for Brest was the rough, dissolute, hot-headed Lieutenant-General Thomas Tollemache or Talmash as Shovell called him. The two men knew each other well from their days in Tangier in 1680 and during the Irish campaign of 1690–1.[42] Shovell was to be second-in-command to John, 3rd Baron Berkeley of Stratton for the Brest operation. Berkeley was 13 years younger than Shovell and a jealous, domineering young man.[43] However, Shovell served loyally under the aristocratic Berkeley until the latter's death three years later. On returning to St Helens with the main fleet, Russell discovered that Shovell had safely embarked the troops. On 29 May, both the main fleet and Berkeley's squadron with its military force sailed. Clearly Russell had misgivings about the attempt on Brest and his own voyage to the Mediterranean: 'I am afraid we shall not have much to brag of for the year is so far advanced and for both our designs.' He continued: 'I am not a very desponding man but I am a little out of hope.'[44] Berkeley's contingent parted from Russell and the main fleet on 5 June.

Russell took the main fleet into the Mediterranean. His presence there led to the withdrawal of the French fleet into Toulon and gave a measure of support to the Spanish army, who were hard pressed in holding the French in Catalonia. Russell had been ordered to spend the winter of 1694–5 in Cadiz, which he was reluctant to do. However, he loyally obeyed William III.[45] Whilst wintering in Spain, Russell gave one of the longest and most celebrated cocktail parties in the whole of history. He converted a fountain into a gigantic punchbowl adding 250 gallons of brandy followed by 250 gallons of Malaga wine. A sailor in a rowing boat refilled the guests' glasses and he had to be relieved every 15 minutes so strong were the alcohol fumes! The party is reputed to have lasted until the fountain was

41 Luttrell, *State Affairs*, Vol. III, p. 293.
42 Aiken, *Nottingham*, pp. 66–7; *DNB*, Talmash.
43 Aiken, *Nottingham*, p. 101; *DNB*, Berkeley of Stratton [Laughton].
44 Richmond, *Instrument of Policy*, p. 252.
45 Richmond, *Instrument of Policy*, pp. 255–7.

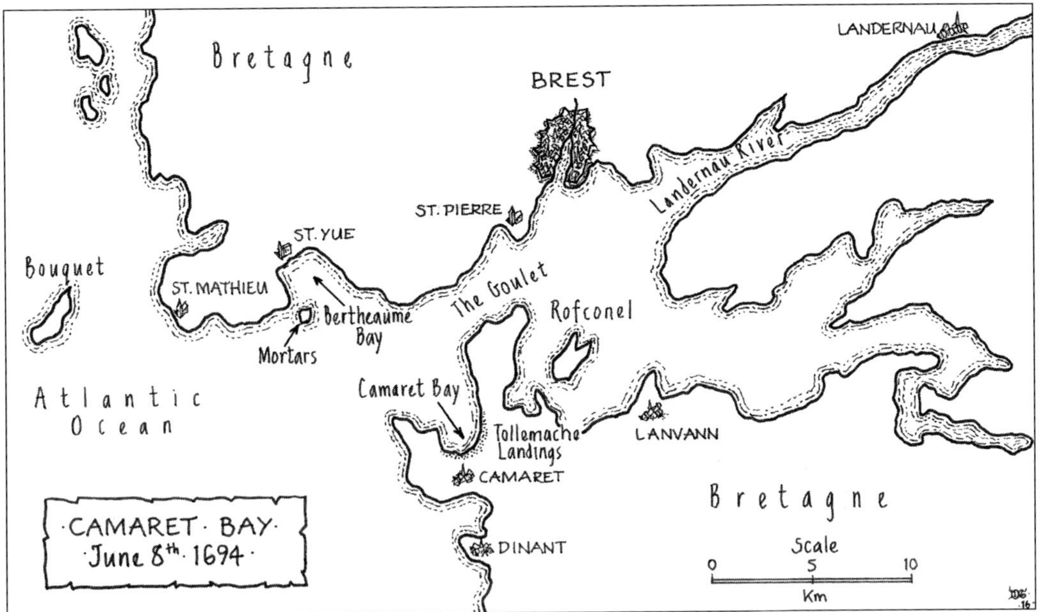

Map 16 Camaret Bay June 8th 1694.

dry.[46] This took a week and a silk canopy was placed over it when it rained. Like John Ashby and Arthur Herbert, Edward Russell was a serious drinking man.

Russell's foreboding of Tollemache's assault on Brest proved to be well founded. When the ex-King James II, who knew of the plan, went to Louis XIV with this choice piece of intelligence, the French king replied: 'sure you are ill-served by your friends in England, for I have long ago had account of it, as the English will find by their reception when they come here.'[47] Tradition had it that John Churchill, later 1st Duke of Marlborough, was the source of the leak. Sébastian Vauban, the celebrated designer of fortifications, had several months to improve the defences of Brest prior to the arrival of Tollemache's expeditionary force. The city of Brest was surrounded with walls, new batteries of cannon were set up and over 8,000 foot soldiers, bombardiers and gentlemen volunteers provided the garrison. Thanks to Vauban the chances of Brest falling into the hands of the English were remote.[48]

In early June, the fleet anchored between Bertheaume and Camaret Bays and a council of war, attended by Shovell was held. On 8 June the landing was made in Camaret Bay, as a stepping stone to Brest and the surrounding area. A document, almost certainly written by Shovell in the *Neptune,* described the action:

My Lord Berkeley was left here with 18 English and 11 Dutch ships of the line of battle, and of both nations there were twelve fireships, six frigates, and five bomb

46 Davies, *Pepys's Navy*, p. 296.
47 Aiken, *Nottingham*, p. 134.
48 Richmond, *Instrument of Policy*, p. 249; Campbell, *British Admirals*, Vol. III, p. 152.

vessels, and we had on board the fleet about 6,000 land soldiers. We directed our course to Ushant, in order to go to Brest, and on the 7th inst we anchored in the evening with our fleet from St Matthews Point towards the narrow going into Brest Sound, keeping out of shot of the shore, but were entertained with bombs from the land on Camarett side, also from both sides going into Brest Sound, and along the north shore almost as far as St Matthews Point, and although we were out of gun shot, yet to my wonder the bombs reached where we rid, which I am confident was two miles and a half, rather more than less: I am also convinced by reasonable argument (contrary to my former opinion) that if one of the great shells fall into one of our ships and burst, it will quite disable if not destroy her. Here we rid all night taking care with our boats and brigantines that the enemy made no insult on our storeships and small vessels.

The 8th instant in the morning, the weather was foggy; but about 7 in the fore-noon it cleared up, and the signal being made, we embarked all our land forces in our boats and tendors in order to land them in Camarett Bay; but discovering there were forts and batteries of guns and lines and trenches all near where we intended to land, we sent seven frigates (three were English and four were Dutch) to batter the aforesaid fortifications, the better to facilitate the landing of the soldiers. The ships that went on this service were commanded by my Lord Carmarthen,[49] who placed them with a great deal of skill, and performed his duty with much bravery and hazard.

Between 3 and 4 this afternoon four or five hundred of our soldiers landed (most of them grenadiers), Lieutenant-General Talmash [Tollemache] landed with them; but they were so warmly received by the enemy that Talmash was shot through the thigh, and with difficulty was got off; and the rest not being able to advance by reason of the shore, in so much that most of our men that landed were either killed or taken prisoner, the rest of our soldiers were returned on board, we having lost five of our well boats which were grounded and left on shore, which the enemy burnt upon the retreat of the soldiers. My Lord Carmarthen came off with the ships all but one of the Dutch frigates of 32 guns. I am pretty well satisfied the French knew of our coming, and may easily be persuaded they knew where we intended to land, they being more particularly fortified at that place, though at other places they had industriously provided to oppose our landing. I suppose about 300 English and Dutch seamen suffered in this skirmish, that is, were killed, wounded or taken prisoners, for several men suffered in our well boats, and other boats, and few men escaped from a Dutchman that was sunk.

This evening at a council of war it was considered whether we could attempt any other place with the land forces; but General Talmash declared he had not power to carry forces anywhere else. It was considered if the fleet could not go into Brest Sound, and bomb the town. It was thought too great a hazard to go in with the fleet, unless we could be certain we could ride without reach of their bombs; for 'tis most of our opinions that if a shell break in any ship it will disable if not destroy

---

49   Peregrine Osborne, Marquis of Carmarthen after his father, Thomas, became the 1st Duke of Leeds in 1694.

her. Then 'twas considered if the frigates and bomb vessels might go in and bomb the town: that was also thought unreasonable and impracticable, first, because our number of frigates are few and those much disabled by the day's action; secondly, we knew not the enemy's strength, which might probably be sufficient to take both frigates and bombs; and thirdly, our number of bomb vessels, being but five, is very insufficient to perform so great an undertaking. In all this you see we make no difficulty of passing their castles, there being no danger other than the hazard of their shot and bombs, which they can ply at you all the way through the narrow land, [from] the rock in the middle of the narrow: therefore 'twas concluded we should return to Spithead and there expect further orders. So that on the 9th, in the morning, we weighed and stood to sea.[50]

The attempted landing by the Anglo-Dutch force at Camaret Bay had been a fiasco, and Berkeley, Shovell and their damaged ships returned to St Helens on 15 June. Tollemache's wounded thigh became infected and he died in England.[51]

The assault on Camaret Bay has rightly gone down in history as a disaster. The proposal to destroy the French fleet in Brest, using Camaret Bay as a stepping-stone was a sound one. However, security had been poor and the French had got wind of the operation. It did not help the situation that the build-up of the Anglo-Dutch force was slow and by the end of May the bulk of the French fleet had already left Brest. Once it was clear that the French defences at Camaret Bay were fully prepared and alerted, Tollemache should have abandoned the attack and looked for an easier target. He and many of his troops, as well as Berkeley's and Shovell's sailors, to a lesser extent, paid for his foolhardiness with their lives.

What of the roles of the principal naval officers in the disaster? Berkeley, Shovell and Peregrine Osborne, Marquis of Carmarthen had attended the various councils of war and must bear a measure of blame for not stopping the operation once it was clear that the French defences were alert and waiting for them. However, the main responsibility for the failed landing lay with the obstinate but brave land forces commander, Thomas Tollemache. The only senior sea officer to enhance his reputation was Carmarthen. For two years running, Shovell's name had been associated with a disaster, firstly the Smyrna convoy and now the landing at Camaret Bay. At least with the latter he was only peripherally involved.

---

50   HMC: Portland MS, Vol. VIII, p. 41; John Laughton, *Naval Miscellany* (London: Navy Records Society 1912).
51   *DNB*, Tollemache [Talmash]; Campbell, *British Admirals*, Vol. III, p. 153.

14

Bombardment of French Coastal Towns and the End of the Nine Years' War 1694–1697

We have seen that the bombardment of French coastal towns began in 1692 and, as we will find out later in this chapter, this would continue until 1696. The rationale was to force the withdrawal of French troops and ships away from other theatres of war, such as Flanders and the Mediterranean. There is no evidence that in this they were in any way successful, the local defence and militia proving capable of dealing with the attacks. The only people to suffer were the civilian inhabitants of the coastal towns, such as Dieppe and Dunkirk, whose homes were destroyed. John, 3rd Baron Berkeley of Stratton, was unhappy about this form of warfare, but Shovell's personal views are unknown. The justification for these barbaric and largely pointless attacks, with little harm done to the French economy, was that they themselves had initiated this form of warfare.[1]

On their return to St Helens, on 15 June 1694, Berkeley and Shovell found instructions from Queen Mary to consider what to attempt next with their ships and troops. A decision was made to attack Dieppe and then to proceed along the French coast to alarm it.[2] In late June–early July, Berkeley's squadron, with Shovell acting as his second-in-command, came across a fleet of Swedish/Danish ships carrying contraband goods and despite their passes took them into harbour. As will be seen this would have repercussions for later in the summer.[3]

Eventually, in mid-July, the bombardment of Dieppe began with the English bomb ketches discharging a mixture of granado shells and carcasses into the unfortunate town. Over 1,000 bombs were thrown into Dieppe over a 12-hour period. The granado shells were explosive in nature and each carcass consisted of a cylinder filled with combustibles to act as incendiaries. Berkeley sent in a machine vessel or infernal filled with explosives in a vain attempt to destroy the wooden pier there. Shovell had no high opinion of machine vessels: 'which some people think absurd.' They were 20–100 tons in size and were towed inshore

---

1   Richmond, *Instrument of Policy,* pp. 254–5, 260–1.
2   Laird Clowes, *Royal Navy,* Vol. II, p. 476; Campbell, *British Admirals,* Vol. III, p. 153; Richmond, *Instrument of Policy,* p. 253.
3   Laird Clowes, *Royal Navy,* Vol. II, p. 476; Richmond, *Instrument of Policy,* p. 253; H of L MS 1693–95 NS, Vol. I, p. 495.

and then detonated.[4] Many of the wooden houses of Dieppe were burnt to the ground, leaving the inhabitants homeless, but having little effect on the finances of France. Next on the list for the bombing treatment was Havre de Grace [in modern times Le Havre]. Although less destruction was done to the port than to Dieppe, the damage was still considerable. At the end of July, the Berkeley/Shovell squadron retired to St Helens to refit and then Berkeley left for London.

At the beginning of August, Shovell took the revictualled squadron to the Downs.[5] Here he was involved in controversy after he ordered a Danish man-of-war, convoy to some merchant ships, to strike his flag. The Dane declined and Shovell instructed the *Stirling Castle* to give him a broadside and was answered in kind. A sharp engagement took place which ended with a successful boarding of the Dane. Forty Danes were killed, including the captain who, initially, Shovell thought must be drunk and the *Stirling Castle* lost eight men in reply. English honour was satisfied.[6] Queen Mary wanted Shovell to make a further attempt on Dunkirk. The infamous Jean Bart with a squadron of eight ships was based in this port and there were 40–50 privateers as well. There were fears that Bart had designs on a large merchant fleet carrying supplies for the navy, such as pitch and hemp, still at Elsinore. If these ships were taken, English naval operations in 1695 would be severely curtailed. The matter was further complicated in that Denmark might hold up the supply fleet in retaliation for their own and Swedish merchant ships having been taken by Berkeley and Shovell near Dieppe earlier in the summer. It was for all these reasons that Dunkirk must be assaulted.[7]

Although loyally prepared to attack Dunkirk again, Shovell was unhappy about the whole business. The eccentric Dutch artillery officer, William Meesters went to Ostend and Neuport to collect pilots for the operation. In mid-September the squadron appeared before Dunkirk once more and an attempt was made to destroy the piers. Meesters' pilots proved to be ignorant, cowardly and insubordinate.[8] Shovell went to the lengths of encouraging the seamen of the machine vessels by saying he would distribute £500 among the crew of any vessel distinguishing itself before Dunkirk. He did not lose his money! The attack failed, Jean Bart, the town of Dunkirk and its piers being untouched. In mid-September, the squadron moved on to Calais which was also bombed and 40 houses were destroyed. The weather was deteriorating and Shovell returned to the Downs, the attacks on Dieppe, Havre de Grace, Dunkirk and Calais having overall been failures. Doctor John Campbell has fairly summarised Shovell's attempts on French coastal towns in the late summer of 1694:

> Sir Cloudesley Shovell, however, took care to demonstrate from his conduct, that there was no fault lay in him; for he went with a boat within the enemy's works and so became an eye witness of the impossibility of doing what his orders directed to be done; and therefore, on his coming home, he was perfectly well received and

4 Le Fevre and Harding, *Precursors*, p. 39.
5 Campbell, *British Admirals*, Vol. VI, p. 186.
6 Luttrell, *State Affairs*, Vol. III, p. 156; HMC: Buccleuch MS, Vol. II, Part I, pp. 116, 240–1.
7 Richmond, *Instrument of Policy*, p. 253; H of L MS 1693–5 NS, Vol. I, p. 495.
8 Campbell, *British Admirals*, Vol. III, p. 157; Laird Clowes, *Royal Navy*, Vol. II, p. 477.

continued to be employed as a man who would command success, where it was possible; and omit nothing in his power, where it was not.[9]

In the autumn, Shovell's last duty of the year was to take a squadron to Gothenburg and then on to Elsinore to escort home Dutch merchant vessels with vital naval stores. So 1694 came to an end and if it had not been a successful year for the English at sea, with the failure at Camaret Bay, at least Shovell had rehabilitated himself after his difficulties of 1693.

William III decided that the strategy for 1695 would be three major land campaigns in Flanders, Spain and Savoy. The main centre of naval activity was to be with Edward Russell in the Mediterranean, where consideration was given to bombing the French fleet in Toulon. Russell thought the defences were too strong and hoped to lure the French to sea and then destroy them in battle. Anne Hilarion de Costentin, Comte de Tourville was too experienced and wily a character to allow this to happen. He effectively contained a greater force without any risk to himself and Russell had to make do with transporting Spanish troops from Genoa to Catalonia. In September 1695, George Rooke came out to the Mediterranean and replaced Russell.[10]

Naval actions in home waters were to be subsidiary to those in the Mediterranean, with Berkeley of Stratton in command and Shovell under him. Their remit was threefold: to stop naval supplies reaching France from the Baltic; to counteract Jean Bart and the privateers; to alarm the French coast with continued bombing from the sea.

In the early months of 1695, Shovell, based at Chatham, was kept busy with a succession of courts-martial, escorting a convoy to Flanders and investigating allegations that some captains were claiming wages for fictitious members of their crews. Judging by his letters to Shovell, Berkeley spent his time in London. When Queen Mary died of smallpox, Shovell was given permission to come to London to attend the funeral, on 5 March. A chamber was taken for Shovell and his wife but it is unlikely that he was able to pay his final respects to the late queen. On the 6th, Berkeley wrote to Shovell, informing him that at present it was not possible for him to come to London, as he was to take a squadron out to the Mediterranean with troops and supplies for Russell.[11]

In the event Shovell did not take the squadron to the Mediterranean as in mid-March he was taken seriously ill. According to Luttrell, he was suffering from a quinsy and had been let blood no less than four times.[12] Two days later, Shovell was reported to be out of danger. In the 17th century, a quinsy was a very serious matter with death often occurring from an uncontrolled infection or asphyxia. By the standards of the 21st century, blood-letting was pointless. On 25 April, Shovell wrote a letter to Thomas Shorting, the collector of customs at Cley-next-the-Sea, Norfolk, who was married to his half-sister and only surviving sibling. In the letter, he prayed for his sister's delivery and was pleased that his mother had got 'well home.' He ended the letter: 'I bless god I am pretty well on my recovery.' Clearly this is a

9   Charnock, *Biographia*, Vol. II, p. 20.
10   Richmond, *Instrument of Policy*, pp. 258–9.
11   KCA: Marsham MS U1515.17, Berkeley to Shovell, 6 March 1695.
12   Luttrell, *State Affairs*, Vol. III, p. 451.

reference to his quinsy and possibly his mother had visited him in view of the seriousness of his condition.[13]

In early June, Shovell, still as vice-admiral of the red, transferred to the newly built 80-gun *Cambridge* and by the middle of the month was at Portsmouth. Here he was joined by Berkeley and a Dutch squadron under Philip Almonde. The English disagreed with the Dutch over which part of the French coast should be attacked first. The Dutch, with the support of William III, favoured Dunkirk, but Berkeley felt that St Malo was an easier prospect. After threats of independent action, the opinionated Berkeley had his way.[14]

At the end of June, the combined squadrons sailed for St Malo, a base for privateers, on the coast of Britanny. Early in July, the bombing attack on St Malo was led by John Benbow who would become a popular hero and die in tragic circumstances, in the West Indies, seven years later. A great deal of damage was done to the town, although at considerable cost to the Anglo-Dutch force in men and small ships. Shovell had been in the *Cambridge* for most of the attack on St Malo but, for a time, he calmly ventured close to the shore in a boat in order to encourage the sailors and bomb vessels. Following the attack on St Malo, the bombing expert, Benbow, was sent with a small force of frigates and bomb vessels to burn nearby Granville. Whilst this was accomplished, Berkeley and Shovell returned to Spithead and then on to the Downs.[15] During the month of July, Benbow had a falling out with Berkeley, feigned illness and was not involved in the coming assaults on Dunkirk and Calais.

Here, in the Downs, final preparations were made for the attack on Dunkirk which had more military and naval significance than St Malo. As well as serving as a base for the able Jean Bart and privateers, a successful attack on the port would take pressure off William III's land forces in Flanders.[16] The attack on Dunkirk was not to go well, as the French had strengthened the defences since the previous year. Another complicating factor was the presence, once more, of the Dutch artillery officer, William Meesters. He was to command the machine vessels and wherever he went trouble was close at hand. Neither Berkeley nor Shovell had any time for the man. Sir John Laughton has aptly described Meesters as at least as much a charlatan as an inventor![17] Perhaps fantasist is closer to the mark.

Shovell has left a personal record of the attack on Dunkirk in his own hand:

> Tuesday 30th [July]. All the small frigates and vessels sailed in nearer Dunkirk and anchored a little to the westward of the brake. Preparations were made for attacking the pier-heads and risbank;[18] and a council of war was called, at which it was resolved (if the weather proved fine) to begin the attack on the morrow morning.

---

13   NMM: RMT MS, MAT 25, copy of a letter from Shovell to Thomas Shorting, 25 April 1695.

14   TNA: ADM 6/3, f. 59, Admiralty commission and warrant book; Burchett, *Transactions at Sea*, p. 293; Campbell, *British Admirals*, Vol. III, p. 173.

15   Campbell, *British Admirals*, Vol. VI, pp. 187–8; *The London Gazette*, No 3096; Anon, *Secret Memoirs*, pp. 66–9.

16   Richmond, *Instrument of Policy*, pp. 261–2.

17   Campbell, *British Admirals*, Vol. III, p. 177; Evan Fyers, 'Machine Vessels', *Mariner's Mirror*, Vol. 11 (United Kingdom: Society for Nautical Research 1925), pp. 58–9; *DNB*, Berkeley of Stratton [Laughton].

18   Risbank was the name given to a man-made bank strengthened with brushwood.

Wednesday 31st. This morning the weather not promising fair we did not begin.

Thursday 1st August. This morning the weather being fair, the frigates, and bomb vessels appointed to go with them, went in and began to bombard about seven in the morning. About the same time I went with my lord [Berkeley] in a boat, and we rowed about to observe in what readiness each vessel was to begin the attack. We met Mr Meesters, he told my lord he would be ready between ten and eleven o'clock; but I very well remember, after eleven, some of the captains of the machines, and with whom my lord spoke, said they had no other orders but to keep near Mr Meesters.

As I have observed, the pilots which Mr Meesters had provided, and undertaken to conduct the ships appointed for the battery, now would not take charge of them, though they draw but sixteen or seventeen feet Flemish. This, admiral Allemonde acquainted my lord Berkeley with, who sent captain Wassenaer to Mr Meesters, to inform him of the same.[19] As I understood captain Wassenaer, upon his return from Mr Meesters, he brought word Mr Meesters said he could do his business without battering ships; and most certain it is, when we met Mr Meesters in his boat afterwards, he made no complaint for want of them, nor did he lay any thing to my lord about altering this disposition of his attack.

Tis further observable that the pilots, notwithstanding the assurance given that they would take charge of the frigates to carry them in to the attack, and out at the east channel, yet when they were to the eastward of the forts, they rather chose to turn the ships back to the westward, though they again passed the enemy's shot, than trust to their judgement to sail through the east channel, which makes me of the opinion none of the pilots knew the east channel; for I generally find pilots had rather trust their judgement, where they have knowledge, than encounter the enemies shot.

Indeed as I understood admiral Allemonde, these pilots of Mr Meesters were men of no account, or reputation, for their skill in pilotage, all their pretentions to their knowledge of this place being only grounded upon their having been there once or twice in ships as sailors, never as masters, or having charge of any ships, and therefore could not reasonably be thought sufficiently skilled, or fitly qualified to undertake such a difficult and hazardous enterprize.

I am pretty positive, that when my lord met Mr Meesters in his boat the first time, it was near eleven o'clock; and upon his lordships doubting whether his smoke ships were ready (having observed his men in a hurry) Mr Meesters replyed, then tomorrow will be as well: and my lord said, he would not lose that opportunity for ten thousand pounds, therefore would have it done, if possible, alledging, the weather being good and the bombardment having been begun; Mr Meesters then assured his lordship all was ready. After this I went with my lord to the machine and smoke ships which lay about a mile without Mr Meesters, some of their captains said they had no other orders than, when they had fitted their vessels

---

19   Probably Jan Gerrit van Wassenaer who rose to become an admiral and died, in 1723, from a spontaneous rupture of the oesophagus, the first time in medical history the condition had been described.

(which they were in hand with) they were to anchor near Mr Meesters. After my lord had hastened them all towards Mr Meesters, his lordship met Mr Meesters in his boat again; it was then one o'clock, and we judged upon the pitch of high water, or rather falling water which my lord told Mr Meesters, and said he thought it was too late; but he pertly replied that there was nothing, that he knew of, to hinder the attack. He spake this with so much boldness and confidence, that I must needs say, I was then, as I am now, of opinion, that if my lord had not immediately ordered the attack, he would have thrown the miscarriage upon his lordship.

Upon the signal being made, the other frigates weighed and did their duty, as far as their knowledge of the place and skill of the pilots would permit: but no machine, or smoke ship went with the frigates, neither did they begin the attack, though contrary to the method prescribed, lord Berkeley ordered the Lime to cut and support them in their disorderly attack.

I remember capt. Carleton, who commanded one of the machines, did cut, but did not sail in, having anchored amongst other bomb vessels, or frigates, that supported them: and Carleton has since told me himself, that he rid near them out of danger of any but random shot from the enemy.

I further remember Mr Meesters was very fond of a ship he said he would make shot proof, and said he would lye with her within a cable's length of the pier-head and take care to order the attacks aright; but I saw no such vessel in that dangerous post.[20]

The attack on Dunkirk can only be described as a failure with little damage done to the town and three French half-gallies sunk. Meesters quietly slipped away with his machine vessels under the cover of darkness. This infuriated Berkeley, who sent orders after him to have him brought back a close prisoner. Succinctly, he wrote on 4 August: 'he is afraid to stand trial of his machines, and now his business is done, with what money he has got, he is packing off, but I hope to stop him. All his actions and words have been every day nothing but contrariety, and his design to cheat his majesty and the nation.' Then Berkeley and Shovell with their squadron returned to the Downs.[21]

Meesters on arrival back in England, wasted no time in laying the blame for the failure of the enterprise squarely at the door of the admirals.[22] He was immediately answered by Berkeley in a letter to the Secretary of State, Charles Talbot, 1st Duke of Shrewsbury:

As for Mr Meesters, it has been my ill fortune to have to do with him; I foresee [foresaw] it, and did all I could to avoid it, but it was inevitable. My Lord, he is certainly akin to the father of falsehood; but to lay down such matters for truth, as in some cases I can bring a hundred witnesses, and in others his own hand to

20   Charnock, *Biographia*, Vol. II, pp. 21–3; NMM: SMF 221 (PHB17), Shovell's account of the action for Berkeley and the Commissioners of the Admiralty, 14 September 1695.

21   Campbell, *British Admirals*, Vol. III, p. 177; Laird Clowes, *Royal Navy*, Vol. II, p. 482; *DNB*, Berkeley of Stratton [Laughton].

22   HMC: Buccleuch MS, Vol. II, Part I, p. 211.

vouch the contrary, I protest, though I pretty well know the man, I wonder at his confidence or forgetfulness; sure he takes no notes.

Later in the letter, Berkeley would describe Meesters aptly as 'a prating fellow.'[23]

The defences at Dunkirk were strong enough to stop any but the most overwhelming assault. Meesters had arrived late in the Downs, failed to provide the promised experienced pilots, failed to organise or use his machine vessels and ran away at the first opportunity. Despite this, unbelievably, an enquiry was held to determine where the blame lay! The contemporary view was that there had been a misunderstanding between Meesters and the sea officers. Certainly no responsibility could be attached to the admirals, Berkeley, Shovell and Almonde, who had done their best. It is possible that Meesters was being protected by some high ranking figure such as William III. He had served with the king in the recent Irish campaign and had narrowly escaped death in 1690, by hiding in a bed of nettles. According to his son, Meesters always received his orders verbally, directly from William, and there were never any written instructions. Even if the machine vessels had been used in a determined fashion against Dunkirk, it is still doubtful whether they would have been a success in view of the strength of the defences there. In strategic terms, the attempt on Dunkirk did little to reduce the pressure on William's troops in Flanders as it had been on too small a scale to be a real threat. In all it was a costly failure.[24]

In the Downs, Berkeley and Shovell prepared their squadron and bomb vessels for a further attack on the French coast at Calais. No doubt the two admirals were delighted to learn that Meesters had declined to accompany them. Coming before Calais, Berkeley held a council of war at which it was resolved to burn the wooden fort at the entrance of the pier heads. The fort had 14 cannons and there were several other batteries, making an assault near impossible until they were neutralised. This was accomplished on 17 August 1695 and then the bombardment began in earnest with 600 bombs being thrown into the town during the day. The magazine and the risbank were burnt and the houses of Calais suffered considerable damage. French retaliation consisted of sending out half-gallies to break up the line of bomb vessels, but Berkeley's frigates and brigantines forced them away. Also, there was prodigious fire from the French batteries but, despite this, English loses were slight.[25]

While still before Calais, Berkeley had decided to relinquish his command to Shovell and return to London. Shovell, too, wrote to the Admiralty asking to do the same. Possibly, the two admirals were still trying to refute Meesters' ludicrous allegations of their failure to support him in front of Dunkirk. Another factor, in Berkeley's case, was that George Rooke was being sent out to the Mediterranean to relieve Edward Russell. Berkeley had already commented on the subject: 'since it has been thought fit to appoint Sir George Rooke to command in the Straits, I suppose care will be taken that he and I may not meet at sea without he will obey, for I can own no superior at sea but admiral Russell.' This was odd

23   HMC: Buccleuch MS, Vol. II, Part I, p. 212.
24   Campbell, *British Admirals*, Vol. III, pp. 177–180; Burchett, *Transactions at Sea*, p. 298; *The London Gazette*, No 3102.
25   Campbell, *British Admirals*, Vol. III, pp. 178–9; Burchett, *Transactions at Sea*, p. 303; *The London Gazette*, No 3107; Laird Clowes, *Royal Navy*, Vol. II, p. 482.

to say the least, as Rooke and Shovell were both considerably older and more experienced naval officers. It says much for Shovell's equable temperament that he could serve under such a self-seeking and opinionated commander without apparent rancour.[26] Calais was the last coastal town to be attacked that year and both sides subsequently struck commemorative medals.

On 1 September, Shovell spent the night ashore at Knowlton, near Deal and close to the anchorage of the Downs. Knowlton Court was the country home of his early patron, John Narbrough, until his death in 1688 and under the terms of his will, his eldest son, another John, a boy rising 11 years at the time, had inherited the estate. Of course Shovell was now the boy's stepfather after his marriage to Elizabeth Narbrough in 1691. It is not clear whether the Shovells were regularly using Knowlton at this time, as they had a town house, in Soho Square, at its junction with Frith Street and, from 1694, a country house, May Place, Crayford. No doubt Knowlton Court was an ideal refuge for Shovell whilst he was based in the Downs. Shovell wrote a letter to Rooke, from Knowlton, asking him to pay particular attention to a merchant ship, owned by friends of his, which was going out to the Mediterranean. It is difficult not to believe that Shovell, or possibly his father-in-law, John Hill, had some financial interest in the ship. Hill was a very wealthy man and had been trading with Smyrna since 1675.[27] One of the few criticisms made of Shovell was that his covetousness knew no bounds.

As well as the Narbroughs, it is clear that Shovell never forgot the debt that he owed to his first patron, Christopher Myngs, and in September 1695 he wrote to Josiah Burchett, Secretary to the Admiralty, lobbying for Myngs' son, another Christopher, to be given a larger ship. 'I own myself under manifold obligation to Capt. Myngs his friend and therefore think my selfe bound in confidence as well as gratitude.' Young Christopher would go on to serve under Shovell, as a captain, at the Battle of Malaga in 1704.[28]

At the end of September, Shovell, in the 70-gun *Northumberland*, went to the Netherlands to bring William III back to England and was safely home by mid-October.[29] The king dissolved parliament and called for a new one to meet on 22 November. This was to be the start of Shovell's parliamentary career, although it was not to be a very active one in view of his duties at sea. He became one of the two Members of Parliament for Rochester in Kent which was close to both his country home, May Place, and also to the naval port of Chatham. Over a month before polling day a newsletter announced that Shovell was to be elected for Rochester! One member was normally a local dignitary and the other a naval man like Shovell who was mildly supportive of the Whigs. He served from 1695–1701 and then again from 1705 until his death in 1707. During the first three parliaments in which Shovell represented Rochester, his companion member was Sir Joseph Williamson, a substantial Kentish landowner through his wife, who had been an Under Secretary of State

26   *DNB*, Berkeley of Stratton [Laughton].
27   NMM: SMF 221 (PHB/17), Shovell to Rooke, 1 September 1695; NMM: RMT MS, MAT 24, will of Sir John Narbrough; KCA: Marsham MS U1515.01, account book of John Hill.
28   NMM: SMF 221 (PHB/17), Shovell to Burchett, 13 September 1695.
29   NMM: SMF 221 (PHB/17), Shovell to the Commissioners of the Admiralty, 20 September and 10 October 1695; Luttrell, *State Affairs*, Vol. III, p. 526.

as early as 1665.[30] Perhaps to mark his election, Shovell paid for the magnificent decorative ceilings in the Guildhall of the city. Work began in 1695 and was completed the following year. Shovell was a generous benefactor to the city and paid for the town clock and the frontage of the Clock House/Corn Exchange.

In 1694, the year before Shovell became a member of parliament for Rochester, he purchased the nearby May Place estate, at Crayford and he became a great supporter of his local Anglican Church, St Paulinus, where his wife, two daughters and their husbands would be buried. The Shovells also had a town house in Soho Square at its junction with Frith Street. In the late 1690s, the square was the height of elegance and the executed Duke of Monmouth had previously owned a mansion close to where the Shovells lived. They had moved up in the world since starting married life in Prescot Street, Goodman's Fields, to the north of the River Thames where the poorer tarpaulin officers often had their homes. It was here that their elder daughter Elizabeth was born.

Towards the end of the year came the first rumblings of a possible French invasion from Dunkirk and Calais. Louis XIV had decided to make a rapid invasion of England, before the Anglo-Dutch fleet was ready for sea in 1696. An invasion force of 20,000 men was quietly collected at Calais and Dunkirk and would be transported across the Channel by André, Marquis de Nesmond, and the redoubtable Jean Bart. The invasion force was to be led by ex-King James in person and his son-in-law, William III, was to be assassinated. Enhanced activity in the French channel ports confirmed William's suspicions and Edward Russell, back from the Mediterranean, with Shovell as his vice-admiral of the red, together with all available ships were sent to put a stop to James' latest attempt to regain his throne.[31]

In January 1696, Shovell was ordered to get the ships of his division ready for sea. Many of his letters at this time were endeavouring to help former members of his crews or their families. There was support for a disabled man who had been with him in both the *James Galley* and the *Anne* for the position of cook. Also there was assistance for the son of the late boatswain of the *Dover*, whose mother was a distressed widow. It is unsurprising that Shovell had little difficulty manning his ships, for he gave great care to his men and was also a successful officer.[32]

In mid-February, Russell went to sea with 50 ships, in order to prevent the potential French invasion and a few days later he was followed by Shovell, in the 52-gun *Montagu*, with a further 13 vessels. Shovell's original ship, the 90-gun *Duchess*, was too large to risk in the winter storms. On 1 March, Shovell and some of the senior captains were sent by Russell to see if it was possible to attack French shipping in Dunkirk. Having looked into the port, after consultation with Russell, the captains, William Meesters and the engineers, it was deemed impractical.[33] The decision was a sensible one, but it is astonishing after his bizarre behaviour of the previous year that Meesters was involved at all. Whilst at sea off Dunkirk, on 2 March, Shovell found the time to write to his brother-in-law, Thomas Shorting, who

30   Campbell, *British Admirals*, Vol. III, p. 183; Burnet, Vol. II, p. 160; Frederick Smith, *Rochester in Parliament 1295–1933* (London: Simpkin Marshall 1933), p. 16.

31   Laird Clowes, *Royal Navy*, Vol. II, p. 487; Richmond, *Instrument of Policy*, p. 262; *The London Gazette*, No 3161.

32   NMM: SMF21 (PHB/17), Shovell statements to the Navy Office, 15 and 29 January 1696.

33   Campbell, *British Admirals*, Vol. III, p. 189.

was at home in north Norfolk. As was recorded earlier he was married to Shovell's sole surviving sibling, his half-sister, Anne:

> Brother,
> On French coast with 50 men of war and have happily prevented an invasion from France for James II ready to embark 20.000 french in order to make a bloody war in our country. I hope ye gentlemen about you will not handle the Jacobites so tenderly since they take part with him who was bringing a foreign army of papists to lay our country in blood and ashes and all ye plagues and misfortunes that attend war. Pray deliver the inclosed to Cap. Brittife and let me know from you how to behave himself as to this present government.[34] This with my duty to my mother, humbly craving her blessing also my love to my sister and your self and all friends.
> I remain,
> Your loving brother,
> C.S.[35]

Captain Charles Britiff lived in Cley-next-the-Sea and it would be fascinating to know what the 'inclosed' [sic] was.

Soon after writing the letter to Thomas Shorting, Shovell was ordered by Russell to remain on station with 31 ships and to blockade Calais and Dunkirk.[36] Shovell did his level best to stop the egress of French ships from the two ports but was hindered by inclement weather and the ability of the shallow-draught, French privateers to slip out over the sand bars. On 23 March, he was recalled to the Downs and went aboard the *Duchess*. His time in port was to be brief as William III was not happy that a proper attempt had been made to bomb Calais and ordered his return to the French coast. Transferring once more to the 52-gun *Montagu*, Shovell sailed for Calais in early April 1696. After three days he was back off the North Foreland and wrote this report for the Commissioners of the Admiralty:

> Pursuiant to your lordship's orders of 31st of March, we, the 3rd instant, having very fair weather, got before Calais with our bomb vessels; and the wind being southerly, which made a smooth sea, we laid our bomb vessels in a line and about noon began to heave shells at the town, and continued so doing till evening; in all which time we expended upwards of 300 bombs and carcasses, many of which were seen to fall and break both in the town and among their embarkations at the pier. I suppose they have done considerable damage to the enemy, though nothing appeared to us more than a vessel being on fire in the harbour, and the town in two or three several places, which were immediately extinguished.

---

34   This is likely to be Captain Charles Britiff of Cley-next-the-Sea. In October 1692, in the 32-gun *Portsmouth*, with Captain William Kerr in the 50-gun *Deptford*, he took a French privateer, the *Hyancinthe* from Nantes, in the Channel. As he was still at sea in 1696, he cannot have been an overt Jacobite. He died in 1703 and was buried at Cley.

35   NMM: RMT MS, MAT 25, copy of a letter from Shovell to Thomas Shorting, 2 March 1696.

36   KCA: Marsham MS U1515.18, Edward Russell to Shovell, 5 March 1696; HMC: Buccleuch MS, Vol. II, Part I, pp. 310–11.

The enemy were very active with their row-boats and half-galleys; but to prevent them from hindering or injuring our bomb vessels, the frigates and brigantines kept very near as indeed they were obliged to do.

The damage we received is, the bomb vessels have their rigging much shattered, and two of them are very leaky by reason of shot received under water; the mortars all spoiled but two; the brigantines have their rigging much shattered too, and two of them have lost their top masts; the Jersey has both main mast and fore mast shot through and spoiled, as also a shot under water which makes her leaky; a bomb fell into her, broke in her hold, and set her on fire; it was soon extinguished; but it is requisite they should go into some port to refit. The Norwich has her mizzen mast shot through and spoiled; her foremast is also spoiled. She has been a ground near Calais, and has knocked away a part of her halfe keel, and her rudder, since which she makes more water than usual.

The Captain's fore-yard was broke by a bomb from the enemy. Captain Benbow had the flesh torn from his leg, by an accident on board one of the bomb-vessels in the action, and, I doubt, will hardly be able to stir within a fortnight.

I have an account of fifteen men killed and wounded.[37]

John Benbow appears to have been singularly unfortunate with his legs, as he was to die, in 1702, from a shattered right leg in the West Indies.

Shovell remained in the Downs during April still with overall command of the ships blockading Calais and Dunkirk. Francis Wivell, who had been left by Shovell, as commodore, to command the ships off the two ports, complained that he had insufficient ships for the task, but was not supported by Shovell who thought that he had enough. Whilst in the Downs, Shovell had to take part in several courts-martial. The unfortunate Robert Ball had disobeyed a superior officer:

Where as at a Court Martial held on board his majesty's ship Dutchess in the Downs on the 9th day of April instant a sentence was passed that Robert Ball, boatswain of the Southampton shall be carried in a boat with a halter about his neck and yet he shall receive 11 lashes on the bare back by ye side of each of those English flagg ship in the Downes and the like ye side of ye Southampton whereon he belonged and his crime to be then declared with beat of drum.[38]

The *Southampton* was having problems with discipline; for example, Shovell was forced to court-martial the stewards for buggery.[39] He also had to investigate the bizarre behaviour of Captain Smith of the *Hind Pink*, who had been found wandering aimlessly in the fields and been detained near Deal Church. Although Shovell gave no explanation for this strange behaviour, it is difficult not to think alcohol must have played a part in it.[40]

37 Charnock, *Biographia*, Vol. II, p. 24; NMM: SMF21 (PHB/17), Shovell to the Commissioners of the Admiralty, 5 April 1696.

38 NMM: SMF 21 (PHB/17), document signed by Shovell, 10 April 1696.

39 NMM: SMF21 (PHB/17), Shovell to the Commissioners of the Admiralty, 1 April 1696.

40 NMM: SMF21 (PHB/17), Shovell to the Commissioners of the Admiralty, 24 April 1696.

At the end of April, Rooke returned to the Downs with the Mediterranean squadron in order to reinforce the English vessels in home waters. In reality, the invasion threat was already over with the French realising that Russell's and Shovell's ships, off Calais and Dunkirk, had stymied them. However, Rooke's departure from the Mediterranean allowed the French Toulon squadron to move to Brest and thus the main sphere of naval activity for the year switched from the Mediterranean to the Channel. On arrival back in England, Rooke was immediately ordered to prepare his own ships as well as those of Shovell for sea. His instructions were to block the path of the Toulon squadron, consisting of 47 ships under Louis Châteaurenault, from getting into Brest. For this expedition, Rooke was to be commander-in-chief and Shovell the admiral of the blue. In a sense it was a role reversal from 1693 and Rooke's star was now in the ascendency. The English fleet sailed to St Helens and here Shovell changed ships, joining the 100-gun *Queen*. He took with him from the *Duchess* his captain James Stewart and several lieutenants.[41]

Early in May, the fleet under Rooke and Shovell reached Ushant only to discover that Châteaurenault's squadron had already safely entered Brest. Thus they were too late and decided that, as they were outnumbered by the combined Brest fleet and Toulon squadron, it would be prudent to return to England. At Torbay, they were reinforced by further vessels, this bringing their number to 115 of which 85 were larger men-of-war.[42]

While at Torbay, Shovell's uncle, Cloudesley Jenkenson, died and he was buried at St Mary Matfelon, commonly called St Mary's Church, Whitechapel, on 21 May, in his 66th year. Almost exactly 30 years before, Christopher Myngs' funeral had been held in the same church. Jenkenson had also had a naval career as midshipman, captain's clerk and probably deputy judge-advocate as well. Uncle and nephew shared the same Christian name, the surname of their mutual maternal grandfather and great-grandfather, Thomas Cloudesley. They were close and Jenkenson's three children, William, Anne and Abigail received minor legacies under Shovell's will. It is likely that both men had lived near to St Mary Matfelon, in Goodman's Fields, just to the north of the River Thames, an area popular with the poorer tarpaulin naval officers of that era. But, in the mid-1690s the Shovells had moved to much grander accommodation in Soho Square which was the Mayfair of the late 17th century.[43]

On 27 May, Rooke was recalled to London to become one of the commissioners of the admiralty. Strangely, Shovell was overlooked as his replacement and John, 3rd Baron Berkeley of Stratton was given command of the fleet. Possibly Shovell was still not fully rehabilitated from his part in the Smyrna convoy disaster of three years earlier. Both Rooke and Berkeley favoured an attack on Brest, but were turned down by the central authorities. However, Berkeley was not a man to remain inactive for long and in late June he took the fleet over to the French coast. Shovell, in the *Queen*, was his second-in-command, and they proposed to assault several islands in the Bay of Biscay. While passing Camaret Bay, the English fleet made contact with French merchantmen convoyed by André, Marquis de Nesmond. Sensibly, the French hurried back to port in Brest to await a more favourable opportunity to sail.

41   NMM: SMF21 (PHB/17), Shovell to the Commissioners of the Admiralty, 24 April 1696.
42   NMM: SMF21 (PHB/17), Shovell to Admiral David Mitchell, 23 May 1696.
43   Marsham-Townshend, 'Parentage of Cloudesley Shovell', p. 42; Davies, *Gentlemen and Tarpaulins*, p. 56.

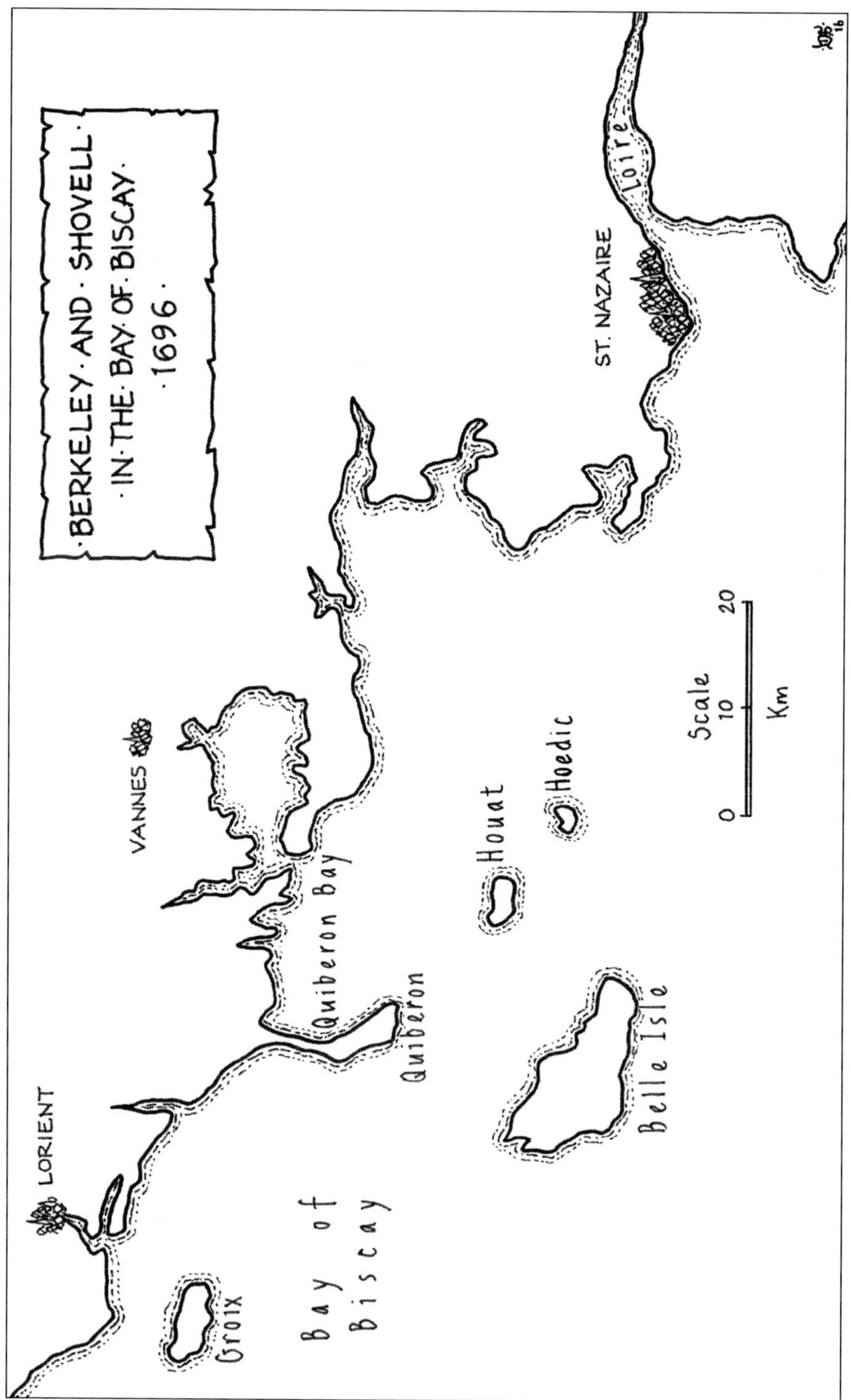

Map 17 Berkeley and Shovell in the Bay of Biscay 1696.

In early July, Berkeley detached several ships to the Island of Groix, where numerous villages were destroyed and over 1,000 head of cattle taken. Berkeley took the main contingent of ships to Belle Isle and landings were made on the lesser islands of Houat and Hoedic. Small bodies of ships were also sent further south to the Ile de Ré and to Olonne on the French mainland. A great number of bombs and carcasses were hurled into the latter, these causing considerable damage to the unfortunate town. Shovell's ship, the *Queen*, was anchored off Belle Isle with the main fleet from 5–9 July and there is no evidence that he was involved with the attack on the Ile de Ré which is implied in his *Secret Memoirs*. On arrival at Belle Isle, Shovell ordered Vice-Admiral David Mitchell to send longboats to help with the landings and young Christopher Myngs, captain of the 90-gun *St Michael,* was in his patron Shovell's division. By the end of July, they were forced to return to Torbay and then to Spithead as supplies were running low.

Victor Amadeus II, Duke of Savoy had abandoned the allies in June 1696 and had made a separate peace with France. With Rooke's return in the spring, the Mediterranean had been largely abandoned to the French. In mid-August, plans were made to send a squadron to the Mediterranean, principally to discourage Spain from throwing in its lot with the French and also to confirm peace treaties with the various Barbary regencies. The expedition was of a size to require a vice-admiral to lead it, but the only two available, David Mitchell and John Neville, both asked to be excused on the grounds that they had served there recently and declined to return at that time. Shovell was senior to both of them, having served as a full admiral, and loyally volunteered to go in their place. He could easily have pointed out his long service in the Mediterranean from 1674–86. In the event insufficient funds and provisions stopped a large squadron from being sent out.[44]

In mid-September, Shovell received a certificate to register himself as a seaman. The responsible office had been set up earlier in the year to help make seamen available for manning the fleet and John Hill, Shovell's father-in-law, served as one of its commissioners. The scheme was abandoned in 1699 as a failure. The certificate is of interest in that it described Shovell's physical appearance at the time: 'These are to certify that Cloudesley Shovell aged forty five years being tall and well set man of a fair complexion ----.' In later life he would run to fat.[45] Five years later, John Macky described him: 'a very large, fat, fair Man, turned Fifty Years old.'[46]

In the autumn of 1696, the House of Commons considered the alleged miscarriages of the fleet during the summer and more specifically why the French Toulon squadron had been allowed to get into Brest. Both Rooke and Shovell were subjected to several strict examinations. Shovell defended himself vigorously and nothing could be found against the naval officers who had been following the orders they had been given. Undoubtedly this was an anxious time for Shovell as, during the autumn, further allegations about the Smyrna convoy disaster of 1693 had been made by Sir John Fenwick.[47] He alleged that Killigrew and

---

44   Richmond, *Instrument of Policy,* p. 264; HMC: Buccleuch MS, Vol. II, Part I, p. 385.

45   NMM: RMT MS, MAT 25, certificate dated 18 September 1696.

46   Macky, *Secret Services*, p. 122.

47   Fenwick was a Jacobite conspirator, implicated in a plot to assassinate William III and on trial for his life. He claimed he was prepared to reveal all he knew about the Jacobite conspiracies in order to save his life. Fenwick's evidence was farcical and he was beheaded early in 1697.

Delaval were planning to keep the fleet out of the way of a proposed landing, in England, of James II. Insultingly, it was suggested that Killigrew and Delaval were able to master Shovell as they pleased. Fortunately, Fenwick's evidence does not seem to have been taken seriously.[48] No wonder Shovell was quoted by James Vernon, a prominent politician: 'Sir Clowdesley says there is no storm so bad as one from the House of Commons.'[49] Vernon was a near neighbour of Shovell's in Frith Street, Soho, and father of the future famous admiral, Edward Vernon, 'Old Grog'.

During this anxious period in the autumn of 1696, Shovell's second daughter, Anne, was baptised at St Olave, Hart Street, having been born earlier in the month. This was the church of the parish of her maternal grandfather, John Hill, and where her mother, Elizabeth, had been married firstly to John Narbrough. All five of Elizabeth's children by Narbrough had also been baptised in St Olave's. In 1718, Anne would marry the Honourable Robert Mansell and after his death she married, for a second time in 1726, John Blackwood of Charlton.[50]

Shovell's final duty of 1696 was to take to sea an Anglo-Dutch fleet of 42 ships to stop Admiral Bernard Desjean de Pointis from leaving Brest with his squadron. In England, there was speculation that it was to be invaded by de Pointis but, in reality his destination was the West Indies. Shovell missed de Pointis by six days and returned to Spithead in the middle of January.[51] The voyage, even in the dangerous seas of winter, must have been a relief for Shovell after his trials and tribulations in the House of Commons.

In February 1697, John Berkeley of Stratton died of 'a violent and obstinate pleurisy.' In modern terms, it seems likely that he died from pneumonia in his 34th year. For much of the previous three years, Shovell had served as second-in-command to this haughty, much younger man with equanimity. He also managed to have excellent relationships with other difficult naval characters such as Arthur Herbert and Edward Russell. But a notable failure was with the influential Samuel Pepys who had disapproved of Charles II awarding Shovell a valuable medal of gold for his exploits off Tripoli in 1676. In addition, Pepys was not impressed by Shovell's lowly parentage, despite the fact that he himself was the son of a tailor! Berkeley's premature demise allowed Shovell to replace him as Colonel of the Second Marine Regiment.[52]

On 9 April 1697, Shovell wrote to John Conney, the Mayor of Rochester, the City that he had been representing in Parliament for the last two years. Conney, a former naval surgeon, who served twice as mayor,[53] was lobbying for a man for the post of surgeon in Shovell's marine regiment. Shovell may have had the reputation of being a blunt, unsubtle naval man, but he could be quite the diplomat when the occasion required it:

48   Campbell, *British Admirals*, Vol. III, p. 196; Luttrell, *State Affairs*, Vol. IV, p. 152; HMC: Buccleuch MS, Vol. II, Part I, p. 396.

49   Cruikshanks, *History of Parliament*, Shovell entry.

50   Marsham-Townshend, 'Parentage of Cloudesley Shovell', p. 43. Robert Mansell was an active Jacobite and it was fortunate that Anne's father was not alive to see this union.

51   Richmond, *Instrument of Policy*, p. 273; Luttrell, *State Affairs*, Vol. IV, pp. 156–9, 161; Campbell, *British Admirals*, Vol. III, pp. 223–4.

52   Luttrell, *State Affairs*, Vol. IV, pp. 170, 191; Campbell, *British Admirals*, Vol. VI, p. 195; Edye, *Royal Marines*, p. 495.

53   *The Parentage and English Progenitors of Nathaniel Coney of Boston, Massachusetts* in Hills 1906, internet archive.

I have yours of the 26th instant and desire you be pleased to do me the justice to believe it is that I have been diverted by the business of some more than ordinary importance that it is so long unanswered especially in the matter that might naturally cause an expectation as to which I must acquaint you that I have been engaged by several friends to continue the surgeon that did belong to my Regiment. But leave me withal to assure you that nothing need have been added to your recommendation to engage me to the choice of a person for that employment where I not under a preengagement as after that I am.[54]

Possibly 'business of more than ordinary importance' was Shovell's preparation for escorting William III to the Netherlands which he undertook later in April.[55]

At about this time a Captain John Shovell of Ratcliff died. Ratcliff was a hamlet on the north bank of the River Thames to the east of Goodman's Fields, where originally Cloudesley Shovell had lived. It was a poor area with ship building, lodgings, opium dens and brothels and much frequented by the ordinary sailor. John Shovell was mentioned in Cloudesley's account book as a cousin and he had served in the same squadron with him, as captain of the 70-gun *Expedition*, a year earlier. The death of John Shovell left a vacancy in the *Expedition* which Cloudesley filled by appointing his flag captain in the *Duchess* and *Queen*, James Stewart to the post.[56]

The summer campaign of 1697, in home waters where Shovell served in the fleet under George Rooke, was an inauspicious one. The main centre of naval activity that year was in the West Indies where Bernard de Pointis sacked Cartagena, in modern day Colombia, before returning to France. John Neville followed him with a squadron but was unable to bring him to action.[57] In the Channel, Rooke with Shovell and the fleet had little success beyond convoying merchant vessels. The ships were usually foul, poorly manned and never properly provisioned. Rooke's and Shovell's views are recorded in a letter from James Vernon, the prominent politician, to Charles Talbot, 1st Duke of Shrewsbury:

June 24th 1697
Sir G. Rooke sailed to St. Helens two days ago. He writes very melancholy accounts to the Admiralty and Cloudesley Shovell speaks yet plainer not only of the small quantity of their provisions but the quality too is not very good especially of the bread and the want of pease and oatmeal is so visible that already the scurvy exceedingly increases in the fleet to a high degree.[58]

Rooke was ever the politician and diplomat with Shovell being much more forthright.

Although being Colonel of the Second Marine Regiment was a well-rewarded sine-cure, Shovell took his duties seriously. In September 1697, he wrote to the Navy Board

---

54   Bod Lib: Rawlinson MS, A 289, f. 144, letter from Cloudesley Shovell to John Conney, 9 April 1697.

55   Lutterell, Vol. IV, p. 221.

56   NMM: RMT MS, MATs 3, 24, inscriptions of Shovell family memorials, Shovell family wills; Laird Clowes, *Royal Navy*, Vol. II, p. 496.

57   Laird Clowes, *Royal Navy*, Vol. II, pp. 487–8; Richmond, *Instrument of Policy,* pp. 273–4.

58   Laird Clowes, *Royal Navy*, Vol. II, p. 365.

complaining about the payment of his marines and their clothing deduction. He wished them to be paid in the same manner as were seamen when their ship reached the end of a voyage.[59] Shovell received an unsatisfactory reply from the Navy Board, although the Admiralty Commisioners did rectify matters to a degree.

The situation in the summer of 1697 was one of stalemate: Barcelona had fallen and Catalonia, without the support of the English fleet, was at the mercy of France. In September 1697, Louis XIV offered reasonable peace terms and the Nine Years' War came to an end with the Treaty of Ryswick.[60] The English navy had not added to the reputation it had gained under Cromwell and Charles II. The only successful flag officers of the war had been George Rooke and Cloudesley Shovell, usually as subordinates to Edward Russell.[61]

1697 ended with Shovell finding time for his parliamentary duties as the naval estimates were considered in committee. In December, Robert Harley proposed that 10,000 men were necessary for maintaining a winter and summer guard. Shovell seconded William St Quintin's proposal for 12,000 men, but they were defeated. Normally, the House would listen carefully to Shovell's views on naval matters in view of his vast experience at sea.[62]

59 National Maritime Museum (NMM): Sergison (Serg) MS, Sept 18th 1697; Edye, *Royal Marines*, pp. 500–2.
60 Richmond, *Instrument of Policy*, p. 274.
61 Laird Clowes, *Royal Navy*, Vol. II, p. 365; Ehrman, *War of William III*, p. 605.
62 Cruikshanks, *History of Parliament*, Shovell entry.

15

Vigo and the Great Storm 1698–1703

The Nine Years' War had come to an end with the signing of the Treaty of Ryswick [1697] and under its terms, Louis XIV withdrew his support of ex-King James II, whilst recognising William III as the King of England. In addition, the main fortresses in the Netherlands were handed over to the Dutch and peace of a sort reigned in Europe.[1] The years 1698–1702 were relatively quiet from the naval viewpoint and so allowed Cloudesley Shovell considerable time for his own affairs.

Early in 1698, Shovell found time for family business as he gave £2 for the christening of one of the 11 children of his half-sister, Anne Flaxman, and her husband, Tom Shorting. In the high summer of 1698, Shovell and Joseph Williamson were returned to the House of Commons and continued in post until further elections in 1700.[2] They had been the members for Rochester since 1695. In the 1699–00 parliamentary session, Shovell was active in the Commons serving on several committees dealing with naval affairs.[3] At about this time, William III had become unhappy with the management of his two marine regiments and they were reformed into a single unit under Colonel Thomas Brudenell. Peregrine Osborne, Marquis of Carmarthen, who had commanded one of them was said to be dilatory and indifferent to admiralty orders! Shovell, who also lost his regiment, was unfortunate as he had taken a practical and useful share in the development of the service.[4]

In July 1698, Shovell commanded the squadron carrying William III to the Netherlands and in the following October brought him back to England.[5] For the remainder of the summer, Shovell served as admiral of the blue and commander-in-chief in the Thames and Medway, a period which must have given him an opportunity to see his family on a regular basis. In February 1699, he was able to spare the time to attend parliament and participated in the debate over the Navy Estimates, making the point that in his view, it was useful to continue recruiting soldiers as marines, as they 'would in due course turn into sailors.'[6] The following month, Shovell, who had been an extra commissioner of the Navy Board since

---

1   Laird Clowes, *Royal Navy*, Vol. II, pp. 365–6.
2   Smith, *Rochester in Parliament*, pp. 16, 127–9.
3   Cruikshanks, *History of Parliament*, Shovell entry.
4   Edye, *Royal Marines*, pp. 536, 544.
5   Luttrell, *State Affairs*, Vol. IV, pp. 441, 446, 449.
6   Le Fevre and Harding, *Precursors*, p. 61.

1693, exchanged positions to become a principal officer, as the Controller of Victualling Accounts. In 1700, he joined the other commissioners in refuting false charges of embezzlement made by a former clerk of the Treasurer's accounts. Shovell would remain in the post until Christmas Day 1704.[7] Later in the spring of 1699, he continued at sea as admiral of the blue and by May there was concern in England, at the possible hostile intentions of the French. Consequently, a squadron of 14 ships under his command put to sea and probably led to a continuation of the peace.[8]

In May 1699, there were suggestions that Shovell should move to the Admiralty Board, the very epicentre of overall naval strategy and command. In the end nothing came of it, but he was so alarmed by the proposal that he wrote to James Vernon, the Whig politician and by now Secretary of State:

> Before I came to the fleet it was talked that I should be removed to the admiralty board; I then solicited my Lord Orford [Edward Russell] that he would be so far my friend as to let me continue at the navy board, from whence, if I fell, my fall would be easy.
>
> I hear Lord Orford is out of all his employment; and still the report holds that I shall remove from the navy to the admiralty board. If such a thing be designed (as I hope not) I humbly and heartily beg you will excuse me to his majesty. I am now easy and quiet in an unenvied employment; but to put me into the admiralty is to set me up where I am pretty sure to be tumbled down – for if my Lord Orford cannot stand, whose services have been so eminent, what can poor I expect?[9]

In a further letter on the same subject, Shovell wrote to Orford himself:

> I do hear, from several hands, that I shall be removed to the admiralty. I have written to secretary Vernon, to desire he will excuse me to his Majesty; and do beg of your lordship, if you meet the secretary in your walks, that you will engage him to excuse me. I know your lordship can do anything with him, he having expressed much honour and friendship for your lordship.[10]

At this juncture in his career, Shovell showed a curious lack of ambition and indeed confidence in his own ability. He understood only too well that the politicians surrounding the admiralty board could well be likened to a den of vipers. No doubt Shovell recalled vividly the enquiries following the Smyrna convoy of 1693, Camaret Bay and the bombing of French coastal towns. Perhaps, this straightforward, brave to a fault seaman was more at home on the quarterdeck of a battleship than moving in the London corridors of power. As will be seen in later chapters, Shovell would soon become a successful commander-in-chief

---

7   Le Fevre and Harding, *Precursors*, p. 61; R. Merriman (ed), *The Sergison Papers* (London: Navy Records Society 1950), pp. 7, 14, 56.

8   Charnock, *Biographia*, Vol. II, p. 25; Luttrell, *State Affairs*, Vol. IV, pp. 510–32.

9   Charnock, *Biographia*, Vol. II, p. 30.

10   Charnock, *Biographia*, Vol. II, p. 30.

in the Mediterranean, skilfully dealing with the likes of Victor Amadeus II, Duke of Savoy, and Prince Eugene.

During the summer of 1699, Shovell again commanded a squadron in the English Channel as admiral of the blue. In May, he escorted William III to the Netherlands and his squadron, the following September, carried the king back to England. A note, dated 12 August, addressed to a Sir Richard and written by the celebrated scientist, Isaac Newton, suggested a meeting with Shovell to discuss longitude. Newton was acting as an informal advisor to Parliament on the difficulty of accurately calculating longitude. From 1703, as President of the Royal Society and later, as a commissioner of the Longitude Act of 1714, Newton worked tirelessly in the search for an accurate determination of longitude at sea. Presumably, Shovell was chosen to meet him as a genuine professional seaman, who was quite capable of navigating his own ship, unlike many of the aristocratic and gentry captains. Of course there was a certain irony with the invitation, in that Shovell's eventual demise in 1707, was as a result of faulty navigation and the inaccurate determination of longitude would appear to have been a factor.[11] It is not known whether the meeting took place or not. Certainly there was an opportunity for the two men to have met.

In the summer of 1700, Shovell once more commanded a squadron in the Channel as admiral of the blue. December saw the dissolution of Parliament and in elections early in the New Year of 1701, Shovell and Williamson were again returned as the members for Rochester. Later, in January 1701, his stepdaughter, Elizabeth Narbrough [daughter of Sir John] married Thomas D'Aeth, who was made a baronet in 1716.[12] The present day descendants of Sir John Narbrough are through this line because Elizabeth's two brothers, John and James, drowned with their stepfather in 1707.

Late in 1700, Charles II, the last Spanish king of the Habsburg dynasty, died without an heir and this would ultimately lead to the outbreak of the War of the Spanish Succession [1701–14].[13] On his demise it had been envisaged that his large empire would be peacefully divided amongst France, Austria and Bavaria. However, Louis XIV proceeded to claim the Spanish crown and empire for his grandson, Philip of Anjou, but many of the other nations of Europe, including England and the Netherlands, were unhappy with such a close link between the thrones of France and Spain. In the Spanish American Empire, the French soon took over its management with the potential to inhibit English and Dutch trade in the area. A counter claim for the Spanish throne was made by the Holy Roman Emperor, Leopold I, on behalf of his son Charles, and eventually England sided with the Emperor against Louis XIV; this led to the formal declaration of war in May 1702. Louis XIV had foolishly compounded the problem in 1701, after the death of ex-King James II, at St Germain-en-Laye, by proclaiming Prince James Edward Stuart [1688–1766], the Old Pretender, King of England, Scotland and Ireland; this was despite the fact that he had previously recognised

11   Note written by Newton to a Sir Richard, on 12 August 1699, from the Mint Office. Sir Richard may well have been Sir Richard Haddock who was the Controller of the Navy at the time. Mullock's Auctions, Shropshire, Catalogue of Historic Ephemera, 13 August 2015, lot 73. Hammer price £3,400.

12   John Burke, *A Genealogical and Heraldic History of the Landed Gentry* (London: Henry Colburn 1838), p. 86; NMM: RMT MS, MAT 16c, chart pedigree of the Shovell family.

13   Charles II of Spain suffered from genetic mandibular prognathism which meant that he could neither speak clearly nor chew his food. This unfortunate condition was a result of inbreeding and became known as 'Habsburg jaw'.

William III as the legitimate King. Understandably, the latter and indeed England were greatly offended by this base act.

In the summer of 1701, Shovell, in the 90-gun *Barfleur;* served once more in the Channel as admiral of the blue and on this occasion was under the overall command of George Rooke. On 29 April, Shovell signed what transpired to be his final will which would be proved after his death, some six and a half years later.[14] In September, he paid a rare visit to Rochester and was royally entertained to dinner by the mayor of the city. The fare put before Shovell consisted of bread, beer, wine, six fowls with bacon and sprouts, a rump of beef, two geese with apple sauce, two pigs, a pigeon pie, a leg of mutton and turnips, a dish of wild fowl, a shoulder of mutton and pickles, a large apple pie and cheese, mince pies and tobacco.[15] He would have been in his element as he appeared to enjoy his food, often taking his cook with him from ship to ship and eventually running to fat himself. In the autumn, Shovell undertook his customary duty of escorting William III back to England from the Netherlands for what would transpire to be the last time.[16] When Parliament was dissolved in November 1701, Shovell did not stand for re-election in the following December.[17]

In February 1702, William III's horse stumbled over a mole-hill and the king fell heavily and fractured his collar bone. Early the following month, William's weakened body gave up the fight for life and he died.[18] He was succeeded on the throne by his sister-in-law, Anne, and her husband, the dim-witted Prince George of Denmark, replaced Thomas Herbert, 5th Earl of Pembroke, as Lord High Admiral. Rooke became his senior adviser and Shovell was made admiral of the white, a more senior post than his last one. The Prince's new appointment coincided with the Anglo-Dutch entry into the War of the Spanish Succession.

In June, Rooke and Shovell were at Spithead with their respective squadrons and the former had been instructed to make an attempt to seize the Spanish Atlantic port of Cadiz. It was looked upon as a stepping stone to an attempt on the crucial French naval port of Toulon. If Cadiz, the key to trade with America, was unobtainable, Rooke and Ormonde were to attack Vigo, Corunna or Gibraltar. Rooke's force consisted of 160 ships and around 14,000 English and Dutch soldiers under the command of James Butler, 2nd Duke of Ormonde. Whilst Rooke sailed with the main fleet, Shovell was to take command of the remaining ships at Spithead and to put John Munden on trial. At the end of May 1702, Munden had commanded a squadron which failed to stop a French one under Admiral Jean-Baptiste du Casse from getting into Corunna. On 13 July, Shovell sat as president of the court-martial which found Munden innocent of all charges against him. However, in a travesty of justice, Queen Anne reversed the decision, Munden was discharged from his

---

14   NMM: RMT MS, MAT 24, copy of Cloudesley Shovell's will.

15   Frederick Smith, A *History of Rochester* (London: C.E. Daniel and Co 1928), p. 91. Walter Raleigh had brought back potatoes from the New World over a century before. Perhaps the mayor mistrusted this foreign food as it was not served at the dinner.

16   Charnock, *Biographia*, Vol. II, p. 25; Luttrell, *State Affairs*, Vol. V, pp. 36, 95; Oscar Browning (ed), *The Jounal of Sir George Rooke, Admiral of the Fleet, 1700-02* (London: Navy Records Society 1897), p. 60; Burchett, *Transactions at Sea*, p. 587.

17   Smith, *Rochester in Parliament,* p. 16; Cruikshanks, *History of Parliament,* Shovell entry.

18   Macaulay, *History*, Vol. VI, pp. 3000–6.

post and he never served at sea again.[19] It is likely that the government, acting in the queen's name, was responding to public pressure. What Shovell thought about this disgraceful decision is unknown, but brave straightforward man that he undoubtedly was, it is likely he was shocked by it.

A little earlier in the month of July, Shovell had received orders to take three recently careened ships and to search for a French squadron of which the Admiralty had intelligence. As an admiral of the white he looked upon these orders as humiliating and he was even angrier when he heard that Admiral George Churchill was trying to displace various naval persons from their posts in order to advance his own candidates. Having discussed the matter with one of his captains, George Byng, Shovell wrote a stiff letter of complaint to the Admiralty and knowing how much he might expose them, Queen Anne was asked to write him a placatory letter. Loyal to his queen and country, it was most unlike Shovell to act in this way, perhaps he had an inkling of Munden's unhappy fate. In the event, Shovell sailed with only two ships besides his own and a fireship! He was soon back at Spithead.[20]

Initially, on 20 July, Rooke, Ormonde and the troops sailed for Corunna on the northwest coast of Spain. Shovell, with by now 11 ships, was left to command in the Channel and was instructed to stop French ships from Brest following Rooke in his voyage to the south. Matters were further complicated by John Benbow's news from the West Indies that the French admiral Francois Châteaurenault, had sailed for Europe with the valuable Spanish plate fleet. Soon the Admiralty instructed Shovell and his squadron to intercept them, with the freedom to cruise in any station north of Cape Finisterre.[21] His slender resources were very much in his mind and the scandalous fate of Munden cannot have helped. Well might Shovell write to Daniel Finch, 2nd Earl of Nottingham and Secretary of State:

> ---- the misfortune and vice of our country is to believe ourselves better than other men, which I take to be the reason that generally we send too small a force to execute our designs; but experience has taught me that, when men are equally inured and disciplined in war, 'tis without a miracle, numbers that gain the victory. For both in fleets, squadrons and single ships of nearly equal force, by the time one is beaten and ready to retreat, the other is also beaten and glad his enemy has left him. To fight, beat and chase an enemy of the same strength I have sometimes seen, but rarely seen at sea any victory worth the boasting when the strength has been near equal.[22]

Unsurprisingly Shovell was concerned about the impracticability of his orders for he wrote to the Admiralty:

19   Browning (ed), *Rooke's Journal*, pp. 157, 165; Richmond, *Instrument of Policy,* pp. 286–7; John Owen, *War at Sea under Queen Anne 1702–1708* (Cambridge: Cambridge University Press 1938), p. 72; Le Fevre and Harding, *Precursors*, p. 63.

20   Laughton, *Torrington*, p. 87.

21   Corbett, *Mediterranean*, Vol. II, pp. 210–13; H of L MS 1702–4 NS, Vol. V, p. 111.

22   Le Fevre and Harding, *Precursors,* p. 64.

> This order directs me to take all possible care to prevent the French from proceeding to the southward after that part of the fleet that's gone with Sir George Rooke, as also to obstruct their coming into and committing insults in the Channel; and it further directs me to look out for and endeavour to intercept Mons. Château Rénault who [probably] will be in these seas very shortly. To do either of which three services, modestly speaking, will require three times as many ships of the line of battle as are in that list of his squadron.[23]

Shovell pointed out that he had only 10 ships in his squadron and that Châteaurenault was reported to have 30 ships of the line of battle. In reality the French had 34 ships. Shovell intended to place his meagre number of ships in the Chops of the Channel to discourage the French from, as he put it, 'insulting the Channel.'[24] However, he warned that in this position he would be unable to stop French ships sailing south after Rooke and also that it would not be possible to block Châteaurenault from reaching Brest or Rochefort if that was his destination. His final comment was: 'And as I esteem Admiral Churchill and it as a great favour and service to me and the country that they will send me word that they approve my design, or direct me where they think I made a misjudgement.'[25] In the current climate, Shovell was wise to involve the Admiralty in his plans in case of later criticism or worse. The smallpox-scarred George Churchill was an influential part of the council of the Lord High Admiral, Prince George of Denmark. Shovell was extremely wary of his political machinations.

Shovell's small force was to spend the latter part of July, August and September 1702, in the western approaches of the Channel and the Bay of Biscay. By August his contingent was further depleted by sickness amongst his seamen, although in September, efforts were made to send him six more ships.[26]

Whilst Shovell was commanding his squadron in the Channel, Rooke, Ormonde and their troops reached Corunna before proceeding to Cadiz. Here they found that the port was too strongly held to be taken by a coup-de-main and on 15 August 1702, Ormonde landed his troops on the other side of the bay at Rota, intending to take Cadiz from the flank. Soon a general disagreement between soldiers, sailors and the Dutch contingent occurred over the plan of attack. Prince George of Hesse Darmstadt, representing the interests of the Holy Roman Emperor Leopold I, vetoed any idea of bombardment or anything that might conceivably offend the Spanish inhabitants against the Habsburg cause. Rooke spent most of his time bedbound in his cabin suffering from the ravages of gout and his second-in-command, Thomas Hopsonn made most of the decisions on his behalf. For three weeks aimless and disorderly attacks were made around the suburbs of Cadiz, with drunkenness and plundering rife. It was quite clear that Cadiz was not going to fall into Rooke's hands and a variety of other targets were suggested. Rooke, by now suffering from a fever as well as gout, would accept none of them and decided to return to England. Ormonde and

---

23   Owen, *War at Sea*, pp. 74–5; BL: ADD MS 29591, Shovell correspondence and papers, ff. 199–247, 257, 269.
24   Chops of the Channel: the western approaches of the English Channel.
25   Owen, *War at Sea*, pp. 74–5; BL: ADD MS 29591, Shovell correspondence and papers, ff. 199–247, 257, 269.
26   Luttrell, *State Affairs*, Vol. V, pp. 186, 214, 216; Richmond, *Instrument of Policy*, pp. 288–9.

Hesse Darmstadt disagreed with the decision and would later be fearfully critical of the unhappy Rooke.[27]

Meanwhile Shovell, in the Channel, was ordered by the Admiralty to sail down in the direction of Corunna as they considered all the conceivable options for the destination of Châteaurenault and the rich Spanish plate fleet. In fact, on reaching the Azores, Châteaurenault with 56 ships in all, received intelligence of Rooke's fleet and wanted to change his destination from Cadiz, the usual port, to Brest. Unsurprisingly, his Spanish charges were underwhelmed with that suggestion, suspecting that it would be the last they saw of their silver and merchandise. As a compromise, Vigo in Galicia, north-western Spain, was selected as their final destination and they quietly slipped in there on 11 September, with Shovell to the north and Rooke to the south. Franco-Spanish luck had held.[28] Shovell was particularly unfortunate as, if Brest had been accepted as the destination port, the silver would have fallen into his hands, although it would have been a hard fight against a superior force.

During September, Rooke's fleet sailed up the western side of the Iberian Peninsula and on the 18th, Paul Methuen, the English Ambassador at Lisbon, was given intelligence about the plate fleet having safely reached Vigo. Realising what a wonderful opportunity had been presented to Rooke, he sent messenger after messenger out to the fleet. Eventually, whilst Rooke was off northern Portugal, the intelligence reached him but he was most reluctant to attempt an assault on Vigo, wishing only to go home. The Dutch admiral Philip Almonde finally persuaded the unhappy Rooke that he must set a course for Vigo. The government in London had also received intelligence that the plate fleet was in Vigo and hurriedly sent off letters to Rooke and Shovell, but these did not reach them until too late.[29]

On 10 October 1702, as Rooke approached Vigo, he made contact with George Byng with his small division of ships who were looking to reinforce Shovell's squadron. Byng, who was thirsting for action, was reluctantly sent away to inform Shovell of the situation so that his ships could be added to those of Rooke for the assault on Vigo. Fortuitously, the very next day, Byng came across part of Shovell's squadron and ordered them to find their admiral and bring him to Vigo. Having only partially followed Rooke's orders, Byng hurried back to Vigo so as not to miss all the action and possible glory.[30] Although Shovell had been sent orders on 5 October from England, it is likely that he did not receive them until after getting Byng's instructions from Rooke. In the event, Shovell did not reach Vigo until 16 October, some five days after the onset of the action.[31]

Rooke's fleet reached the bay, Ria de Vigo, on 11 October, and discovered that the plate fleet was in its innermost recesses, off the town of Redondela, protected by a strong boom of chains and timber plus forts at either end. Surprisingly, Rooke made no attempt to await Shovell, ordered Hopsonn to lead the assault and retired once more to his sick bed. On the 12th, with great courage, Hopsonn's *Torbay* charged the boom and broke it. Initially, the

27   Corbett, *Mediterranean*, Vol. II, pp. 212–7; Richmond, *Instrument of Policy*, pp. 287–90; H of L MS 1699–1702 NS, Vol. IV, p. 115.

28   Corbett, *Mediterranean*, Vol. II, p. 221; Owen, *War at Sea*, p. 82; Richmond, *Instrument of Policy*, p. 90.

29   Corbett, *Mediterranean*, Vol. II, pp. 222–3.

30   Corbett, *Mediterranean*, Vol. II, pp. 223–4; Laughton, *Torrington*, pp. 90–1.

31   Burchett, *Transactions at Sea*, pp. 628–31; H of L MS 1702–4 NS, Vol. V, p. 113.

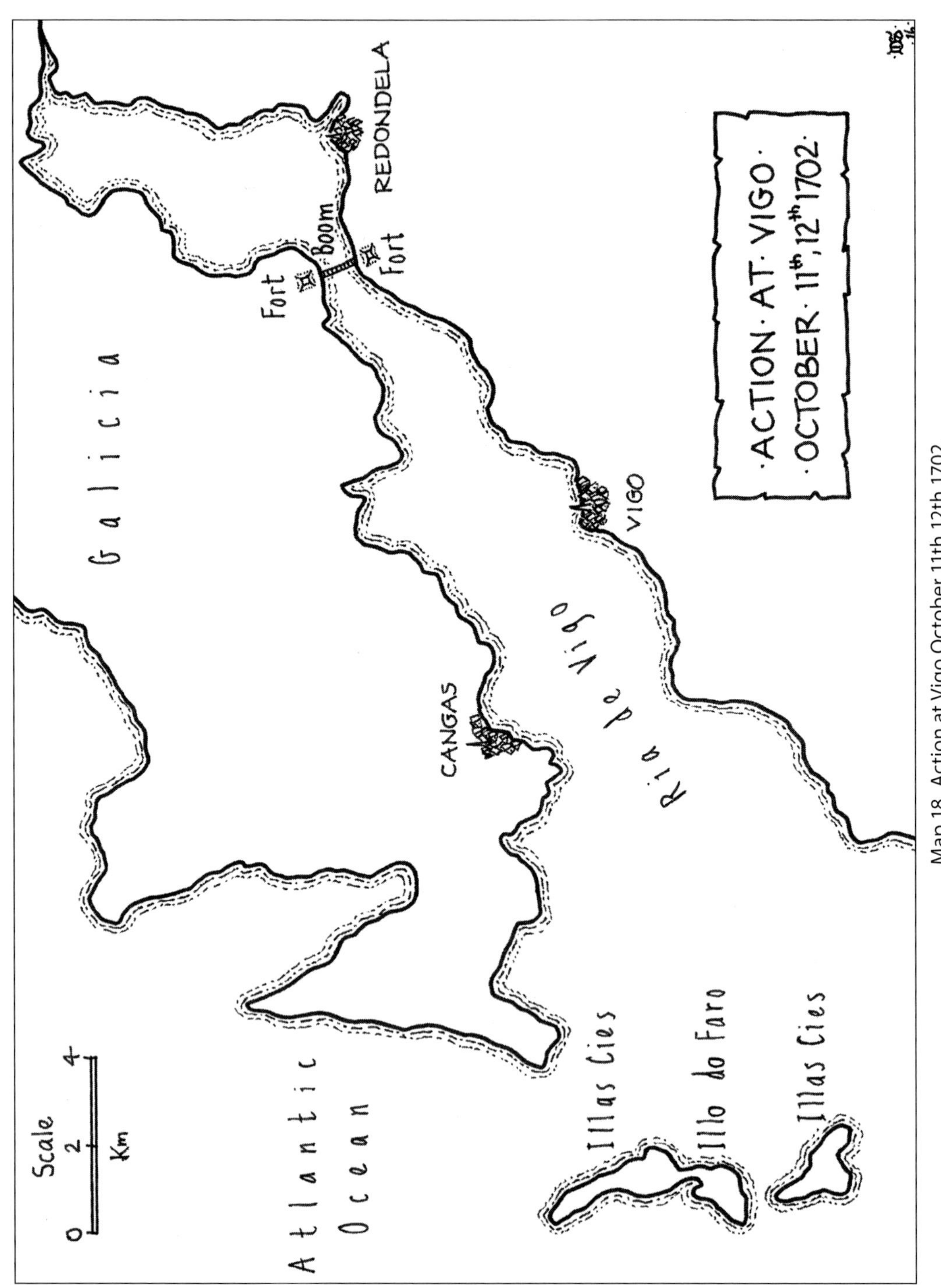

Map 18 Action at Vigo October 11th 12th 1702.

Torbay was isolated beyond the broken boom, with two French men of war in attendance, and suffered about 60 casualties. Gradually, the breeze returned and reinforcements came to the heavily-engaged Hopsonn's aid. Ormonde's troops took the surrounding batteries and the scene became one of carnage. Stephen Martin, who was present at the action, described the scene: 'for some time there was nothing to be heard or seen but cannonading, burning, men and guns flying in the air, and altogether the most lively scene of horror and confusion that can be imagined.' By the end of the day many of the outnumbered Châteaurenault's squadron and the plate ships had been destroyed.[32]

Unfortunately, much of the treasure had been unloaded already and was on the way up country before Rooke's men could lay hands on it. Some had been lost in the waters off Redondela as ships sank under English fire. However, it was reported that around £1,000,000–£1,750,000 worth of goods were salvaged by the English.[33] Modern research has indicated that the Spanish had actually saved an enormous 6,994,293 pesos, whilst later the English Treasury recorded only some £14,000 of captured silver. Although this had been a fine and successful combined military and naval operation, the rewards were not nearly as great as first thought.[34] The unfortunate Shovell arrived some five days after the action and received orders from Rooke:

> To remain at Vigo till he should get the prizes rigged and in a condition to sail, and unlade those galleons that were ashore, and such of them afloat as cannot be brought away, with a strict order against embezzlement and a power to suspend immediately any officer he should find so doing and to lose no time on that service, but to burn and destroy all the ships he could not bring with him and make the best of his way to Spithead.[35]

Rooke was set on returning to England, despite Ormonde and Hesse Darmstadt begging him to leave a strong squadron at Vigo for the winter. On 19 October, Rooke sailed for England without a backward glance.

No doubt Shovell was disappointed to have missed the action but, as was his custom, he loyally set about the collection of the silver treasure, captured ships and cannon. In a single week, he organised the collection of 60 iron cannons from the destroyed forts, plus a further 60 bronze guns from beached French ships. The five French ships brought home to England were: *Le Prompt*, *Le Ferme*, *Le Modéré*, *L'Assuré* and *Le Triton*.[36] Later a petition would be made to Queen Anne on his behalf for a reward, recognising his diligence and the retrieval of the brass guns. His task completed, Shovell left Vigo on 26 October for home waters, only to have his ships scattered widely by bad weather. Despite further inclement weather in the Soundings, he got into Spithead on 11 November. Rooke, possibly with thoughts of his

32   Corbett, *Mediterranean*, Vol. II, pp. 223–4; Richmond, *Instrument of Policy*, pp. 290–1; Laughton, *Torrington*, pp. 93–4; Burchett, *Transactions at Sea*, pp. 628–31.
33   Richmond, *Instrument of Policy*, p. 225; *DNB*, Rooke [Laughton]; Larn and McBride, *Shovell's Disaster*, p. 9.
34   Le Fevre and Harding, *Precursors*, pp. 64–5; Henry Kamen, 'The Destruction of the Spanish Silver Fleet at Vigo 1702', *Bulletin of the Institute of Historical Research* 39 (London: 1966), pp. 165–73.
35   Browning (ed), *Rooke's Journal*, pp. 235–6; Corbett, *Mediterranean*, Vol. II, p. 225.
36   Kamen, 'Silver Fleet at Vigo', p. 168.

share of the treasure, sent out cruisers [frigates] to guide him in. Perhaps, if this had been done successfully five years later, the Shovell disaster off the Isles of Scilly might never have occurred.[37] It was no mean feat, so late in the year, to bring safely home the captured ships, silver and cannons in appalling weather.

Queen Anne's England treated the action at Vigo as a great victory, but in reality this was not the case. It is true that many French and Spanish ships were destroyed and a further five brought home to England. But the principal losers in both ships and goods were the merchants rather than the Spanish government, a vast quantity of cocoa, cochineal, pepper, snuff, indigo and hides having vanished into the waters of Vigo Bay. Ironically, the English and Dutch merchants were amongst the greatest losers as they had been quietly trading with the West Indies and northern South America using Spanish ships as a means of transport. In 1703, Philip V of Spain [previously Duke of Anjou] decreed that as a reprisal he was seizing 4,000,000 pesos of silver that had been transported in the fleet for the English and Dutch merchants and was now safely in his hands! Only silver worth some £14,000 was actually brought home by Shovell. Modern examination of the action at Vigo in 1702, shows that it was not the spectacular success that it was thought to be at the time.

Ormonde and others complained bitterly about Rooke's conduct and the House of Lords held an enquiry. Rooke calmly stated that his orders were contradictory and that the expedition had been badly planned. He escaped censure and was made a privy councillor! Ormonde was silenced with the lucrative Lord Lieutenancy of Ireland and Hopsonn deservedly received a pension of £500 a year for life from Queen Anne.[38] Shovell had done everything that could possibly have been expected of him. As Campbell has written, bringing the treasure home under difficult circumstances was a remarkable service, and it was resolved to employ him in affairs of the greatest consequence for the future.[39]

In early March 1703, Shovell had been ordered to take a strong squadron into the Mediterranean, one Rooke had already declined to command as being 'too small for his character.'[40] Shovell spent the spring getting his squadron ready for sea and studying his instructions for the voyage which were complicated and constantly being added to. In essence they were to bring pressure to bear on the French in the Mediterranean: by assisting the Holy Roman Emperor Leopold I and Victor Amadeus II, Duke of Savoy; to attack Cadiz or Toulon if he had the chance; to persuade Cosimo III de Medici, Grand Duke of Tuscany, to maintain a strict neutrality; to review the peace treaties with the Barbary regencies and to persuade them to declare war on France; to give aid to the Cevennois; to provide a convoy for merchant shipping to Lisbon, Genoa, Leghorn, Smyrna and Scanderoon; to prevent the French Toulon squadron from passing through the Strait of Gibraltar.[41] Even a cursory glance at this long wish list demonstrates the impossibility of Shovell fulfilling his orders in the time available.

In the middle of May 1703, Shovell raised his flag in the 90-gun *Triumph* and on 1 July the combined Anglo-Dutch fleet set sail from Spithead for the Tagus. John Leake was left

---

37   Laughton, *Torrington*, pp. 96–7; Browning (ed), *Rooke's Journal*, p. 237; Larn and McBride, *Shovell's Disaster*, p. 9.
38   Corbett, *Mediterranean*, Vol. II, pp. 225–6; Luttrell, *State Affairs*, Vol. V, p. 234.
39   Campbell, *British Admirals*, Vol. IV, p. 247.
40   Corbett, *Mediterranean*, Vol. II, p. 230; BL: ADD MS 29591, f. 193, 3 March 1703.
41   Corbett, *Mediterranean*, Vol. II, pp. 230–1; Laughton, *Torrington*, pp. 98–100.

to follow with eight further ships, but he discovered that there were over a thousand sick sailors in these vessels. Sensibly, Leake manned only five of the ships with fit men and hurriedly set off in the wake of Shovell. The many delays had been caused by the late arrival of the Dutch and inclement weather.[42] Shovell was supported by the junior flag officers, Stafford Fairborne, George Byng and with the Dutch contingent under Philip Almonde. The fleet consisted of 40 major ships, fireships, bomb vessels and 160 merchantmen.[43] The traders with Smyrna and Scanderoon may have influenced the strengthening of the convoy, threatening not to sail as they had intelligence that France and Spain were intending 'to disrupt our passage into the Straits.'[44] On 5 July, Shovell and his ships were briefly forced to put into Torbay by a gale.

Eventually, on 24 July, Shovell's ships reached the entrance of the Tagus and Fairborne was sent to pay his respects to Pedro II of Portugal and to Catherine of Braganza, widow of Charles II. Pedro viewed the Anglo-Dutch fleet from the fort of St Anthony and sent Shovell a present which he did not receive, as the boat carrying it arrived after his departure.[45] Soon the fleet was underway again and on 4 August Cape Spartel was in sight. But they were then met by a fresh easterly wind which precluded their sailing through the Strait of Gibraltar. Shovell put into Tangier road and was well received by the hospitable Alicaid and a demonstration skirmish, with no less than 400 horses, was put on for the benefit of the visitors. However, the Alicaid pointed out that Queen Anne still owed them 86 barrels of gunpowder for a previous redemption of English captives.[46] Wisely Shovell rectified the matter.

On 12 August, the fleet sailed again and with a westerly wind swept through the Strait of Gibraltar that night.[47] The wind then unkindly swung round to the east and progress became difficult against it, leaving the fleet strung out along the Barbary Coast. After a week, water was in short supply and Shovell sent Byng to look for supplies on the Moroccan coast. Byng had little luck in his search with one of his boat crew killed and only then to discover that the local ruler had just been beheaded. After Byng reported to Shovell, a decision was taken to look for water on the coast of Spain at Altea Bay as their situation was becoming desperate with men dying of thirst. The fleet arrived at Altea Bay on 31 August, but it required the protection of a force of marines to get ashore to fill the water barrels. However, once Shovell had informed the local governor that they would pay for their food and water, the Spaniards' attitude changed and they became friendly.[48]

Part of Shovell's complicated orders instructed him to make contact with the Cevennois in the Bay of Narbonne and to supply them with arms. In 1702, the Protestants living in the Cevennes Mountains, in south-west France, had rebelled against Louis XIV. The Duke of Savoy had been wavering about whether to support the allies or not and joint action by him and the Cevennois would disrupt French communications with their naval base at Toulon. In addition, it was hoped that the Cevennois could be persuaded to destroy the salt works at

---

42   Martin-Leake, *John Leake*, Vol. I, pp. 118–9; Laughton, *Torrington*, p. 100.
43   Laughton, *Torrington*, pp. 100–1.
44   Luttrell, *State Affairs*, Vol. V, p. 307.
45   Anon, *Secret Memoirs*, p. 85.
46   Anon, *Secret Memoirs*, p. 86.
47   Martin-Leake, *John Leake*, Vol. I, p. 121.
48   Laughton, *Torrington*, pp. 103–5; Martin-Leake, *John Leake*, Vol. I, pp. 121–3.

Peccais, salt being essential for preserving meat at sea. As the Bay of Narbonne was shallow and potentially dangerous for his major ships, Shovell wisely sent only Robert Airis, in the 60-gun *Pembroke,* and John Cooper, in the *Tartar,* to communicate with the Cevennois.[49] Although both ships, carrying three French gentlemen familiar with the terrain, got into the bay, no contact was made. The salt works at Peccais were not destroyed and the English ships, fearful of a change in the direction of the wind, did not show much resolve in getting close to the shore, let alone setting foot on it.

On 3 September, Shovell, having sent the *Pembroke* and *Tartar* away, sailed with the remainder of his fleet for Leghorn in north-western Italy. Off the Balearic Islands, he allowed the merchant vessels to sail independently for Smyrna and Scanderoon as he judged that there were no French ships in the vicinity to interfere with them. He would not have been human if his mind did not go back 10 years to an earlier disastrous Smyrna convoy as the merchantmen disappeared over the horizon. At this juncture, Almonde told Shovell that he must soon leave the Mediterranean with his Dutch contingent in order to be back in the Netherlands by 11 November as his orders stipulated. Almonde asked Shovell what his plans were for the immediate future. Shovell replied that he intended to sail to Leghorn and he pointed out the inherent dangers of dividing the fleet. Almonde agreed to stay a little longer depending on the direction of the wind which could make sailing home difficult.

Leghorn road was reached at night on 19 September and there was an immediate altercation with the Governor over saluting. They had been greeted by a paltry five-gun salute which Shovell had not answered as he considered it inadequate. The Governor told him that it was an identical salute to the one given to, amongst others, Shovell's friend and patron John Narbrough. This did not satisfy Shovell, and led to much 'toing and froing' between Leghorn and Florence to diffuse the matter. A compromise was agreed: Leghorn fired 11 guns as a salute to the Queen's flag and a further 23 in honour of Shovell's person. Shovell replied in kind and similar arrangements were made for the Dutch. Honour was satisfied after three days of hard negotiations. In the 17th and early 18th centuries, saluting was a matter of national prestige and taken very seriously indeed.[50]

Part of Shovell's orders required him to remind the Grand Duke of Tuscany to maintain his neutrality. Through the Governor of Leghorn and General Teriesi, Shovell made a number of demands: English subjects must be free to embark on Queen Anne's ships; English ships must be able to leave Tuscany's ports without being hindered and the French must not be allowed to sail after them for a minimum of 24 hours; the Governor was to be removed as he was favouring the French enemy. If Shovell's demands were not met, he threatened to use the firepower of the fleet to enforce them and, in the event, Shovell was successful with most of his requests. Unsurprisingly, the removal of the Governor was not among them as he had been a conduit for the one-sided negotiations.[51]

On 28 September, Shovell was informed that Emperor Leopold I had declared his second son Charles, King of Spain, as Charles III and a royal salute was fired in his honour. It was said that the thundering of Shovell's guns that could be heard far inland, in salute of the

---

49   Corbett, *Mediterranean,* Vol. II, p. 237.

50   Martin-Leake, *John Leake,* Vol. I, p. 124; Laughton, *Torrington,* p. 107.

51   BL: ADD MS 29591, ff. 213, 217, 225, 226, 233, Shovell correspondence and papers whilst commanding in the Mediterranean, 1703.

Habsburg King of Spain, had shown the Grand Duke of Tuscany how he lay between the devil and the deep blue sea. Had Shovell been bombarding Leghorn, his guns could not have spoken with a louder voice.[52]

The combined Anglo-Dutch fleet left Leghorn on 2 October and Almonde and his ships soon went their separate ways home. Shovell had wanted to visit the Barbary regencies, Tripoli, Tunis and Algiers, in order to renew their peace treaties and persuade them to declare war on Louis XIV's France. However, it was now dangerously late in the year and Shovell sent Thomas Swanton to Tripoli, Robert Airis to Tunis and George Byng to Algiers to act in his place. Then Shovell decided to sail to Altea Bay to replenish his water supplies before returning to England.[53] Having done so, the fleet sailed through the Strait of Gibraltar and headed to the north and home. The first members of Shovell's fleet reached England on 16 November and reported that all the crews were sickly. On sighting land, Shovell hauled down the union flag from the main mast head, as commander-in-chief and replaced it with the correct flag for an admiral of the white. Over 500 men had died on the voyage and the survivors were in a poor state of health.[54]

The Mediterranean campaign of 1703 cannot be looked upon as an overwhelming success. It is true that: the Toulon fleet had been kept in port by Shovell's presence; the Grand Duke of Tuscany had been pressurised into being less partial to the French; peace treaties had been renewed with the Barbary regencies. However, no attack had been possible on the coasts of Spain or France and no contact made with the Cevennois. That little was accomplished by Shovell is unsurprising as his orders were constantly changed before sailing and he did not get away until the beginning of July with a return through the Strait of Gibraltar anticipated by the end of September. Although questions were asked in the House of Commons, all members agreed that Shovell had done his duty in every respect. After his earlier clashes with both Houses of Parliament, Shovell was entitled to breathe a sigh of relief. The campaign can be simply summarised as too much expected in too short a time.[55]

The late arrival of the fleet in England would prove to be almost fatal for Shovell and certainly so for many of his men who had been out to the Mediterranean with him. On the evening of 24 November, Shovell still in the *Triumph*, sailed with the 90-gun *Association*, 96-gun *St George*, 80-gun *Cambridge*, 80-gun *Russell*, 80-gun *Dorsetshire*, 70-gun *Royal Oak* and 70-gun *Revenge* from the Downs.[56] That same evening they all anchored in the Gunfleet. Two days later, on the evening of Friday 26 November, a great storm broke with a fierce gale blowing from the south-west.[57] The storm reached its peak in the early hours of Saturday morning, wreaking havoc over the south and west of England in particular. The centre of the storm was in the Downs and away to the north-east caused catastrophic

52 Corbett, *Mediterranean*, Vol. II, pp. 238–9.
53 BL: ADD MS 29591, ff. 227, 228, 230, 237, Shovell correspondence and papers whilst commanding in the Mediterranean, 1703.
54 Martin-Leake, *John Leake*, Vol. I, p. 126.
55 Campbell, *British Admirals*, Vol. IV, p. 248.
56 BL: ADD MS 5440, f. 3, Shovell order to John Leake, 3 December 1703.
57 Luttrell, *State Affairs*, Vol. V, p. 363.

damage to Shovell's ships in the Gunfleet, as well as shipping in general in the English Channel.[58]

No one in living memory could recall a storm of this intensity and it became known as the Great Storm. A vast number of chimneys and the roofs of houses were blown off. Queen Anne was forced to take shelter in a cellar at St James's Palace. Trees were uprooted in nearby St James's Park, the Temple and Gray's Inn. Many people were killed by falling debris, including the unfortunate Richard Kidder, Bishop of Bath and Wells and his lady who were struck down by two falling chimney stacks whilst asleep in bed. An East India ship and several merchant vessels were cast away near Blackwall. Over 100 ships from Yarmouth Broad, mainly colliers, were missing.[59] The church put the storm down to the vengeance of God for a sinful nation.

Shovell, anchored at the Gunfleet, was caught up in the height of the storm. In a letter to his fellow admiral, John Leake, he has left us a graphic description of what happened to him personally:

> Triumph near Gunfleete
> Dec 3rd 1703
> Genm
>
> The 24th ultimo the day wee sayled out of the Downes with the ships in the Margine about the Long head,[60] we anchored in the evening in twelve fathome water, the North Foreland South West, distant about six leagues, On Saturday last soone in the morning wee had a most miserable Storme of Wind, which drove us to some streights, for after wee had veered out more than three cables of our best bower that Anchor Broke, soon after our Tillar broke, and before wee could secure our Rudder, it broke from our sterne, and has shaken our Stern Post that we prove very leakey, and had our four Chaine Pumps and a hand Pump going to keep us free, Wee let go our Sheete Anchor and Veeredout all the Cables to it, butt that did not ride us, butt wee drove neare a Sand called the Galloper of which we saw the breach, I directed the Maine Mast to be Cutt by the Board, after which we ridd fast of Eight Ships that came out of the Downes four are mifsing, the Association, Rufsel, Revenge and Dorsetshire, pray God they drove clear of the Sands, Wee have now fitted a Jury Maine Mast & Rudder, and the ship works very well with them, and the Carpenter has stopt some of our Leakes, We are got in neare the Gunfleete, and if the Weather proves faire I hope we shall get neare in, the Cambridge is now with us and I have ordered her to stay by us till we get up,
> I am
> Gen:m
> Yr & C
> Clo Shovell

---

58 Burchett, *Transactions at Sea*, p. 656; Martin-Leake, *John Leake*, Vol. I, p. 127.
59 Luttrell, *State Affairs*, Vol. V, p. 363.
60 The ships were *Triumph, Association, St George, Cambridge, Rufsell, Dorsetshire, Royal Oake, Revenge.*

PS I doubt it has fared worse with the four ships that have drove away than it has done with us. I have some hopes that some of them have drove to Sea, but if they are without Anchors or Cables and may be without Masts, I judge it will be of service if some Friggts: were sent out to look for them.

C:S[61]

Shovell's *Triumph* had been very lucky to survive the storm with the anchors not holding the ship and the loss of the rudder making steering, in a near hurricane, impossible to achieve. Undoubtedly his personal decision to cut down the main mast had saved the ship from becoming a wreck.

Other ships had miraculously survived the atrocious weather. Stafford Fairborne, in the 90-gun *Association*, the ship that Shovell would later lose his life in, had an equally eventful time. The *Association*'s cables parted at 4:00 a.m. on 27 November and the ship drove over the Galloper sand where, in shallow water, a great sea tilted her over. Fortunately, she progressed into deeper water and the crew managed to bring her head around to the north. Later on the night of the 27th, Fairborne thought they were on the coast of Holland. In fact by 11 December, the *Association* had been driven all the way to Gothenburg in Sweden. It would be another month before Fairborne managed to return to the Gunfleet.[62]

Vice-Admiral John Leake, in the 90-gun *Prince George,* had been part of Shovell's fleet, but had remained in the Downs on the night of 26–27 November. The Downs had been a forest of ship's masts, but within two hours of the storm hitting them, it had become a desert. Leake had managed to ride out the storm, when at 3:00 a.m. the *Restoration* drove down upon them and the two ships became locked together. Desperate attempts, without success, were made by the crew of the *Prince George* to free themselves from the *Restoration*. Finally, the *Restoration* broke free and was then smashed to pieces by the violent sea with the loss of all hands. Leake's *Prince George* survived the battering without having to cut down her masts.[63]

When day broke, Leake had the melancholy sight of 12 ships ashore on the Goodwin, Burnt Head and Brake Sands. Amongst them were the 60-gun *Mary,* 70-gun *Stirling Castle,* 70-gun *Northumberland* and 70-gun *Restoration.* During 27 November, Leake ordered all available boats to the *Stirling Castle*'s wreck where over 70 men were clinging to the remains of the poop. The single survivor from the *Mary,* the coxswain, had managed to swim to the poop of the *Stirling Castle* in mountainous seas. He was able to report on the deaths of Admiral Basil Beaumont, his lieutenant and clerk, who had lashed themselves to a piece of the ship and had been swept out to sea to drown.[64] In all between 2,000 and 3,000 men had been lost from these ships. Leake instituted a search for distressed shipping in the vicinity of the Downs and later this was extended to the North Sea.

Perhaps one of the unluckiest men in the Great Storm of 1703 was George Byng. Having concluded his protracted negotiations with Algiers he had the great misfortune to be off the Lizard on 26 November, when the storm broke over him. His ship, the 80-gun *Ranelagh,*

61   BL: ADD MS 5440, f. 3, Shovell order to John Leake, 3 December 1703.
62   Burchett, *Transactions at Sea*, p. 657.
63   Martin-Leake, *John Leake*, Vol. I, pp. 126–8.
64   Martin-Leake, *John Leake*, Vol. I, p. 129.

had started to leak partly because a gun had broken free and penetrated the hull of the ship. The vessel started to fill up with water and was six feet deep in the hold. Only frantic bailing by the crew, supported by frequent tots of brandy, kept the ship afloat. Miraculously, the *Ranelagh*, with two of her masts cut down, limped into St Helen's Roads on the Isle of Wight. Byng was made commander-in-chief at Spithead and found himself responsible for two men who had been condemned to death for desertion. So affected was he by the enormous loss of life that pardons for the unfortunate sailors were requested and granted. This must have been one of the few happy events at this grim time.[65]

The Great Storm of 1703 was one of the worst disasters in the annals of the Royal Navy and Shovell had indeed been fortunate to survive it.

65 Laughton, *Torrington*, pp. 116–8.

16

The Siege of Gibraltar and the Battle of Malaga 1704

In late 1703, George Rooke had taken a squadron to collect Archduke Charles, the second son of Emperor Leopold I, from the Netherlands and transported him to Spithead. Early in January 1704, the newly proclaimed Charles III, the Habsburg claimant to the throne of Spain, was escorted by Rooke out to Lisbon, where he remained as a guest of the Portuguese royal family. In March, Rooke received orders from home to proceed into the Mediterranean with his ships. He was instructed to: support the Duke of Savoy; prevent a junction between the French ships from Toulon and Brest; if possible capture Toulon; 'alarm the coast of Spain', particularly Catalonia which was thought to favour Charles III; support the Cevennois.[1]

At the end of April, Rooke left Lisbon with a combined Anglo-Dutch fleet of 31 ships, entered the Mediterranean and the following May proceeded to bombard Barcelona. The Catalonians, although sympathetic to the cause of Charles III, were not prepared to declare themselves in his favour. Rooke set sail for Nice, but his frigates reported the presence of about 40 French vessels, thought to be from Brest and under the command of Louis Alexandre de Bourbon, Comte de Toulouse, a natural son of Louis XIV. Following a council of war, a dilatory chase was made before the French slipped safely into Toulon. At the end Rooke rather gave up on his pursuit, thinking that the French were about to be reinforced, and returned to the Straits with his fleet. Although there was no enquiry into his actions, Laird Clowes has severely criticised Rooke for not making the most of an opportunity to deny their entry into Toulon.[2]

Shovell had narrowly escaped death in the Great Storm of November 1703 and he spent the early part of 1704 in England. On 13 February, he was made an Elder of Trinity House,[3] which had been responsible for pilotage and later lighthouses since its original charter in 1514. In April, Prince George of Denmark, the Lord High Admiral, gave orders for Shovell's squadron to proceed to sea and to prevent French shipping from Rochefort and Port-Louis, near Lorient, from reaching Brest. If he found that the French fleet had left Brest and had

---

1   Richmond, *Instrument of Policy,* pp. 301–2; Le Fevre and Harding, *Precursors,* p. 67.
2   Laird Clowes, *Royal Navy,* Vol. II, pp. 390–1; Le Fevre and Harding, *Precursors,* p. 67.
3   Trinity House (TH): Court Minutes of 1704.

good reasons for thinking that it had sailed for the Straits, he was to detach a sufficient number of ships to give Rooke superiority over a combined West France/Toulon fleet.[4] If he judged that a large number of ships were required to support Rooke, Shovell himself was to sail with them and then put himself under the former's command.[5]

In early May, Shovell left Portsmouth with his squadron and at St Helens called a council of war. After due deliberation, it was decided to sail to Plymouth to reinforce themselves with further men-of-war and to pick up the merchantmen for the West Indies. Following this Plymouth rendezvous, they would join their frigates between the Lizard and Forne Head and ascertain whether the French had left Brest or not.[6] If they had, Shovell would search for them in the Soundings. Failure to find the French there would lead Shovell to position his squadron 140–150 leagues west-south-west of the Isles of Scilly. If the French had still not appeared, ships up to 22 in number would be sent to reinforce Rooke. During May no sign of the French was found and the plans listed above where put into effect with the addition of the West Indies ships leaving under William Kerr and Stafford Fairborne.[7] The French fleet from Brest, under the Comte de Toulouse, was well ahead of them and as we saw earlier would slip into Toulon with Rooke in ineffectual pursuit.

On 28 May, Shovell's squadron split up with him, taking the maximum 22 ships that he was allowed under his orders, to join Rooke. Early in June, he reached Lisbon and found no sign of Rooke who was eventually identified, on the 16th of the month, off Lagos. Then Rooke and Shovell decided to seek the combined Brest and Toulon squadrons in the Mediterranean and possibly also make an attempt on Cadiz or Barcelona if they had sufficient forces. In July, Rooke called a council of war at which Shovell, John Leake, George Byng, James Wishart and the Dutch flag officers were present. Rooke pointed out that Queen Anne had given instructions that the fleet should undertake nothing without the support the kings of Spain and Portugal. Cadiz was rapidly ruled out as being too strongly defended and anyway Rooke had burnt his fingers badly there two years earlier. However, Gibraltar was a very different matter and the two kings raised no objections.[8]

Gibraltar was an attractive target for Rooke and his newly formed fleet. Oliver Cromwell had considered taking it and in the reign Charles II careening hulks had been stationed there in preference to Tangier. William III had coveted the place and every admiral passing by had been instructed to capture it if at all possible. Above all else, it controlled the Straits and thus the entry and exit to the Mediterranean.[9] Gibraltar was familiar to both Rooke and Shovell from their time in the Mediterranean in the 1670s and '80s.

On this occasion precisely who first suggested that Gibraltar should be attacked is unclear. A case has been made for both John Leake and Prince George of Hesse Darmstadt. Stephen Martin with his close connections to Leake recorded 'the admirals determined to attack

4   West France ships: from Brest, Port-Louis and Rochefort.
5   Laughton, *Torrington*, pp. 122–3; Burchett, *Transactions at Sea*, p. 673.
6   Forne Head is Portsall in north-western Brittany.
7   Burchett, *Transactions at Sea*, p. 675; Laughton, *Torrington*, pp. 124–5.
8   Burchett, *Transactions at Sea*, p. 677.
9   Corbett, *Mediterranea*n, Vol. II, p. 255.

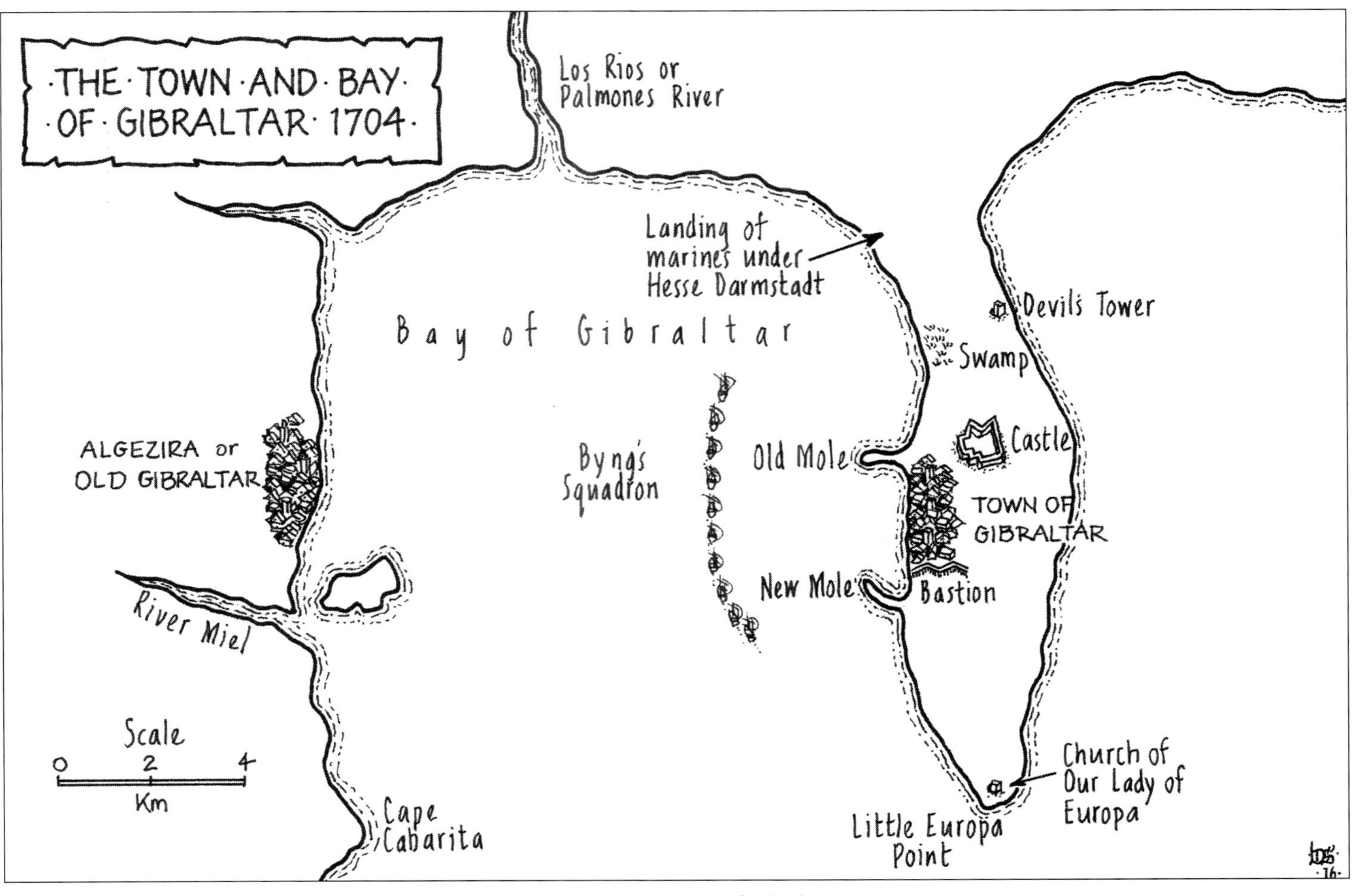

Map 19 The Town and Bay of Gibraltar 1704.

Gibraltar ----',[10] giving the impression that it was a collective decision. Shovell's anonymous biographer tells a different tale:

> The two admirals [Rooke, Shovell] returned forthwith into the Mediterranean and whereupon a council of war being called, it was argued by Cloudesley Shovell that since the French had got into Toulon and secured themselves from any attempt to be made upon them in that impregnable city it was expedient for the good of this Catholick Majesty and the honour of our arms to make some sudden attempt upon the Spanish Coast, that if the town of Gibraltar could be taken, it would easily be made tenable, that it would be a sure retreat for such Spaniards in the interest of Charles III would give him a strong place of arms and be an inlet into the Conquest of Spain, from which Town if it fell into our hands, we might easily penetrate into the heart of Andalusia and without enumerating all the advantages which seemed material, such a harbour would be a refuge for our merchant ships too frequently exposed to the insults of the French and Spaniards in those foreign seas.
>
> These arguments being very solid, had so strong an influence over the officers that composed this Council of War, that they without hesitation sailed for Gibraltar in order to attempt the reduction of that place.[11]

Here rests the case for Shovell.

The honour of leading the amphibious assault on Gibraltar fell to George Byng, a strange choice as he was said to be a vocal critic of the enterprise. On 21 July 1704, the land forces consisting of 1,800 marines, commanded by Hesse Darmstadt, were put ashore on the neck of land to the north of the town with the effect that Gibraltar was isolated from Spain. Hesse Darmstadt summoned the Governor, Don Diego de Salinas, to surrender the town in the name of Charles III and was immediately rebuffed as the defenders owed their allegiance to the Bourbon cause. The next day, the 22nd, Rooke ordered Byng, with a combined Anglo-Dutch squadron of 22 ships, to bombard the town from the sea, but a contrary wind precluded this for 24 hours. On the 23rd, Byng oversaw an intense bombardment from the sea with the result that the enemy were blasted from their guns, particularly at the south mole directly in front of the English ships. Captain Edward Whitaker with the ships' boats crammed full of sailors was sent ashore and the first man to land was William Jumper. Despite a considerable loss of life following the detonation of a mine at the south mole, the enemy were driven from their cannons. A small bastion situated halfway between the south mole and the town was also captured. For a second time, Hesse Damstadt called upon the Governor to surrender and this time he did so. No doubt his mind was concentrated by the fact that the town's women and children were trapped in the Church of Our Lady of Europa, at the most southern tip of the peninsula. Somewhat to his surprise, Hesse Darmstadt discovered that the defending force was only 150 men strong, although 100 guns had been mounted against his forces.[12] However, 61 of his men had been killed and about 260 were wounded.

---

10   Markham (ed), *Stephen Martin*, p. 75.
11   Anon, *Secret Memoirs*, pp. 90–1.
12   Martin-Leake, *John Leake*, Vol. I, pp. 154–5; Laughton, *Torrington*, pp. 138–45.

What of Shovell's part in the taking of Gibraltar? He was a participant in the council of war which decided to make an attempt on the place and may have been instrumental in getting Rooke to agree to the siege. During the action Shovell went on board Byng's ship, the 80-gun *Ranelagh*, and viewed the action from there. At the stage that the boats were being sent in, priests, women and children attempted to run back from the Europa Church to the protection of their menfolk in the town. Shovell suggested that the *Ranelagh's* cannons be fired in their direction, not with a view to harming them, but to drive them back into the church. He thought that that the Governor would soon surrender with the knowledge that their womenfolk were separated from safety by rough English sailors and in this matter he was proved to be correct. The sailors did not harm the women and children in the Europa Church, but they broke off the head of the wooden Madonna and Christ carving from the altar and threw it down a cliff. The remains were found and kept hidden for many years, in Algeciras, across the bay. Finally, in recent years, it was restored and returned to the refurbished Europa Church.[13]

It has be acknowledged that Shovell's part in the taking of Gibraltar was a minor one as second-in-command of the fleet to his rival Rooke. However, in the Battle of Malaga which rapidly followed, he was to play a major role. Gibraltar remains a British Overseas Territory but, in 1704, it did not cease to be an integral part of Spain as it had been captured in the name of Charles III. Eventually, Philip V was successful in claiming the throne of Spain over Charles III, and it was the former, in 1713, who was forced to allow the cession of Gibraltar in return for recognition by the allies.[14]

On 25 July, Rooke held a council of war with his flag officers to discuss their plans for the immediate future in the light of their recent success at Gibraltar.[15] Letters had been received from London and the ambassador at Lisbon, Paul Methuen, informing them that the Comte de Toulouse had arrived at Toulon with the Brest fleet. This fact was already known to Rooke but he was also instructed to make an attempt on either Barcelona or Cadiz. The former was soon laid aside as being too late in the year although the admirals were prepared to co-operate with action at Cadiz provided they were given sufficient troops by the kings of Spain and Portugal.[16] In the meantime, whilst the sovereigns deliberated, the fleet would water on the Barbary Coast.[17]

The news of the fall of Gibraltar reached a startled Madrid and Francisco Castillo Fajardo, 2nd Marquis of Villadarias, was dispatched with 8,000 men to reclaim the place or, at the very least, hinder the progress of the allies into the interior of Spain.[18] The authorities back in London believed that Toulouse's fleet was inferior to the Anglo-Dutch one and that he would shut himself up safely in Toulon. The admirals were wary of this mistaken view and were proved to be correct as he had taken the combined French fleet to Barcelona which

<hr>

13   Anon, *Secret Memoirs,* pp. 91–3; Laughton, *Torrington,* p. 193. When the author visited the church, in 2005, and photographed the carving, he was greeted by a very loud, in English, 'what do you think you are doing?' Only the rapid production of a suitably large euro note for church funds allowed peace and tranquillity to return to the holy place. Also he was only too aware of an ancient whipping post just outside the church!

14   Laird Clowes, *Royal Navy,* Vol. II, p. 396.

15   Martin-Leake, *John Leake,* Vol. I, p. 157.

16   Corbett, *Mediterranean,* Vol. II, p. 262; Laughton, *Torrington,* p. 146.

17   Martin-Leake, *John Leake,* Vol. I, p. 157.

18   Anon, *Secret Memoirs,* pp. 92–3.

Louis XIV thought was Rooke's prime objective. Toulouse was told the shattering news that Gibraltar had fallen and he was ordered to sail south to rectify matters.[19]

Prince George of Hesse Darmstadt was left at Gibraltar with 1,800 marines as a garrison while the fleet watered by squadrons on the African shore.[20] On 1 August, Rooke took most of his ships to Ceuta whilst Shovell and his division plied up against the wind to Reifi, some nine miles to the east of Tetuan where the river runs into the sea.[21] A great sea was running and stopped Shovell from filling his casks and so he was forced to join Rooke at Ceuta to complete the task. On the 3rd, most of the fleet had completed their watering and by degrees returned to Gibraltar.[22]

Early in the morning of 9 August, one of Rooke's ships, the *Centurion*, on the way back from watering, spotted the French to the east of Gibraltar and signalled to that effect.[23] George Byng was the first to see the signal and reported to Rooke who was doubtful about its authenticity but a number of officers shinned up the mast and confirmed the proximity of the French fleet.[24] A council of war was then again called with the English represented by Rooke, Shovell, John Leake, George Byng, Thomas Dilkes, James Wishart and the Dutch by Gerrit Callenburgh, Jan Wassenaer. It was agreed to return to Gibraltar and to re-embark half the marine force left behind under Hesse Darmstadt. If the wind was easterly, they would wait for the French to attack, and if westerly, they would seek out the enemy, but sail no further than Cape Malaga. Wishart, Rooke's captain of the fleet, was against the plan and wanted the fleet to return to Gibraltar to await the French. If this course of action had been followed it could have led to disaster for the English, at anchor in Gibraltar Bay and in no position to see off the French fleet. A further complicating factor was that 12 English ships were still watering on the Barbary Coast.[25]

Toulouse had the advantage of an easterly wind, but made no attempt to engage, slipping quietly away to collect his galleys from Malaga. On 10 August, Rooke took the opportunity to re-embark 1,000 marines from Hesse Darmstadt's garrison and sailed away from Gibraltar. On the 11th, a French ship which had been keeping a close eye on Rooke's vessels was chased on shore by English frigates and burnt. Rooke summoned another council on the 12th, at which it was decided to sail to the Strait of Gibraltar for 48 hours and if the French still had not appeared to return and further fortify Gibraltar. At 11:00 a.m., soon after the council had broken up and the participants had returned to their own ships, the French were observed to the north-west of Rooke's fleet, off Cape Malaga, and going away in the direction of the Straits with the easterly wind. This was a most worrying turn of events as the French fleet had been missed by Rooke, in a sweep to the south-east, and it was now between him and his recent capture, Gibraltar. Immediately, Rooke signalled for his ships to form the line of battle and engage the enemy. However, at this juncture, the wind slackened and battle was delayed until the next day.

19   Corbett, *Mediterranean*, Vol. II, p. 263; Anon, *Secret Memoirs*, p. 93.
20   Laughton, *Torrington*, p. 147.
21   The name Reifi appears to have been lost. It probably lay just to the north of Sidi Abdeslam Beach.
22   Martin-Leake, *John Leake*, Vol. I, p. 158; Laughton, *Torrington*, p. 147.
23   Owen, *War at Sea*, p. 92.
24   Laughton, *Torrington*, pp. 147–8.
25   Laughton, *Torrington*, p. 148.

During the night of 12–13 August, the two fleets lay separated by three leagues of sea [nine miles] and anxiously awaited the morrow. As dawn broke on the 13th, Rooke and Toulouse's fleets were situated some eight to 10 leagues to the south of Cape Malaga with the wind still from the east. The only major fleet action of the War of the Spanish Succession, the Battle of Malaga, was about to begin in earnest.[26] The French line faced south towards the Barbary Coast and was shaped with a concavity in its centre, similar to a half moon. Byng and others thought that this configuration would allow the French van and rear, with the aid of their galleys, to gain the advantage of the wind.[27] Fourteen years earlier, at the Battle of Beachy Head, Tourville had drawn up his ships in a similar fashion.

The French had 50 major ships of the line supported by galleys with a total of 3,577 guns and 24,275 men. Their van was commanded by Philippe, Marquis de Villette-Mursay with 16 ships of the white and blue squadron, supported by the Duke of Tursis in the second line with 12 galleys, two frigates and four fireships. In the centre was the white squadron of 16 ships under Toulouse himself, supported by four galleys, four frigates, two fireships and two flutes as the second line.[28] The rear was made up of the blue squadron of 18 ships under Joseph Andrault, 2nd Comte de Langeron, supported by eight galleys, three frigates and three fireships in the second line.[29]

The Anglo-Dutch fleet had 53 major ships divided into the now traditional three squadrons with a total of 3,614 guns and 22,543 men. Cloudesley Shovell, admiral of the white, commanded the van of 15 ships with the assistance of his junior, John Leake, vice-admiral of the blue and their second line consisted of two frigates, three fireships and a hospital ship. Unusually there was no rear-admiral in the van. In the centre was Rooke, as commander-in-chief, with 24 ships aided by rear-admirals George Byng and Thomas Dilkes. The second line in the centre was made up of two frigates, four fireships, two bomb vessels, a yacht and a hospital ship. There was also a third line in the middle with two 50-gun ships, two frigates and two fireships. The rationale behind their presence was to block the possibility of galleys and fireships pushing through Rooke's line. The rear was made up of a Dutch squadron of 12 vessels under Admiral Gerrit Callenburgh with Jan Wassenaer as second-in-command.[30]

In Shovell's division of the van were several ships commanded by close associates and protégés. He was himself in the 90-gun *Barfleur* with his long time captain, James Stuart, and with the 90-gun *Namur* under Christopher Myngs, the son of Shovell's first great patron of the same name, as the next ship ahead. Immediately behind was the 70-gun *Orford* under John Norris, who had been a midshipman under Shovell in the *Edgar* some 15 years earlier at the Battle of Bantry Bay. Three years after the Battle of Malaga, Shovell would die off the Isles of Scilly after his ship, the *Association*, was wrecked on the Gilstone rock. Both the captain of the *Association* that fatal day, Sam Whitaker, and Shovell's personal flag-captain, the nephew of John Narbrough, Edmund Loades, were with him at Malaga commanding the 60-gun *Nottingham* and 70-gun *Warspite* respectively. Robert Hancock whose ship, the

---

26   Martin-Leake, *John Leake*, Vol. I, pp. 159–60; Laughton, *Torrington*, pp. 149–151; Anon, *Secret Memoirs*, pp. 93–105.

27   Martin-Leake, *John Leake*, Vol. I, p. 160; Laughton, *Torrington*, p. 151.

28   Flute or Fluyt was a vessel of Dutch origin with round stern which often carried cargo.

29   Martin-Leake, *John Leake*, Vol. I, pp. 160–1; Anon, *Secret Memoirs*, pp. 97–101.

30   Martin-Leake, *John Leake*, Vol. I, pp. 161–3; Anon, *Secret Memoirs*, pp. 96–7, 101.

Eagle, sank at the same time as the *Association* was also present, in Shovell's division, at Malaga, as captain of the 66-gun *Assurance.* Edward Vernon, the future renowned admiral, was a member of the crew of Shovell's flagship, the *Barfleur.* When Shovell died in 1707, Vernon was part of his fleet as captain of the 32-gun *Rye.* Patronage was very much the order of the day in the early 18th century navy.[31]

Shovell's immediate opponent in the white and blue squadron, de Villette was in the 88-gun *Fier* and had fought on the same side as the English, at Sole Bay in 1672, and against them at Barfleur in 1692. He was supported in the van's leading division by Louis Le Roux, Marquis d'Infreville, in the 90-gun *St Philippe* and by Jean Erard, Comte de Belle-Isle, in the 86-gun *Magnifique.*[32] These three French admirals were in their 77th, 62nd and 67th years respectively, giving a combined age of some 206 years. Shovell and Leake were in their 54th and 48th years of age. Perhaps the poor performance of the French van in the coming battle can at least partially be laid at the door of anno domini.

The two fleets were well-matched in numbers of ships, men and guns. However, there was a glaring disparity in available ammunition as the English ships had been profligate in their bombardment at the siege of Gibraltar. To compound the error, Rooke had made neither an attempt to collect more ammunition, in the form of powder and balls, nor to uniformly redistribute such as he already had in the fleet. As will be seen, this would have serious repercussions during the battle.

Early on Sunday 13 August, with the easterly wind behind them, Rooke's Anglo-Dutch fleet bore down obliquely on Toulouse's semi-circular line of battle which was still facing south. At 10:00 a.m., the English van led by Leake and with Shovell in overall command came up with de Villette's white and blue squadron and, as was often the case in the age of sail, the various Anglo-Dutch squadrons became separated, leaving gaps between them. Shovell, appreciating that the French might slip through the inviting space and 'double' his van, hove to within half a gunshot of de Villette's *Fier* and awaited Rooke with the English centre to close up and block this potential danger. Shovell, in the *Barfleur,* was the fourth ship in his division, whereas, de Villette's *Fier,* was third in his, which meant that the English van overlapped the French by one ship. De Villette's captain in the leading ship of his van, Jacques-Auguste de Bellefontaine in the *Eclatant,* realised that there was a possibility of the English 'doubling' them. He informed de Villette who ordered that he must come up level with the English line to preclude this happening.[33] The movement ahead by the French van made Shovell feel uneasy and in fear of being 'doubled' himself, particularly as he had only 15 ships to de Villette's seventeen. Consequently, Shovell ordered a similar movement forward of the English van with the effect that his ships became further separated from those of Rooke and the centre squadron.

The 43-year-old Victor-Marie d'Estrées, in name Toulouse's chief adviser, but in reality the originator of the tactics adopted by the French fleet, saw his opportunity. He, with Toulouse's assent, ordered part of the French centre to slip through the widening gap

---

31   Laird Clowes, *Royal Navy,* Vol. II, p. 399.

32   Martin-Leake, *John Leake,* Vol. I, p. 162, recorded that Belle-Isle was in the *Monarque.* However, Laird Clowes, *Royal Navy,* Vol. II, p. 399 indicated that he was in the *Magnifique.*

33   Philippe Villette-Mursay, *Mémoires du Marquis de Villette* (Paris: for the Société de l'Histoire de France by Jules Renouard 1841), p. 350.

between the English van and centre squadrons. D'Estrées' intention was to 'double' the English van and destroy it with a local superiority of force before the rear Dutch squadron could come up to influence the action. It would be the only significant move that the French made all day. Rooke saw the danger, although he took the movement of the French centre to be an attempt to weather his own squadron and he made the signal to engage the French.[34] Dilkes, in the 70-gun *Kent*, commanding the leading division of the English centre, moved up on Belle-Isles' ships at the rear of the French van and thus produced an equality of strength between the two vans. Vigorous battle commenced all down the line, with the exception of the Dutch in the rear who were still too distant.

Shovell and Leake fought a fierce battle of attrition against their opponents in the French van. Towards the head of the line, Leake, in the 90-gun *Prince George*, with Stephen Martin as his captain, was heavily engaged with d'Infreville's 92-gun *St Philippe*. Shovell, in the 90-gun *Barfleur*, made every effort to come up with the de Villette's 88-gun *Fier*, but the elderly French admiral appeared to have been wary of engagement with a ship commanded by such an aggressive younger man with a reputation of being brave to a fault. The *Fier* pulled away until at around 2:00 p.m. her stern blew up after the attention of English bomb vessels and de Villette was forced out of the line to extinguish the resulting fire. Quite inexplicably, the rest of his division followed de Villette's example and retired from the line of battle.

Leake, who had been hammering d'Infreville's ships, sent Stephen Martin across to the *Barfleur* in a boat to suggest to Shovell that they follow the French van out of the line and annihilate it. If this happened, the French centre would have to fall back too, to avoid the possibility of being 'doubled' themselves. This was excellent advice and under normal circumstances, Shovell would have undoubtedly followed it, if he were not already in hot pursuit of the French. However, it was apparent to Shovell that Rooke was under great pressure in the centre and several of his ships had been forced to pull out of the line. Subsequently, it was shown that they had run out of shot, as a result of the intense bombardment of Gibraltar a few weeks before. Consequently, Shovell ignored Leake's advice and ordered part of his own division in the van to move astern and aid the hard-pressed Rooke. This tricky sailing manoeuvre, under backed topsails, was carried out with panache and allowed Shovell to assist Rooke in stabilising the English centre. It is likely that Shovell's action at this juncture saved the day for the English. Meanwhile a furious Leake fumed at the head of the English line with little to do and never forgave Shovell.

Prior to the critical phase of the battle described above, at around 10:30 a.m., Rooke with the English centre had engaged their opposite numbers. As was the custom, Rooke in his 90-gun *Royal Katherine* sought out the French nominal commander-in-chief, Toulouse, in the huge 104-gun *Foudroyant*, and opened fire. The battle continued for most of the day with the *Royal Katherine* getting the worse of it. Not only was she out-gunned by the *Foudroyant*, but both Rooke's seconds were weaker than Toulouse's two supporters, who had almost 100 guns apiece. Matters became even more problematical when the various ships of Byng's and Dilkes' divisions pulled back from the line because of lack of shot. Some had actually fired solely powder from their cannons to hide the fact that they had run out

---

34   To weather means gain the wind.

of ammunition. In particular, John 'Jack' Jennings, in the 96-gun *St George* fought heroically against Toulouse and one of his supporters. At one point Jennings had no less than 25 guns dismounted on one side and was forced to transfer guns across the deck to make up the deficit. Another captain to enhance his reputation was Josiah Crowe of the 80-gun *Shrewsbury* who was also in the thick of the action in the centre.

As we have already seen, in the afternoon, Shovell and part of his division came to the assistance of Rooke and the English centre. Some of Shovell's ships gave de Belle-Isle in the 86-gun *Magnifique* and Alain Emmanuel de Cöetlogon, vice-admiral of the white squadron, in the 92-gun *Tonnant* such a hard time that they declined to face a single personal broadside from Shovell's *Barfleur*. Instead, they sailed away from him, being clean and thus faster through the water. At 7:00 p.m., Toulouse's *Foudroyant* was towed out of the line and the battle for the day was at an end in the centre.

The Dutch, under Callenburgh, in the rear, were not involved in the battle until the afternoon of 13 August and reputedly required some persuasion from Byng to enter the action. However, they then fought bravely a fierce battle with the French rear under de Langeron until dusk. At this point the French towed out of the line bringing the fighting to a close.[35]

Although neither side is thought to have lost a major ship during the battle, casualties on both sides were heavy. The *Paris Gazette* gave the total French casualties as 1,500 although it was very much a propaganda tool of Louis XIV. The Anglo-Dutch contingent were reputed to have had over 2,700 casualties which is odd as normally the French concentrated on destroying rigging, whereas the English put most of their fire through the hull of a ship. It can be well imagined that hull shots were likely to cause more damage to the enemy sailors either directly or through splinters than cannonballs through the rigging. In Shovell's division the casualties were: one officer killed and seven wounded; 105 sailors killed and 303 wounded. Leake's division suffered slightly lighter casualties than Shovell's. The greatest number was in Rooke's own division in the centre with no less than six officers and 219 sailors slain. The Dutch squadron in the rear had 360 casualties. The number of casualties gave an indication where the fighting was fiercest which was in the centre.

If French casualties had been fewer than in the Anglo-Dutch contingent, there were certainly more 'persons of quality' among them. De Belle-Isle, the rear-admiral of the white and blue squadron, three captains, and 32 other persons of distinction died. Toulouse was slightly wounded and four of his pages had the misfortune to be killed whilst close to his person. This was not a dissimilar situation to the loss of members of the Duke of York's retinue at the Battle of Lowestoft in 1665. The English had two captains slain: Byng's captain of the *Ranelagh*, John Cowe, and the popular Sir Andrew Leake [no relation of John], of the *Grafton*. Andrew Leake had his wound dressed and then bravely sat in a chair on deck until his demise. In addition, John Leake 'spilt blood' for the first time and three English captains, including Christopher Myngs, were wounded. Shovell himself was unharmed. The Dutch lost a single captain.

---

35   The principal sources for the Battle of Malaga: Martin-Leake, *John Leake*, Vol. I, pp. 158–80; Laughton, *Torrington*, pp. 151–60; Corbett, *Mediterranean*, Vol. II, pp. 268–73; Laird Clowes, *Royal Navy*, Vol. II, pp. 396–404; Anon, *Secret Memoirs*, pp. 92–105; Burchett, *Transactions at Sea*, pp. 678–80; Owen, *War at Sea*, pp. 86–96.

By neither side was a ship taken in battle. The later loss of the Dutch flagship, the *Albemarle*, was unrelated to the battle. The French were thought to have lost the 44-gun *Cheval Marin* and two galleys during the engagement and a further four ships as a result of it.[36]

On the evening of 13 August, the Battle of Malaga had closed inconclusively with both the Anglo-Dutch and French fleets still in being. During the early hours of the 14th, the wind switched around to the north-west, giving the French the weather gage. At daybreak, through the misty haze, Rooke and his fleet could make out the French, some nine miles away to the west and forming a line of battle, this time with their heads to the north. The situation was a serious one for Rooke as the French still barred his route back to the newly taken Gibraltar. He immediately gave instructions for his ships to prepare to receive the French and placed his most disabled ships to leeward. However it soon became apparent that the French were not going to continue the action by descending on Rooke's fleet with the wind at their backs. Some of the French ships were so badly damaged that they required their galleys to tow them out of harm's way.

Rooke summoned a council of war which was attended by Shovell, Leake and the other admirals. A wise decision was made to share out the small amount of remaining shot and Leake reported that some ships had been firing powder only to hide their weakness. Once the shot had been redistributed, the admirals were determined to fight their way through the French to Gibraltar, come what may. Apart from lack of ammunition, the Anglo-Dutch fleet was also at the disadvantage of being far from a friendly port and with ships that had not been careened for some time, this making them slower through the water than their opponents. Dusk came on 14 August with no further battle and, during the hours of darkness, Toulouse slipped away to the north with the aid of his galleys. Clearly, he was ignorant of the parlous state Rooke's fleet was in through lack of shot and absolutely no attempt was made by the French to re-engage. The Anglo-Dutch fleet was not in a position to renew hostilities, even had they been capable, as a suitable wind was lacking.

Sunrise on 15 August, showed the French to be about 12–15 miles to windward. At noon, the wind shifted to the east, a slight breeze then giving Rooke the opportunity to force his way through the French and make his way to Gibraltar. It took until 4:00 p.m. for Rooke's fleet to come up with the French and by then it was considered too late in the day for battle. The Anglo-Dutch fleet lay with their heads to the north overnight. In reality the sweep towards the French had been one of sheer bravado as they were in no condition for battle and it was reported that some captains were prepared to burn their ships, rather than fail to reach Gibraltar.

On 16 August, the wind continued from the east and so leaving the initiative still with the Anglo-Dutch fleet. However, the French had vanished and the initial inference was that they had sailed towards Cadiz. Intelligence was received that the French fleet had not sailed through the Straits and on further reflection it was thought that they must be beating a hasty retreat to the safety of Toulon. This surmise later proved to be correct. At a further council, initiated by Rooke, a decision was made to take the Anglo-Dutch fleet to Gibraltar. Gibraltar was reached on the 19th, but not before Callenburgh's flagship, the *Albemarle*,

---

36   Laird Clowes, *Royal Navy*, Vol. II, pp. 402–3; Laughton, *Torrington*, pp. 163–4; Martin-Leake, *John Leake*, Vol. I, pp. 168–9.

had blown up with the loss of all hands bar nine. Fortunately, Callenburgh was absent from his ship at the time of the explosion and the catastrophe was put down to the accidental ignition of gunpowder whilst making cartridges. The fortifications at Gibraltar were improved, Leake with a small squadron based on Lisbon was left behind to act as a winter guard, and the fleet sailed for England on 25 August.[37]

Reports and letters from the fleet were sent home to England. A number, including one from Shovell personally, were published.[38] On 28 August, Shovell wrote from the *Barfleur* his own account of the Battle of Malaga:

> This brings the News of my Health, and that we are on our way Homeward: That which sends us home so soon is, a very sharp Engagement we have had with the French; our Number of Ships that Fought in the Line of Battle were pretty equal, I think they were 49, and ours 53, but Sir George Rooke reserved 2 or 3 of the 50 Gun-ships, to observe if they attempted any thing with their Gallies, of which they had 24. Their Ships did far exceed in bigness, I judge they had 17 Three Deck Ships, and we had but 7. The Battle began on Sunday the 13th Instant, soon after 10 in the Morning, and in the Center and Rear of the Fleet it continued till Night parted; but in the Van of the Fleet, where I Commanded, and Lead by Sir John Leake, we having the Weather-Gage, gave me opportunity of coming as near as I pleas'd, which was within Pistol-shot, before I fir'd a Gun, thro' which means, and God's assistance, the Enemy declin'd us, and were upon the Run in less than 4 hours, by which time we had but little Wind, and their Gallies tow'd off their lame Ships, and others, as they pleas'd, for the Admiral of the White and Blue [de Villette], with whom we fought, had 7 gallies tended on him. As soon as the Enemy got out of reach of our Guns, and the Battle continuing pretty hot astern, and some of our Ships in the Admiral's Squadron towed out of the Line, which I understood afterwards was for want of Shot, I order'd all the Ships of my Division to slack all their Sails to close the Line in the Centre; this Working that had good effect, that several of the Enemy's Ships astern which had kept their Line having their Top-sails and Fore-sails set, shot up abreast of us, as the Rear Admiral of the White and Blue [de Belle-Isle], and some of his Division; and the Vice Admiral of the White [Cöetlogon], and some of his Division; but they were so warmly receiv'd before they got a Broad-side, that with their Boats a-head, and their Sprit-sails set, they Tow'd from us, without giving us the opportunity of firing at them.
>
> The Ships that suffer'd most in my Division were, the Lenox, Warspright, Tilbury, and Swiftsure, the rest esca'd pretty well, and I best of all, tho' I never took greater pains in all my Life to have been soundly beaten; for I set all my Sails, and tow'd with 3 Boats a Head to get a Long side with the Admiral of the White and Blue; but he out-sailing me, shun'd Fighting, and lay a Long-side of the little Ships: Notwithstanding the Engagement was very sharp, and I think the like between two Fleets never has been in any time. There is hardly a Ship that must not Shift

---

37 Laughton, *Torrington*, p. 165.

38 Anonymous, *A Review of the Late Engagement at Sea A Collection of Private Letters never before printed* (London: John Nutt 1704), pp. 1–23.

one Mast, and some must shift all, a great many have suffer'd much, but none more than Sir George Rooke, and Capt. Jennings in the Monk. God sends us well Home, I believe we have not three spare Top-Masts, nor three Fishes in the Fleet, and I judge there is ten Jury Top-Masts now up. After the Fight we lay two days in sight of the Enemy, preparing for a second Engagement, but the Enemy declin'd and stood from us in the Night. I am of Opinion the Enemy wou'd have given way in the Center before Night, had not several of our Ships tow'd out of the Line of Battle for want of Shot, and the Dutch were in the Rear with little Ships (the Admiral carrying but 64 Guns) they fought very well, but had not weight enough to make the Enemy give way. We did not lose one Ship, nor can I say the Enemy lost any: Of our Captains Sir Andrew Lake [Leake] and Cow [John Cowe] were kill'd, and Mings [Christopher Myngs], Kirton [Robert Kirton], Jumper [William Jumper], and Baker [John Baker] were wounded, but are like to do well: Of the Lieutenants, Capt. Jennings's [John 'Jack' Jennings] Son, and Lestock's [Richard Lestock] youngest Son, and some others, kill'd. Among the wounded are Edisbury, my 3d and 5th Lieutenants, but like to do well. Mr Cary tells there is about 3000 kill'd and wounded, 300 of which are Dutch. Two days after the Engagement, the Dutch Admiral's Ship, by an unknown Accident, blew up, only 9 Men sav'd. They lost none in the Fight. 'Tis Reported in Spain, that the Enemy had 4 Ships and Gallies sunk.[39]

It is clear from the above record just how hard Shovell had attempted to engage de Villette without success.

On 23 August, a member of Shovell's crew in the *Barfleur* wrote to his parents giving a flavour of the action:

After my Duty to you both, my Writing at this time is, to let you know we have had a Bloody Engagement with the French Fleet in the Streights, and several old Men in our Ship, who have been in all the Engagements say, that none was ever so sharp; it continued all day long very furious on both sides, for the French fought very well, but run away at last, as they did from us by 2 a-Clock. I was in the Boat the greatest part of the time to Tow our Ship up to the French Admiral, who out-sail'd us. We had about 30 Men Kill'd and Wounded. I can say no more of it, than that we had the Honour of the Day, and chas'd them. The 13th of August is not to be forgot. Pray tell Mr Manning, his Man John is kill'd.[40]

This letter showed how Shovell had used his boats to try and engage the reluctant de Villette and that his part in the action ceased in the early afternoon. The author of the letter believed that Rooke and his fleet had won the day.

On 23 August, a member of the crew of the 70-gun *Swiftsure*, under Captain Robert Wynn, gave his account of the battle. The *Swiftsure* was part of Shovell's division in the van:

39   Anon, *A Review of the Late Engagement at Sea*, pp. 1–3.
40   Anon, *A Review of the Late Engagement at Sea*, p. 16.

> ---- we have had a most bloody Engagement with the French Fleet off Malaga, which lasted from Morning till Night, but not so long in the Van, where we were, for Sir Cloudsly, who Commanded it, broke the French Line by two a-Clock, one or two of which were fired by the Bombs; no Ship suffer'd more than we have, being three great Ships on us at once, bigger than ourselves, and had suffer'd worse, had not Sir Cloudsley Shovel came up to our Assistance; we had two Captains kill'd, and three or four wounded. The next day the French had the Weather-Gage, but did all they could to avoid Engaging us again, which makes us believe they had their Bellyful. The two Admirals [Rooke and Toulouse] Fought one another all day, but the Admiral that Commanded the French Van [de Villette], did not Engage Sir Cloudsley Shovel.[41]

This eyewitness account confirms that de Villette did not engage Shovell at all. The 'one or two fired by bombs' may well have referred to the blowing up of the stern of de Villette's flagship *Fier*.

On 24 August, a member of the crew of George Delaval's *Tilbury* wrote to a friend:

> You remember the Fight at Beachy-Head, but that was nothing to which we have had with the French off of Malaga. We have some on Board who have been in all the Engagements since Bantry-Bay, who say, that none of 'em were so sharp; the Van, where we were in the hottest for the time, but we got little respite, for in three hours we made some of the French Line keep their distance.[42]

This letter is ample evidence of the intensity of the fighting at Malaga. Shovell had been fortunate to miss the debacle in 1690 at Beachy Head, but he had been prominent in 1689 at Bantry Bay.

One man who had a fortunate escape in the *Assurance*, under Robert Hancock, wrote to his wife on 25 August: '---- yet thro' Mercy am very well in Health, and received no hurt at all, more than that a shot went thro' my Breeches, and broke a Knife that was in my Pocket.'[43] The *Assurance* was also in Shovell's division in the van.

A less fortunate crew member in the *Shrewsbury*, part of the centre with Rooke, wrote to his wife in an undated letter from Gibraltar Road:

> Tho' I am unwilling to let you know I am wounded, being in hopes I shall recover again; yet I could not forbear writing to you by this Opportunity; I was wounded by a Splinter in my Thigh at the beginning of the Engagement, and carried down to be dressed; don't be disheartened, for the Chyrurgeons give we [sic] great hopes, I shall soon be well again.[44]

History does not relate whether he survived his wound or not.

41 Anon, *A Review of the Late Engagement at Sea*, p. 17.
42 Anon, *A Review of the Late Engagement at Sea*, pp. 13–4.
43 Anon, *A Review of the Late Engagement at Sea*, p. 8.
44 Anon, *A Review of the Late Engagement at Sea*, p. 12.

Rooke's fleet reached St Helens on 24 September and Shovell took the major ships on to the Medway to protect them against the autumnal and winter storms.[45] So ended the naval campaign of 1704: the Battle of Malaga would prove to be the only major naval encounter of the War of the Spanish Succession. Both sides claimed a victory and after Toulouse returned to Toulon with his severely battered fleet, Louis XIV ordered a celebratory *Te Deum* to be sung in Notre Dame, Paris. On the Danube, the Duke of Marlborough, still flushed with his success at the Battle of Blenheim, fought on the same day as the naval action off Malaga, had his spirits dampened by rumours of a French naval victory in the Mediterranean.[46] Although reports had reached England claiming an Anglo-Dutch success at Malaga, Queen Anne gave a cold reply when Malaga was bracketed with Blenheim as a double success.[47]

The fine performances of some of the naval officers were recognised with knighthoods for George Byng, Thomas Dilkes, John Norris and John Jennings. Shovell was presented to Queen Anne and, by family tradition, received from her a gold snuffbox. Its lid was adorned with a portrait of the Queen surrounded by diamonds. In the 19th century, the box was still with the Romney family with supposedly some of Shovell's snuff still present in it. Its whereabouts are no longer known.

The Battle of Malaga is generally considered to have had no victor. The advantage should have been with Toulouse. His fleet roughly matched Rooke's in ships, guns and men but were cleaner and thus faster through the water; furthermore they were closer to their home ports. The Anglo-Dutch fleet had been away from home for many months and a considerable number of the men were sickly. Although the French were unaware of its usage at the time, their greatest advantage lay in ammunition as Rooke's men had been profligate of it at the earlier siege of Gibraltar. Toulouse and his fleet had come to support Villadarias in the retaking of Gibraltar and while Rooke's fleet was in being, this could not be achieved. Following the battle, Toulouse and his ships slunk back to Toulon, never to risk another fleet action during the whole war. Gibraltar is still technically a British protectorate: Rooke was the strategic victor.

What of Shovell's role at Malaga? He commanded the van and forced de Villette's French van to give way. At a crucial point in the battle, in a skilful demonstration of seamanship, he and part of his division had been able to back their ships to shore up the hard-pressed Rooke in the centre. If Shovell had failed with this difficult manoeuvre the outcome of the battle might well have been very different. The only real criticism of Shovell came from his subordinate admiral in the van, John Leake, who wished that Shovell had continued to drive the French van out of the line rather than support Rooke. History has justified Shovell's actions and Laird Clowes recorded that 'Shovell throughout the engagement greatly distinguished himself both as an able and brave officer.'[48] This was abundantly true. Perhaps the inconclusive result of the Battle of Malaga was not unexpected. On numerous occasions, Shovell stated that where two fleets were of equal size, then no result could be expected.

In the three remaining years of his life, Cloudesley Shovell was to be at the very height of his considerable powers as Rear-Admiral of England and Commander-in-Chief of the Anglo-Dutch naval forces in the main theatre of war, the Mediterranean.

<hr>

45   Laughton, *Torrington*, p. 165.
46   Corbett, *Mediterranean*, Vol. II, p. 276.
47   Martin-Leake, *John Leake*, Vol. I, p. 171.
48   Laird Clowes, *Royal Navy*, Vol. II, p. 402.

17

The Siege of Barcelona and a Winter in Lisbon 1705–1706

Early in 1705, the general strategy for the coming year was considered and it was decided that the principal naval activity was to be in the Mediterranean in order to draw enemy forces away from the main area of military activity in Flanders. Henri de Massue, 1st Earl of Galway, who had been sent to support the Portuguese, was in need of reinforcements and Victor Amadeus II, Duke of Savoy, might be persuaded to attempt an assault on the key French naval base of Toulon. The Emperor, Leopold I, was selfishly endeavouring to seize Naples and Sicily and would not be of much assistance. Finally, it was thought that the inhabitants of Catalonia were in favour of Charles III and might be stimulated into activity in his cause. Above all these considerations was the vital control of the sea which allowed the freedom of movement for military forces. However, a major strategical error was made in that no serious consideration was given to taking the fine harbour at Port Mahon, Minorca, which would have allowed an all-year-round naval presence in the Mediterranean.[1]

In late 1704, George Rooke's pre-eminent position in the Royal Navy came to an abrupt end. In England, there was a general feeling of disappointment that the naval battle off Malaga, had not been an overwhelming victory over the French. Early in the New Year of 1705, Rooke wrote: 'some of my services of the last year have been so ill received by some and so ill rewarded by others that I could no longer forbear my inclinations to quit command of the fleet.' In reality, it was not just the disappointments of 1704 that affected him, but his health had broken down. In December 1704, Rooke had undergone the painful surgical removal of chalk from his joints and the next month his secretary recorded that he had resigned his commission 'weakened and crippled by gout.'[2] In effect Rooke retired on the grounds of ill-health.[3]

If Rooke's star had faded, Shovell's would shine brightly in 1705 with his contemporary and chief rival no longer playing an active part in naval affairs. On Christmas Day 1704, Shovell left his position as Controller of Victualling and the next day he was made

---

1   Richmond, *Instrument of Policy,* p. 314; Owen, *War at Sea,* p. 130.
2   Removal of chalk: in modern terms, it was probably the removal of gouty tophi made up of urate crystals. It says much for Rooke's staunch character that he was able to continue in command for so long with this painful affliction.
3   Le Fevre and Harding, *Precursors* p. 70.

Rear-Admiral of England, a post that had not been filled since 1688. On 13 January, Shovell became admiral and commander-in-chief of the fleet in succession to Rooke, his flagship being the 100-gun *Britannia,* with his protégé John Norris as captain. Shovell's appointment was considered to be less controversial than either George Churchill's or that of Arthur Herbert, Earl of Torrington, and also he was popular with the Dutch, making it more likely that there would be harmonious relations with England's main naval ally.[4]

In early 1705, one of Shovell's first duties was to court-martial several sea-captains who had left the line of battle at Malaga, claiming they had run out of ammunition. Subsequently, in one ship, shot was found underwater in the flooded hold and in another the captain had been wrongly informed by his lieutenant, now dead, of the situation. Sensibly, these two men were cleared of wrongdoing.[5]

At the end of March, the diminutive Charles Mordaunt, 3rd Earl of Peterborough, was given a warrant by Queen Anne to be commander-in-chief of the troops that were being sent out to the Mediterranean. A month later, Peterborough was also made joint admiral-of-the-fleet with Shovell, both to command the Anglo-Dutch contingent bound for the Mediterranean. The subordinate admirals were to be Stafford Fairborne, John Leake [already at Lisbon] and Thomas Dilkes and the Dutch squadron was to be led by Philip Almonde. Peterborough was a strange choice for either command as he was no soldier and had very limited experience at sea. Johann Hoffmann, envoy in London to the Emperor Leopold I, commented on Peterborough's appointment: 'he is of such a temperament that he can not brook an equal. He is a thoroughly restless and quarrelsome character, incapable of dealing with anybody ---- and on top of that he has no war experience on land or sea.'[6]

Such was the man with whom Shovell was to share the command of the fleet. In fact the two men were known to each other from their time in the Mediterranean in the period 1674–80. Additionally, Peterborough was related to Arthur Herbert, Earl of Torrington, a known admirer and patron of Shovell.[7] The only advantage that Peterborough had was that as a peer he might open doors in foreign courts. Joint commissions were far from unknown in the navy and in 1693 Shovell had held one with Henry Killigrew and Ralph Delaval. What was unusual about Peterborogh's appointment was his complete lack of experience in a senior naval post. Since the Restoration only the Duke of York had held the supreme command with so little experience; but he was of royal blood.

As was recorded in an earlier chapter, Shovell had been a Member of Parliament for Rochester from 1695–1701. In May 1705, he thought the time was propitious for a return to Parliament and was elected as one of the two members for Rochester with Stafford Fairborne as the other. Previously, Shovell had been the naval member, but for this Parliament he was indulgently looked upon as the local landowner and Fairborne the naval person.[8] This was not stretching the truth too much as he did indeed own the May Place estate in nearby

4   Le Fevre and Harding, *Precursors*, p. 70.

5   Laughton, *Torrington*, p. 161; H of L MS 1704–6 NS, Vol. VI, pp. 187–8.

6   Winston Churchill, *Marlborough his Life and Times*, Vol. II (London: George Harrap 1936), p. 57; Heinrich Kuenzel, *Das Leben und der Briefwechsel des Landgrafen Georg von Hessen-Darmstadt*, Hoffmann's despatch on 7 April (Friedberg and London: John Ritwell 1859), p. 555, quoted in Klopp, *Der Fall des Hauses Stuart*, XI, p. 489.

7   Herbert was Peterborough's mother's stepbrother.

8   At the time, Rochester had two MPs: one a naval man, the other a local dignitary.

Crayford. Earlier Fairborne had asked Shovell to support his candidature, but he declined on the honourable grounds that he had previously refused others. Shovell's re-election was looked upon as a gain for the Whigs. After his death in 1707, Shovell was replaced in Parliament by another admiral, John Leake.[9]

In the first week of May, Peterborough and Shovell were given their orders for the forthcoming campaign in the Mediterranean. They were to join Leake at Lisbon, and then review the possibility of taking Cadiz and Barcelona. Additionally, if possible, they were to support the Duke of Savoy in his designs on Toulon. Shortly, further secret orders were sent to Peterborough and Shovell that made Toulon their prime objective. To complicate matters for the joint admirals, Queen Anne instructed that at councils of war they would have only a single joint vote.[10] At the end of May, the fleet sailed from Spithead with 5,000 soldiers on board and the joint admirals soon to be cooped up together for the campaign season in their flagship, the *Britannia*.[11]

The fleet of around 23 vessels sailed down the Channel and then George Byng and John Jennings were detached to look into Brest. They reported that Alain Emmanuel de Cöetlogon had 18 ships in the harbour there and separate intelligence also showed that Toulouse had a further 40 ships at Toulon. Leake's ships based at Lisbon would be used to reinforce the fleet once that port was reached. The admirals were reluctant to divide their ships for the sound reason of potentially making Cöetlogon's 18 ships a superior force to either of the two English squadrons, but felt that they had little choice. Byng and John Jennings were left on station to shadow Cöetlogon and the joint admirals nervously sailed for Lisbon. An additional worry was that Toulouse's ships might join those of Cöetlogon whilst the English fleet was in the Mediterranean. If the Dutch ships under Almonde had not been sailing independently, the problem would not have been as acute.[12] In the event, neither the Brest squadron nor Toulon fleet came out of their harbours in any strength. The first allied ships to arrive at Lisbon were the Dutch ones of Almonde on 3 June, followed by Peterborough in the *Swallow* on the 9th and Shovell, in the *Britannia* a day later. Leake and his squadron were already at Lisbon so that the Anglo-Dutch fleet was now united.[13]

Soon after their arrival at Lisbon, on 15 June, the admirals conferred with the Earl of Galway, commander of the Anglo-Dutch troops in Portugal, and also the courts of Spain and Portugal. It was decided to await further troops being convoyed from Ireland by William Jumper before the expedition entered the Mediterranean. In the meantime Shovell would take part of the fleet to cruise between Cadiz and Cape Spartel, to prevent a junction of the Brest and Toulon ships. Thus Shovell was absent from Lisbon whilst earnest debate took place about how best to employ the expeditionary force. The Duke of Savoy was too hard-pressed defending Turin to attempt Toulon and the Portuguese court refused to join in any design on Cadiz or indeed anywhere else. Prince George of Hesse Darmstadt arrived from his successful defence of Gibraltar and proposed a landing at Valencia with a march

---

9   Cruikshanks, *History of Parliament,* Shovell entry.

10   H of L MS 1706–08 NS, Vol. VII, pp. 361–3.

11   Burchett, *Transactions at Sea,* p. 684; Owen, *War at Sea,* p. 130; Campbell, *British Admirals,* Vol. IV, p. 245; *DNB,* Mordaunt [Laughton].

12   Burchett, *Transactions at Sea,* p. 685; Owen, *War at Sea,* p. 132.

13   Martin-Leake, *John Leake,* Vol. I, pp. 277–8; Owen, *War at Sea,* p. 132.

on Madrid. Peterborough supported Hesse Darmstadt, but Charles III was adamant that Barcelona, the main city of Catalonia, should be their goal. The die was well and truly cast.[14]

Shovell had been at sea whilst a landing at Barcelona was being considered and thus was unable to partake in the discussions. Once more the opportunity of taking Port Mahon was missed, although the subject had been raised and dismissed as being too late in the year. Perhaps, if Shovell had been present at the councils, as an experienced naval officer, he might have pushed the matter. A fine chance was lost.

By this time, William Jumper's ships and soldiers had arrived from Ireland and, on 20 July, the ships at Lisbon joined those of Shovell who was still at sea. Some of the raw battalions of troops from England were exchanged for more experienced ones who had been garrisoning Gibraltar; the fleet then set sail to water at Altea Bay, on the south-eastern coast of Spain.[15] The Bay was reached on the 30th and watering took place over the next few days. On 4 August, the fleet sailed for Catalonia with Hesse Darmstadt sent ahead in James Dursley's *Devonshire* to establish whether the people of Catalonia really were supportive of Charles III or not. Another Shovell protégé, Edmund Loades, was sent to Denia with a small squadron and made threats with shot and bomb, the governor then hastily declaring for Charles III. It was a most august opening to the Anglo-Dutch campaign.[16]

On 11 August, the fleet, for practical purposes commanded by Shovell, anchored off Barcelona. The city was the largest and most prosperous in Spain with a waterfront extending for one and a half miles. There were strong walls with eight bastions surrounded by a ditch of moderate depth. The key to the whole city was the 700-foot hill called Montjuic which was situated to the south west. It was crowned by a fort whose walls fell away to a precipitous cliff down to the sea shore. The weather was stormy on the 11th, with thunder, lightning and a high sea which precluded a landing. The next day, after a disturbed night, the landing was effected some four miles north-east of Barcelona. Hesse Darmstadt who had sailed 50 miles to the north with Dursley, whilst testing the reactions of the Catalonians to rule by Charles III, arrived back in time for the landings. They have been described by Shovell in person:

> Sunday 12th, the army landed, and the Prince of Hesse [Darmstadt] came time enough to get ashore with them. There was no manner of opposition, not so much as a musket fired to interrupt our landing, and the people in the neighbouring towns and villages keep in their habitations, and esteem us their friends, and the garrison their enemies. We landed from the fleet of our ships' complements about 1150 who were all marines.[17]

Over the next few days, soldiers were brought ashore and Peterborough set up camp to the north-east of the city, at St Martins.[18]

---

14   Owen, *War at Sea*, pp. 135–6; H of L MS 1706–8 NS, Vol. VII, pp. 365, 409.

15   H of L MS 1706–8 NS, Vol. VII, pp. 409–10.

16   H of L MS 1706–8 NS, Vol. VII, pp. 410–11.

17   H of L MS 1706–8 NS, Vol. VII, pp. 410–11.

18   Owen, *War at Sea*, pp. 138–9; H of L MS 1706–8 NS, Vol. VII, p. 411; Colin Ballard, *The Great Earl of Peterborough* (London: Skeffington and Son 1929), p. 138.

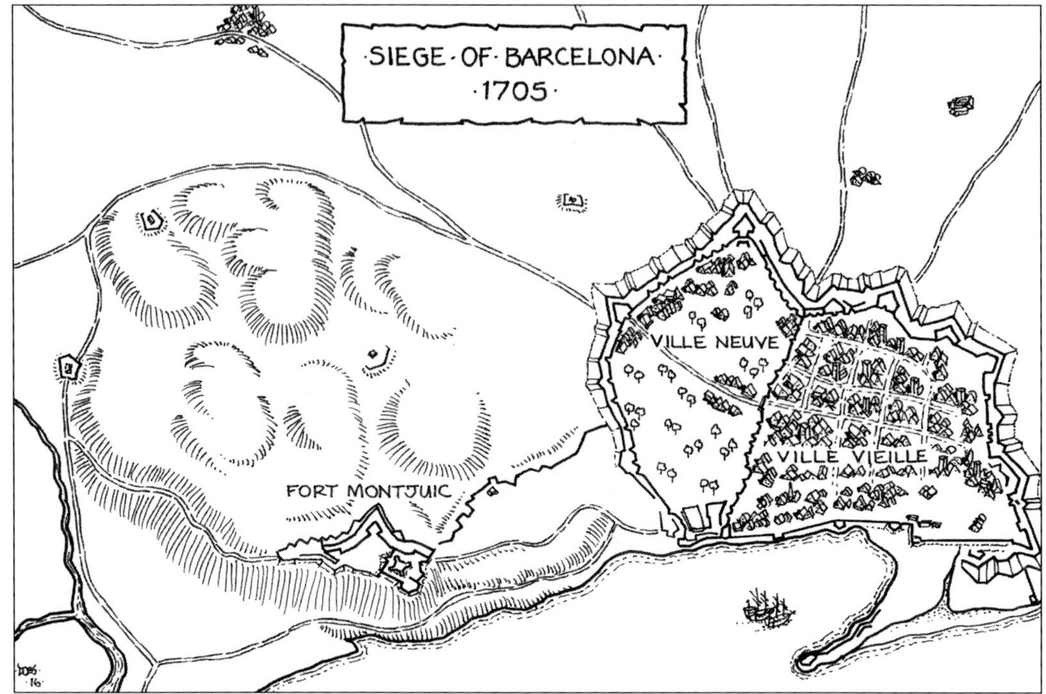

Map 20 Siege of Barcelona 1705.

Don Francisco Velasco, the Viceroy of Catalonia, governed Barcelona with 3,200 foot soldiers and 800 horse and he was dedicated to the Bourbon cause. Peterborough's position was a delicate one as he was hindered from either starving the city into submission or using an undue bombardment and so perhaps alienating the inhabitants. If he received no help from the citizens of Barcelona, he was supported by an irregular force of fierce Miquelets in the surrounding countryside. While Peterborough was ashore undertaking the siege, Shovell had sole command of the fleet. He did not think that it was necessary to watch Toulon for French naval activity as he had been given good intelligence that there were few ships fit for sea service. However, Shovell did use a small number of frigates to screen his current anchorage.[19]

A week after the first landings, 19 August, the senior land officers told Peterborough bluntly that the siege should be called off and that the fleet should carry them to support the Duke of Savoy, in Italy, instead. Not unreasonably, they argued that Hesse Darmstadt had promised an open city and this was far from the case. On hearing the military opinion, Shovell called his own council of the sea officers who agreed with his view that the attempt on Barcelona be continued and only if it proved to be unfeasible should something else on the Spanish coast be attempted.[20] The naval officers, led by Shovell, had no intention

19   Owen, *War at Sea*, p. 139.
20   H of L MS 1706–8 NS, Vol. VII, p. 411.

of deviating from their original orders. Peterborough, in a letter to Sidney Godolphin, 1st Baron Godolphin,[21] has left an accurate description of Shovell's personality at this critical juncture:

> Sir Cloudesley Shovell is a man of many good qualities ----. He is brave if I may say to a fault, and in matters he does not understand thinks that whatever is directed first must be begun, and when begun must be carried on what accidents soever occur, or whatsoever improbabilities come in the way. He sticks close to what he calls orders, and will conceive no latitude in such instructions that I think were calculated for the greatest.[22]

This letter with its waspish comments about the rigidity of Shovell's personality has the ring of truth about it. However, as will be seen, the fortitude of Shovell and the sea officers would ultimately lead to the capitulation of Barcelona. If the land officers had got their way, the siege would have failed and they would have been far away in Italy.

On 24 August, Peterborough came aboard the *Britannia* to discuss with the admirals a letter he had received from Charles III, who was now ashore with the troops. The king wished the siege to continue for a further 18 days despite the land officers wanting to give up. Peterborough was now happy to accede to Charles III's wishes, but asked the admirals whether it would be possible to take troops to Italy once this time had elapsed. After due debate, Shovell and the admirals broadly agreed to the plan, but would only carry the troops to Nice rather than Italy.[23] The senior land officers reluctantly fell into line, although they covered themselves by stating that it went against their professional judgement.

A council of the admirals was summoned and Shovell offered the support of the fleet in the continuation of the siege for the next 18 days. He had sent Edmund Loades to Peterborough to request his presence at the meeting. But Peterborough did not deign to put in an appearance and Shovell officially recorded: 'the Earl of Peterborough not thinking fit to afford us his company at this great council.' Later, Peterborough added a memorandum to Shovell's report for Prince George of Denmark in which he acknowledged his failure to attend the admirals' discussions, but added lamely that he did not want to stop the flags from showing their zeal for King Charles! Shovell generously agreed to send 1,500 naval men to the besieging trenches and also supplied 52 cannons to batter Barcelona's walls.[24]

A few days later, the despondent land officers reverted to their original view of the impracticability of taking Barcelona. There was also a row with the admirals over just how many men were being supplied by the ships to man the siege trenches. Once more they were hankering after going to Italy to support the Duke of Savoy.[25] Poor Charles III was only too well aware of the views of the disheartened land officers in wishing to give up the attempt on Barcelona. He used Hesse Darmstadt as a conduit to Shovell to express his gratitude for

---

21   Created the 1st Earl of Godolphin in 1706.
22   Churchill, *Marlborough*, Vol. II, pp. 244–5.
23   H of L MS 1706–8 NS, Vol. VII, pp. 411–3; Owen, *War at Sea*, p. 141.
24   H of L MS 1706–8 NS, Vol. VII, pp. 411–5; Owen, *War at Sea*, p. 142.
25   H of L MS 1706–8 NS, Vol. VII, pp. 411–6.

the unswerving support that he was getting from the fleet. On 30 August, Hesse Darmstadt wrote to Shovell on behalf of the king:

> His Catholic Majesty [Charles III] relies in every part on your good zeal and particular love you have showed in all occasions to his person, shall always owe to you the good success of this present undertaking, which, if well supported, will lead him to the possession of this Monarchy.[26]

By 29 August, even Charles III was beginning to accept the reality of the situation and was looking for a way out. He considered marching the troops south to Tarragona or even as far as Valencia and once more Shovell agreed to support such a march from the sea. However, the admirals had now come to the conclusion that it was too late in the year to sail to Nice in support of the Duke of Savoy and they had every intention of sailing for home no later than 20 September. No doubt this concentrated the generals' minds.[27] At this juncture, Hesse Darmstadt asked Shovell to consider taking the Balearic Islands. Of course Minorca had Port Mahon with its all-year-round port. But once again the opportunity was lost, although through no fault of Shovell's. Then events unfurled at Barcelona making it impossible for him to leave and by the time he was free it was too late in the year.[28]

During late August and early September, there was an air of confusion in the leadership of the Anglo-Dutch forces with the leading participants vacillating in the course of action to take. Personality came into it with Peterborough considering that Shovell was too much under the influence of Hesse Darmstadt. John Norris, the first captain of the *Britannia*, was used by Shovell as his emissary ashore and he fell foul of Peterborough who rudely described him as 'a governing coxcomb.' Peterborough believed that it was Norris who had persuaded Shovell that Barcelona must come before any other scheme. At this unhappy juncture, on 3 September, a surprise attack on the fort on Montjuic led to the breaking of the stalemate around the city.

Early on 2 September, the fleet and the army were preparing to withdraw to Tarragona. That night Peterborough and Hesse Darmstadt planned to take an Anglo-Dutch force of around 1,000 men on rocky paths, to the west of Barcelona, and attack Montjuic the next morning. Norris was sent to inform Shovell of the plan and to prepare scaling ladders. Philip Cavendish of the 54-gun *Antelope* was ordered to assist the assault from the sea. But in the event rough seas precluded him from helping a great deal. On the 3rd, Peterborough's troops managed to take the outworks of Montjuic, although Hesse Darmstadt was mortally wounded by a musket ball through his right femoral artery. The poor man, who may have originally planned the attack,[29] continued marching steadfastly for another 50 paces before dropping dead from exsanguination. The next day, Peterborough wrote to Shovell asking for further support from the fleet. The capture of Barcelona was now a distinct possibility.[30]

---

26   H of L MS 1706–8 NS, Vol. VII, pp. 423–6.
27   H of L MS 1706–8 NS, Vol. VII, pp. 411–7.
28   H of L MS 1706–8 NS, Vol. VII, p. 424.
29   H of L MS 1706–8 NS, Vol. VII, p. 425; Owen, *War at Sea*, p. 140.
30   Owen, *War at Sea*, pp. 147–51; Martin-Leake, *John Leake*, Vol. I, pp. 288–90; Ballard, *Peterborough*, pp. 146–51.

Peterborough would get everything he asked for. Forty guns, 18 and 24 pounders, were sent ashore and the fleet would start firing on the city. Shovell sent Fairborne, with eight men of war plus bomb vessels, to undertake the bombardment from the sea. On the 6th, a lucky bomb from a mortar hit a powder magazine in the isolated citadel of Montjuic and killed the governor of the place. Vigilant Miquelets rushed in through a rent in the wall and the fort of Montjuic fell into a grateful Peterborough's hands. Immediately, he concentrated on taking the City of Barcelona as well.[31] Whilst the fleet's guns ashore were being set up as batteries, Fairborne supervised the bombardment from the sea. His bomb ketches threw a large number of bombs and carcasses into the city, although Fairborne's men-of-war merely threatened from the sea without actually firing their guns.[32] Amongst his captains was Christopher Myngs who had long been associated with Shovell. Shovell sent the three youngest captains and six lieutenants to command the guns of the naval batteries ashore. In addition, Shovell allowed Peterborough to use 40,000 dollars of naval money to finance the continuation of the siege.

On 19 September, Shovell and the admirals convened once more, in the *Britannia,* and a decision was made to send further guns and their crews ashore. Taking a calculated risk, Shovell reduced the reserves of shot in the fleet to a bare minimum. In all 20,872 of 18-pounder shot, 12,146 of 24-pounder shot and 1,423 barrels of powder were transported ashore. Also, the admirals' earlier decision to sail for England by 20 September was rescinded in light of the successes ashore. On the 23rd, three weeks after a decision was made to assault Montjuic, a breach was made in the city walls. Eventually, on the evening of 28 September, the terms of capitulation of Barcelona were signed. These stated in particular that the garrison would march out in four days' time. However, shortly before it was due to do so, a prisoner called out 'Viva Carlos Tercero' and was shot dead by his French guard. This led to general disorder in the city and Velasco, the defeated governor, had to be taken aboard the *Britannia* under Shovell's protection. In the city, the ever gallant Peterborough was supposed to have saved the life of the young, beautiful Duchess of Popoli from licentious soldiery, and to have received a shot through his wig for his trouble! Her unpopular husband, the Duke, was Velasco's deputy. The defeated garrison was to be transported to Malaga or Almeria as they did not feel safe anywhere else.

Now that the siege was finally over, the admirals considered at councils of war what to do with the fleet. They correctly decided that it could not be left in the Mediterranean all winter with no suitable port to hand and that Shovell would take the bulk of the ships back to England. Leake would remain at Lisbon with a small winter squadron and Peterborough would stay in Barcelona. He might have use of Leake's squadron 'if it shall be thought advisable by a council of war.' Possibly, this clause was inserted by Shovell to stop the quixotic Peterborough interfering too much with Leake. Shovell sailed with his fleet on 12 October and was back, at Spithead, on 26 November – very late in the year indeed.[33]

---

31   H of L MS 1706–8 NS, Vol. VII, pp. 412–7; Owen, *War at Sea,* p. 150; Ballard, *Peterborough,* pp. 148–9.
32   Carcass: cylinder filled with combustibles to act as incendiaries.
33   H of L MS 1706–8 NS, Vol. VII, pp. 417–22; Owen, *War at Sea,* pp. 151–5; Ballard, *Peterborough,* pp. 153–5; Martin-Leake, *John Leake,* Vol. I, pp. 291–5; Burchett, *Transactions at Sea,* pp. 687–8; Markham (ed), *Stephen Martin,* pp. 83–4.

Charles III made a formal entry into Barcelona on 12 October and was officially proclaimed King of Spain. By the end of October all Catalonia was in his hands and this period would be his high point in Spain. Hesse Darmstadt had been essentially correct in believing that the Catalans would rise against Bourbon rule, but he had not lived to see it. The taking of Barcelona was a spectacular success and was announced, on 15 November, to Parliament, by Queen Anne in person. Perhaps she could now forget about the drawn Battle of Malaga, a year earlier. If Peterborough was given the lion's share of the credit, the part played by Shovell and the fleet was absolutely crucial. With Peterborough ashore for the siege, Shovell had sole command at sea and when the land officers were all for deserting Barcelona for Italy, Shovell never wavered in his support for Charles III in its continuation. Whether it was shot, powder, gunners, money or bombing from the sea, the army was never let down by Shovell and the fleet.

The year 1705 ended quietly for Shovell at home with his family in England. That December his mother-in-law, Elizabeth Hill, née Kingsman from Maldon in Essex, died. It would be the last Christmas of his life that he would spend in England with his wife and young daughters.[34]

Early in the New Year of 1706, family matters must have been very much at the forefront of his mind as his father-in-law, John Hill, died on 18 January, a month after his wife. Hill who lived in the parish of St Olave, Hart Street, London, was a very wealthy man and left the bulk of his estate, of around £100,000, to his daughter, Elizabeth Shovell. By this time, Shovell was rich in his own right from 'good voyages' in the Mediterranean and his investments. In any event, Hill's untimely demise so soon after his wife's made the Shovell family fabulously rich.[35]

Also in January 1706, Shovell was summoned to appear before a House of Lords Committee to discuss the difficulties of manning the fleet. Perhaps he was drawing on his own early career when he recommended that the age boys were recruited for the navy be raised from 10 to 12 years.[36] The next month, his recent bereavement not withstanding, Shovell was charged with the preparation of a bill in the Commons to increase manning in the fleet and this was passed in March.[37]

During 1706, Shovell generously paid for renovation work on what was then the Butcher's Market,[38] in Rochester, the city he represented in Parliament. Although an impressive plaque on the facade of the building still informs us that it was 'Erected at the Sole Charge and Expence of Sir Cloudsley Shovel Knight. A.D. 1706', in reality he only paid for the market bell, town clock and facade of the building. On first representing Rochester, in 1695, Shovell paid for a magnificent ceiling in the Guildhall. In 1700, he also paid for extensive renovations and presented a new reredos to his local church, St Paulinus, Crayford.[39] In

---

34   NMM: RMT MS, MATs 24, 25, copies of the wills of the Shovell family, parentage and children of Elizabeth Shovell née Hill.
35   NMM: RMT MS, MAT 24, copies of the wills of the Shovell family.
36   H of L MS 1704–6 NS, Vol. VI, pp. 386–7.
37   Cruikshanks, *History of Parliament*, Shovell entry.
38   More recently known as the Corn Exchange or Clock House.
39   Smith, *History of Rochester*, pp. 90–1; *A Short Account of St Paulinus Church*, p. 6.

due course, many members of his immediate family would be interred in a vault under the south transept of the church.

In early 1706, Louis XIV had begun preparations to retake Barcelona and Marshal René de Froulay Tessé had been sent there with an army of 25,000 men, supported by the Comte de Toulouse's fleet from the sea. Much of Peterborough's force was scattered around Valencia and the garrison at Barcelona now numbered only 4,000 men. The city was in great peril when, on 21 March, Charles III summoned Leake to come to his aid from Lisbon. Leake carrying troops in the ships of his squadron set sail for Barcelona, but then received contrary orders from the unpredictable Peterborough, who wished the troops to be landed at Valencia. Sensibly, Leake ignored these orders and then had the great misfortune to be joined by Peterborough, himself, from the shore. As the senior officer from the previous year, Peterborough tactlessly raised the union flag on the main mast of Leake's flagship. The siege of Barcelona was broken and Peterborough coolly claimed the credit, much to Leake's chagrin. Toulouse's ships had slunk back to Toulon at the first indication that Leake had returned to the Mediterranean. Peterborough's high-handed behaviour had been deplorable and it is not surprising that Leake wrote to Prince George of Denmark, the Lord High Admiral, on the subject. It is also clear from the letter that he was expecting Shovell to rejoin him that summer.[40]

From his town house in Soho Square, Shovell wrote a generous letter to Leake congratulating him on saving Barcelona. Their little spat at the Battle of Malaga was hopefully a thing of the past:

> I congratulate you with all my heart on your success in the afaire of Barcelona, and wou'd not slip this opportunity without acquainting you, that you have a great many friends here who rejoice as well as I in your good fortune, and will not suffer the great fatigues and pains you have taken to pass unregarded, but will improve them to your service: the last winter with the assistance of Mr Churchill [George Churchill] who is much your friend, we sett forth your services to the Prince [George of Denmark] and his highness was mighty well satisfied with your prudence and good management. His highness directed a present as an acknowledgement of your good services, which I dout [sic] not will be a leading card to draw the same honour from her Majtie [sic]; I shall not come abroad, so wish your health and a safe return.[41]

Leake was to have a successful summer on the coast of Spain with the taking of Cartagena, Alicante, Ibiza and Majorca. He returned to England that October and missed meeting Shovell by a few days. The two men would never meet again.

Peterborough's influence in the Mediterranean was in decline and he eventually returned to England in 1707. The taking of Barcelona, in 1705, was the pinnacle of his military career in Spain. Leake was not the only naval man to be upset by the absence of Shovell from the coasts of Portugal and Spain that summer. Philip Almonde, the Dutch admiral, returned

40   Richmond, *Instrument of Policy,* pp. 319–20; H of L MS 1706–8 NS, Vol. VII, p. 438.
41   BL: ADD MS 5441, f. 185, Shovell to Leake 1706.

home from Lisbon in July 1706; he was unprepared to serve under an inferior flag, Leake, if Shovell was not to command that year. Possibly, the reason for Shovell getting on so well with the Dutch was related his own origins in the Low Countries. A contemporary account showed him socialising with the Dutch:

> His covetousness goes beyond reason, and his courage beyond the bounds of good conduct; he will venture the fleet on any occasion, and it is feared further than Allemonde will sometimes be willing. If we be much superior his forwardness maybe of good consequence. He eats and drinks much with the Dutch and is generally beloved amongst the sailors, for his familiar conversation with them, which Sir George Rooke never affected but was very reserved.[42]

Since the late autumn of 1705, Count Louis de Guiscard, a French refugee in England, had been proposing a landing on the west coast of France, near Bordeaux, to encourage an uprising of the Cevennois. It would take place between Blaye and the mouth of the River Charente at Rochefort. Nearby Saintes was to be fortified and French Huguenot officers from there would be used to foment rebellion in this most unstable part of France. The Duke of Marlborough supported the venture, hoping that it would take pressure off the allies in Catalonia and Italy.[43] It was for this scheme that Shovell, by then indisputably the leading admiral in Queen Anne's navy, was held back from command in the Mediterranean.

In May 1706, Stafford Fairborne made a reconnaissance in force to the area and destroyed some French shipping in the mouth of the Charente.[44] Nearly 10,000 troops were collected at Portsmouth under Richard Savage, 4th Earl Rivers, one of the greatest rakes in England in his youth, and with Shovell to command the supporting fleet. By 10 August, preparations were complete and that very day the fleet sailed from Portsmouth with the transport vessels carrying the troops. In all Shovell, in his flagship, the *Britannia*, commanded 19 large men-of-war, 10 frigates, 148 transports, plus some bomb vessels and fireships. Several thousand declarations in French had been printed for distribution to the local population after the descent on their coastline. All seemed to be going smoothly to plan, until on the 14th, inclement weather forced Shovell to seek shelter in Torbay.[45] He was intending 'to take the first opportunity to sail' when orders to cancel the operation came from Queen Anne.[46] The Queen and her advisors had had a change of heart and decided their ships and troops would be better employed in Spain. As a result, de Guiscard became mentally disturbed and in 1710 attempted to assassinate the Chancellor of the Exchequer, Robert Harley, by stabbing him with a penknife.[47]

---

42   HMC: Portland MS, Vol. VIII, p. 302; Luttrell, *State Affairs*, Vol. VI, p. 70.
43   Churchill, *Marlborough*, Vol. II, pp. 80–1; Richmond, *Instrument of Policy*, pp. 322–3; Campbell, *British Admirals*, Vol. III, p. 466.
44   Laird Clowes, *Royal Navy*, Vol. II, pp. 509–10.
45   Churchill, *Marlborough*, Vol. II, p. 162; Campbell, *British Admirals*, Vol. III, pp. 466–7; Luttrell, *State Affairs*, Vol. VI, p. 70.
46   HMC: Portland MS, Vol. VIII, p. 240.
47   Churchill, *Marlborough*, Vol. II, pp. 80–1, 162; H of L MS 1706–8 NS, Vol. VII, p. 515.

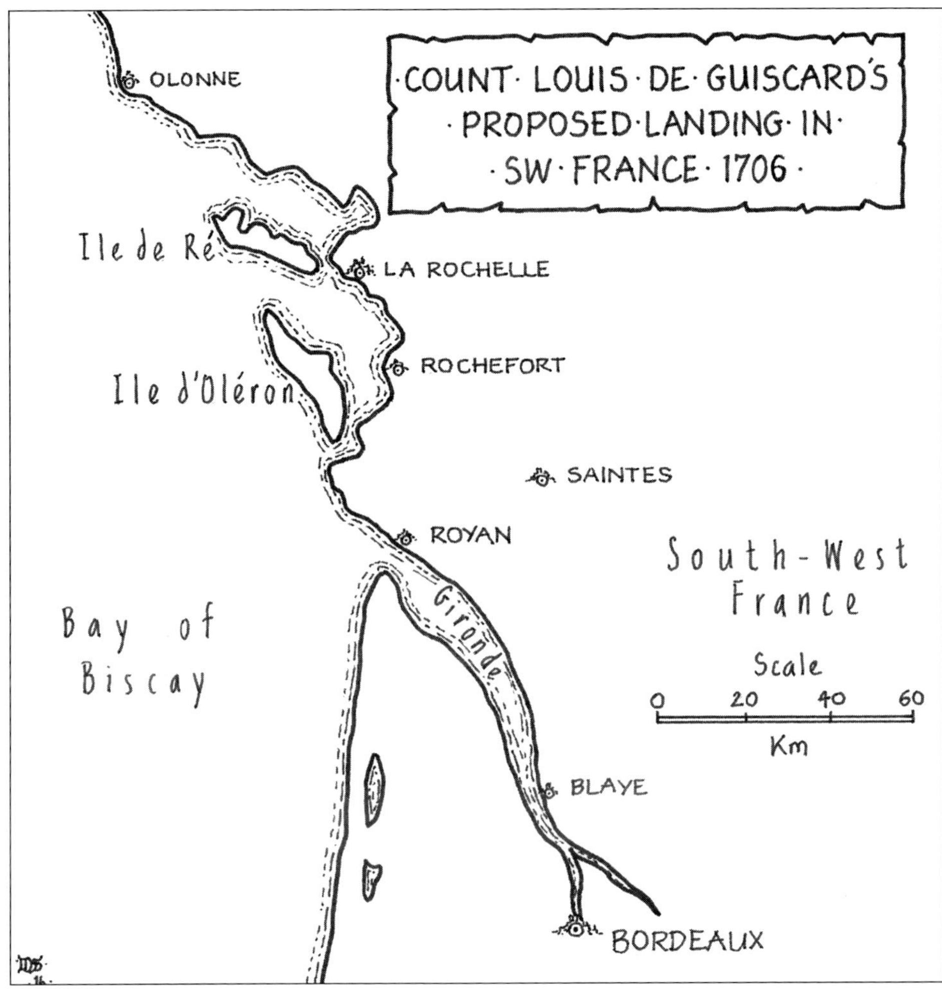

Map 21   Count Louis de Guiscard's proposed landing in SW France 1706.

On 20 August, the Queen sent fresh instructions for Shovell to follow. Initially, he was ordered to attempt Cadiz as this was thought to be the most satisfactory objective for confirming Charles III on the throne of Spain. Rivers produced a manifesto to be distributed amongst the Spaniards. In order to make it more attractive to them, he inserted a clause giving them freedom of trade and navigation which Shovell was decidedly unhappy about. Later, Rivers had the good sense to rescind this unfortunate clause.[48]

Three days after receiving his orders, Shovell joined the 90-gun *Association* from the *Britannia*. The newer *Association* had been built at Portsmouth, in 1697, and would be Shovell's ship when he drowned in the autumn of the next year. The captain of the

48   Historical Manuscripts Commission (HMC): Bath MS, Vol. I, pp. 91, 98, 104–5, 129–31.

Association was Sam Whitaker and Shovell's two flag captains were trusted friends, John Norris and Edmund Loades, a nephew of John Narbrough senior. The fifth lieutenant was a son of Matt Aylmer and Shovell's stepsons, John and James Narbrough, were also part of the *Association's* crew.[49]

Eventually, Shovell sailed with the fleet and Rivers' troops on 1 October, dangerously late in the year for his first and second rates. Torbay would be the last part of England that Shovell saw before his death. Bad weather plagued them all the way to Lisbon which was reached at the end of the month. Two ships had sunk and others were driven to Ireland with the result that men and horses all had suffered greatly. Time would be required to repair the ships and for the soldiers to recover from their difficult voyage. Shovell found that he was in somewhat of a dilemma as the affairs of Charles III and the Earl of Galway were in disarray on the east coast of Spain.

During the summer of 1706, Charles and Galway had actually held the capital, Madrid, but subsequently had been forced to retire to Valencia. Should Shovell follow his orders to assault Cadiz or should he attempt to support Charles III by sailing to Valencia? Matters were further complicated by the King of Portugal, Pedro II, choosing this unfortunate moment to die.[50] He was succeeded by his son, John V, and there were concerns that the new king might withdraw from the war. In the event he did not, but there was an unpleasant altercation between a royal prince and some of the English ships' crews whom he chose to insult. Matters were inflamed even more when the Portuguese forts opened fire on the English ships. Shovell was having none of this disrespectful behaviour and remonstrated with the Portuguese authorities, forcing John to issue orders for his subjects to behave in a more becoming fashion. Poignantly, Rivers commented: 'I refer you to Cloudesley Shovell who on this occasion has exerted himself in a manner becoming an English admiral ----.'[51]

Word had got back to England of the difficulties facing Rivers and Shovell, who were then told to drop the Cadiz operation and to strengthen the forces already in Spain. Shovell was instructed to settle communications between Lisbon and the coast of Spain and so, despite the fact that his ships were under repair, he ordered that they be got away quickly with the troops for Alicante. However, as Shovell was about to embark Rivers' troops, contrary orders arrived from England to the effect that they were to remain at Lisbon. The Portuguese were cunningly behind this change and, following a council of war, Shovell and Rivers courageously stuck to the original plan of sailing to Alicante, to reinforce Charles III. Later Queen Anne was to approve their decision. On 11 January 1707, Shovell sailed with the troops and had reached Alicante by the end of the month. In mid-February, he started the return journey to Lisbon and arrived there a month later. Then Shovell concentrated on planning for his next great exploit; for the summer of 1707, an attempt on the formidable French naval base of Toulon.[52]

In these trying times it is interesting to read Rivers' opinion of Shovell: 'I cannot help upon this occasion saying that never any man was more zealous for her Majesty's service,

---

49   Larn and McBride, *Shovell's Disaster*, pp. 47–53.
50   Campbell, *British Admirals*, Vol. III, pp. 467–8.
51   Martin-Leake, *John Leake*, Vol. II, p. 165; Campbell, *British Admirals*, Vol. IV, p. 254; HMC: Bath MS, Vol. I, p. 144.
52   Campbell, *British Admirals*, Vol. III, pp. 468–9 and Vol. IV, pp. 254–5; H of L MS 1706–8 NS, Vol. VII, pp. 516–7.

nor more kind to her troops in assisting them with everything that is necessary.' In connection with leaving three or four frigates on the coast of Spain under Charles III: 'I do not say this to offend Sir Cloudesley Shovell, who is very forward and zealous in whatever relates to public service, that this precaution would not be necessary if we were always sure of having him here.'[53]

53   HMC: Bath MS, Vol. I, p. 144.

18

The Siege of Toulon 1707

By the end of 1706, the allies were in possession of Flanders and the Duke of Marlborough contemplated an offensive from the weaker southern region rather than to try to batter a way through to Paris from the north. If Toulon were taken and the French fleet destroyed, southern France would be ripe for invasion with Prince Eugene having broken the siege of Turin and the French no longer threatening Savoy. The campaign in Spain continued and held French troops there who otherwise might have been used to defend Toulon. If Toulon were assaulted, then the withdrawal of French troops from the Iberian Peninsula would be advantageous to Charles III and open the way to Madrid. Having two major campaigns running at the same time was potentially dangerous, but the new Holy Roman Emperor, Joseph I, had self-indulgently sent troops to take Naples. Hence the allies were now involved with no less than three major undertakings. In essence, the capture of Toulon would be a catastrophic blow to France and might conceivably lead to the end of the war.[1]

While refitting his ships in Lisbon, Shovell received orders from Queen Anne to attack Toulon. The plan for 1707 was more appropriate than that considered in 1705. The lifting of the Siege of Turin would allow the forces of the Duke of Savoy to sally forth on land whilst Shovell and the fleet supported them from the sea. Shovell's instructions for the operation against Toulon ran to some 15 paragraphs and the main ones were: the capture of Toulon was their principal aim; the assault should start in May; the fleet and troops would obey Savoy's orders; 40 ships of the line and transports would be provided by England; Shovell would supply cannons for the shore batteries and Savoy their carriages; ammunition would be supplied by Savoy and powder from the fleet; Queen Anne would pay for 28,000 men to be recruited locally; ships captured at Toulon were to be the property of England.[2]

Despite the agreement, Emperor Joseph I selfishly continued with his attempt on Naples and was supported by Prince Eugene who believed that there were sufficient troops for both enterprises. This was despite the fact that Marlborough had written to him repeatedly to take one thing at a time. This crucial decision was to fatally undermine the siege of Toulon from the start.[3] Meanwhile, at Lisbon, Shovell organised his Anglo-Dutch fleet which consisted of 46 vessels in total. Under Shovell's command, Vice-Admiral Philips van

---

1   Richmond, *Instrument of Policy*, pp. 324–5.
2   Campbell, *British Admirals*, Vol. IV, pp. 255–6; Owen, *War at Sea*, pp. 158–61.
3   Campbell, *British Admirals*, Vol. III, p. 515; Owen, *War at Sea*, p. 161.

der Goes commanded the Dutch contingent until his untimely death in June, when he was replaced by Captain Johan van Convent. The subordinate English admirals were George Byng, Thomas Dilkes and the newly promoted John Norris. It would be May before Shovell and his fleet left from Lisbon.

At the end of March 1707, Byng and Norris got to sea with an advance force of 22 ships. On hearing of the Earl of Galway's decisive defeat at Almansa, an event that allowed the Bourbons to reclaim most of Eastern Spain, Byng diverted to the Spanish coast to give support to the defeated army. Norris stopped off briefly at Barcelona before sailing to Italy to perform the duties of Shovell's trusted emissary at the court of the Duke of Savoy. He had held a similar position with Charles III, at Barcelona, two years earlier. At this time, Shovell was closer to Norris than any other naval officer and their relationship went back 18 years to Bantry Bay, where the younger man had served as a midshipman in the *Edgar*. Norris was married to Matthew Aylmer's eldest daughter and was known in the Navy as 'Foul Weather Jack.' The only blemish on his distinguished career had been in 1702 when he had drawn his sword in an altercation with another officer on the deck of George Rooke's flagship. Rooke and Norris had a history by having fought a duel in 1700 with the latter suffering a wound of the arm. After Shovell's death Norris was supportive of his widow and eventually acted as a trustee to her estate. This was the man who would play a key role in the siege of Toulon.[4]

Norris carried a letter for the Duke from Shovell in which he described his emissary: 'a man of great fidelity, honour and experience with whom you may entirely confide.'[5] Shovell informed Savoy that the fleet would carry out his orders as per Queen Anne's instructions, but privately Norris had been told to make certain that there were no improper ones. Norris was received in Savoy's bedchamber before lodging with John Chetwynd, the British Minister at Turin. After the return of Prince Eugene, a council of war took place consisting of the Duke, his cousin Eugene, Chetwynd and Norris. They went through Queen Anne's 15 articles for the project, line by line. The main problem was lack of powder and cannonballs for which Savoy, despite the agreement, expected the English to pay for. Norris, as Shovell's representative, took it upon himself to write home directly to the Secretary of State, Charles Spencer, 3rd Earl of Sunderland, requesting further supplies.[6]

Eventually, on 10 May, Shovell led his fleet out of the Lisbon River and sailed through the Straights for the Mediterranean. Off Alicante he was joined by Byng and steered for Italy. Whilst still in Spanish waters, Shovell heard from Norris about the ammunition difficulties and, acting immediately, he ordered two ships to return to Gibraltar for powder and shot. By the end of June, they were able to return with 12,000 cannonballs in time for the crossing of the River Var. In addition, Shovell, encouraged from afar by Marlborough, had to pledge his own private credit to purchase ammunition locally. No wonder Shovell complained: 'it is with great difficulty that I procure these things, and I do not doubt it might have been done with more ease and despatch by his Royal Highness's [Duke of Savoy] Ministers and

---

4   Campbell, *British Admirals*, Vol. III, pp. 512–3 and Vol. V, pp. 155–6; Owen, *War at Sea*, p. 162; Larn and McBride, *Shovell's Disaster*, p. 50; *DNB*, Norris [Laughton]; Cruikshanks, *History of Parliament*, Norris entry.

5   BL: ADD MS 28153, f. 19, Shovell to Duke of Savoy, 1707.

6   BL: ADD MS 28153, f. 23, Norris to Sunderland, 1707; Owen, *War at Sea*, pp. 162–3.

agents.' The inadequate supply of shot was amongst the reasons that the land attack on Toulon was delayed. It would have far-reaching consequences.[7]

At about this time matters were further complicated by Charles III asking both Emperor Joseph I and the Duke of Savoy for troops to be sent to help him in Spain. Norris, once made aware of this new development, was concerned about a diversion of forces away from the Toulon project and he wrote to both the Secretary of State, Sunderland, and Marlborough on the subject. Marlborough, in particular, was adamant that troops should not be sent to Spain. At Barcelona, Byng went through an elaborate subterfuge of pretending to get his ships ready for the transfer, whilst awaiting the arrival of Shovell and the fleet.[8]

When Shovell arrived, on 20 May, he was able to persuade Charles III that the fall of Toulon would indirectly be of great benefit to him in Spain. As Shovell explained to the king: 'the most advantageous measures ---- to repair the loss in Spain, and for the good of the common cause and the interest of the Allies and honour of their arms.' More firmly he added Charles and his court would: 'endure a great deal than that any number of troops be withdrawn from his Royal Highness that might in the least obstruct the vigorous prosecution of this project.' As Shovell controlled the only means of transporting troops to Spain, he was in a strong negotiating position. Perhaps the unfailing support that he had given the king two years before, at the Siege of Barcelona, helped his cause. The yeoman farmer's son from North Norfolk was now capable of making monarchs change their mind if the necessity arose.[9]

On 2 June, Shovell sailed from Barcelona, with the fleet of 43 ships with 57 transports, and anchored at Finale Ligure, about 60 miles east of Nice. At this juncture Norris informed him that the land forces would be ready in one week. In a graceful reply, obviously meant for Savoy's eyes, Shovell laid on his best diplomatic flattery:

> You have done me particular satisfaction by letting me know the great esteem and regard his Royal Highness has for her Majesty's [Queen Anne] friendship and alliance. I am sure her Majesty and the people of England have equal friendship for his Royal Highness ---- and am further sure his Royal Highness [Duke of Savoy] has already so great and just esteem of the Allies, but in particular of her Majesty's subjects, the vigorous prosecution of this great and acceptable design will for ever make his friendship and alliance memorable and grateful to the English nation. I esteem it the greatest honour of my life that I have the happiness to serve under his Royal Highness's direction for carrying on a service so agreeable to the public.[10]

Before arriving at Finale Ligure, Shovell had sent the transports on to Leghorn and Genoa. A great deal of work had to be done in loading ammunition and supplies. Unfortunately, the English tars made the most of their time ashore by imbibing a surfeit of alcohol to the detriment of the speed of supply to the ships. The subordinate admirals did their best to hurry

---

7   Campbell, *British Admirals*, Vol. IV, p. 256; Owen, *War at Sea*, pp. 162–3.

8   Owen, *War at Sea*, pp. 164–5; H of L MS 1706–8 NS, Vol. VII, p. 443.

9   Owen, *War at Sea*, p. 165.

10   Owen, *War at Sea*, pp. 165–6; Campbell, *British Admirals*, Vol. III, p. 515; *The London Gazette*, No 4343.

things along.[11] Shovell was perturbed at the delay in getting the expedition underway and urged the Duke of Savoy to march without waiting for the transports. He knew that Savoy intended to take Monaco, Villefranche and Antibes on the way before assaulting Toulon. Shovell believed that the army should advance on Toulon without neutralising the towns on the route. On 10 June, he informed the Duke:

> It is no new thing for us to be sometimes three weeks or a month getting to a place which at times we may get to in twenty four hours, which will show your Royal Highness that our motions are not so regular nor cannot be so timely as marches by land.

A week later, on the 17th, Shovell wrote to Norris a letter for the Duke of Savoy to see:

> If these accounts be true, that there are so few troops about Toulon, I cannot forbear to offer my judgement that we fall first upon that place; for if we secure Toulon, which is a harbour for our ships, and his Royal Highness should think of keeping it, I would venture to leave a squadron of twenty sail there all winter, which should be at his Royal Highness's commands for such services as he should think proper on these coasts. And the taking and keeping of Toulon would be so well liked in England and Holland that, if his Royal Highness should think it practicable from Toulon to penetrate into France next spring, I dare venture my reputation and all I am worth in the world that his Royal Highness will neither want men, money, ships, nor other materials to execute his designs.[12]

Shovell had the support of Marlborough in the possibility of a captured Toulon acting as an Anglo-Dutch naval base. He also agreed with Shovell that the land forces should march directly to Toulon and ignore the intervening towns. Savoy and his army commander, Prince Eugene, rejected this view commenting: 'they passed some jest how they should get back again, if the enemy proved too strong.' It is quite understandable that they did not respect a sailor's opinion on a land attack, but to ignore Marlborough, one of England's greatest strategists, is an entirely different matter.[13]

Instead of the forecast seven days after Shovell's arrival at Finale Ligure, it was to be a full 17 days until Eugene was ready to march. His army consisted of 35,000 men, made up of ardent Savoyards, German mercenaries paid for by England and, a paltry 6,000 supplied by Emperor Joseph I whose mind was fixated on Naples. Until the last moment Eugene attempted to persuade the Anglo-Dutch commanders to abandon thoughts of Toulon and to send 5,000 men to Spain. He raised the matter in person with Shovell who flatly refused to alter his plans. Come what may, Shovell's orders from Queen Anne were for action at Toulon and as he controlled the ships, men and money, there was little Eugene could do

11   Owen, *War at Sea*, pp. 166–7; Churchill, *Marlborough*, Vol. II, p. 247.
12   Owen, *War at Sea*, p. 167.
13   Owen, *War at Sea*, p. 168.

about it. Shovell understood the strategic importance of Toulon and, in retrospect, here was an indication of Eugene's irresolution which would bedevil the whole enterprise.[14]

Shortly after Eugene left Turin with the army, Savoy, Norris and the English minister, Chetwynd followed. The mountains were crossed at a rate of 10 to 15 miles a day through Tenda, Briel, Sospel and L'Escarere to Nice, which was reached on 29 June. At Sospel only a nominal effort was made to defend the town and Norris related to Shovell that it had been indicated to the officer on the gate that it would be lawful to hang him if he stopped a royal army![15] At Savoy's request, Shovell had taken the fleet westwards to a point between Nice and the River Var. On the night of 29 June, Shovell entertained Savoy and Eugene aboard his flagship, the *Association*. This memorable occasion has been described by Campbell:

> Sir Cloudesley Shovell, though he was not one of the politest officers we ever had, showed a great deal of prudence and address, in the magnificent entertainment he made upon this occasion. The duke, when he came on board the Association, found a guard of halberdiers, in new liveries, at the great cabin door. At the upper end of the table was set an armed chair, with a crimson velvet canopy. The table consisted of sixty covers, and every thing was so well managed that his royal highness could not forbear saying to the admiral at dinner.[16] 'If your excellency had paid me a visit in Turin, I could scarcely have treated you so well.'[17]

At the end of the dinner a council of war was conducted at which it was resolved to force a passage across the River Var.[18]

The Var was a rapidly flowing river, arising in the Alps and, flowing into the Mediterranean to the west of Nice, some 70 miles to the east of their destination, Toulon. The French had dug trenches on the western bank of the river, stretching some four miles inland. The soldiers placed along the banks of the river were to be reinforced by a further three battalions under the experienced Irish general, Arthur Dillon. The Var, meaning waterway in Ligurian, was a formidable barrier to an advance on Toulon. It was Shovell who pointed out to Savoy that the French trenches, at the mouth of the river, could be bombarded by his ships. So it was agreed that while the fleet occupied the French at the mouth of the river, the army would force its passage further inland.[19]

Shovell's right hand man, Norris, was given the honour of leading a small squadron of six ships, plus two bomb vessels and the armed boats of the fleet to undertake the bombardment of the French trenches. At noon, 30 June 1707, Savoy sent word to Norris for the engagement to begin in two hours' time. Norris hoisted his flag in the 70-gun *Monmouth* and was surprisingly followed on board by all the other English admirals, Shovell, Byng and

---

14   Owen, *War at Sea*, p. 168; Churchill, *Marlborough*, Vol. II, p. 248.

15   Owen, *War at Sea*, pp. 168–9; Churchill, *Marlborough*, Vol. II, p. 247.

16   Legend has it that there was a dinner service of gold aboard the *Association*. Divers on the wreck site have been using sophisticated sonar to try and find it. To date, 2017, without success.

17   Campbell, *British Admirals*, Vol. III, p. 516.

18   Campbell, *British Admirals*, Vol. III, p. 516; Owen, *War at Sea*, p. 169; Charnock, *Biographia*, Vol. II, p. 27.

19   Campbell, *British Admirals*, Vol. III, p. 516 and Vol. IV, pp. 256–7; Owen, *War at Sea*, p. 169; Burchett, *Transactions at Sea*, pp. 731–2; Anon, *Secret Memoirs*, pp. 112–4.

Dilkes. Clearly, the thought of action against the French was difficult to resist, particularly for a man of Shovell's temperament.[20]

The heady lure of battle meant that Shovell took over command of the action from his subordinate, Norris. Having spotted, with his keen tactical eye that some French dragoons were moving away from the mouth of the river, Shovell sent Norris with 600 men ashore in boats under covering fire from his ships. The French emplacements were soon in English hands and Shovell suggested to Savoy and Eugene that this might be an opportune moment for their army to cross the Var, further inland. The 8,000-strong army effected the crossing in relative peace, although around 100 men were swept away and drowned.[21] The panicking French retreated and met Dillon and his reinforcements about eight miles west of the Var. Dillon was taken aback to see them, and allowed himself to be persuaded to retire on Toulon. The way to Toulon was now open to Savoy and his army. It had been a most auspicious opening to the campaign.[22]

The River Var had been successfully crossed on 2 July and that night, once again, Shovell entertained Savoy and Eugene to dinner in the *Association*. After the meal, earnest debate took place amongst the assembled company on the best way to continue the expedition. Shovell was adamant that the army should march straight for Toulon without neutralising the French garrisons at Monaco and Antibes. A rapid advance on Toulon was essential, before French troops freed up, by their success at Almansa, were able to reinforce the port from Spain. Leaving the enemy in the rear of the advance was potentially dangerous as a threat to their lines of supply and Shovell did his best to reassure Savoy and Eugene by promising, if things went badly on land, then the fleet would carry them back by sea. Shovell tried to pacify Savoy: 'I hope better things from your Royal Highness's fortune; but, if there should be any appearance of such an event's happening, your highness may rely upon me, I will take care to supply a sufficient number of transports to embark all your troops.' Shovell's view was accepted.[23]

Savoy's army set off, on 4 July, for the march to Toulon and the weather proved to be scorching hot. Two days rest was required at Fréjus and, scores of men died of heat stroke with others apparently shooting themselves in despair. At last, La Valette, two miles to the north-east of Toulon, was reached on the 15th of the month. Criticism has been made of Savoy in that his army took 11 days to reach Toulon and only seven days in their eventual retreat. Suggestions have been made that this was a further sign of irresolution, particularly with Eugene, or that Shovell may have withheld subsidies on crossing the Var, thus angering Savoy. There is no evidence for the latter explanation and, in any case, it would have been out of character for the straightforward admiral.[24]

Shovell had been instructed by Savoy to make his base for the fleet in the Iles d'Hyères, around 20 miles to the east of Toulon. Once the army reached the port, he would be summoned there; meanwhile Byng with a small squadron, including supply ships, would

20   Owen, *War at Sea*, pp. 169–70; Campbell, *British Admirals*, Vol. III, p. 516 and Vol. IV, p. 257.

21   Owen, *War at Sea*, p. 170; Brian Tunstall, *The Byng Papers*, Vol. I (London: Navy Records Society 1930), p. 220; *The London Gazette*, No 4532; Campbell, *British Admirals*, Vol. III, p. 517; Anon, *Secret Memoirs*, pp. 112–4.

22   Owen, *War at Sea*, p. 170; Campbell, *British Admirals*, Vol. IV, p. 257.

23   Campbell, *British Admirals*, Vol. III, pp. 517–8; Owen, *War at Sea*, pp. 170–1.

24   Owen, *War at Sea*, pp. 171–2; Campbell, *British Admirals*, Vol. III, p. 518.

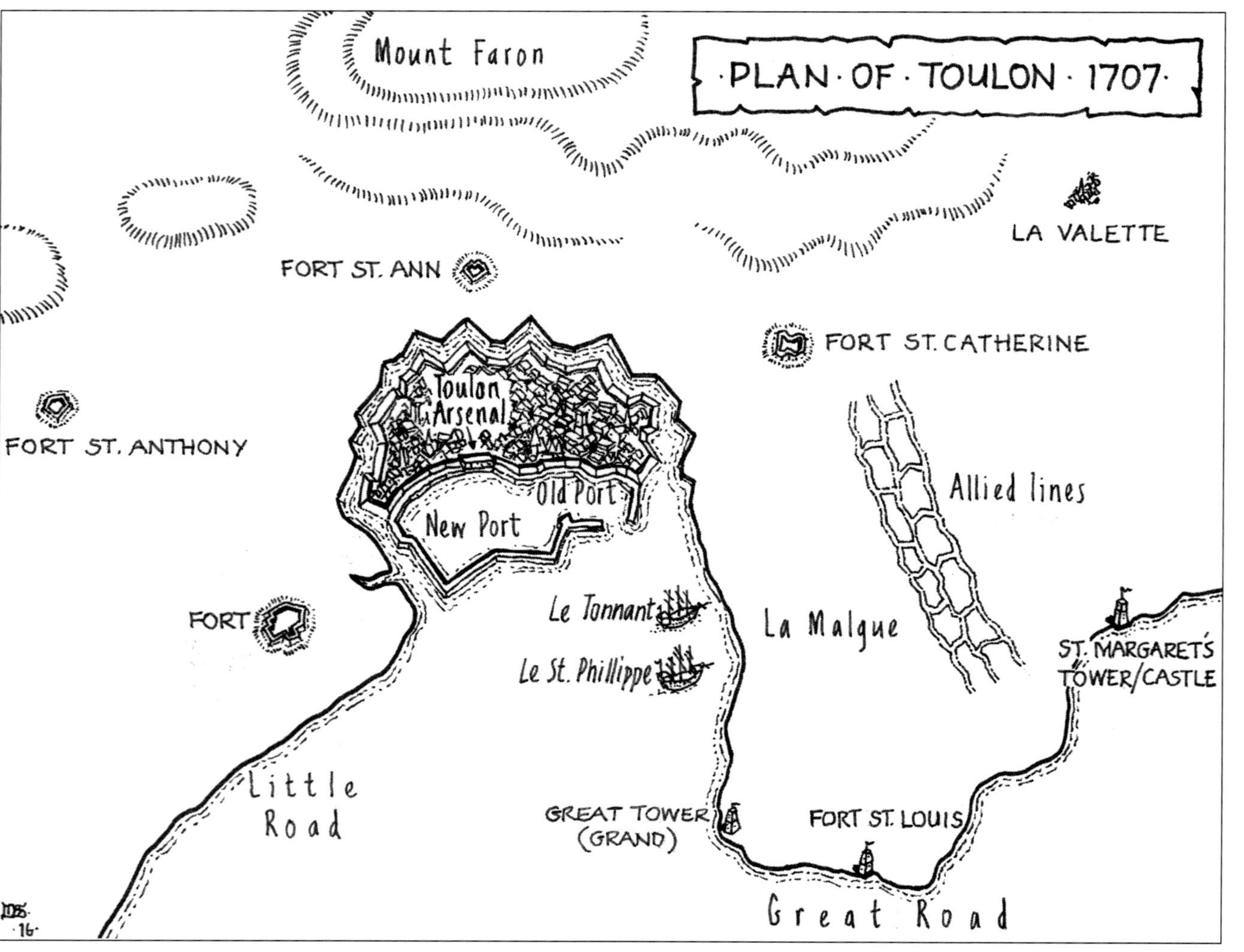

Map 22 Plan of Toulon 1707.

follow the army along the coast. At Fréjus, Byng took off no less than 500 sick soldiers. On 13 July, a violent storm precluded Shovell from using the Iles d'Hyères as a fleet anchorage and he was forced to sail to the town of Hyères on the mainland, which was ready to capitulate. The townspeople were friendly in providing ovens for baking bread, hospitals for the sick and oxen for transport.[25]

Savoy's advance from Turin threw the French into confusion as they could not be certain of his final objective. It was not until the crossing of the Var that they woke up to the fact that their premier Mediterranean naval port of Toulon was under threat. At this juncture the French tried to fortify the place and, by some accounts, it was the local inhabitants who did more in its defence than their king or generals. Plate and jewels were sold to pay for the fortifications and servants were armed. In consternation, Louis XIV, turned to Marshal Nicolas Catinat, reputedly France's finest soldier, for advice and he, with the aid of female intrigue, suggested Marshal René de Froulay de Tessé should command the defending forces. He was in the Dauphiné [Dauphiny] and immediately marched south and, despite having further to go, reached Toulon one day before the allies. At this stage, Tessé had about 20,000 men and by the end of July he had collected a further 10,000 foot soldiers and 1,000 horse to pit against the allies, who had begun the march with 35,000 men. Sickness had depleted the allies to a certain extent and had left the two sides well matched. However, if Savoy and Eugene had not procrastinated for so long, they would have found Toulon virtually undefended.[26]

In the harbour of Toulon were no less than 46 major ships plus fireships and other smaller vessels. In fact they posed little threat to Shovell and his fleet as Louis XIV was so short of money that he was unable to provide funds for their manning, repair and victualling. The French king so feared that Shovell might set fire to his ships with shells and carcasses that he had ordered them to be temporarily sunk to protect them from incineration. The three deckers would lie with their upper decks above water and the remainder would be completely submerged.[27]

On arrival outside Toulon, near La Valette, the allies' senior army officers climbed Mount Faron to view the port from on high. Norris, having returned ashore as Shovell's emissary, accompanied them and has left a record of the scene below him:

> The town has ten bastions, a shallow dry ditch, but no palisades or outworks to the bastions and curtains. In the two basins lay their ships without mast or anything, I believe, on board them. I endeavoured to count them, but could not distinguish them; but I judge the number of men-of-war to be upwards of forty sail; they seem to lay lashed on board each other, and mostly in the West Basin. The front of the basins to the water is walled as high as a ship and has an entire range of cannon placed upon it; and at each end of the town was placed a three decked ship to help flank any attack that should be against the town. Between the two land gates of the town toward the mountain [Faron], their army lay encamped in two lines; but the

---

25   Owen, *War at Sea*, p. 172; Tunstall, *Byng Papers*, pp. 199–207, 224–5.

26   Owen, *War at Sea*, pp. 170, 174; Tunstall, *Byng Papers*, pp. 219–220; Charles de la Roncière, *Histoire de la Marine Francaise* (Paris: Plon-Nourrit 1906), p. 392; Campbell, *British Admirals*, Vol. III, pp. 518–9.

27   Owen, *War at Sea*, pp. 173–4; Roncière, *Marine Francaise*, pp. 391–4; Campbell, *British Admirals*, Vol. III, p. 519.

tents looked thin, our officers did not judge them above seven thousand men; and they made entrenchments and were working at them. There are many forts and batteries that command the two roads [harbours], and they seemed to be so narrow that a ship cannot any ways ride, but is commanded by one shore or the other.[28]

Three forts were particularly important for their defence of Toulon: Fort St Catherine in the foothills of Mount Faron; Fort St Ann between the north wall of the town and the mountain; Fort St Anthony controlled the approaches from the west. The French had made further entrenchments in a roughly north-south direction facing La Valette and Savoy's army proceeded to dig their own trenches facing them. However, they were lethargic about it. On 17 July, Savoy summoned Shovell from his land base at Hyères and a private meeting took place between the two of them in the presence of Eugene and Norris. Laconically, Savoy told Shovell that he was glad to see him as the maritime powers had made him wait a long time. A bristling Shovell replied that he had not delayed a minute to wait on the Duke. At this, Savoy smiled and said: 'I did not say you, but the maritime powers had made me wait; for this expedition I concerned so long ago as 1693; and fourteen years is a long time Sir Cloudesley.'[29]

At this meeting on the 17th, Shovell bluntly told Savoy that Toulon should be stormed immediately, before the French had a chance to strengthen their defences further. Savoy was inclined to Shovell's viewpoint but deferred to his army commander, Eugene, who feared being cut off by the French and wanted to retreat. Shovell absolutely disagreed with him, leading Eugene to report back to Emperor Joseph I in Vienna: 'in spite of the representations I have made to the Admiral [Shovell], he absolutely insists upon carrying on with the enterprise of Toulon.' Later, in another letter to the Emperor: 'although the Admirals [Shovell, Byng, Dilkes, Norris] do not understand the land service, they refuse to listen to facts, and adhere obstinately to their opinion for good or ill everything must be staked on the siege of Toulon. Yet the clear impossibility of this is clearly before their eyes.' Finally, it was agreed that there would be no grand storming, but, instead, a bombardment and local assault at a single point of the defences.[30]

Having come to a compromise, Savoy and Eugene wanted to know how Shovell's fleet could help them further. There was a shortage of shot ashore and Shovell readily agreed to land cannons, shot and powder. As he had done two years earlier at Barcelona, Shovell took a calculated risk by reducing the standard reserve of the fleet's shot to a new minimum and he also agreed to blockade the harbour of Toulon from the sea. Moreover, Shovell reluctantly agreed to send three ships to carry artillery from Genoa to Naples. When Savoy and Eugene asked what he would do if the French land forces proved too strong for the allies, Shovell again promised to evacuate their soldiers by sea, the naval cannons ashore having to be abandoned.[31]

28   Owen, *War at Sea*, p. 173.
29   Owen, *War at Sea*, p. 175; Campbell, *British Admirals*, Vol. IV, p. 259; *Mercure Historique et Politique*, Vol. II (Netherlands 1707), p. 331.
30   Owen, *War at Sea*, pp. 175–6; Churchill, *Marlborough*, Vol. II, pp. 251–4.
31   Owen, *War at Sea*, pp. 175–6; Churchill, *Marlborough*, Vol. II, p. 247.

Later, Shovell explained to Byng that he had agreed to ship artillery to Naples purely to keep Eugene in the fold. He said: 'in order to engage Prince Eugene to go vigorously on with this affair here, for I believe it stops most on his account.' There can be little doubt that Shovell had accurately assessed Eugene's pessimistic frame of mind, although it was also possible that he had been instructed by Emperor Joseph I not to risk his troops. Certainly, it was not the bold Eugene that had broken the siege of Turin the previous year.[32]

On 12 and 13 July, Fort St Catherine in the foothills of Mount Faron was taken by Savoy's men and the allies began setting up batteries and extending their trenches towards Toulon. Shovell proposed attacking Fort St Louis and St Margaret's Castle which were both close to the shoreline and could be softened up by bombardment from his ships. But the ever-reliable Norris was sent to investigate and the engineer who was with him thought that the fort and castle could easily be taken from the land and a cannonade might damage the allies' camp. Norris carefully noted the possibility of bombarding Toulon over the narrow neck of land facing the harbour.[33]

By 23 July the batteries were in place and Savoy then asked for naval gunners to help man them. Shovell readily agreed to this request and with Norris suggesting that they man the batteries closest to the shore in order to make their resupply easier. More importantly, if the allies' army were in difficulty, the French fleet could be bombarded in their protected harbour. At this juncture Savoy joined Eugene in losing faith with the naval commanders. This was precipitated firstly by galleys slipping into Toulon from Marseilles and secondly by his paranoid fear that Shovell and the fleet might abandon them. Norris did his best to reassure the Duke that Shovell would stay with the fleet, off Toulon, until at least September. Privately, in a letter written 27 July to Charles Montagu, 4th Earl of Manchester, the English ambassador at Venice, even Shovell began expressing doubt about the outcome of the siege of Toulon.[34]

Two days after writing to Manchester, Shovell was summoned ashore to see Savoy in his private quarters at La Valette. With Chetwynd interpreting, in view of Shovell's ignorance of the French language, it was clear that Savoy had lost all heart as he explained that the army had been before Toulon for 15 days with little accomplished. This pessimistic view would not have come as a surprise to Shovell who had been forewarned by Norris of the Duke's state of mind. Eugene joined the meeting and somewhat surprisingly was non-committal, suggesting the generals should express a view. Finally, spurred on by Shovell, it was agreed to land further naval cannons to bring the number up to 90 and, then assault Fort St Louis and St Margaret's Castle. The taking of the latter would improve communications between the army and the fleet. Norris has left an account of Shovell's views at this critical juncture:

> The Admiral [Shovell] in the discourse used all means possible to persuade the continuance of the siege, alleging, if the town could be taken, that, as the enemy were daily sinking their ships, we should by degrees so disable them as not suddenly to be in any condition to put to sea.[35]

---

32 Owen, *War at Sea*, pp. 175–6; Tunstall, *Byng Papers*, pp. 207–8; Churchill, *Marlborough*, Vol. II, pp. 246–7, 252.
33 Owen, *War at Sea*, p. 177.
34 Owen, *War at Sea*, pp. 178–9.
35 Owen, *War at Sea*, p. 181.

Around this time Shovell wrote to George Byng:

> Everything has almost been at a stand ashore. I find neither officers nor soldiers very forward; these great guns don't well agree with them; but now they seem to design to proceed more vigorously, and resolve to attack Fort Louis and St Margaret's. We continue to land every day ammunition and provisions for them, and we are going to land more guns to make up the whole number between ninety and one hundred, and I believe I shall in a little time be ready to come to you.[36]

Shovell's fleet had been active in the blockade of Toulon and with the transport of supplies from Hyères. On land, seamen operating batteries from La Malgue, bombarded Fort St Louis and, by 2 August, much of the facade of the Fort had been destroyed; but progress against St Margaret's Castle was slower. Although both fort and castle were well within range of the fleet, inclement weather precluded greater bombardment from the ships. Savoy told Norris that he now had only 18,000–20,000 troops, as a result of battle-injuries, diseases and desertion and the allies were outnumbered by Tessé's forces. Clearly, the situation was extremely grave.[37]

Then, early in the morning of 4 August, 12,000 French troops sallied forth and attacked the allies' lines from Mount Faron in the north to La Malgue in the south. Fort St Catherine and St Margaret's Castle fell, although the allies repulsed the French from their own batteries at La Malgue. The losses on land were not catastrophic, but certainly appeared to be so in the minds of Savoy and Eugene. The French advance had confirmed to them that Toulon could not be taken however hard Shovell and the other admirals drove them. Shovell now accepted that Toulon would not fall, but he was determined to do the maximum damage to the French ships and dockyard at Toulon before he sailed for home with the fleet.[38]

Shovell planned to use his bomb ketches to hurl bombs over the narrow neck of land between Fort St Louis and the Grand Tower in order to destroy the harbour area of Toulon. Firstly, the fort and batteries near the unmanned Grand Tower would have to be silenced for fear that they would sink the bomb ketches and Byng and Dilkes were ordered to effect this operation. On 5 August, Byng boldly attempted the destruction of Fort St Louis with his small squadron, but his ships were hampered by a gale and they failed to silence the fort. Dilkes' ships concentrated on a battery halfway between the Grand Tower and Fort St Louis and, two days later, when the ships' boats went ashore the battery was found to be abandoned. That same day, the 7th, seamen manning a shore battery blew a large hole in the wall of Fort St Louis and troops subsequently found that the fort was free of Frenchmen. Norris was soon on the scene and having ascertained that the way was clear for the bomb ketches to strike at the harbour of Toulon, he hurried back to appraise Shovell of the situation.[39]

Shovell ordered Dilkes to take the frigates and bomb ketches off the neutralised Fort St Louis and to bombard Toulon harbour and dockyard. Poor weather prevented Dilkes from going ashore to place markers in the ground to aid the bomb ketches until 9 August. Then

---

36   Owen, *War at Sea*, pp. 179–81; Tunstall, *Byng Papers*, pp. 209–10.
37   Owen, *War at Sea*, pp. 181–4.
38   Owen, *War at Sea*, pp. 184–5; Campbell, *British Admirals*, Vol. III, p. 522.
39   Owen, *War at Sea*, pp. 185–8.

he shifted his flag to the 48-gun *Romney* and took the fleet's frigates to provide covering fire for the bombardment which lasted from the afternoon of 10 August through to the next morning. During the night, the French set up new batteries to provide an answering fire and thus forced Dilkes to withdraw. He had acted bravely by going ashore with the masters of the bomb ketches to correct the fall of the bombs. Five hundred shells and carcasses were hurled into Toulon harbour, making a great deal of noise, but little damage was done to the partially underwater French shipping. Two French ships, the 54-gun *Sage* and the 52-gun *Le Fortuné,* were destroyed by fire and the 58-gun *Le Diamant* plus two frigates were badly damaged in the action. In addition, some of the naval storehouses were destroyed. Dilkes reported back to Shovell and a council of war was called which concluded that no further bombardment was feasible. Shovell succinctly told Byng: 'I would we had more time, but they brought guns to the water side and mauled our bomb vessels.'[40]

While Shovell was striving mightily to do as much damage as possible to the French men-of-war, plans were being drawn up to evacuate Savoy's army. On 5 August, Savoy sent Norris to find a suitable beach to embark cannon and stores and, the following day, the Duke told Shovell to expect 3,000 sick and wounded soldiers. There was concern that the bread supply should be maintained and Byng was sent to Hyères, where it was baked, to enforce its continued production. He did so by threatening to burn down the town if bread was not forthcoming. In fact, the English marine garrison at Hyères was so popular with the local populace that they were allowed to leave peacefully by the French commander Tessé and presents were exchanged! Clearly the marines' behaviour was very different from that seen at the siege of Gibraltar in 1704.[41]

From 7–9 August, the fleet took aboard men and their equipment off St Margaret's Castle. Savoy then told Shovell that he and Eugene had decided to retreat immediately and so, on the morning of the 10th, Savoy's army set off for Fréjus, to the east of Toulon, leaving a 4,000 man rearguard to follow. The fleet sailed from the Bay of Toulon on the 12th, and true to his word, Shovell accompanied the retreating army as far as the River Var. On 20 August, off Nice, he offered to carry 5–6,000 of Savoy's men to Spain for further action. But both Savoy and Eugene declined the invitation on the grounds that they had no spare men. Finally, the forces dispersed on the 23rd, Savoy to his homeland, Eugene to Lombardy and Shovell with the fleet to Gibraltar. Shovell would take the main part of the fleet home, leaving Dilkes and a small squadron, in the Mediterranean. Dilkes, like Shovell too, had little time to live, dying on the following 12 December, at Leghorn, possibly having been poisoned.[42]

The bid to take the crucial French naval port of Toulon in 1707, despite exemplary efforts by Shovell and his subordinate admirals, had failed. The reasons behind the failure were multifactorial: the unfortunate dispatch of troops to Naples by Emperor Joseph I; delay in the fleet reaching Italy; delay in the start of the expedition; delay in getting to Toulon after the River Var was successfully crossed; the irresolution of Prince Eugene. Perhaps the most important factor of all was the last one, certainly Marlborough, closely monitoring events as they unfolded, believed that Toulon would have fallen if Savoy's army had arrived a mere

40   Owen, *War at Sea*, pp. 188–9; Tunstall, *Byng Papers*, pp. 213–4.
41   Owen, *War at Sea*, pp. 187–8; Tunstall, *Byng Papers*, pp. 210–3.
42   Owen, *War at Sea*, pp. 189–90; Tunstall, *Byng Papers*, pp. 215, 243–5; Campbell, *British Admirals*, Vol. III, p. 522 and Vol. IV, p. 260.

five days earlier. Some good came out of the Toulon operation, as Marlborough consoled the disappointed Shovell: '---- has been of great use to the King of Spain [Charles III], and likewise put a stop to the successes of the French in Germany by the detachments they were obliged to make from all parts of Provence.' Additionally, two major French ships had been destroyed and the remainder scuttled in the harbour of Toulon for fear of what Shovell might do to them.

Shovell in his straightforward manner had done everything in his power to drive the enterprise on and his support of the army was beyond praise. As Winston Churchill wrote in the biography of his illustrious ancestor, John Churchill, 1st Duke of Marlborough: 'in our history the Navy has sometimes stood by to watch the Army do the work. Here was a case where a navy tried by its exertion and sacrifice to drive forward an army.' Never was a truer word spoken, but unfortunately they did not succeed. Shovell was at the very height of his considerable powers as commander-in-chief in the Mediterranean; but as we shall see shortly, the failure to capture Toulon, would arguably, cost him his life.[43]

43   Churchill, *Marlborough*, Vol. II, p. 247. John Churchill had served with Shovell in the *Prince* at the Battle of Sole Bay in 1672.

19

The Disaster of 22 October 1707

Cloudesley Shovell departed from Gibraltar on 29 September with 20 ships bound for the ports of England and a winter at home. Off Tangier, the fleet was increased to 21 with the addition of the 54-gun *Panther*. The following day, their last sight of land as they sailed north-west into the Atlantic, was the promontory of Cape Spartel, a thousand feet above sea-level in Morocco. As might be expected, the weather that October was inclement with squalls and gales for much of their journey home. However, contrary to popular belief, the sky was not continually overcast and thus preventing observations from being made. On 15 of the 24 days of the voyage, including 21 October, at least one officer in the fleet was able to make an observation.[1] Thus at 6:00 p.m. on 22 October 1707, with a strong south-westerly gale behind his fleet, Shovell made the fatal decision to sail on into the darkness. He believed that his fleet was entering the western approaches of the English Channel with their homes and families beckoning them. Unfortunately, Shovell, his two captains, Edmund Loades and Samuel Whitaker, plus the master, Hend Whitfield were categorically and fatally wrong. Why had these highly experienced mariners made such a catastrophic error in their navigation from the Mediterranean?

Did faulty charts play a part in the coming disaster? For much of the 17th century, the English mariner was dependant on Dutch charts produced by Lucas Waghenaer and known as 'waggoners'. However, they were inaccurate and although John Sellers produced a new set of charts in 1731, they still left a great deal to be desired. In 1680, Greenvile Collins who had been to the South Seas with John Narbrough and to the Arctic, searching for a north-eastern passage, with John Wood, was commissioned to prepare more accurate charts. After seven years' work, Collins produced his *Great Britain's Coasting Pilot*, which was greatly superior to anything that had come before and was finally published in 1693. However, Collins still gave the position of the lighthouse on St Agnes as 50°02' N: still nine miles in error compared with the modern calculation of 49°53' N. If the navigators in Shovell's ships were using Collins' work, they would have had a false sense of security. It is not known which charts were used that fateful 22 October, but it is likely that many different varieties were consulted by the ships' navigators.[2]

---

1 The taking of the sun's or another celestial body's altitude to calculate latitude or longitude.
2 Davies, *Pepys's Navy*, p. 146.

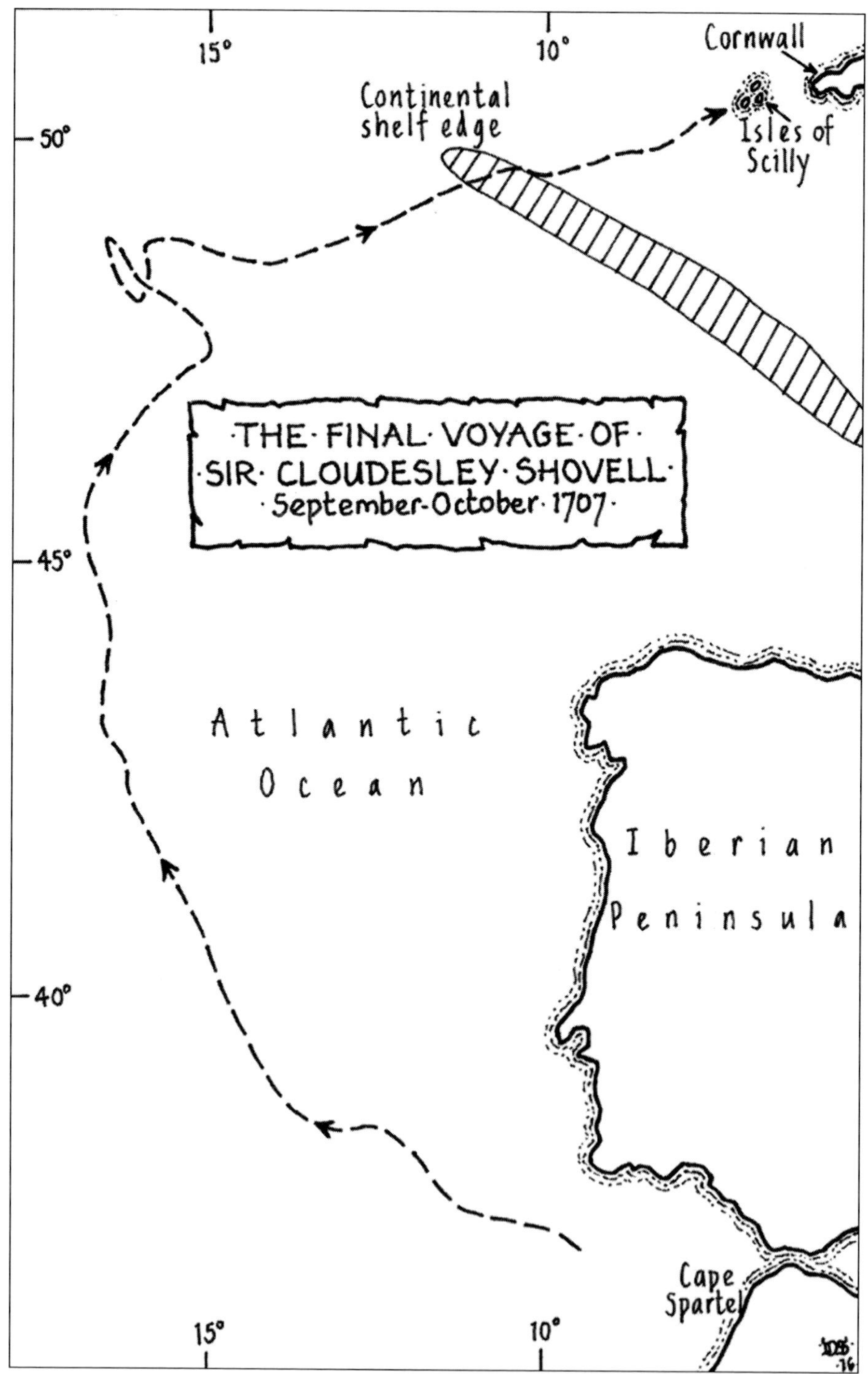

Map 23 The Final Voyage of Sir Cloudesley Shovell September–October 1707.

What part did poor navigation play in the tragedy? Latitude, in this case the distance travelled north, was calculated with a backstaff or by dead reckoning.[3] During Shovell's final voyage, the greatest difference between the most northerly and southerly figures, measured by the navigators in the fleet, was 41 miles and calculations by dead reckoning were even worse, averaging 72 miles. Longitude, the measurement of the distance travelled from west to east, was even more difficult to ascertain.[4] Indeed one of the outcomes of the Shovell disaster was the setting up of the Longitude Committee in 1714 and John Harrison's eventual production of an accurate chronometer that allowed longitude to be determined with confidence. But in Shovell's time, the speed, direction of travel and thence final position of a ship was gauged by repeated usage of a log line together with an unreliable hour-glass together with leeway adjustment. From such recordings, the position was calculated relative to the point of departure – dead reckoning.[5] The then favoured log line, 42 feet was knotted at regular intervals,[6] had long been in use and continued to be greatly preferred despite a more recent and superior line by then being available. The latter, by introducing a different total length [50 feet] and knot interval, allowed more accurate assessments; but most mariners adhered to the old familiar system and attempted ad hoc corrections.[7]

Most navigators in Shovell's fleet used Cape Spartel as their reference point although a few appear to have used Tenerife in the Canary Islands. In the 1960s, Commander W.E. May made a detailed study of the surviving logs of Shovell's fleet. Many were grossly inaccurate, although he considered that the log of Lieutenant Anthony Lochard of the *Orford* was amongst the best and it is illustrated in this account.[8] The map of the route of the *Orford* shows, at about 10 degrees of longitude, a small kink that suggests some hesitation before sailing on to the Isles of Scilly. At that point, they had, as they knew from soundings, just crossed the continental shelf edge, a feature that stretches across the Channel approaches from north-west to south-east. Knowing they were on the shelf edge and expecting to use the prevailing wind to sail north-east into the Channel, they must have thought they were some 1 degree of latitude and 2 degrees of longitude from their actual position. The conclusion is therefore that errors in both latitude and longitude occurred but the latter was the larger.

3   Latitude is a geographic coordinate that specifies the north-south position of a point on the surface of the earth. It is an angle which ranges from 0° at the Equator to 90° N or S at the poles.

4   Longitude is a geographic coordinate that specifies the east-west position of a point on the surface of the earth. It is an angular measurement and is expressed in degrees. By convention, British then and worldwide much later, the Prime Meridian passed through the Royal Observatory, at Greenwich, and was designated 0° and the longitude of other places was shown as the angle ranging from 0° to 180° either eastwards or westwards from it.

5   Peter McBride and Richard Larn, *Admiral Shovell's Treasure and Shipwreck in the Isles of Scilly* (Penryn, Cornwall: Troutbeck Press 1999), pp. 3–4.

6   A wooden log was attached to the end of a rope which was knotted at regular intervals. The sailors counted the number of knots passing through their hands in a given time to calculate the speed of the ship.

7   Davies, *Pepys's Navy*, p. 149; Eva Taylor, *The Haven-Finding Art* (London: Hollis and Carter 1956), pp. 230-1.

8   Whilst considering the navigational failures of Shovell's fleet, it is worth noting that one man, the master of the *Panther*, was nearly correct in his estimated position. Surely this was the reason that the *Panther* remained on the southern flank of the fleet and did not have to alter course to avoid the rocks.

What role did the compass play in the Shovell's fate? Sir William Jumper, captain of the *Lenox,* part of the fleet, afterwards made the comment: 'I am surprized to find my ship so far to the northward ---- and indeed can impute it to nothing but the badness of the compass which was old and full of defects.'[9] At an inquiry after the disaster only four out of 112 compasses from nine of Shovell's surviving ships were found to be working accurately.[10] Compasses were contained in a binnacle on the quarterdeck of a ship. Normally, the binnacle was divided into three compartments, the outer ones each with a compass and a lantern in the centre. By the early 18th century, the bowl containing the compass needle was gimballed to keep it level in rough seas. Azimuth compasses were not popular, although John Narbrough had used one on his voyage to the South Seas in 1669–71.[11] When it came to navigation he was a man before his time. Part of the problem with ships' compasses was that they were kept in the boatswain's store and suffered from damp. After the loss of Shovell's ships, recommendations were made that the Navy should switch to brass compasses, these to be stored in the dry bread-room.[12] Up to a point, Jumper was right: 'the badness of the compass[es]' was a contributory factor in the disaster.[13]

Did magnetism play a part in Shovell's death? A final potential influence of the compasses was that no allowance had been made for magnetic variation. This would have increased from 4° to 7° west as the voyage progressed, and if not allowed for would have placed the fleet one or two degrees to the westward of their reckoning – away from the rocks. Early in the 18th century little was understood about the possible deviation of a compass caused by magnetic material in the ship itself. However, any magnetic deviation from within a ship steering from west to east would have led them to the southward of their course – again away from the rocks. Thus magnetic effects played no part in Shovell's demise.[14]

We saw earlier that John Narbrough, in May 1673, had found himself in a similar position to Shovell's fleet and one of the reasons he used to explain the faulty navigation was: 'the indraught of a current that set into the estuary of River Severn and St George's Channel.' Mariners in the 17th and 18th centuries were aware of the current that might sweep them obliquely across the Channel approaches, but it was not until 1815 that James Rennell formally described it – hence it became known as the Rennell Current.[15] This can run at a rate of 1.5 knots, which meant that if it was running strongly, Shovell's ships, at noon on 22 October, could have been as much as 24–36 miles north of their estimated positions. However, for the current to run it required exceptionally heavy or prolonged westerly gales:

9   G. Marcus, 'Sir Clowdisley Shovel's Last Passage', *RUSI Journal,* Vol. CII (London: RUSI 1957), p. 547; W. May, 'The Last Voyage of Sir Clowdisley Shovel', *Journal of Navigation,* Vol. XIII (Cambridge: Royal Institute of Navigation 1960), pp. 331–2.

10   Larn and McBride, *Shovell's Disaster,* p. 32.

11   An azimuth compass is a nautical instrument used to measure the magnetic azimuth, the angle between the direction of the sun or some other celestial object and of the magnetic north.

12   Larn and McBride, *Shovell's Disaster,* p. 32.

13   Captain Sir William Jumper [1660–1715], an experienced naval officer, and one of the first men ashore during the Siege of Gibraltar in 1704. A bastion there, still to be seen today, was named after him. He was captain of the *Lenox* on Shovell's final voyage.

14   May, 'Last Voyage of Sir Clowdisley', p. 332.

15   James Rennell was an ex-naval officer, geographer and oceanographer.

this vital pre-condition was not met. If the Rennell Current was a factor in the coming tragedy, it must have been a minor one.[16]

Did the sounding line feature in Shovell's decision to sail on into the night? Probably it did in view of the inadequacies of the coastal charts. Certainly, until Greenvile Collins' time, the early 18th century mariner was still very dependent on his sounding line. A lead weight with tallow on its base was run out from a boat, beside the man-of-war, until it came into contact with the bottom of the sea. The depth of the sea was measured and the tallow examined for the type of sand and shell that was embedded in it. What they were searching for was a belt of fine sand, at a depth of 64 fathoms and a latitude of 49°40' north, known as 'The Sleeve' – hence the Soundings. Here a ship could safely turn east and sail up the English Channel.[17] It is known that men from the *Association*, Shovell's flagship, made soundings between 4–6:00 p.m. on 22 October, but the records were lost when the ship was wrecked. The *Monmouth* found 60 fathoms, fine white sand; the *Torbay* 55 fathoms, rocky ground; the *Cruizer* 53 fathoms, branny sand with pieces of red masked shells; the *Panther* 47 fathoms, fine white sand. With soundings of 55–60 fathoms the fleet might equally have been to the west or south of the Isles of Scilly, as the depths are not materially different. As can be readily understood the reliance on sounding was unreliable in the extreme. In all probability the soundings made by the *Association* between 4–6:00 p.m. on the 22nd, were a significant factor in Shovell's decision to sail on into the night.[18]

Was the coal-burning lighthouse on St Agnes functioning that night? This lighthouse had been operational since 1680 and was working normally on 22 October 1707. It was seen by several of Shovell's fleet, but too late; poor visibility meant that the ships were amongst the rocks and in mortal danger before they could act. In 1790, a revolving light was put into the St Agnes lighthouse and it is likely that this would have prevented the disaster. Certainly, the relatively modern lighthouses on Bishop Rock [1887] and Peninnis [1911] would have done so.[19]

What was the role of frigates in the coming disaster? Often the commanding admiral would send his smaller ships out ahead of the fleet to warn of approaching danger. On this occasion Shovell does not appear to have done so although it was said to have been his customary practice. In fact he only had two 6th rates, the *Cruizer* and *La Valeur* in his fleet. *La Valeur* was detached with the *Lenox* and *Phoenix*, by Shovell's command, on the morning of 22 October, and sent to Falmouth. Also, it was standard practice for frigates to be sent to the western approaches of the Channel to guide home the returning Mediterranean fleet. Edward St Lo, in the *Tartar*, had been ordered to do just this and had sailed from Plymouth on 21 October. Unfortunately, the *Tartar* did not come across Shovell and his fleet. If they had done so the tragedy might have been averted.[20]

16 James Rennell, 'Some Farther Observations, on the Current, That Often Prevails, to the Westward of the Scilly Islands', *Philosophical Transactions of the Royal Society*, Vol. 105 (1 January 1815), pp. 182–202; May, 'Last Voyage of Sir Clowdisley', p. 331; Marcus, 'Last Passage', p. 540; John Laughton, *Physical geography in relation to the prevailing winds and currents* (London: Potter 1873), p. 214; Larn and McBride, *Shovell's Disaster*, pp. 13, 32.

17 Davies, *Pepys's Navy*, pp. 149–50.

18 Marcus, 'Last Passage', p. 545.

19 Harris, *Cloudesley Shovell*, pp. 337–8.

20 Owen, *War at Sea*, p. 192.

Shovell's late return to England with the Mediterranean fleet and his attempt to sail up the English Channel at night, are both open to criticism. As regards the late return, according to Horace Walpole, he had hoisted himself on his own petard.[21] He quoted Shovell as having said: 'an admiral would deserve to be broke, who kept great ships out after the end of September, and to be shot if after October.'[22] As was demonstrated in the previous chapter, the reason for the fleet's late return was the hope that the key French port of Toulon could be finally captured. Indeed, in 1703 and again in 1705, Shovell had brought the Mediterranean fleet home even later in November without mishap. If he had had an excellent reason for the late return, the same cannot be said for attempting the English Channel in darkness.[23] In mitigation it can be said that other admirals had blithely sailed up the Channel at night. For example, in 1684, Lord Dartmouth did so with his officers arguing over whether they were still to the west of the Isles of Scilly or not![24] It is surprising that Shovell's memories of May 1673, with John Narbrough, did not register in his mind 34 years later. Alarm bells should have been ringing loudly.

Two major legends have come down through the three centuries since Shovell's untimely death. Both owe their origins to Edmund Herbert's expedition, in 1709, to recover lost property from the 1707 shipwrecks in the Isles of Scilly. In the first legend Shovell was alleged to have held a council of sailing masters, in the *Association,* at some point on 22 October. The surviving ships' logs show that there were regular visits by boat to the admiral's flagship during the voyage, but none were recorded for the 22nd. The most likely explanation for this erroneous theory was the taking of soundings by the crew of the *Association* around 4:00 p.m. that day. This involved lowering a ship's boat into the sea in order to drop the sounding weights and line into the water. Possibly this action was mistaken for boats carrying sailing masters to the *Association* for consultation.[25] Before leaving the phantom meeting of the sailing masters, it is worth recording some hearsay evidence in favour of it having taken place. In the 1880s, a Frederick Locker owned a document in the hand of an ancestor pertaining to Shovell's shipwreck:

> In a conversation with Admiral Forbes who had been Sir John Norris's Lieut: in the Britannia at Lisbon – he told me he had often heard Sir John say, that the evening before the Admiral brought too [sic] many of the captains and himself went on board him with their different Reckonings which disagreed from each other very much and that he was determined when they left him to lay too [sic] all night, but

---

21   Horace Walpole [1717–1797], 4th Earl of Orford, was a man of letters, antiquarian and art historian. As he was born 10 years after Shovell's death, this piece of mischievous and widely quoted information, cannot have been obtained directly from the admiral himself.

22   Marcus, 'Last Passage', p. 542; Mrs Paget Toynbee (ed), *The Letters of Horace Walpole Fourth Earl of Orford,* Vol. IV (Oxford: Clarendon Press 1904), p. 340.

23   Burchett, *Transactions at Sea,* p. 733.

24   George Legge, 1st Baron Dartmouth [1647–91].

25   James Cooke, *The Shipwreck of Sir Cloudesley Shovell on the Scilly Islands in 1707* (Gloucester: John Bellows 1883), pp. 7–8; J. Pickwell, 'Improbable Legends Surrounding the Shipwreck of Sir Clowdisley Shovell', *Mariner's Mirror,* Vol. 59, Part 2 (United Kingdom: Society for Nautical Research 1973), pp. 221–2.

> Sir John Norris supposed he was persuaded by his captain to make sail, which he did, and the unfortunate accident happened before morning.[26]

Second-hand reports of this type must be treated with caution. However, Norris was a protégé, colleague and family friend of the Shovells'. He would become one of the executors of Lady Elizabeth Shovell's will. In all probability, his promotion to rear-admiral had saved his life. Until 18 March 1707, he had been Shovell's confidant and flag-captain in the *Association*. His replacement, Edmund Loades, drowned on 22 October.

The second legend regarding the faulty navigation of Shovell's fleet is more colourful. One of the crew of the *Association*, a native of the Isles of Scilly, is supposed to have warned Shovell that they were sailing too far to the north and were in danger of running on to the infamous Western Rocks to the south-west of St Agnes. For his insubordination the mariner was hanged at the yardarm on Shovell's orders. Prior to his execution he was allowed to read from Psalm 109: part of which reads 'Let his days be few; and let another take his office. Let his children be fatherless; and his wife a widow.' In effect the seaman was putting a curse on Shovell and his unfortunate family. It is a romantic myth which does not fit the known facts. Firstly, Shovell was kind and merciful to his men. It would have been completely out of character for him to have behaved in this draconian manner. Secondly, more importantly, even if the story were true, it could never have been told as all the crew to a man lost their lives that night. For the same reason the allegation that the crew of the *Association* were all drunk was a false one.[27]

Around 6:00 p.m. on 22 October, Shovell gave the signal to wear and the fleet sailed into the darkness, to the north-east, with a favourable south-westerly gale behind them.[28] But instead of an open English Channel ahead of them, many of the fleet were steering directly on to the Western Rocks to the south-west of the Isles of Scilly. From 7–8:00 p.m. the majority of Shovell's fleet found themselves amongst some of the most treacherous rocks of the entire English coastline. Cannons were fired as a signal of danger and it was every man for himself. The ships steered in all directions attempting to escape being wrecked and their crews suffering an almost certain watery grave.[29]

Of the 21 ships of Shovell's fleet, six struck the rocks and four sank. The ships lost were the 90-gun *Association*, the 70-gun *Eagle*, the 48-gun *Romney* and the 8-gun, fireship, *Firebrand*. Another 8-gun fireship, the *Phoenix*, was beached and the fortunate 96-gun *St George* luckily escaped from the rocks with little damage. Shovell's *Association*, leading the fleet, was one of the first ships to find itself in mortal danger. According to Francis Percy, the captain of the *Firebrand*, the *Association* collided with the rocks at 7:45 p.m. and sank almost immediately:

---

26   NMM: RMT MS, MAT 25, Section 12. Admiral John Forbes [1714–96]. He became an expert on the Navy and passed much information to his friend Captain William Locker, the probable ancestor of Frederick Locker. Forbes refused to sign the death warrant of Admiral John Byng in 1757.

27   Edmund Herbert MS; Cooke, *Shipwreck*, p. 5; Rex Bowley, *The Fortunate Islands* (Reading: Bowley Publications 1964), pp. 75–6.

28   Wear: to bring a ship about by turning its head away from the wind.

29   Harris, *Cloudesley Shovell*, p. 343.

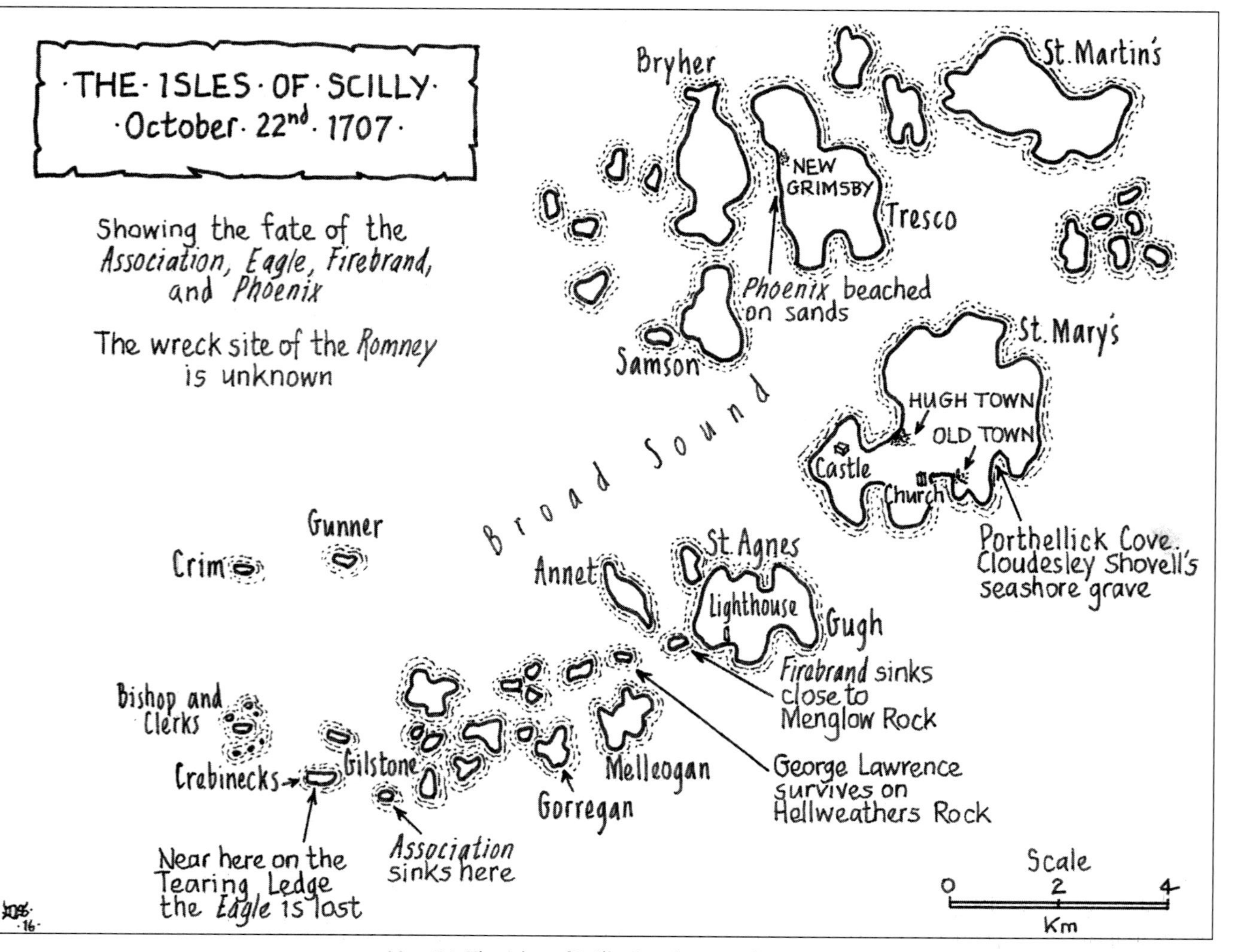

Map 24 The Isles of Scilly October 22nd 1707.

> Captain Francis Percy reports, that on the 22nd instant sailing with Sir Cloudesley Shovell, and Her Majesty's fleet, about three quarters past 7 at night, he heard the Admiral fire a gun, and immediately lost sight of his lights. He soon after perceived that the Admiral was lost, being then close aboard the Rocks call'd the Bishop and Clarks ----.[30]

Although the Bishop and Clerks was a name formerly attached to part of the Western Rocks, it was the Outer Gilstone Rock which sank both the *Association* and Percy's own *Firebrand*. For obvious reasons it has sometimes been known as the Shovell Rock.

Sir George Byng, Shovell's deputy, in the *Royal Anne,* had a narrow escape himself which was reported in the same edition of *The London Gazette* as Percy's account quoted above:

> We made sail under our courses. Soon after several ships made Signal of Danger, as did Sir Cloudesley himself. The Royal Anne that was not then half a mile windward of him, saw several Breaches, and soon after the Rocks above water: Upon one of which she saw the Association strike, and in less than two minutes disappear. The Royal Anne was saved by great presence of mind both in Officers and Men, who in a Minutes time set her top sails, one of the rocks not being a Ship's length to leeward of her, and the other on which Sir Cloudesley was lost, as near, and in a Breach of the Sea.[31]

Byng reported that 'the sea ran so very high that it was impossible to send him [Shovell] any succour.'[32]

Francis Percy's fireship, the *Firebrand,* had run on to the same Gilstone Rock as the *Association*, but a large wave had washed her off with a badly holed hull. Percy got his men to work frantically at the pumps as he steered his crippled craft along the southern edge of the Western Rocks aiming for the now visible light on St Agnes. However, despite their best efforts the ship filled with seawater and sank in 10 fathoms of water in the vicinity of the Menglow Rock. Around 23–24 men saved themselves in one of the ship's boats by rowing to the Island of St Agnes. Other reports suggested that some of the men had got ashore on pieces of wreckage and Percy on a hencoop![33]

Francis Percy was a romantic character and known to Queen Anne as her handsome lieutenant. In an engagement with the French, thinking that the action was over, Percy bent down to buckle his shoe, when a cannon was fired at his ship. The ball penetrated his cabin wall, but he received only a small laceration on his back from the wind of the projectile. Percy kept the cannonball as a weight to his kitchen jack, a fitting memorial to his narrow escape. Like Shovell, he was associated with Rochester, Kent, and there is a monument to him in St Margaret's Church there.[34]

---

30 *The London Gazette,* No 4380 Oct 30th–Nov 3rd 1707.

31 *The London Gazette,* No 4380.

32 NMM: RMT MS, MAT 2, copy of a letter from Joseph Addison, the essayist, playwright and politician to Charles Montagu, 4th Earl and later 1st Duke of Manchester, 28 October 1707.

33 Larn and McBride, *Shovell's Disaster,* p. 19.

34 St Margaret's Church is now a Chapel of Ease.

Both the *Eagle*, Captain Robert Hancock, and the *Romney*, Captain William Coney, sank that night. It is believed that a wreck found on the Tearing Ledge close to the Crebinicks is the *Eagle* but the final resting place of the *Romney* remains a mystery. No one escaped from the *Eagle*, and George Lawrence, Quarter Master, was the sole survivor from the *Romney* and indeed from any of the three major ships lost that night. Lawrence saved himself from drowning by clinging to an oar and then had the good fortune to be swept on to Hellweathers Rock, off Annet Island. Here the poor man was found the next morning:[35]

> ---- & but one soul sav'd from off the rock, call'd – who was Quarter Mr of ye Rumney, a north country-man near Hull, a butcher by trade, a lusty fat man but much batter'd with ye rocks. (Most of ye Captains, Lieutenants, Doctors & c of ye Squadron came on shoar and ask'd him many questions in relation to ye wreck, but not one man took pity on him, either to dress or order to be dress'd his bruises & c, wherefore had perish'd had not Mr Ekins, a Gentm of ye Island, charitably taken him in; and a doctor of a merchant ship then in ye road under convoy of Southampton & c, search'd his wounds and applied proper remedies).[36]

Lawrence was treated in a cavalier fashion with little thought given to his personal comfort and injuries. As the sole survivor from the *Association*, *Eagle* and *Romney*, he was able to give a little more information on their tragic loss with so many men:

> ---- only the man saved out of the Rumney tells that Sir Cloudesley was to windward of all the ships and fired three guns when she struck, and immediately went down, as the Rumney a little after did. Upon hearing the guns, the rest of the fleet, that were directly bearing on the same rocks changed course and stood to the Southward or else in all probability they had run the same fate, as never enough to be admired ----.[37]

Perhaps the most fortunate ship of all Shovell's fleet was the *St George*, commanded by his young friend and protégé, Lord James Dursley, later 3rd Earl of Berkeley. The *St George* was dashed on to the Gilstone with the *Association* and the same wave which Dursley saw extinguish all of Shovell's lights, set his own ship afloat again. It was a truly miraculous escape.

The final ship of Shovell's original fleet to fall foul of the rocks of Scilly was the fireship *Phoenix*. We saw earlier that, at 11:00 a.m. on the 22nd, the *Phoenix* had been dispatched by Shovell with the *Lenox* and *La Valeur* for convoy duty at Falmouth. Sir William Jumper, in command of this small contingent, ordered a course to the north-east until early that evening when, thinking himself at risk of running on to the coast of Cornwall, he altered course to the south-east. Jumper's actions had been logical but, at 3:00 a.m. on the morning of the 23rd, to his horror, he found himself among the rocks to the south-west of Samson Island. The fortunate *Lenox* and *La Valeur* escaped into Broad Sound and away from the

---

35   Larn and McBride, *Shovell's Disaster*, pp. 18–9.
36   Edmund Herbert MS; Cooke, *Shipwreck*, p. 4.
37   T. Quiller Couch, 'Shipwreck of Sir Cloudesley Shovell', *Journal of the Royal Institute of Cornwall*, Vol. II, letter from John Ben to Jonathan Trelawney, Bishop of Winchester, 16 November 1707 (1866–7).

rocks more by luck than good judgement. Captain Michael Sanson of the *Phoenix* was not as fortunate because his ship was penetrated by a sunken rock and he was forced to lay her on sand somewhere between Samson and Bryher Islands. It was not until 25 October that Sanson was able to get the *Phoenix* off and move her to the sands at New Grimsby, Tresco Island. Surprisingly not a single member of the crew of the *Phoenix* lost his life in this incident.[38]

Some of the surviving officers serving in Shovell's fleet gave graphic accounts of that night of tragedy. For example Lieutenant Arthur Field, in John Norris' *Torbay*, recorded in his journal:

> 1707 23 October.[39] Hard gales with hazey weathr and rain ---- att 6 the Gener. ll made the Sigll to wear: wch we repeated at 7 the Monmouth made the Sigll of Danger: at ½ past 7 on our weather bow we unexpectedly see ye breaks on the Bishop & Clarks we Immediately wore and made the Sigll of Danger, wch was very Emminent, in which we had infallible Demonstrations of Almighty providence, first our wearing sooner than usuall with main and fore course 2dly when we judg'd our selves inevitably on ye rocks yet preserved from ye mighty danger: at 9 ye light of Scilly bore E by S ½ S, about 3 miles: we then steer'd between ye wt and ye NW till 7 this morning: ye wind shifting to ye WNW, we wore, sett small saile, and steer'd S by W at 9 sounded and had 60 fathom water, brown sand, then told [counted] 11 Saile who followed us: God preserve the rest.[40]

The crew of the *Torbay* had seen 'ye light of Scilly', the lighthouse on St Agnes, but only at 9:00 p.m. by which time most of the carnage had already taken place. Joseph Lyne, Master of the *Somerset,* had seen the lighthouse about half an hour earlier: 'at ½ after 8 we lost sight of our Admiral's light at once & saw Silly Light.'[41] He went on 'ye Royal Anne who was ½ a Mile leeward of us Extinguisht her lights and did not light them again in an hour ----.'[42] No doubt George Byng had his stern lanterns put out in order to avoid other ships following him into danger.

Considering how close James Dursley's ship, the *St George*, had come to destruction, his Fifth Lieutenant, Benjamin Wiscard was remarkably circumspect in his journal: 'October 23rd ---- at ½ past 7 we heard severall Gunns fired & 8 wee discovered ye breakers off from ye Island of Scilly we wore ship and stood to ye Wnd ----.'[43] One of the first ships to see the Western Rocks was John Baker's *Monmouth*. His Second-Lieutenant, John Furzer recorded: 'Oct. 23rd ---- at 7 last night saw ye Rocks of Scilly bearing ENE a Stones throw. Wee fired sevll Guns and showed lights and gave the fleet Notice of being in Danger & afterwards bore

---

38   Marcus, 'Last Passage', pp. 546–7; Larn and McBride, *Shovell's Disaster*, pp. 19–20.

39   Confusingly, in the early 18th century navy, the date changed at the preceding noon, and not at midnight. i.e. the day at sea was measured from noon to noon. This meant that Shovell's *Association* sank at around 7:45 p.m. on 23 October. On land it was still the 22, the correct date.

40   Cooke, *Shipwreck*, pp. 8–9, Lieutenant Arthur Field journal in the *Torbay*.

41   Time at sea was measured to the nearest half hour and was notoriously inaccurate.

42   Cooke, *Shipwreck*, p. 10, Joseph Lyne journal in the *Somerset* [master].

43   Cooke, *Shipwreck*, p. 9, Lieutenant Benjamin Wiscard journal in the *St George*.

away.'[44] Captain Richard Griffiths of the *Swiftsure*, saw the end of the *Association*: 'at ½ past 7 fell in with the Islands of Scilly; the Generall fired one Gun, as we plainly saw, and immediately lost sight of him.' Griffiths appeared not to know that Scilly light was on St Agnes Island and not St Mary's; 'ye Light on St Mary's under our lee bow ----.'[45]

Perhaps the fullest contemporary account of the disaster was that of Captain Finch Reddall of the *Isabella Yacht*:

> October 23rd. This 24 houres hard gails of wind until 10 at night (22nd) then weather somewhat Moderate. at 4 in ye Afternoon (of the 22nd) ye Admiral brought to & sounded we likewise Sounded & had between 50 and 55 Fathom water a Course Sand intermint with Shells he lay by till six foll (following) at which time we heard Several guns fired to ye Soward of us supposing they had Discovered danger at 8 at night saw ye Light of Silly bearing SE by S Dist to Judgt about 4m, we took it to be one of our Admiral's lights we steered after it till we Perceived it to be a fixed light it being very thick dark Rainey weather. We Perceived ye Rocks on both sides of us we being very near to them we immediately wore our yacht & layed our head to ye Westward Crowding all ye Sail we Could to weither ye Rocks under our lea. We filled full & full & by God's Mercy we got Clear of them all for which Deliverance God's holy Name be Blest & Praised which caused a great Separation in ye fleet for happy was he that Could Shift for himself some Steering wth their heads to ye Soward & others to ye Nthward & those that lay wth their heads to ye Soward ware most of the lost.[46]

Sir William Jumper, in the *Lenox*, had reached Falmouth, where he was given a first-hand account, by the master's mate of the *Orford*, of two ships actually lying on the rocks on the night of 22 October:

> about 9 his company cried out a Rock on which he set his foresail and weather it but a very little, which he says was the body of a great ship wreck and many crying out for God's sake save them which he could nott, but standing on them soon cried out Another Rock which bit he says was a wreck of a ship ----.[47]

Shovell's fleet were not the only vessels in the vicinity of the Isles of Scilly at this time. On 21 October, the Welsh fleet had arrived from Milford Haven with 60 coasters. In addition, the *Salisbury*, *Antelope* and the *Charles Galley* had come into the Roads of St Mary's having been cruising out to the west.[48] During the hours of darkness, on the night of 22–23 October, cannon fire from the direction of the Western Rocks was heard repeatedly. It was clear that a large number of ships were in distress, but the gale from the south-west made

---

44   NMM: RMT MS, MAT 26, Second-Lieutenant John Furzer journal in the *Monmouth*.

45   Cooke, *Shipwreck*, p. 9, Captain Richard Griffiths journal in the *Torbay*.

46   Cooke, *Shipwreck*, pp. 9–10, Captain Finch Reddall journal in the *Isabella Yacht*.

47   NMM: RMT MS, MAT 26 Jumper's account of the tragedy.

48   NMM: RMT MS, MAT 26, extract from David Jones, *Compleat History of Europe 1707* (London: Rhodes, Nicholson and Bell 1708), pp. 343–4.

assistance quite impossible. On the morning of 23 October, a vast amount of wreckage and many bodies floated down Broad Sound and on to the Islands. Boats went out and in one place the head of a mast projected above water but could not be moved. It was suspected that a whole ship had foundered at this spot. Captain Joseph Soanes, of the *Southampton*, was able to confirm that the *Association* had sunk by finding a paper in the sea with Ral. Fatherington's name on it. Although no Fatherington appeared on the *Association*'s crew list, a Ralph Farrington was a midshipman in her and it is likely that the document was his.

The precise number of men lost on 22 October 1707 will never be known. According to the muster lists, officially, the sunken ships were carrying 1,363 men in total: *Association* 702; *Eagle* 377; *Romney* 236 with one man saved; *Firebrand* 48 men of whom 23 or 24 were saved.[49] However, many men who had fought in the Toulon campaign plus the sick and wounded were not on the muster lists. Hence the true loss of life that night was at least 1,600 and perhaps more. Their corpses floated around the Western Rocks and were washed on shore. St Agnes, the island closest to the site of the disaster, had the greatest number to deal with. It is thought that mass graves were dug on the island close to the old lifeboat station and the suspected site can be can be seen to this day.[50]

What are the details of the demise of Shovell and his close entourage? They were: his flag-captain Edmund Loades [the son of Sir John Narbrough's favourite sister, Anne]; John and James Narbrough [stepsons]; Henry Trelawney [second son of Jonathan Trelawney, the newly consecrated Bishop of Winchester]; his Fifth Lieutenant Edward Aylmer [son of Matthew Aylmer].[51] Without question the fullest contemporary account of Shovell's death and that of most of his immediate followers is that of Edmund Herbert. In 1709, he was charged with reclaiming property lost in the wrecks of 1707 and was able to give a near contemporary account of the disaster:

> Sir C. Shovel cast away 8 br 23, being Wednesday, between 6 and 7 at night, (others say between 4 and 5, bet: night and day,) off Guilstone (south) by west, was found on shoar (at Porthellick Cove) in St Marie's Island, stript of his shirt, wc by confession was known, by 2 women, wch shirt had his name at ye gusset at his waist; (where by order of Mr Henry Pennick was buried 4 yards off ye sands;[52] which place I myself view'd, & as was by his grave, came by sd woman yt first saw him after he was strpt;) His ring was also lost from off his hand, wch however left ye impression on his finger, as also of a second.[53] The Lady Shovel offered a considerable reward to any one [who] should recover it for her, and in order thereto wrote Cpt. Benedick,

---

49 These figures are taken from *Admiral Shovell's Treasure and Shipwreck in the Isles of Scilly* [1999] by McBride and Larn. TNA: ADM 33/249, TNA: ADM 33/257, TNA: ADM 33/258. In their earlier work, *Sir Clowdisley Shovell's Disaster* [1985], they quoted 1,649 men being carried. Made up of: the *Association* 739; *Eagle* 500; *Romney* 365; *Firebrand* 45. TNA: ADM 8/10. The figures were based on *Admiralty Treasury Musters*.

50 The *Association* was carrying more gentlemen volunteers than perhaps ever before.

51 McBride and Larn, *Admiral Shovell's Treasure*, pp. 157–172.

52 The Reverend Henry Penneck, who had been a clergyman on St Mary's for only a short time before the disaster. Apparently he left the same year and Richard Larn has suggested that dealing with so many burials was too much for him.

53 The first ring was the famous emerald one. [See below]. The second ring has never been found and folklore has it that if it leaves the Isles of Scilly, they will sink into the sea.

Dep. Governor & Commander in Ch. Of Islands of Scilly, (giving him a particular description thereof,) who used his utmost diligence both by fair and foul means, though could not hear of it. Sr Cloud. Had on him a pr of thread stockings and a thread waistcoat. (Others say a flannel waistcoat and a pair of drawers.) Mr Child (Mr Paxton) Purser of ye Arundel caused him to be taken up and knew him to be Sr Cloudesley by a certain black mold under his left ear, as also by the first joynt of one of his forefingers being broken inwards formerly by playing at Tables; the sd joint of his finger was also small and taper, as well as standing somewhat inwards; (he had likewise a shot in his right arm, another in his left thigh.) Moreover he was well satisfied 'twas him, for he was fresh when his face was washt as if only asleep; his nose likewise bled as tho' alive, wch Mr Child (Paxton) said was bec. Of himself, for Sr C. had preferred him to Purser of Arundel and was his particular friend. They carried him to Mrs Bant's in ye island, & had on shoar sevrll Doctors of ye ships of ye fleet, but none could embalm or embowel him; (neither did any of ye fleet take much notice of him, but as Mr Paxton was carrying him on board ye Arundell, Capt – (Hosier) Commander of ye Salisbury ordered him on board his ship;) wherefore they put him on board ye Salisbury on a bare table, (the table was Mrs Bants,) and a sheet only to cover him; the table they kept but the sheet was sent on shoar; and on board the Salisb. They carried him to Plimo where he was embalmed, and afterwards conveyed to London by land carriage.[54] (Sir Cloudesley was the first man came on shoar, saving one, of the almost 1800 lost in the wreck. His Commission was brought on shoar by one –, and his chest wch was by him taken up floating.) Many that saw him sd his head was the largest that ever they had seen, and not all swell'd with the waters, neither had he any bruise or fear about him, save only a small scratch above one of his eyes like that of a pin. Was a very lusty, comely man, and very fat.

Capt. Loades, Commander of ye Association, (Sir Cloudesley's Captain as Admiral, but Capt. Whitacre was Captain of ye ship) wch Sr C. was on board of wn cast away, was also taken up on St Marie's island, (in ye same cove near Sir C.) and buried in Old-town Ch. Whose burial 'twas reported cost £90, but Mr With who was manager of it says ½ that sum.

(This Mr Withe rais'd a report by Mr Pennick buried Sr C. before cold, but had sd gent. liv'd 'twould have cost him dear, but himself had misfortn to be cast away, A.D. 170-.) Mr James Narborough, (others say Sr John Narborough) and the Ld Bishop Trewlawney's son, was likewise buried in sd Church very honourably.[55] Sir C. had a naked small greyhound cast on shoar in ye same cove with, and not far distant, (as about a bowshot,) from him, with a collar of his name &c. round its neck.[56] (There came on shoar in or very near ye same cove the stern of Sir C.'s barge, wch gives ground to believe he had time to get in it with some of his crew, tho' most

---

54   Plimo is Plymouth.

55   Edmund Loades, Henry Trelawney and James Narbrough were all buried in the chancel of Old Town Church, on St Mary's. In all probability James' brother, Sir John Narbrough, was buried there too. In the 19th century, the church was reduced in size and the chancel became part of the churchyard, outside the walls of the building.

56   Shovell's mentor, Sir John Narbrough, also took a greyhound to sea with him.

people are not of that mind; Captain Loades, Sr John and Mr James Narborough, also the Bishop Trelawney's son, being all cast on shoar on St Marie's island, give further matter of credit;)[57]

Shovell's body was found in Porthellick Cove, on the south side of St Mary's Island, some eight miles by sea from the Gilstone.[58] This was odd in itself as the majority of drowned corpses, from the Western Rocks, are swept on to St Agnes Island or up Broad Sound. This stretch of water lies with Samson and Tresco Islands to the north and St Agnes and St Mary's Islands to the south. On that fateful October night, this is largely what happened to the bodies. Over the centuries, it has been rare for drowned corpses, from the Western Rocks, to be washed up on the south side of St Mary's. Perhaps, the corpulent Shovell drowned close to the Gilstone and it was pure chance that his body found its way into Porthellick Cove. A more likely scenario was that Shovell was able to get away from the sinking *Association*, in his barge, with the closest members of his entourage. In that case all would have been drowned as the barge broke up to the south of St Mary's with their corpses being washed up on the island. The fact that the bodies of Edmund Loades, Shovell's flag-captain, and his pet greyhound were washed up in Porthellick Cove would support this theory.[59] In addition, the stern of a barge resembling his was found near Porthellick, although more recently it has been thought to be the coat of arms from the stern of the *Association* itself.[60] However, if the admiral's barge was launched, why did they not steer for St Agnes Island which was much closer than St Mary's?[61]

Did Shovell drown or was he murdered on the seashore? According to legend in the Romney family, the half-drowned Shovell was murdered by an elderly woman, on the sands of Porthellick, for the sake of the emerald ring on his finger.[62] He was then buried close to the sands for the next three days, before being dug up on 26 October and carried to Plymouth, as described by Herbert in his article related earlier. The alternative theory was that he was washed ashore dead, the emerald ring removed and then he was temporarily buried near the sands as before. Murder seems most unlikely, if only on the balance of probabilities. The *Salisbury* carried Shovell's corpse to Plymouth where Doctor James Yonge embalmed him in the citadel. Yonge's diary entry stated:

> 1707 In November this yeare the corps of Sir Cloudesley Shovell was brought into the Citadell. he had unfortunately drowned 9 days and I embalmed him and had

---

57   Edmund Herbert MS; Cooke, *Shipwreck*, pp. 3–5.

58   Some six and a half miles as the crow flies.

59   The two Narbrough young men, John and James, were also washed up on to St Mary's and Shovell's chest was found floating in the sea near his body. Could all these facts be pure coincidence?

60   The coat of arms is now displayed in Penzance Magistrate's Court.

61   *The London Gazettes*, Nos 1783, 1945, 4380; Edmund Herbert MS; Cooke, *Shipwreck*, pp. 3–5; Harris, *Cloudesley Shovell*, pp. 354-64.

62   Robert Marsham-Townshend, 'Death of Sir Cloudesley Shovell', *Notes and Queries* (London: John Francis 27 December 1884), pp. 518–9. The Romney legend that Cloudesley Shovell was murdered on the beach, for the sake of his emerald ring, came from a draft letter, written around 1792 by Robert, the 2nd Baron Romney to a Captain Locker. As Lord Romney was the grandson of Shovell he should be taken seriously. His mother, Elizabeth, was the elder daughter of Shovell and had married Robert Marsham in 1708. He became the 1st Baron Romney in 1716.

50£ for it. The Corps was carried to London and buryed in Westminster Abbey at the Queenes Cost.[63]

Whilst the inhabitants of the Isles of Scilly were burying the dead mariners and taking stock of the situation, George Byng led most of the survivors of the broken fleet along the English Channel to Spithead, which was reached on 25 October. It was not until they went on board the *Royal Anne* and spoke to Byng that some captains, such as John Price of the *Somerset* and Finch Reddall of the *Isabella Yacht*, learned for the first time about the death and destruction they had left behind in the Isles of Scilly.[64] Once news of the disaster reached London, bank stock fell on the exchange.[65] The campaign season of 1707 had ended disastrously.

Lady Elizabeth Shovell sent a hearse to Plymouth to collect her husband's mortal remains. The horse-drawn hearse left Plymouth on 10 November for the long journey to London. On the way, for a single night, the coffin was left in an ale-house at Honiton Cleft. What the abstemious Shovell would have thought about this does not bear contemplation! The misery of Elizabeth Shovell, who had lost her husband, two sons [John and James Narbrough] and nephew [Edmund Loades], on the Western Rocks cannot easily be imagined. No doubt her grown-up daughter, Elizabeth [by Sir John Narbrough] and her husband Thomas D'Aeth, must have been a great support to her. Her younger children, Elizabeth and Anne, by Shovell, were only 15 and 11 years old at the time. They had not seen their father for the best part of two years. Shovell's body lay in state in his town house, on the west side of Soho Square, at its junction with Frith Street, until his funeral.

William Gregg, spy and sometime clerk to James Vernon and also Robert Harley, confessed: 'Shovell had only gone on the expedition because otherwise the world might think that he had abandoned the government after he had got an estate by it.'[66] In 1708, Gregg was hanged, drawn and quartered for passing information to the French. It is difficult to take Gregg's comments seriously: Shovell spent the winter of 1706–7 in Lisbon when the final decision to attack Toulon was made; Shovell has been described as brave to a fault; Shovell was subsumed with duty to his queen and country.

Exactly two calendar months after Shovell's death, at night, on 22 December, the funeral was held in Westminster Abbey, at Queen Anne's expense. The funeral was something of a disappointment as it was imagined that it would be pompous and make a great show. The streets were expected to be lined with a vast crowd, and the houses adorned with tapestries and full of lights and spectators. None of this happened. At the end of the funeral Shovell's body was interred in a large vault in the south choir aisle, to the west of the east cloister door of the Abbey. The humble Norfolk boy had found rest amongst his country's great and good. In 1708, the celebrated Grinling Gibbons received £322-10s-0d for executing the carved memorial over the tomb.[67] After the funeral the following verses were surreptitiously laid on the tomb:

<hr>

63   Yonge's diary is to be found in Plymouth Museum.
64   *Daily Courant,* No 1779; *The London Gazette,* No 4379.
65   Cruikshanks, *History of Parliament,* Shovell entry.
66   Cruikshanks, *History of Parliament,* Shovell entry.
67   Larn and McBride, *Shovell's Disaster,* p. 23. The tomb and carved memorial did not meet with universal approval. Joseph Addison wrote: 'instead of the brave rough English admiral, which was the distinguishing character of that

> As Lambeth pray'd, so was the dire event
> Else we had wanted here a monument;
> That to our fleet kind heaven would be a rock;
> Nor did kind Heaven the wise Petition mock:
> To what the metropolitan did pen,
> The Bishop & his Clerks reply'd Amen.

In April 1707 Archbishop Tenison had prepared a formulary to be used for imploring divine blessing on England's fleets and armies.[68] Unfortunately, an unguarded expression 'the rock of our might' had slipped in, which the wits of the time did not fail to recollect. Hence the above epigram.[69]

After the funeral, Lady Elizabeth Shovell wrote to the Deputy Governor of the Isles of Scilly requesting his help in returning any possessions belonging to her late husband that had been garnered by the locals and, in particular, the emerald ring stolen from his finger. Eventually, the ring surfaced in the hands of James, 3rd Earl of Berkeley [the former James Dursley, captain of the *St George* and a Shovell protégé]. Lady Elizabeth Shovell died in 1732 and Berkeley in 1736 and it has been suggested that the ring was returned at some stage during this period. The rationale was that if the ring had been found before Elizabeth's death, it would have been given back to her. According to the tradition in the Romney family, an elderly woman on her deathbed in St Mary's gave up the ring. Having admitted killing Shovell for plunder, she handed the ring to the minister. 'This, ring which she delivered to the minister, was by him given to James Earl of Berkeley at his particular request, Sr Cloudesley Shovell and himself having lived on the strictest footing of friendship.' The ring descended through the Berkeley family and was converted into a locket by Mrs Caroline Mary Rumley, in the Victorian era. Its whereabouts are no longer known.[70]

Let the final valedictions of Sir Cloudesley Shovell be those of his sovereign, Queen Anne, and his contemporaries, Sir John Molesworth, Tory Member of Parliament, and Abel Boyer, the historian and editor of the *Post-boy* news-sheet. Queen Anne, on appointing Sir John Leake to be Rear-Admiral of Great Britain, said 'she knew of no man so fit to repair the loss of the ablest seaman in her service.'[71] Molesworth recorded: 'he is universally regretted for his courage, capacity and honesty, which it will be very hard to parallel in another commander.'[72] Boyer wrote of Shovell's demise:

> This was the fatal end of one of the greatest sea commanders of our age, or, as ever this island produced; of undaunted courage and resolution, of wonderful presence of mind in the hottest of engagements, and of consummate skill and experience:

plain gallant man, he is represented on his tomb by the figure of a beau, dressed in a long periwig, and reposing on velvet cushions under a canopy of state.'

68   Archbishop of Canterbury, Thomas Tenison [1636–1715], attended the Duke of Monmouth before his execution, ministered to William and Mary on their death beds and crowned Queen Anne. 'The rock of our might' was an unfortunate slip.

69   Harris, *Cloudesley Shovell*, p. 369.

70   Harris, *Cloudesley Shovell*, pp. 394–6.

71   Campbell, *British Admirals*, Vol. IV, p. 263.

72   Cruikshanks, *History of Parliament*, Shovell entry.

But more than all this, he was a just, frank, generous, honest, good man. He was the artificer of his own fortune, and by his personal merit alone, rais'd himself to almost the highest station in the Navy of Great Britain.[73]

Let Sir Cloudesley's reputation be returned to him.[74]

73   Abel Boyer, *History of the Reign of Queen Anne*, Vol. IV (London: A. Roper 1703–13), p. 242.
74   Harris, *Cloudesley Shovell*, pp. 366–373.

Bibliography

Manuscript Sources

All Souls College, Oxford (ASC): MS 240
Bodleian Library, Oxford (Bod Lib):
    Rawlinson MS: A 181, A 189, A 190, A 214, A 215, A 216, A 289
British Library (BL):
    ADD MS: 5440, 5441, 5442, 19872, 22546, 25374, 28056, 28141, 28153, 29591, 35855, 35898, 39757, 88980
    Egerton MS: 2518, 2621
    Sloane MS: 819, 2755
    Stowe MS: 305
Herbert Manuscript: The manuscript of Edmund Herbert, describing the loss of Cloudesley Shovell, and presented by James Cooke to the Society of Antiquaries on 1 February 1883. The manuscript was published in Cooke's book *The Shipwreck of Sir Cloudesley Shovell on the Scilly Islands in 1707* (Gloucester: John Bellows 1883)
Huntington Library (HL), San Marino, California, USA: MS SR 1–85
Kent County Archives (KCA), Maidstone, Kent: Marsham MS U1515: 01, 03, 011, 012, 17 [This material is now in the National Maritime Museum, Greenwich]
Pepysian Library (PL), Magdalene College, Cambridge: Pepysian MS 2555, 2556, 2877
The National Archives (TNA), Kew:
    ADM: 1/4080, 2/1741, 6/3, 6/4, 8/10, 33/91, 33/98, 33/104, 33/121, 33/135, 33/247, 33/257, 33/258, 51/49, 51/489, 51/857, 51/4125, 52/35/2
National Maritime Museum (NMM), Greenwich:
    ADM/L/F/198
    Journal of Edward Barlow 1659–1703, JOD/4
    Sir John Narbrough's letterbook 1687–88, LBK/1
    Robert Marsham-Townshend (RMT) MS MATs 1–64
    Sergison (Serg) MS
    SMF 221 (PHB/17)
Norfolk Record Office (NRO):
    All Saints Church, Cockthorpe Baptismal Register, NRO PD 493/1
    Saint Nicholas Church, Salthouse Parish Register, NRO PD 23/1
Scott Polar Research Institute, Cambridge (SPRI):
    William Chambers' Journal of the Batchelor 1669–70, MS 1636

Trinity House (TH): Court Minutes 1704
Yale University Library (YUL):
    Herbert letterbook 1678–83, James Marshall and Louise Osborn Collection shelf no
        fb 96

Historical Manuscripts Commission (HMC) [Now part of The National Archives]:
    Bath MS, Vols. I–III (London: HMSO 1904–8)
    Buccleuch MS, Vol. II (London: HMSO 1903)
    Dartmouth MS, Vols. I and III (London: HMSO 1889, 1899)
    Finch MS, Vols. II, III, IV (London: HMSO 1922–65)
    Heathcote MS, (London: HMSO 1899)
    Portland MS, Vols. III, IV, V, VIII, X (London: HMSO 1891)

House of Lords (H of L) Manuscripts (MS) New Series (NS), Vols. I–VII (London: HMSO
    1900–21)

Printed Sources

William Aiken, *Conduct of the Earl of Nottingham* (New Haven: Yale University Press 1941)
Richard Allyn, *A narrative of the Victory obtained by the English over that of France in the year 1692* (London: J. Robinson 1744)
Roger Anderson, *Journals and Narratives of the Third Dutch War* (London: Navy Records Society 1946)
Anonymous, *An Account of the late Great Victory at sea, against the French by their Majestie's Fleet, Commanded by Admiral Russell; and the Dutch Commanded by Admiral Allemond, near the Cape of Barfleur in May, 1692* (London: J. Rawlins 1692)
Anonymous, *A Review Of the Late Engagement at Sea Being A Collection of Private Letters never before printed* (London: John Nutt 1704)
Anonymous, *The Life and Glorious Actions of Sir Cloudesley Shovell* (London: D. Brown 1707)
Anonymous, *Secret Memoirs of the Life of the honourable Sir Cloudesley Shovell* (London: 1708)
A Short Account of St Paulinus Church
Philip Aubrey, *The Defeat of James Stuart's Armada 1692* (Leicester: Leicester University Press 1979)
Colin Ballard, *The Great Earl of Peterborough* (London: Skeffington and Son 1929)
John Barratt, *Cromwell's Wars at Sea* (Barnsley: Pen and Sword Books 2006)
Blakeney Area Historical Society Booklet
Francis Blomefield, *County History of Norfolk*, Vols. 2, 8, 9 (London: W. Miller 1805, 1808)
Rex Bowley, *The Fortunate Islands* (Reading: Bowley Publications 1964)
Abel Boyer, *History of the Reign of Queen Anne* (London: A. Roper 1703–13)
T. Brett, *St Leonards and Hastings Gazette* (6, 13 May 1893)
Oscar Browning (ed), *The Journal of Sir George Rooke, Admiral of the Fleet, 1700–1702* (London: Navy Records Society 1897)
Josiah Burchett, *A Complete History of the most remarkable transactions at Sea* (London: J. Walthroe 1702)

John Burke, *Genealogical and Heraldic History of the Landed Gentry* (London: Henry Colburn 1838)

James Burney, *A Chronological History of Voyages and Discoveries in the South Sea or Pacific Ocean* (London: Luke Hansard and Sons 1817)

Calendar of State Papers Colonial, America and West Indies (British History Online)

Calendar of State Papers Domestic: Interregnum; Charles II; James II; William and Mary; William III; Anne (British History Online)

Calendar of State Papers Relating to English Affairs in the Archives of Venice (British History Online)

Doctor John Campbell, *Lives of the British Admirals,* Vols. III, IV, VI (London: C.J. Barrington 1817)

Bernard Capp, *Cromwell's Navy: The Fleet and the English Revolution 1648–60* (Oxford: Clarendon Press 1989)

Edward Carter, *The Norwich Subscription Books 1637–80* (London: Nelson 1937)

Edwin Chappell (ed), *The Tangier Papers of Samuel Pepys* (London: Navy Records Society 1936)

John Charnock, *Biographia Navalis*, Vol. II (London: R. Faulder 1794–8)

Winston Churchill, *Marlborough His Life and Times*, Vol. II (London: George Harrap 1936)

James Clarke, *The Life of James II*, Vol. II (London: Longman 1816)

Cockthorpe Hall, *Eastern Daily Press,* 17 October 1986

James Cooke, *The Shipwreck of Sir Cloudesley Shovell on the Scilly Islands in 1707* (Gloucester: John Bellows 1883)

Julian Corbett, *England in the Mediterranean 1603–1713*, Vol. II (London: Longman 1904)

Henry Cousins, *Hastings: Of Bygone Days and the Present* (Hastings: Parsons 1920)

Gilbert Crockatt, *Consolatory Letter to Lady Shovell* (London: George Strahan 1708)

Eveline Cruikshanks (ed), *By Force or Default? The Revolution of 1688–89* (Edinburgh: John Donald 1986)

Eveline Cruikshanks, Stuart Handley, David Hayton, *The History of Parliament 1690-1715* (Woodbridge: Boydell and Brewer and online 2002)

Galbraith Crump (ed), *Poems on Affairs of State* (New Haven: Yale University Press 1968)

Francis Davenport (ed), *European Treaties Bearing on the History of the United States and its Dependencies* (Washington: Carnegie Institute 1917)

J. David Davies, 'James II, William of Orange and the Admirals' in Eveline Cruikshanks (ed), *By Force or Default? The Revolution of 1688–1689* (Edinburgh: John Donald 1989)

J. David Davies, *Gentlemen and Tarpaulins* (Oxford: Clarendon Press 1991)

J. David Davies, *Pepys's Navy* (Barnsley: Seaforth Publishing 2008)

Esmond De Beer (ed), *The Diary of John Evelyn*, Vol. V (Oxford: Oxford University Press, 1955)

Gavin De Beer, *Sir Hans Sloane and the British Museum* (London: Oxford University Press 1953)

Dictionary of National Biography (Oxford: Oxford University Press 1885–2004)–Berkeley [James Dursley]; Berkeley of Stratton; Berry; Brooks [Liu]; Grafton; Mordaunt; Myngs [Laughton, Knighton]; Narbrough [Laughton, Davies]; Norris; Rooke; Tollemache

George Duckett, *Naval Commissioners* (Published by the author 1889)

Florence Dyer, *The Life of Admiral Sir John Narbrough* (London: Philip Allan 1931)

Florence Dyer, 'Captain Myngs in the West Indies', *Mariner's Mirror*, Vol. 18 (United Kingdom: Society for Nautical Research 1932)

Peter Earle, *The Wreck of the Almiranta* (London: Macmillan 1979)

Lourenco Edye, *Historical Records of the Royal Marines*, Vol. 1, 1664–1701 (London: Harrison 1893)

John Ehrman, *The Navy in the War of William III 1688–97* (Cambridge: Cambridge University Press 1953)

Alexandre Exquemelin, *Buccanneers of America* (London: Folio Society 1972)

Charles Firth, 'The Capture of Santiago, in Cuba, by Captain Myngs, 1662', *The English Historical Review* (Oxford: Oxford University Press 1 July 1899)

Charles Firth, *Naval Songs and Ballards* (London: Navy Records Society 1908)

Frank Fox, *The Four Days' Battle of 1666* (Barnsley: Seaforth Publishing 2009)

Evan Fyers, 'Machine Vessels', *Mariner's Mirror*, Vol. 11 (United Kingdom: Society for Nautical Research 1925)

Anchitell Grey, *Debates of the House of Commons 1667–1694* (London: Henry and Cave 1763)

Clarence Haring, *The Buccaneers in the West Indies in the XVII Century* (New York: E.P. Dutton 1910)

Simon Harris, *Sir Cloudesley Shovell Stuart Admiral* (Staplehurst: Spellmount 2001)

William Harvey, *History of the Parish of Linkinhorne* (Bodmin: written in 1727 and published in 1876)

Timothy Hawes, *Norwich City Officers 1453–1835* (Norwich: Norfolk Record Society 1986)

Henry Horwitz, *Parliament, Policy and Politics in the Reign of William III* (Manchester: Manchester University Press 1977)

International Genealogical Index: Norfolk; Gimingham

Gertrude Jacobsen, *William Blathwayt: A Late 17th Century English Administrator* (New Haven: Yale University Press 1932)

David Jones, *Compleat History of Europe 1707* (London: Rhodes, Nicholson and Bell 1708)

Rachel Jones [Mrs H], 'Historic Memorials of the Norfolk Coast', *Fraser's Magazine*, (September 1881)

Henry Kamen, 'The Destruction of the Spanish Silver Fleet at Vigo 1702', *Bulletin of the Institute of Historical Research*, 39 (London: 1966)

Paul Kennedy, *The Rise and Fall of British Naval Mastery* (USA: Random House 1976)

Charles Knight, *Popular History of England*, Vol. V (Boston: Estes and Lauriat 1874)

Heinrich Kuenzel, *Das Leben und der Briefwechsel des Landgrafen Georg von Hessen-Darmstadt* (Friedberg and London: John Ritwell 1859)

William Laird Clowes, *The Royal Navy A History From the Earliest Times to the Present*, Vol. II (London: Sampson Low and Marston 1898)

Richard Larn and Peter McBride, *Sir Clowdisley Shovell's Disaster in the Isles of Scilly* (Plymouth: Historic Maritime Series 1985)

John Laughton, *Physical geography in relation to the prevailing winds and currents* (London: Potter 1873)

John Laughton (ed), *Memoirs relating to Lord Torrington* (London: Camden Society 1889)

John Laughton, 'The Battle of La Hogue and Maritime War', *Quarterly Review*, Vol. CLXXVI (1893)

John Laughton, *Naval Miscellany* (London: Navy Records Society 1912)

Peter Le Fevre, 'Sir Cloudesley Shovell's Early Career', *Mariner's Mirror,* Vol. 70 (United Kingdom: Society for Nautical Research 1984)

Peter Le Fevre, 'Tangier, the Navy, and its connection with the Glorious Revolution of 1688', *Mariner's Mirror,* Vol. 73 (United Kingdom: Society for Nautical Research 1987)

Peter Le Fevre, 'The Battle of Bantry Bay 1 May 1689', *The Irish Sword*, Vol. XVIII (Dublin: The Military History Society of Ireland 1990)

Peter Le Fevre and Richard Harding (eds), *Precursors of Nelson* (London: Chatham 2000)

C. Linnell, *A Guide to St Nicholas Church, Salthouse* (2009)

London Gazette, issue nos: 18, 39, 1080 supplement, 1783, 1945, 2454, 3096, 3102, 3107, 3161, 4343, 4379, 4380, 4532

Narcissus Luttrell, *A Brief Historical Relation of State Affairs from September 1678–April 1714*, Vols. II–VI (Oxford: Oxford University Press 1857)

Thomas Macaulay, *The History of England*, Vol. IV (London: Macmillan and Co 1914)

Peter McBride and Richard Larn, *Admiral Shovell's Treasure and Shipwreck in the Isles of Scilly* (Penryn, Cornwall: Troutbeck Press 1999)

John Macky, *Memoirs of the Secret Services of John Macky Esq* (London: Spring Macky 1733)

G. Marcus, 'Sir Clowdisley Shovel's Last Passage', *RUSI Journal*, Vol. CII (London: RUSI 1957)

Clements Markham (ed), *Life of Captain Stephen Martin* (London: Navy Records Society 1895)

David Marley, *Pirates Adventurers of the High Seas* (London: Arms and Armour Press 1995)

David Marley, *Wars of the Americas: A Chronology of Armed Conflict in the New World* (Santa Barbara: ABC–CLIO 2008)

Robert Marsham-Townshend, 'Death of Sir Cloudesley Shovell', *Notes and Queries* (London: John Francis 27 December 1884)

Robert Marsham-Townshend, 'Death of Sir John Narbrough', *Notes and Queries* (London: John Francis 29 December 1888)

Robert Marsham-Townshend, 'Parentage of Cloudesley Shovell', *Notes and Queries* (London: John Francis 19 January 1895)

Stephen Martin-Leake, *The Life of Sir John Leake Rear-Admiral of Great Britain,* Vol. I (London: Navy Records Society 1918)

W. May, 'Naval Compasses in 1707', *Journal of Navigation*, Vol. VI, No 4 (Cambridge: Royal Institute of Navigation 1953)

W. May, 'The Last Voyage of Sir Clowdisley Shovel', *Journal of Navigation*, Vol. XIII (Cambridge: Royal Institute of Navigation 1960)

Mercure Historique et Politique, Vol. II (Netherlands 1707)

R. Merriman (ed), *The Sergison Papers* (London: Navy Records Society 1950)

Mullock's Auctions, Shropshire, Catalogue of Historical Ephemera, 13 August 2015, Lot 73

John Narbrough, *A particular Narrative of the Burning in the Port of Tripoli, Four men of War belonging* to *those Corsairs 14 Jan 1675/6* (1676)

John Narbrough, *An Account of Several Late Voyages and Discoveries to the South and North* (Tennessee: General Books 2009, original publication 1694)

Simon Ockley, *An Account of South West Barbary* (London: J. Bowyer and M. Clements 1713)

Richard Ollard, *Cromwell's Earl* (London: Harper Collins 1994)

John Owen, *War at Sea under Queen Anne 1702–1708* (Cambridge: Cambridge University Press 1938)

Matthew Parker, *Willoughbyland* (United Kingdom: Hutchinson 2015)

Samuel Pepys, *Tangier Papers of.* Reprint 1980

J. Pickwell, 'Improbable Legends Surrounding the Shipwreck of Sir Clowdisley Shovell', *Mariner's Mirror*, Vol. 59, Part 2 (United Kingdom: Society for Nautical Research 1973)

David Plant, *The Battle of Scheveningen 1653* (Self-published 2010)

Robert Playfair, *The Scourge of Christendom* (London: Smith, Elder and Co 1884)

John Powell, *The Rupert and Monck letter book 1666* (London: Navy Records Society 1969)

Edward Powley, *The English Navy in the Revolution of 1688* (Cambridge: Cambridge University Press 1928)

Edward Powley, *The Naval Side of King William's War* (London: John Baker 1972)

T. Quiller Couch, 'Shipwreck of Sir Cloudesley Shovell', *Journal of the Royal Institute of Cornwall*, Vol. II (1866–7)

James Rennell, 'Some Farther Observations, on the Current, That Often Prevails, to the Westward of the Scilly Islands', *Philosophical Transactions of the Royal Society of London*, Vol. 105 (1 January 1815)

Herbert Richmond, *The Navy as an Instrument of Policy 1558–1727* (Cambridge: Cambridge University Press 1953)

Charles de la Roncière, *Histoire de la Marine Francaise* (Paris: Plon-Nourrit 1906)

Walter Rye, *Norfolk Familes* (Norwich: Goose and Son 1913)

Frederick Smith, *A History of Rochester* (London: C.E. Daniel and Co 1928)

Frederick Smith, *Rochester in Parliament 1295–1933* (London: Simpkin Marshall 1933)

Dava Sobel, *Longitude: The True Story Of A Lone Genius Who Solved The Greatest Scientific Problem Of His Time* (New York: Walker and Co 1995)

Thomas Spalding, *The Life and Times of Richard Badiley* (Westminster: Archibald Constable and Co 1899)

Lucie Street, *An Uncommon Sailor a Portrait of Admiral Sir William Penn* (Bourne End: Kensal Press 1986)

Joseph Tanner (ed), A *Descriptive Catalogue of the Naval Manuscripts in the Pepysian Library*, Vols. I, II, III, IV (London: Navy Records Society 1903–32)

Eva Taylor, *The Haven-Finding Art* (London: Hollis and Carter 1956)

Henry Teonge, *Diary of 1675–79* (London: Charles Knight 1825)

The Hastings and St Leonards Pictorial Advertiser and Visitors List (Hastings 1914)

The Parentage and English Progenitors of Nathaniel Coney of Boston, Massachusetts (Internet:www.archive.org/stream/parentageenglish1906hill/parentageenglish-1906hiII_djvu.txt)

Claire Tomalin, *Samuel Pepys the Unequalled Self* (London: Viking 2002)

Mrs Paget Toynbee (ed), *The Letters of Horace Walpole Fourth Earl of Orford* (Oxford: Clarendon Press 1904)

Brian Tunstall (ed), *The Byng Papers*, Vol. I (London: Navy Records Society 1930)

Frances Verney, *Memoirs of the Verney Family*, Vol. IV (London: Longmans, Green and Co. 1892)

Philippe Villette-Mursay, *Mémoires du Marquis de Villette* (Paris: for the Société de l'Histoire de France by Jules Renouard 1841)

David West, *Admiral Russell and the Rise of British Naval Supremacy* (Forres, Scotland: Librario 2005)

William Winks, *Lives of Illustrious Shoemakers.* (New York: Funk Wagnalls 1883)

Index

The Century of the Soldier series – Warfare c 1618-1721

www.helion.co.uk/centuryofthesoldier

'This is the Century of the Soldier', Falvio Testir, Poet, 1641

The 'Century of the Soldier' series will cover the period of military history c. 1618–1721, the 'golden era' of Pike and Shot warfare. This time frame has been seen by many historians as a period of not only great social change, but of fundamental developments within military matters. This is the period of the 'military revolution', the development of standing armies, the widespread introduction of black powder weapons and a greater professionalism within the culture of military personnel.

The series will examine the period in a greater degree of detail than has hitherto been attempted, and has a very wide brief, with the intention of covering all aspects of the period from the battles, campaigns, logistics and tactics, to the personalities, armies, uniforms and equipment.

Submissions

The publishers would be pleased to receive submissions for this series. Please contact us via email (info@helion.co.uk), or in writing to Helion & Company Limited, 26 Willow Road, Solihull, West Midlands, B91 1UE.

Titles

No 1 *'Famous by my Sword'. The Army of Montrose and the Military Revolution* Charles Singleton (ISBN 978-1-909384-97-2)*

No 2 *Marlborough's Other Army. The British Army and the Campaigns of the First Peninsular War, 1702–1712* Nick Dorrell (ISBN 978-1-910294-63-5)

No 3 *Cavalier Capital. Oxford in the English Civil War 1642–1646* John Barratt (ISBN 978-1-910294-58-1)

No 4 *Reconstructing the New Model Army Volume 1. Regimental Lists April 1645 to May 1649* Malcolm Wanklyn (ISBN 978-1-910777-10-7)*

No 5 *To Settle The Crown – Waging Civil War in Shropshire, 1642-1648* Jonathan Worton (ISBN 978-1-910777-98-5)

No 6 *The First British Army, 1624-1628. The Army of the Duke of Buckingham* Laurence Spring (ISBN 978-1-910777-95-4)

No 7 *'Better Begging Than Fighting'. The Royalist Army in Exile in the War against Cromwell 1656-1660* John Barratt (ISBN 978-1-910777-71-8)*

No 8 *Reconstructing the New Model Army Volume 2. Regimental Lists April 1649 to May 1663* Malcolm Wanklyn (ISBN 978-1-910777-88-6)*

No 9 *The Battle of Montgomery 1644. The English Civil War in the Welsh Borderlands* Jonathan Worton (ISBN 978-1-911096-23-8)*

No 10 *The Arte Militaire. The Application of 17th Century Military Manuals to Conflict Archaeology* Warwick Louth (ISBN 978-1-911096-22-1)*

No 11 *No Armour But Courage: Colonel Sir George Lisle, 1615–1648* Serena Jones (ISBN 978-1-911096-47-4)

No 12 *Cromwell's Buffoon: The Life and Career of the Regicide, Thomas Pride* Robert Hodkinson (ISBN 978-1-911512-11-0)

No 14 *Hey for Old Robin! The Campaigns and Armies of the Earl of Essex During the First Civil War, 1642–44* Chris Scott & Alan Turton (ISBN 978-1-911512-21-9)*

No 15 *The Bavarian Army during the Thirty Years War* Laurence Spring (ISBN 978-1-911512-39-4)

No 16 *The Army of James II, 1685–1688: The Birth of the British Army* Stephen Ede-Borrett (ISBN 978-1-911512-39-4)*

No 17 *Civil War London: A Military History of London under Charles I and Oliver Cromwell* David Flintham (ISBN 978-1-911512-62-2)*

No 18 *The Other Norfolk Admirals: Myngs, Narbrough and Shovell* Simon Harris (ISBN 978-1-912174-22-5)

Books within the series are published in two formats: 'Falconets' are paperbacks, page size 248mm × 180mm, with high visual content including colour plates; 'Culverins' are hardback monographs, page size 234mm × 156mm. Books marked with * in the list above are Falconets, all others are Culverins.